# CONTESTED PASTS

In contemporary political and intellectual debates, memory is a constant reference point. From debates about traumatic memory to nationalist accounts of the past, memory is invoked to justify, explain or challenge familiar histories. Bridging the gap between public and private, between scholarly and popular uses of history, it has become a key term in our culture's engagement with the past.

This engagement is a complex one and has important political and theoretical implications. The essays in this book explore the way in which memory is involved in contesting the meanings of the past. While memory challenges or subverts dominant accounts of history, *Contested Pasts* shows how it may also disguise and reinvent, serving to cover up as well as to reveal. The contributors to this international interdisciplinary volume investigate the work of memory in contemporary culture, interrogating a wide variety of memorial cultural forms, from museums to television, and ranging from the Basque country to Cambodia, from Hungary to South Africa. This book is divided into parts – Transforming memory; Remembering suffering: trauma and history; Patterning the national past – which demonstrate the complex cultural work and struggles over the meanings that are at the heart of memory today.

*Contested Pasts* will be of essential interest to those working in the fields of cultural studies, history and anthropology.

**Katharine Hodgkin** teaches in the School of Cultural and Innovation Studies at the University of East London. Her research centres on questions of autobiography, memory and madness, particularly in the early modern period. She has published several articles on these topics, including most recently 'The Labyrinth and the Pit' (*History Workshop Journal* 51, 2001), a study of madness in seventeenth-century autobiography, and is currently completing an edition of a seventeenth-century manuscript for Ashgate, (*Women, Madness and Sin in Early Modern England: the autobiographical writings of Dionys Fitzherbert*).

**Susannah Radstone** teaches in the School of Cultural and Innovation Studies at the University of East London. Her research interests are in cultural theory, memory studies and psychoanalysis. Her previous publications include *Memory and Methodology* (2000) (ed.) and she is currently completing *On Memory and Confession*, to be published by Routledge.

# ROUTLEDGE STUDIES IN MEMORY AND NARRATIVE

Series editors: Mary Chamberlain, Paul Thompson, Timothy Ashplant, Richard Candida-Smith and Selma Leydesdorff

## NARRATIVE AND GENRE
*Edited by Mary Chamberlain and Paul Thompson*

## TRAUMA AND LIFE STORIES
International perspectives
*Edited by Kim Lacy Rogers and Selma Leydesdorff with Graham Dawson*

## NARRATIVES OF GUILT AND COMPLIANCE IN UNIFIED GERMANY
Stasi informers and their impact on society
*Barbara Miller*

## JAPANESE BANKERS IN THE CITY OF LONDON
*Junko Sakai*

## MEMORY AND MEMORIALS, 1789 – 1914
Literary and cultural perspectives
*Edited by Matthew Campbell, Jacqueline M Labbe and Sally Shuttleworth*

## THE ROOTS OF ENVIRONMENTAL CONSCIOUSNESS
Popular tradition and personal experience
*Edited by Stephen Hussey and Paul Thompson*

## THE POLITICS OF WAR MEMORY AND COMMEMORATION
*Edited by T G Ashplant, Graham Dawson and Michael Roper*

## LINES OF NARRATIVE
Psychosocial perspectives
*Edited by Molly Andrews, Shelley Day Sclater, Corinne Squire and Amal Treacher*

## THE ETHIOPIAN JEWISH EXODUS
Narratives of the migration journey to Israel 1977–1985
*Gadi BenEzer*

## ART AND THE PERFORMANCE OF MEMORY
Sounds and gestures of recollection
*Edited by Richard Candida-Smith*

## CONTESTED PASTS
The politics of memory
*Edited by Katharine Hodgkin and Susannah Radstone*

## REGIMES OF MEMORY
*Edited by Susannah Radstone and Katharine Hodgkin*

## LIVING THROUGH SOVIET RUSSIA
*Edited by Daniel Bertaux and Paul Thompson*

# CONTESTED PASTS

## The politics of memory

*Edited by Katharine Hodgkin and*
*Susannah Radstone*

Routledge
Taylor & Francis Group

LONDON AND NEW YORK

First published 2003
by Routledge
11 New Fetter Lane, London EC4P 4EE

Simultaneously published in the USA and Canada
by Routledge
29 West 35th Street, New York, NY 10001

*Routledge is an imprint of the Taylor & Francis Group*

Typeset in Baskerville by Taylor & Francis Books Ltd
Printed and bound in Great Britain by MPG Books Ltd, Bodmin

*British Library Cataloguing in Publication Data*
A catalogue record for this book is available from the British Library

*Library of Congress Cataloging in Publication Data*
Contested pasts: the politics of memory /
edited by Katharine Hodgkin and Susannah Radstone.
Includes bibliographical references and index.
1. Memory – Social aspects. 2. Memory – Political aspects.
I. Hodgkin, Katharine, 1961– II. Radstone, Susannah.
BF378.S65 C665 2003
153.1'2–dc21 2002035844

ISBN 0–415–28647–6

# CONTENTS

# CONTENTS

# ILLUSTRATIONS

# NOTES ON CONTRIBUTORS

**Robert Burgoyne** is Professor of English and Film Studies at Wayne State University. He is author of *Film Nation: Hollywood Looks at U.S. History* and co-author of *New Vocabularies in Film Semiotics*. His work revolves around questions of history and memory in contemporary media culture.

**Graham Carr** teaches US and Canadian history at Concordia University in Montreal. His research deals with twentieth-century North American cultural and public history. In addition to work on war and commemoration, he has published on various topics in literary history and historiography, and has written on public policy issues such as the implications of trade liberalisation for national cultures. His current research focuses on music, society and politics in Canada and the US in the 1950s-60s. The main focus of this work is on the neglected relationship between culture and security issues in Cold War narratives of East–West performer exchanges.

**Christopher J. Colvin** is currently completing his dissertation in sociocultural anthropology at the University of Virginia's Department of Anthropology. He conducted ethnographic research with an apartheid victim support and advocacy group as well as with a psychological trauma clinic in Cape Town, South Africa. His work explores the role of memory-making about traumatic events in post-conflict societies with a particular emphasis on the intersection of medical, politico-legal and religious discourses of memory and trauma. His dissertation focuses on the post-apartheid 'political economy of story-telling' in South Africa.

**Carrie Hamilton** teaches Spanish History in the School of Modern Languages at the University of Southampton. Her research focuses on women's political activism in contemporary Spain. She has conducted an oral history project on women in ETA, the radical Basque nationalist armed organisation, and has published several articles on the topic. She is currently completing a book based on this research, titled *Remembering ETA: women, family and conflict in the Basque country, 1959–1982*.

**Paula Hamilton** is Associate Professor of History and Research Director in the Faculty of Humanities at the University of Technology, Sydney. She has published widely on memory, history and popular culture and is currently involved with a team completing a national survey on how Australians use and understand the past. From mid-2002 she will take up a university reader-ship to complete a book of collected essays on the culture of memory in Australia.

**Chris Healy** teaches Cultural Studies at the University of Melbourne. He is the editor of *The Lifeblood of Footscray: working lives at the Angliss Meatworks* (1986), co-editor, with Sarah Ferber and Chris McAuliffe, of *Beasts of Suburbia: reinterpreting cultures in Australian suburbs* (1994), and author of *From the Ruins of Colonialism: history as social memory* (1997). He is currently co-editor, with Stephen Muecke, of *Cultural Studies Review*.

**Anne Heimo** is a tutor in the Department of Cultural Studies at the University of Turku, Finland. Her forthcoming doctoral dissertation examines the memory of the 1918 Finnish Civil War at local level and how it has changed since the Reds were given recognition in the 1960s.

**Marianne Hirsch** is Professor of French and Comparative Literature at Dartmouth College in Hanover, NH, USA. Among her works on cultural memory are *Family Frames: photography, narrative and postmemory* (1997), *The Familial Gaze* (1998), and a special issue of *Signs* on 'Gender and Cultural Memory' (2002). She is currently writing a book with Leo Spitzer, *Ghosts of Home: Czernowitz and the Holocaust*.

**Katharine Hodgkin** teaches in the School of Cultural and Innovation Studies, University of East London. Her research centres on questions of autobiography and memory, particularly in the early modern period, and she has published various articles on these topics. She is also the editor of *Women, Madness and Sin in Early Modern England: the autobiographical writings of Dionys Fitzherbert* (Ashgate, 2003), an edition of an early-seventeenth-century manuscript.

**Rachel Hughes** is a doctoral student in the School of Anthropology, Geography and Environmental Studies at the University of Melbourne. Her previous work has examined the relevance of post-colonial fiction to (human) geography's inquiry into migration, tourism and colonialism. Her current research interests include the local politics of memory in post-1979 Cambodia, the international articulation of memorial sites and cultural representations of Democratic Kampuchea, and tourisms of war in southeast Asia.

**Maya Nadkarni** is a Ph.D. candidate in cultural anthropology at Columbia University, where she is working on a dissertation titled 'Remains of Socialism: memory, mass culture, and fantasies of the new in postsocialist Hungary'. She has also written on Holocaust film and memory, Hungarian mass media and popular culture, and the marketing of socialist nostalgia. Her article, 'The "Whisky Robber": criminality as a moral discourse in post-'89 Hungary' appeared in the *Anthropology of East Europe Review*.

**Luisa Passerini** is Professor of Twentieth-Century History at the European University Institute in Florence. She has published extensively on themes of memory, including work on the Resistance, on fascism and the working class, and on the political history of the last few decades. Her books include *Fascism in Popular Memory: the cultural history of the Turin working class* (1987), *Autobiography of a Generation. Italy 1968* (1996), and *Europe in Love, Love in Europe: imagination and politics in Britain between the wars* (1998).

**Ulla-Maija Peltonen** is a researcher in the Finnish Literature Society and a lecturer in the Department of Cultural Studies at the University of Helsinki, Finland. She is author of *Naisia turvasäilössä* (Female political prisoners in Finland 1930–1944) (1989) and *Punakapinan muistot* (Memories of the 1918 Civil War) (1996) and is co-author of *To Work, to Life, or to Death. Studies in Working-Class Lore* (1996). She is currently researching the relationship between official and unofficial memory of the Finnish Civil War.

**Alessandro Portelli** teaches American literature at the University of Rome 'La Sapienza'. His work in oral history includes *Biografia di una città. Storia e racconto. Terni 1831–1985* (1985), *The Death of Luigi Trastulli and other stories. Form and Meaning in Oral History* (1991), *The Battle of Valle Giulia: oral history and the art of dialogue* (1997), *L'ordine è già stato eseguito. Roma, Le Fosse Ardeatine, la memoria* (1999). In 2002 he was designated as the mayor's representative for historical memory in the city of Rome.

**Susannah Radstone** teaches in the School of Cultural and Innovation Studies at the University of East London. Recent publications include: *Memory and Methodology* (ed.) (Berg, 2000); 'Autobiographical Times', in Tess Cosslett *et al.*, *Feminism and Autobiography* (Routledge, 2000); 'The War of the Fathers: trauma, fantasy and September 11', in Judith Greenberg (ed.), *Trauma at Home* (University of Nebraska Press, 2003). She recently compiled and edited a dossier, 'Trauma and Screen Studies', *Screen* (42: 2, 2001). She is currently completing *On Memory and Confession: the sexual politics of time*, to be published by Routledge.

**Leo Spitzer** is the Kathe Tappe Vernon Professor of History at Dartmouth College. His most recent book is *Hotel Bolivia: The culture of memory in a refuge from Nazism* (Hill & Wang: Farrar, Straus & Giroux, 1998). He is also the author of *Lives In Between: assimilation and marginality in Austria, Brazil and West Africa* (Cambridge, 1990; reprinted 1999, Hill & Wang), *The Creoles of Sierra Leone: responses to colonialism* (Wisconsin, 1974), and is co-editor with Mieke Bal and Jonathan Crewe of *Acts of Memory: cultural recall in the present*. He is currently working in collaboration with Marianne Hirsch on a book, *Ghosts of Home: Czernowitz and the Holocaust*.

**Janet Walker** is Professor of Film Studies at the University of California, Santa Barbara, where she is also affiliated with the Women's Studies Program. Author of *Couching Resistance: women, film, and psychoanalytic psychiatry* (1993), co-editor (with Diane Waldeman) of *Feminism and Documentary* (1999), and editor of *Westerns: films through history* (2001), her book-in-progress studies documentary and fiction films and videos about incest and the Holocaust in light of contemporary psychological theories of traumatic memory.

# PREFACE AND
# ACKNOWLEDGEMENTS

*Contested Pasts* and its companion volume *Regimes of Memory* have been some five years in the making. The seeds of both were sown during a research discussion day held in the Department of Cultural Studies (as it then was) at the University of East London, in 1997. At that meeting, it emerged that we shared an interest in memory, though coming at it from different places and directions and theories. Katharine Hodgkin had a background in research on autobiographical writing (especially early modern), and a general interest in questions of history and memory, as well as history and psychoanalysis. Susannah Radstone worked on cultural theory, psychoanalysis, literature, film and contemporary history, and was already actively involved in research on memory. A further seed was Raphael Samuel's brief presence as a professor in the department, setting up a history research centre that would undoubtedly have been a focus for work drawing on and developing his seminal work on history and memory. His death interrupted that project, along with much else. But for the department as well as personally it seemed a valuable thing to hold some sort of event that would acknowledge that work, and remember him. Susannah Radstone, meanwhile, in the throes of editing an interdisciplinary volume on memory and finding links to work going on in Canada and the USA, was keen to build on those links, and initiate a wider conversation on the subject.

The first outcome of this convergence of interests and wishes was an international interdisciplinary conference, 'Frontiers of Memory', held at the Institute of Education in September 1999. The response to our early calls for papers was disconcertingly large, and over the months that followed, as we worked through and selected from a continuing flood of abstracts, we found ourselves increasingly intrigued by the overview we were acquiring of work on memory in the late 1990s, and by the emphases and the absences these abstracts suggested. We wanted the conference to be as open as possible to interdisciplinary work; we were interested in work about past and present, space and time, objects and fantasies. It quickly became clear that though we were not going to have as many papers from historians as we had hoped, a vast number of people were working on traumatic and holocaust memory; this pattern is reflected on further in the Introduction to *Contested Pasts*. The conference was also firmly based in humanities subjects, in part no doubt a consequence of where it had been publicised; we had few contributions from psychology or geography, for instance, despite the significant work on memory going on in both these fields. Nonetheless, by the time we had managed to select some hundred papers from the three hundred or more abstracts we were offered, it was clear that memory was indeed an immensely motivating and topical subject, drawing contributors from many parts of the world and from many different disciplines, as well as some from outside the academy. The theme of memory seemed to make possible an engagement with both personal and intellectual preoccupations in a way that remains rare in academic work.

The conference itself was a large and successful event, and we quickly proceeded to the even more difficult task of selecting from those hundred papers twenty or so with the aim of publication. Inevitably there were many deserving papers left out; and as the volumes took shape, the agendas and the priorities we had initially envisaged shifted somewhat. Thus the eventual publications have moved quite a long way away from the original conference, and the changed titles of these two volumes reflect that distance, although certain themes and interests have remained constant.

In choosing essays for this volume and its companion, our main aim was innovation: we were looking for papers that would do something new with memory, whether through cutting edge theory, or interesting and unusual applications of more familiar approaches, or indeed both. In addition, an important part of our aim was to bridge what still too often appears as a divide between 'history' and 'theory'. Our different fields of interest cover a great deal of the ground addressed by memory work – from autobiography and oral history to trauma and film, from heritage to psychoanalysis – and our historical and theoretical approaches are differently balanced. Nonetheless for both of us it would be impossible to think about memory simply taking it as a given: to work with memory must entail asking questions about memory itself, how it is conceived in different cultural and historical contexts, and how to understand its extraordinary discursive prominence today. Precisely because of its interdisciplinary breadth, memory as a concept throws light on the unquestioned assumptions and the internal workings of the various disciplines in which it comes to be positioned. 'Memory' as it is mobilised by oral historians is not necessarily identical with 'memory' in the writings of film theorists; different priorities and problems come to the fore. By juxtaposing work from different fields we hope that these two volumes will help us to think across boundaries – as Luisa Passerini suggests, to make dangerous liaisons.

It would have been hard for us to imagine, on that research day in 1997, that the next five years would lead to such a sustained, productive and exhausting engagement with the topic we identified almost casually. Our first thanks should perhaps go to one another, for what has been a collaboration – an intellectual pilgrimage – of exceptional interest, as well as friendship, encouragement and mutual support. But we have many other thanks to give as well.

PREFACE AND ACKNOWLEDGEMENTS

We owe thanks firstly to our department (now part of the School of Cultural and Innovation Studies at the University of East London), and to Mike Rustin, then Dean of Faculty, for giving us encouragement and underwriting the initial conference, despite the constant anxiety about how much money we might be about to lose! Many thanks also to Tina Papoulias, at the time Susannah Radstone's research student, for a great deal of assistance during the planning of the conference – for much of the time during this period we were effectively a triumvirate; and to Joan Tremble for taking over much of the burden of administering the event. Their efficient support kept us sane at various critical points. *History Workshop Journal*, of which Raphael Samuel had been a founding editor, very kindly funded the conference reception; our thanks to the editorial board for buying us lots of wine. We also remember with great gratitude and pleasure the participants, both those who gave papers and those who did not. We thank them all for their time and energy, their enthusiastic responses in discussion, and their good temper when things went wrong. We are only sorry that we couldn't publish a wider range of the papers given; so many merited wider circulation, and we hope by now they have found other homes.

For our contributors, it has been a long haul since the conference, and we are very grateful to them all for staying with us, and for their patience over the many and complex delays. We thank also the Memory and Narrative editors, in whose series the two volumes are appearing, for their support; we are delighted to be in such excellent company as the previous volumes in this series. And thanks to Anna Davin and Abbas Vali, for reading and advising on editorial material.

Finally, personal thanks. From Katharine Hodgkin, thanks to Vian Vali, for (as she suggested I put it) leaving me alone while I am working. The conference and the books have been in the background for half her life, and she has tolerated the consequent parental distractions with impressive patience and good humour, not to mention charm. Thanks also to Abbas Vali; I owe more than he knows to his sustaining presence, as well as to his intellectual rigour.

From Susannah Radstone, thanks to Julia Boutall for helping her keep on track, and to Annette Kuhn, Claudia Lank, Clare Palmer, Sara Radstone and Amal Treacher for friendship and encouragement.

The authors and the publisher would like to thank the following for permission to reprint material:

Hirsch, Marianne and Spitzer, Leo, 'We Would Not Have Come Without You': Generations of Nostalgia originally appeared in *American Imago* 59:3 (2002), 253–276. ©The John Hopkins University Press. Reprinted with permission of The John Hopkins University Press.

J. Walker, 'The Traumatic Paradox' which originally appeared in *Signs*, 22:4 (1997), 803-26. ©1997 by the University of Chigaco. Reprinted with permission of the University of Chicago Press.

# INTRODUCTION

## Contested pasts

*Katharine Hodgkin and Susannah Radstone*

The question of what it means to contest the past is one that has become increasingly charged in the last few decades. It reveals certain presuppositions about the relationship between the present and the past, which have both historical and political purchase; and the discourse of memory has come to have a central part in thinking about that relationship. The idea of contest in the literal sense is apparently a straightforward one: it evokes a struggle in the terrain of truth. If what is disputed is the course of events – what really happened – new answers, particularly by groups whose knowledge has previously been discounted, may challenge dominant or privileged narratives. But to contest the past is also, of course, to pose questions about the present, and what the past means in the present. Our understanding of the past has strategic, political, and ethical consequences. Contests over the meaning of the past are also contests over the meaning of the present and over ways of taking the past forward. Ideas of restitution and reparation, evoking both financial or political justice and more abstruse compensations such as recognition of wrongs done, or readiness to hear and acknowledge hidden stories, all draw on a sense that the present is obliged to accommodate the past in order to move on from it (itself, of course, a historically specific way of thinking about history).[1]

The focus of contestation, then, is very often not conflicting accounts of what actually happened in the past so much as the question of who or what is entitled to speak for that past in the present. The attempt to resolve meaning in the present is thus often a matter of conflicts over representation: where a memorial should be sited, what artefacts a museum should include, whose views should be sought in television interviews. In these debates the contest is often over how truth can best be conveyed, rather than what actually happened. There may be agreement as to the course of events, but not over how the truth of those events may be most fully represented, or what should be the explanatory and narrative context that would make sense of a given episode. And if these arguments are partly historical, memory, in such debates, occupies a particular place. In all the debates over the relationship between memory and history, one constantly recurring theme is that although history is about the present, so too is memory, and much more directly. Memory is still live and active, still charged with the weight

1

of these contests, and it is to memory that one should turn in order to reveal 'what really happened'.

The appeal to memory in determining the truth of the past, then, is widespread. But it is also problematic: both 'memory' and 'truth' here are unstable and destabilising terms. To privilege memory as a tool of truth, through which the statements of authority may be subverted or contradicted, we must assume a direct correspondence between the experience and how it is remembered. The person who remembers, in this model, is able to know and tell the truth of the event, because s/he was there at the time. Experience is the guarantee of certainty; distortion an ideological weapon, opposed to the real facts, and imposed by ideological means (media, academy … ). But for history as for other disciplines, after the critical revolutions of the last decades, the answer cannot be so straightforward. Not only the reliability of memory and experience as exact records of the past, but also the very notion of historical truth, have come into question; the past is constituted in narrative, always representation, always construction. In so far as historians have engaged in memory studies, indeed, they have done so primarily because the concept of memory seems to offer a more cautious and qualified relation to the past than the absolute assertion that for some is associated with history. Working with the concept of memory – provisional, subjective, concerned with representation and the present rather than fact and the past – suggests a way out of the impasse into which historiography might have been driven by the poststructuralist assault on truth.[2]

But if the vocabulary of memory is found with increasing frequency in historical work, this still could not be said to make it more than a minority interest for historians. The relation between memory and history is complex, and has been constituted in many different ways by historians and others in the last few decades.[3] And yet it remains a curiously unrealised relation, as if conversations or conceptualisations are taking place independently of one another, and with little mutual awareness. Within the field of memory studies, 'history' is a key reference point, invoked both in titles and in discussion. A glance at a few titles gives an indication of the characteristic juxtapositions: Felman and Laub's *Testimony: crises of witnessing in literature, psychoanalysis and history* (1992), for instance, or Vivian Sobchack's 1996 collection *The Persistence of History: cinema, television and the modern event*.[4] But 'memory studies' itself, despite its interdisciplinary potential and despite the way in which the idea of memory has become dispersed across many different fields (anthropology, psychology, sociology) is located most firmly in disciplines most accustomed to a concern with representation: literature, film studies, cultural studies.[5]

Arguments about the relation between history and memory have thus to a surprisingly large extent (and of course with exceptions) taken place outside the historical profession. 'History', prominent though it is in these debates, stands for a certain notion of truth and a certain notion of referentiality, to be summoned up as a tool in arguments going on elsewhere, rather than identifying the place where the argument is happening. The academic discipline of history has engaged with issues of memory much less than a brief survey of 'memory studies' might lead one to expect. There have been journal articles and special features, and the word appears in conference titles more than it used to.[6] But a brief survey of recent works on historiography suggests that memory has had surprisingly little impact on historical writing or on theorisations of history.[7] Curiously, although it is often assumed that the rise of 'memory' goes alongside that of 'poststructuralism' (presumably leaving 'history' tied to 'empiricism'),[8] poststructuralist historiographies seem particularly uninterested in memory. With few exceptions, theoretically informed historiographical studies tend to locate memory as a sub-category of oral history, or to ignore it altogether. Of two recent critical readers on history and theory, for example – Geoffrey Roberts's *History and Narrative Reader*, on 'the history and narrative debate' since 1960, and Anne Green and Kathleen Troup's collection *The Houses of History: a critical reader in twentieth-century history and theory* – the first has no index entry for memory, and the second directs the searcher to 'see oral history'.[9] The idea of history, it seems, has been more important to memory studies than vice versa.

In this sense one might argue that the challenge represented by Raphael Samuel's *Theatres of Memory* (1994), widely cited though the book is, has never really been taken up.[10] The book's concern with how the past is represented and engaged with in the present through an extraordinary variety of forms – television, fashions in interior decoration, historical walks, family histories, local museums, school textbooks – has certainly been followed through; but the field is identified primarily as 'public history' – history in the public sphere – not as 'memory', in the sense that Samuel used it.[11] Public history may cover very similar ground to that of *Theatres of Memory*, and may indeed draw on memory discourses; its field might be identified as social or cultural memory, it might look at memorial discourses in museums, and so on. But the very fact that this field has come to be known as 'public history' must say something about the discomfort historians continue to feel in working with the concept of memory. And Samuel's central suggestion, that history might use memory actually to rethink its own conceptual and disciplinary boundaries and practices, and to acknowledge common characteristics rather than setting up the two as opposites, does not appear to have found much of a following.[12] Bill Schwarz's discussion of memory and historical time, in our companion volume *Regimes of Memory*, is a rare example of a historian suggesting that memory might be integrated into historiography.[13] Often, it seems, history is willing to question the epistemological status of its object of study – the past – but less ready to engage with how 'the past' itself is variously conceptualised and constituted as history, memory, or archive.

The remainder of this introduction, then, returns to the question of the relation between history and memory, in the larger framework of the relation between the past and the present: in what fields has the encounter between history and memory been staged? What problems emerge in that encounter? And what is at stake in contests over the past? Implicit in these debates are questions about the social and individual dimensions of memory, and the media through which memory is experienced, produced or conveyed.

## Witnessing history (1): the spoken word

One major exception to the relative reserve of history confronted with memory, of course, is the field of oral history, in which the concept of memory – the idea of memory *as* concept, rather than as given phenomenon – has been increasingly significant over the last couple of decades. This is hardly surprising. Oral historians, whose work involves soliciting the memories of the living, are ideally placed to reflect on and theorise the issues that the processes of remembering and retelling bring forward; and over the last few decades, there has been a shift in the preoccupations of oral history, involving an increasing attentiveness to issues of memory.[14] In its origins, however, oral history's view of memory was less complex. It laid claim precisely to an authentic truth excluded from the historical record.[15] It solicited the voices of those who have been silent and ignored throughout the centuries: the poor and powerless, workers and women, who seldom have speaking parts in the historical drama. It attended to the private, the domestic, the details of daily life, rather than to great events. And it found in the memories evoked a counter-narrative, a corrective to the simplifying and patronising assumptions of the traditional makers of history.[16]

Thus, in the first instance, oral history offers a validation of memory as *more* true and more reliable than other records: these people know what it was like, because they were there.[17] Early distrust of oral history, indeed, expressed itself at times precisely as contempt for the rememberers: old men drooling about their youth, in A.J.P. Taylor's notorious phrase.[18] And it is as a popularising and democratic form of history that it has become most widespread. Along with family history – and often closely allied to it, as family historians tape-record ancient relatives to fill out the picture and get crucial genealogical details before death snatches them out of reach – it has become a grass-roots practice. Schoolchildren are encouraged to interview their grandparents (as Graham Carr notes in this volume); local enthusiasts publish booklets in small presses recording *Memories of Old Poplar*, or *Memories of Highgate from a Keeper's Lodge*, to be sold in local shops and libraries, used by schoolchildren (again) for projects, and so on.[19]

All this activity is founded on, and confirms, a belief that one's own memory is more to be relied on than other forms of knowledge: if I remember something, it must be true; this vivid picture in my mind could not have sprung up at random. But it is precisely in revealing the ways in which memory, even when it seems most real and definite, is not a certain guarantee of truth, that oral history has developed into such a fruitful area for thinking about memory. This is not to return to a dismissive approach to those whose accounts of the past have previously been ignored. If at times people claim memories of what evidently never happened, or happened other than how they remember it, this does not mean their memories are invalid or irrelevant, but that different questions need to be asked. The focus of historical analysis shifts from the notion of memory as either 'true' or 'mistaken', to an emphasis on memory as process, and how to understand its motivation and meaning. How do people recollect events they were involved in or witnesses to, and what can be learned from their narratives? These

4

are the questions now posed by oral history, as several contributors to this volume point out. The very fact that there are divergences, inconsistencies, different versions at different times, is in itself revealing both about the culture in which these memories have been built and emerge, and about the workings of memory itself.[20] The idea of memory as a tool with which to contest 'official' versions of the past, too, shifts from an opposition between the subordinate truth versus the dominant lie, to a concern with the ways in which particular versions of an event may be at various times and for various reasons promoted, reformulated, or silenced. This is not to deny that the dominant versions of the past are inextricably entangled with relations of power in society, but rather to refocus the question around the many ways in which conflict and contest can emerge.

Such work also reminds us that memory is not only individual but cultural: memory, though we may experience it as private and internal, draws on countless scraps and bits of knowledge and information from the surrounding culture, and is inserted into larger cultural narratives.[21] This is a relationship that goes both ways, of course. If individual memories are constructed within culture, and are part of cultural systems of representation, so cultural memories are constituted by the cumulative weight of dispersed and fragmented individual memories, among other things. We may 'remember' the 1960s, or the Second World War, in our own lifetimes; but it would be impossible to remember them without seeing them in the framework established subsequently of what a given decade or event *means*. And what it means is itself an occasion for cultural struggle. If history and oral history are now both inclined to be more cautious about the notion of an absolute historical truth, there remains nonetheless a sharp sense that it is possible to tell lies about the past; and that the meanings and narratives of the past that we live with are of critical importance in establishing our sense of ourselves and our cultures.

Moreover, while the model of authorities imposing false histories (to be countered by memory) may be too simple, it is clear that questions of power and authority do not disappear in thinking about what versions of history come to be identified as true. For history and memory are not abstract forces: they are located in specific contexts, instances, and narratives, and decisions have always to be taken about what story is to be told. Memory as it is invoked in schools, museums, and mass media may be forwarding political agendas which serve particular ideas about the virtues of the nation, the family, or the current government, as several of the pieces in this volume demonstrate.[22] The appeal to memory itself (as opposed to its content) may carry particular ideological assumptions about history and subjectivity, as we shall see below. Thus moving away from a model of 'truth' vs. 'distortion' does not imply moving away from a sense that memory is political; it remains a site of struggle over meaning. This sense of struggle, of contest, indeed, runs through all the chapters in this volume: memory, in both private and public manifestations, makes claims about the past, which will not be acceptable to everybody. And if these differences in some instances seem reconcilable, in others there is a sense of intractability. As examples in this volume indicate, memories of the Finnish Civil War may be moving towards a consensus; memories of the 'adoption' of aboriginal children in Australia will probably prove much harder to agree.

## Witnessing history (2): trauma and history

If oral history is one field in which the notion of memory has been a focus for special interest, another area particularly associated with the vocabulary of remembrance is that of holocaust studies.[23] The two, indeed, at times are hard to separate out. A cluster of politically and emotionally charged concepts – witnessing, testimony, trauma, silence, memory, history, denial – keep recurring in discussions of the holocaust, not so much in relation to the historical event as to its memorial afterlife.[24] Trauma theory, the 'home' of this cluster, in its origins a discourse relating to the psychology of individuals, has become an explanatory apparatus through which to apprehend and analyse the past; partly through the frame of the individual memory, but also through a more general set of arguments about representation, what could be said, what could be remembered and how.[25] Founded on the notion of an originary traumatic event, however, trauma theory returns us to precisely the problems about the nature of the event that memory as it stands in relation to history helps us to rethink. Memory cannot be seen as a simple evasion of the problem of referentiality, since it is itself a referential system. But its relation to historical 'events' is complex and mediated, involving fantasy and wish rather than simply recording what happens. If memory slides uncertainly along a line with history and fantasy at either end, trauma theory has difficulty in acknowledging the place of fantasy.

At the heart of the idea of traumatic memory, as it developed particularly in relation to the sexual abuse of children, is the idea of unrepresentability. Following a terrible event, it suggests, memory goes into crisis, and refuses the knowledge of what has happened. The theoretical crux is the idea of something that cannot be thought, that is inaccessibly closed to memory, because the psychic wound inflicted by the event was intolerable. Thus the notion of trauma complicates referentiality by interposing the disruptions of memory between the event and its representations. But whereas for oral history, as we have seen, those disruptions are intrinsic to memory itself (which distorts, conflates, masks, omits), for trauma theory it is a specific event that disrupts a memory that would otherwise – in its healthy state – be unperturbed. Underpinning the theory of traumatic memory is a particular narrative of the psychic consequences of a real event; and the debates around what can and cannot be spoken, remembered, represented, take place in relation to arguments about whether that event happened or not – so, once again, in the context of a contested past, in which neither events nor their meanings can straightforwardly be known.[26]

These issues will be returned to in the introduction to Part II 'Remembering suffering'. For the moment it is worth noting that, while this conceptualisation of the relation between the traumatic event and its subsequent representation has been hugely influential in the two particular instances of childhood sexual abuse and the holocaust, it is striking how seldom the main concerns of trauma theory appear in other historical or national contexts.[27] Other massacres and genocides, other experiences of violence, loss, suffering, displacement, are either little studied, or studied in other contexts than that of traumatic memory. Despite the association of memory with the capacity of minority or subordinated peoples to generate alternative narratives of their own pasts, academic papers dealing with the experiences of (for example) Rwandans, or Tamils, or East Timorese, or Kurds, or Armenians, or indeed Palestinians, seldom seem to address their sufferings in a framework of either trauma or memory.[28]

To argue for the extension of trauma theory beyond the fields with which it has become associated, as Paula Hamilton suggests in this volume, is however a more problematic suggestion than one might think, even apart from the theoretical questions that are raised by this approach. The specific horrors of the holocaust have generated a sense that it is a problem for representation in a way that no other event can be; that it is set apart, requiring its own language, its own theory; that, ultimately, discussion of holocaust memory should be somehow excused the norms of critical interchange. And this is, clearly, an argument with a politics attached, and one which becomes increasingly problematic as it leaches into debate over the present-day politics of the state of Israel. The tendency to regard the state of Israel as the present-day representative of the Jewish victims of the Third Reich often leads to the implication that to question the policies of that state becomes a direct attack on those who suffered the holocaust.[29] Thus to draw the application of trauma theory out beyond its 'home' in holocaust studies has implications that go beyond the academic.

But equally, the replacement in this context of historical with memorial discourses has direct and significant implications for the meaning of the event in the present. To the extent that trauma theory is a memory discourse, it aims precisely to summon up the presentness of memory, to insist on unfinished business: guilt and reparation remain the dominant themes. So to emphasise memory over history, perversely enough, can mean to remain past rather than future-oriented. It is of course true of states in general, as the chapters in Part III 'Patterning the National Past' remind us, that they find ways of accommodating the difference of the past and moving forward; and it is precisely around such moments that the relation between memory and history becomes particularly fraught.

## Memory, history, empathy

'History', we have suggested, with certain exceptions, has been less willing to engage with 'memory' than one might expect, whether as a methodology or as a perspective from which to examine its own disciplinary constitution. It may be, however, that this is not only a mark of the conservatism of much historical work. The difference between them as modes of engaging with the past seems in certain respects an important one to maintain, and not only for practitioners of history; there are questions to be asked about what happens when discourses of memory so to speak infiltrate the 'historical', which do not always suggest memory's impact will be beneficial. For if in relation to the academic discipline of history memory seems potentially fruitful, a reminder of the complex ways in which we know and live with and through the past, in its more public manifestations – in relation to history in schools, history in politics, history in the public sphere – there is perhaps more unease. To appeal to memory over history can imply the displacing of analysis by empathy, of politics by sentiment, as Carr suggests in his discussion of the tropes of memory in Canadian engagements with the Second World War. Memory, because of its powerful pull towards the present, and because of its affective investments, allows more readily for a certain evasion of critical distance.[30] Thus, although some of the most interesting recent work in the field of memory suggests that the analysis even of powerful personal memories can be carried out without abandoning critical distance[31], memory's public uses often seem problematic. Instead of allowing us to think critically about how divisions between personal and political are constituted, it may be that the political dimensions of memory are discounted in favour of its ability to summon up the personal – a move which has implications for the conceptualisation of civil society, and which we discuss further in the introduction to our companion volume *Regimes of Memory*.

Memory's capacity to bridge thinking about the individual and the social, similarly, can become problematic.[32] Memory in common use is tied to the individual: memory is indeed the defining moment of western subjectivity, that which distinguishes one person from another and anchors social beings in their individual identities. Its extension into a wider sphere of course also has a long history, as the prominent place assigned to the arts of memory in past cultures reminds us; and individual memory is inseparably bound up with cultural memory, as we have seen. Nonetheless it is in certain ways a metaphorical extension, a way of drawing an equivalence from the workings of the mind to the workings of society at large; and when policy is built on that metaphor, questions may be asked about its appropriateness. We need, perhaps, a vocabulary that allows us to think more precisely about the different aspects of memory, while retaining a sense of their connections. The political memory of members of a group is not identical with the personal memories of the individual activist, even though they may share events and concerns in common, as Carrie Hamilton's discussion of the interweaving of public and private memories among Basque nationalists suggests; one person may hold memories from more than one category.[33] The emblems and articulations of memory in flags and films, memorials and museums, are in a different register of memory to that of the single individual's recollections of his or her own life, however the two may interconnect.

The collapsing of personal and public registers is one of the most prominent features of the turn to memory. As we have seen, it has serious implications conceptually as well as politically, and indeed the two cannot readily be separated. Colvin, in his analysis of the workings of the Truth and Reconciliation

Committee in post-apartheid South Africa, suggests that what we see at work in such enterprises is an extension of a 'therapeutic ethic', developed particularly in relation to traumatised individuals, to an entire culture, and correlatively to the production of history. Social policy comes to see its task as one of revealing traumatic secrets in order to cure them. The memory of individual actors in the trauma is solicited in order to cure the entire society; the production of history is thus tied to a narrative of disclosure, closure and reconciliation, along with the particular model of the relation between past and present that the traumatic narrative implies. Colvin's critique of this therapeutic ethic suggests that history should serve other needs than therapy. To think historically implies different orders of causality to those assumed by a model of guilt and reparation. It requires attention to politics and economics, to ideology and culture; it identifies problems which should be addressed through policy rather than therapy. This need not exclude attention to the emotional weight of the past in the present, but it does imply a different relationship to it. What is culturally valuable in such situations is precisely history's distance from the present, its ability to look coolly at the past rather than being drawn into the role of therapist; and memory, by contrast, is perhaps too readily co-opted into this role.

Moreover, implicitly, to assent to a therapeutic relationship between past and present would imply returning to a model of memory in which memory speaks for truth: there was an event, it is remembered (painfully), it must be spoken in order to defuse it. But for history, as we suggested earlier, the recourse to memory has provided a way of rethinking the notion of the originary event, and the teleologies of cause and effect. As a mode of thinking about the past that allows history to acknowledge its imaginary dimension, its own implication in fantasy and the constructedness of its narratives, memory is a useful corrective to history's claims to objectivity. But at the point where memory binds and limits the past into a purely subjective mode, and undoes the distinction between the individual and the collective, then its effects are perhaps more problematic.

## Generations: change, loss, death

As memory is bound up with ideas about subjectivity, so also it has a bearing on death, and the passing away of the subject – which leads to a different set of problems. For if memory, at least in common use, implies a person who is remembering, then with the rememberer, memory dies; and history traditionally might have been seen as that which replaces memory, as generations replace one another. Historians of any period before the twentieth century necessarily have a different relation to the idea of memory to those who focus on the last hundred years: working on any epoch before the modern means that memories cannot be directly solicited from the objects of study. Scholars may work with memory documents such as autobiographies and diaries, or with the signs and symbols of memory in previous cultures (that is to say on the history of memory itself, or on how it has been implicated in for instance the constitution of national identity, or

9

arguments about civil liberties); but they do not converse with people who remember. This is of course the central and self-evident reason why memory has been so much more prominent, and so much more creatively developed, in oral history than in history of other sorts. It also reminds practitioners that those who remember are constantly on the point of vanishing; that memory is a fragile possession, to be seized from its aged and valuable bearers and passed on. And one of the interesting features of the way in which memory is mobilised in contemporary culture is the intense anxiety attaching to this disappearance, as if the inevitable moment when there is no longer anyone left alive who remembers the nineteenth century, or the First World War, must be deferred as long as possible, if not somehow prevented altogether.[34]

Contemporary attempts to preserve as 'memory' things which are in the course of becoming 'history', then, seem to need explanation. Graham Carr's account of the attempt to preserve the memory of the First and Second World Wars in the minds of younger generations as the war veterans themselves die identifies an urge to seize memory at the moment it is on the point of evaporating, as if by direct transmission from old to young it can be kept alive and out of the realm of the 'historical'. Something similar can be seen in the recent renewed interest in Britain in commemorative rituals such as the two-minute silence on Armistice Day.[35] It is not hard to see political agendas in such instances as these, but they are not only political. Physical and ritual memorials are in a sense another means of trying to ensure the preservation of meaning in memory, to prolong an existence in the present, where history is seen to allow it to escape – letting the past bury its dead. There are complex issues at stake here about attachment and letting go, as well as about politics and the contestation of the past; testimony, as Portelli reminds us elsewhere, means among other things the passing on of knowledge that might otherwise disappear.[36] But also, perhaps, the urge to translate memories from one generation to the next signals an inability to think of history as connected with the present. It would be hard to substitute memory for history in idioms such as 'but that's history now', or 'you're history!' – 'but that's memory' would immediately imply a continuing resonance, a continuing ability to command attention in present-day minds.

One way of seeing this desire that memory should continue beyond the lifespan of the rememberer would be as a decentring of the subject, perhaps, and a reminder that memory is also social. Detached from the self who remembers, memory can become a property to be inherited and passed on, continuing to function in the minds of others after the 'original' rememberer has gone. This, indeed, is reminiscent of the Sakalava model described by Lambek in our companion volume.[37] Given the cultural variability of models of subjectivity, the close connection made in western culture between subject and memory can be seen as a historical form now passing; and this has repercussions on conceptualisations of the memory/history pair as well, as the discussion above suggested. But we do not have ways of conceiving of the person that would allow for the transmission of memories from one to another by spiritual means; there must be institutional forms that mediate the transmission of memory, and it seems they often do so in ways that reinforce existing models of the relation between self and social, or self and other. Concepts such as cultural memory, social memory, public memory, important as they are in detaching the idea of memory from its fixation on the individual, seem unstable, too capacious and imprecise to allow for much clarity in all this.[38]

## Charting memories

Memory, of course, does not operate only as an abstract (mental) system: it is generated by and channelled through an endless variety of media and artefacts. Closely related to the anxiety of loss of memory in the persons of the disappearing generations is the anxiety about objects and places, the stuff of memory which itself has power to represent or stand in for the past, and whose destruction must be fended off. The establishment of memorial sites, places where the past is not only preserved as fetish but also transmitted as signification, is inevitably a focus for struggle over meaning: whose monument is permitted, and what meanings may it convey? And since these sites are also often publicly established, or at least sanctioned, they are inescapably implicated in the construction of narratives – or perhaps maps – of national identity.

Memorials and museums are themselves physical locations: people go to them, walk about them. To apprehend the meaning of such a site, to follow its narrative, it is necessary to move about on the surface of the world. This movement in a sense replicates – or at least echoes – one of the most familiar metaphors of memory, that of the map, in all its variety. The journey (from place to place), the memory theatre (from icon to icon); figures such as the garden, the palace, the labyrinth, all evoke this horizontal dimension. If one familiar set of metaphors for memory concerns depth and containment, then – memory as closet, cauldron, archaeological dig – another set emphasises its topographical aspect, reminding us how closely memory is tied to place, and how many of its moments of disjuncture and complexity are associated with changes in a place, registering the uncanniness of being at once the same and different, at once time and space.

The importance of the horizontal dimension – memory as flat surface over which one wanders – is apparent in many of the chapters in this volume: from memorial parks and train journeys to Passerini's imagined itinerary, memory traverses, is spatial as well as vertical. Freud's attempt to imagine the city of Rome as different times co-existing in a single space, discussed in the introduction to *Regimes of Memory*, is a well-known instance. Portelli's Rome, oscillating between the streets of the German occupation (uniforms, queues, people hiding behind heavy doors) and the modern city, adds a couple of later layers to Freud's; his is also a city of the imagination, with its clearly remembered nonexistent warning posters, and its streets swept by rumours.

Place names are one way of insisting on the reality of a particular version of the past, and also (therefore) of the present. To know an area as the Basque country is not the same as knowing it as Euskadi, in the same way as to refer to south-eastern Turkey as Kurdistan evokes a different history, and insists on a different knowledge of place. So for a new regime, the act of renaming attempts to rewrite the past by changing the place that is the present: St Petersburg and its avatars; Cambodia/Kampuchea; or Palestine again.[39] For nationalism, naming and renaming – the continuing transformation of the supposedly eternal physical environment – is one of its most powerful and contentious tools, as well as one of power's most explicit attempts to rewrite the past, literally reinscribing the surface of the world, and changing the name on the map – often while laying claim to something more ancient and authentic than the 'old' one. Memory here may act subversively in refusing to 'remember' the new name, as one may refuse to 'remember' new coinage, or new vocabulary, in a gesture of resistance against unwanted change.

The fact that not only names but places change is somehow one of memory's most intractable problems, or at least one of its most insistent themes.[40] Hirsch and Spitzer's Czernowitz is no longer Czernowitz (even to the name); sites of oppression (Robben Island, Tuol Sleng) are now museums, and yet still able to be what they are only because of what they were before. Identity is often located in a specific physical landscape, and through the changes in that landscape, the memory of times when it was different, changes in the self may be perceived and registered. We measure the passage of time in ourselves against the houses that have been built since we walked down a given road as a child, and the children who have already grown to adulthood in those new houses; we return to landscapes known before they were transformed by some tremendous upheaval, and experience the dislocating impossibility of their difference.

But imaginary landscapes are also important in the construction of identity (and all landscapes are imaginary). Images of the lost homeland – Ireland, Afghanistan – can be passed down generations, summoning up loyalties and nostalgia. In some cases this may produce a powerful identification with the parents' lost physical environment, as nostalgia, or as charge: to go back, to reclaim what was lost. In others it is a more reluctant and ambivalent bond: the children who have come to belong somewhere else will not readily be summoned back. In either instance, what is returned to will not be the same. (Hirsch and Spitzer's chapter in this volume reflects on these problems.) Landscape, in any case, is little touched by human concerns for memory: give or take a few centuries, and the battlefields will be ordinary meadows; the memorials insisting on the reality of the deaths that took place will become illegible and crumble away. In the meantime, though, the urge to put bookmarks all over the physical world attempts to recreate everywhere the palimpsest city, to ensure that nothing is lost – or conversely that only certain things are not; there are desirable amnesias here. Arguments over the preservation or abandonment of particular sites, of course, are embroiled in political and economic interests, as well as abstract and emotional ones.

Memorials and museums represent public statements about what the past has been, and how the present should acknowledge it; who should be remembered, who should be forgotten; which acts or events are foundational, which marginal; what gets respected, what neglected. Because of their visibility, and the authority with which they are invested, they can become a particular focus for resentment and contest, as Heimo and Peltonen's account of Finnish memorials after the Civil War shows; to grant or refuse a monument to the dead is a potent signal of approved (authorised) national values. But even without a background of open conflict, the statements made by memorials are complex and multifaceted; the meanings assigned to and derived from them cannot be guaranteed; and there are difficulties in accommodating the weight of meaning they may be required to carry. The presence of a museum alone cannot guarantee that the conflict is over, as Colvin's description of the Robben Island museum suggests. In asserting the existence of a new nation – whether administratively or territorially – such sites can function instead to focus debates that are often highly charged. And different viewpoints do not disappear when the nation is (so to speak) already established. As an instance of public memory, the museum or memorial attempts to reconcile what Burgoyne refers to as 'the interplay of official, vernacular and commercial cultural viewpoints and expressions' (p.209); official and popular wishes for a memorial site do not always coincide.

## Memory texts

Memory stories, in western tradition, are most familiarly told in narrative. Autobiography is the exemplary instance, and its rise in the early modern period is tied into stories of the emergence of the modern western self, however problematically. The single consciousness that can narrate itself as a continuity over time is replicated and reinvented in diaries, novels, witness statements, confessions – a flood of self-narrative now perhaps at its height. This is perhaps something of a paradox, given that for Jameson the contemporary subject has lost the capacity to construe and narrate itself as continuing through time.[41] If the history of western consciousness has been inextricably tied to this account of the self, the twentieth century has seen an insistence on fracture, multiplicity, discontinuity – the self as episodic rather than continuous; and alongside the decentring of the west has been a reminder of other ways of conceptualising consciousness, identity and the self than through memory. Thus over the last few decades there has been a broadening out of the category of the memory text into collective rather than subjective contexts, and non-narrative as well as narrative forms.[42] Interpretation reaches far beyond the limits of autobiography, finding memory texts in places old – medieval spiritual writings, folk songs, patchwork quilts – and new – photographs, department stores, websites.

In particular, the question of the relation between memory's narrative and metaphorical aspects – what we might think of, again, as its vertical and horizontal lines – is one which may perhaps be most successfully explored or engaged with in non-traditional narrative forms. Film, here, is particularly significant, and both Walker and Healy suggest that film, with its juxtapositions, flashbacks, fadeouts and affective immediacy, may offer a more appropriate medium or model for memory work than more traditional media. Film, memory and history thus intertwine in various ways. Film, of course, is instrumental in producing its own narratives of the past, especially the national past; and if these narratives can be contestatory, as Healy suggests is the case with *Dead Man*, they are also often conservative. Like computer technology, film may provide a new metaphorical language that allows us to rethink memory processes.[43] And it appears also as a model for historical writing that allows full weight to the uncertainties and fractures of the past, rather than depending on the teleology of narrative structures; in particular, Walker suggests, documentary film can subvert the problem of the 'real event' through a 'simultaneous insistence on irrevocable truth and refusal of realist mode' (p.111).[44]

What makes a film a memory text, then, may be not so much a matter of its explicit content as of its form: it may enact mnemonic processes as well as, or instead of, being about memories. But this is perhaps equally true of every medium for memory. The form, the physical and conceptual structure, of the museum, it has already been suggested, is as significant in its representation of memory as the actual objects it contains; the choice and location of a war memorial is as revealing as its explicit injunction of remembrance. And the range of memorial materials and practices represented in this volume are a reminder of the complexity of defining a memory work. School projects, advertising campaigns, television, local traditions, graffiti, journalism; all these contribute to the formation of both individual and cultural memories.

## The past in the present

The relationship between past and present in the chapters in this volume is a problem. The chapters deal with how that problem is negotiated, or denied; how contradictory versions may move towards reconciliation, or how they refuse to; how from one generation to another memory is transmitted, and what are its messages. They also deal with how that problem is mapped onto the physical environment, and how meaning is located in space.

The first part, 'Transforming memory', is concerned primarily with the social and personal transmission of memory, across time and generations. How are memories communicated, and how do they change meaning, both for those who remember and for those who receive their memories? The contexts here are very different. Memories of events that shattered communities or nations may move in the course of a few generations from painful silence to stories that attempt to rebuild consensus and re-establish community, as Heimo and Peltonen demonstrate in their account of memories of the Finnish Civil War. Memory's conservative and reparative effects, or at least its drive towards such effects – not always successful – can be seen also in the other chapters in this part. In Portelli's account of the afterlife of a massacre in Rome during the German occupation, a dramatically misremembered version has achieved hegemony, apparently in the interests of the postwar rebuilding of the Italian state, but his account makes clear the inadequacy of reconciliation as justification for denial. Graham Carr focuses on the tensions arising out of conflicting accounts of Canada's involvement in the Second World War: what is heroism to one generation may appear as morally problematic to another; but the appeal to memorial discourses, he suggests, attempts to smooth over that difference and insists on the unifying and uplifting effects of the war. Finally Hirsch and Spitzer engage with the question of the afterlife of memory from a personal perspective, contemplating the effects of what they identify as 'postmemory' on the children of those who have survived terrible events.

The question of the after-effects of catastrophe is brought to the fore in Part II, 'Remembering suffering'. Here the chapters engage more directly with the questions about trauma raised in this introduction, and also with the more general issue of how cataclysmic events are remembered. Janet Walker identifies the specific features of traumatic memory and explores their representation in film, arguing that trauma poses the problem of referentiality with peculiar starkness: the 'memory' of trauma is often a symbolic or metaphorical representation of the unbearable, rather than an accurately described event. Paula Hamilton, in a wide-ranging reflection on the culture of memory in contemporary Australia, focuses on the case of the 'lost generation', Aboriginal children taken from their parents by the state as part of postwar social policy, and considers the subsequent representation of this in public memory; arguments about suffering and restitution are similarly bound up with questions of reliable testimony and effective ways forward. Chris Colvin's exploration of how memory is mobilised in dealing with the past in post-apartheid South Africa offers a more critical take on memorial frameworks, and specifically on the recourse to the discourse of trauma, suggesting that a model of recovery based on the suffering of the individual cannot adequately engage with the larger historical dimensions of the problem: both individuals and society, he suggests, are being asked to recognise themselves in a discourse of disclosure followed by closure, which is not always successful. And Carrie Hamilton, analysing the complex interplay between private and public memories of violence among Basque women from families engaged in armed struggle, interprets the elisions and evasions of her interviewees' memories as a way of dealing with terrible events in the past, but does so in relation to oral history rather than trauma theory.

In Part III, the relation between nation and memory – an important theme for several chapters in previous parts – is the central issue; and the struggle involved in producing smooth and non-contestatory narratives is repeatedly apparent. The focus in all these pieces is on the media through which the national past may be constructed and represented. Rachel Hughes, investigating the museum of Tuol Sleng, in which victims of the Cambodian genocide are commemorated, emphasises how the complex internal and external politics of the new regime shaped its representation of the past; here again we see an attempt to use memory to repair and move on, which does not always correspond to the wishes of those visiting the museum. Similarly, Maya Nadkarni's account of the construction of the Statue Park in Budapest, simultaneously acknowledging the nation's Communist past and displacing it to the margins of the city, registers the complex ways in which new regimes attempt to come to terms with their predecessors in the public space. Robert Burgoyne, focusing on the centrality of rock music in the construction of America's own narrative of its identity, argues that the museum attempts to manoeuvre a combative and critical musical history into a narrative of accommodation and progress – from contest to consensus, in effect. And Chris Healy, taking another formative myth of American identity – the Western – suggests that film can in fact comment critically on such myths, and offer an anti-consensual memory that reminds America of its own colonial injustices.

The final part contains only one chapter, Luisa Passerini's reflections on the complex and multiple meanings of silence and oblivion. Amnesia is often used as a figure for the denial of shameful pasts; but silence does not always imply either denial or forgetting, and Passerini explores the moments when memory does not speak in order to raise questions about what it speaks for, and how.

The chapters in this volume, then, offer a complex awareness of the workings of memory, and the ways in which different or changing histories may be explained. They explore the relation between individual and social memory, between real and imaginary, event and fantasy, history and myth. If the past is contested, it is not for simple reasons. Institutions, governments, cultures, individuals, are all engaged in the work of making memory and in its repeated transformations. Contradictory accounts, or memories in direct contradiction to the historical record, are not always the sign of a repressive authority attempting to cover something up. Memory itself covers up: it reshapes, attempts to comfort, addresses changing needs. The tension between memory as a safeguard against attempts to silence dissenting voices, and memory's own implication in that silencing, runs throughout the book; but that tension is precisely what gives memory the complex resonance it has in intellectual and political life.

## Notes

1 See, for an exploration of these themes, Stephan Feuchtwang, 'Loss: transmissions, recognitions, authorisations', in S. Radstone and K. Hodgkin (eds), *Regimes of Memory*, London, Routledge 2003.

2 For further discussion of this, see Hayden White, *Tropics of Discourse*, New York, John Hopkins University Press, 1978; Keith Jenkins, *Re-Thinking History*, London, Routledge 1991.

3 This is a relation too large and complex to be traced in any detail here. But for a few contrasting points of reference, see for instance Jacques Le Goff, who in the 1986 Preface to the essays collected in his *History and Memory*, trans. Steven Rendall and Elizabeth Claman, New York, Columbia University Press 1992, states, 'Recent, naïve trends seem virtually to identify history with memory, and even to give preference in some sense to memory' and insists instead that 'Memory is the raw material of history ... it is the living source from which historians draw' (pp. xi–xii). Pierre Nora,

in his influential essay 'Memory and counter-memory', *Representations* 26, Spring 1989, also insists on a firm distinction between memory and history. Raphael Samuel in *Theatres of Memory*, London, Verso 1994, argues polemically for a recognition of the artificiality of the divide, pointing out the resemblances between the two: 'history involves a series of erasures, emendations and amalgamations quite similar to those which Freud sets out in his account of "screen memories"' (p. x). And Ludmilla Jordanova in her recent *History in Practice*, London, Arnold 2000, situating memory in the context of a discussion of historical periodisation, comments: 'At the level of individuals, both historians and those they study, time is managed by memory. ... The practice of history is, after all, a highly specialised form of commemoration. Yet we need to problematise the very notion of memory' (p. 138).

4  Shoshana Felman and Dori Laub, *Testimony: crises of witnessing in literature, psychoanalysis and history*, New York and London, Routledge 1992; Vivian Sobchack, *The Persistence of History: cinema, television and the modern event*, New York and London, Routledge 1996. It's worth remarking that both these books would be generally regarded as key texts in memory studies; yet both prefer the word 'history' to 'memory' in their titles.

5  A few examples: Peter Middleton and Tim Woods (eds), *Literatures of Memory: history, time and space in postwar writing*, Manchester, Manchester University Press 2000; Maureen Turim, *Flashbacks in Film: memory and history*, New York and London, Routledge 1989; Ann Scott, *Real Events Revisited: fantasy, memory and psychoanalysis*, London, Virago 1996. Journals such as *Representations*, *Screen* and *New Formations* have been particularly influential in the development of 'memory studies'.

6  See, for instance, *American Historical Review* 5, December 1997. The Routledge Memory and Narrative series, in which this volume and its companion *Regimes of Memory* appear, is another place where history and memory converge; and *History Workshop Journal* has published a number of articles working with the concept of memory over the last ten years (e.g. Catherine Merridale, 'Death and memory in modern Russia', *History Workshop Journal* 42, Autumn 1996; Heather Goodall, 'Telling Country: memory, modernity and narratives in rural Australia', *History Workshop Journal* 47, Spring 1999).

7  This is a different perspective from that taken by Kerwin Lee Klein in his recent article 'On the emergence of *Memory* in historical discourse', *Representations* 69, Winter 2000, where he argues that memory has become central to historical discourse: '*Memory* is replacing old favorites – *nature, culture, language* – as the word most commonly paired with history, and that shift is remaking historical imagination' (p. 128). It's a very stimulating and thoughtful discussion; but at least in terms of the British history scene, he seems to overstate memory's influence in historical writing.

8  See Klein, 'On the emergence of *Memory*': 'Recent works on memory often tie the rise of the word to the waves of theory that had washed over American human sciences by the 1980s ... [there is a] common sense that "memory" is the new critical conjunction of history and theory' (p. 128).

9  Similarly, the *Routledge Companion to Historical Studies*, (ed.) Alan Munslow, Routledge 2000, a keyword dictionary which claims to identify and explain 'key concepts for the new history', has no entry for 'memory'. John Tosh's *The Pursuit of History*, interestingly, is marked by a distinct shift between the second edition of 1991 – where the index offers only a few references to 'popular memory' – and the third edition of 2000, which introduces a new chapter on historical awareness, including a discussion of memory.

10  Raphael Samuel, *Theatres of Memory*, vol. 1, *Past and present in contemporary culture*, London, Verso 1994.

11  For instance the Public History MA course and associated conferences at Ruskin College, Oxford. The term 'public history' seems to have been used in the USA for some time before arriving in Britain.

12 'Like history,' Samuel declares, 'memory is inherently revisionist and never more chameleon than when it appears to stay the same'; the book 'returns again and again to the idea of history as an organic form of knowledge', *Theatres of Memory*, p. x.

13 Bill Schwarz, '"Already the past": memory and historical time', in Radstone and Hodgkin, *Regimes of Memory*.

14 See Robert Perks and Alistair Thomson (eds), *The Oral History Reader*, London and New York, Routledge 1998, which includes two key essays by Luisa Passerini ('Work ideology and consensus under Italian fascism') and Alessandro Portelli ('What makes oral history different'). Both of these first appeared in English over twenty years ago (in *History Workshop Journal*, 8, 1979; 12, 1981). See also E. Berger Gluck and D. Patai (eds), *Women's Words: the feminist practice of oral history*, New York and London, Routledge 1991.

15 For an overview of this see Paul Thompson, *The Voice of the Past: oral history*, Oxford, Oxford University Press 1988 (second edition).

16 For an example from a feminist position, see Joan Sangster, 'Telling our stories: feminist debates and oral history', in *Women's History Review* 3 (1), 1994, pp. 5–28 (also extracted in Perks and Thomson, *Oral History Reader*). Sangster comments that 'traditional sources have often neglected the lives of women', and suggests that oral history offers the possibility of 'contesting the reigning definitions of social, economic and political importance that obscured women's lives … putting women's voices at the centre of history and highlighting gender as a category of analysis'; these possibilities, along with others, 'offer challenges to the dominant ethos of the discipline'. Similar priorities and aspirations would inform much work on the history of the working class, or of ethnic minority communities.

17 Roy Rosenzweig and David Thelen's study of historical consciousness in America, *The Presence of the Past: popular uses of history in American life*, New York, Columbia University Press 1998, provides some suggestive statistics on the perceived trustworthiness of various sources of information about the past. In their survey of attitudes to historical activities and historical knowledge, respondents rated museums as the most reliable sources of information; personal information, from relatives and from eyewitnesses, came in second and third places, above college professors, high school teachers, and books and films (p. 21). Paula Hamilton's chapter in this volume similarly emphasises the importance of the idea of eyewitness testimony in contemporary culture.

18 'In this matter I am an almost total sceptic. … Old men drooling about their youth – No.' Quoted by Thompson, *Voice of the Past*, p. 70.

19 John Blake, *Memories of Old Poplar*, London, Stepney Books Publications 1977; Liza Chivers, *Memories of Highgate from a Keeper's Lodge*, London, Hornsey Historical Society Occasional Paper 3, 1982. In the 1970s and 1980s these pamphlets were frequently associated with the radical history movement, produced in local history groups, and published by small local co-operative presses (the QueenSpark project in Brighton was one of the longest-running). Subsequently similar publications have emerged in many other contexts – local tourist information, projects with elderly people, and so forth; increasingly they are associated with (and sometimes funded by) urban regeneration projects. (For instance, Eve Hostettler (ed.), *The Island at War: memories of war-time life on the Isle of Dogs, East London*, London, Island History Trust, n.d., c. 1990.) They are often collective, and very often geographically based, with an intense sense of local history. For school projects, see Alistair Ross, 'Children becoming historians: an oral history project in a primary school', in Perks and Thomson, *Oral History Reader*, reprinted from *Oral History*, 12 (2), Autumn 1984.

20 There is now an extensive literature on this approach to oral history. The articles by Alessandro Portelli and Luisa Passerini cited in n. 14 above remain key sources, and more generally, see Alessandro Portelli, *The Death of Luigi Trastulli and Other Stories: form*

*and meaning in oral history*, New York, State University of New York Press 1991; Luisa Passerini, *Memory and Totalitarianism (International Yearbook of Oral History and Life Stories*, vol. I), Oxford, Oxford University Press 1992. See also e.g. Patrick Hagopian, 'Oral narratives: secondary revision and the memory of the Vietnam War', *History Workshop Journal* 32, Autumn 1991; Penny Summerfield, *Reconstructing Women's Wartime Lives: discourse and subjectivity in oral histories of the Second World War*, Manchester, Manchester University Press 1998. This approach is also, of course, used more widely in relation to personal testimony in general. Studies of letters and diaries, etc. can produce very similar readings, see e.g. Michael Roper, 'Re-remembering the soldier hero: the psychic and social construction of memory in personal narratives of the Great War', *History Workshop Journal* 50, Autumn 2000.

21 Again, to select from a very extensive literature, see Pierre Nora, *Les Lieux de mémoire* (7 vols), Paris 1984–92; James Fentress and Chris Wickham, *Social Memory*, Oxford, Blackwell 1992; Samuel, *Theatres of Memory*; the Popular Memory Group paper 'Popular memory: theory, politics, method', in R. Johnson *et al.* (eds), *Making Histories: studies in history-writing and politics*, London, Hutchinson 1982; Susan A. Crane, 'Writing the individual back into collective memory', and Alon Confino, 'Collective memory and cultural history: problems of method', both in *American Historical Review* 5, December 1997.

22 For discussion of this in a British context see the articles collected in the *History Workshop Journal* special feature 'History, nation and the schools', issues 29 and 30, Spring and Autumn 1990; Raphael Samuel, *Island Stories: Unravelling Britain. Theatres of Memory* vol. II, London and New York, Verso 1998.

23 A third area, overlapping these two, where the language of memory and commemoration is extensively appealed to is that of war history more generally. Jay Winter's *Sites of Memory, Sites of Mourning: the Great War in European cultural history*, Cambridge, Cambridge University Press 1995, is a classic example. More generally, see T. G. Ashplant, Graham Dawson and Michael Roper (eds.), *The Politics of War Memory and Commemoration*, Routledge Studies in Memory and Narrative, London, Routledge 2000. Much of this material, however, can be explored in relation to other aspects of the history/memory pair: oral history, for instance, or museums and memorials.

24 For example, Dominick La Capra, *Representing the Holocaust: history, theory, trauma*, Ithaca, NY, Cornell University Press 1994; Cathy Caruth, *Unclaimed Experience: trauma, narrative and history*, Baltimore, Johns Hopkins University Press 1996. See also the articles collected in 'Trauma and screen studies: opening the debate', introduced by Susannah Radstone, *Screen* 42 (2), Summer 2001. Conventional Second World War historiography, however, proceeds more or less untouched by these debates.

25 On trauma theory as a general concept, see Susannah Radstone, 'Screening trauma: *Forrest Gump*, film and memory' in Susannah Radstone (ed.), *Memory and Methodology*, Oxford and New York, Berg 2000; Thomas Elsaesser, 'Postmodernism as mourning work', *Screen* 42 (2), Summer 2001. See also Paul Antze and Michael Lambek (eds), *Tense Past: cultural essays in trauma and memory*, New York and London, Routledge 1996, especially their introduction, 'Forecasting memory'.

26 See Scott, *Real Events Revisited*; Radstone, 'Screening trauma'.

27 On the other hand, at the level of the individual, the language of trauma in medical and legal contexts has expanded hugely over the last ten years or so, with an increasing recourse to the diagnosis of PTSD (post-traumatic stress syndrome) in the wake of accidents of all kinds.

28 For an analysis aiming to conceptualise 'cataclysmic events' in an international perspective without reference to theories of trauma, see Stephan Feuchtwang, 'Reinscriptions: commemoration, restoration and the interpersonal transmission of histories and memories under modern states in Asia and Europe', in Radstone (ed.), *Memory and Methodology*.

29 See Thomas Laqueur, 'Introduction', and Idith Zertal, 'From the People's Hall to the Wailing Wall: a study in memory, fear, and war', both in *Representations* 69, Winter 2000, special issue 'Grounds for remembering'.

30 This point is also made by Klein, 'On the emergence of *Memory*': 'If history is objective in the coldest, hardest sense of the word, memory is subjective in the warmest, most inviting senses of that word', p. 130; and also, he argues, tied problematically to a discourse of the sacred.

31 In particular, the genre of 'revisionist autobiography', as Annette Kuhn calls it (Kuhn, 'A journey through memory', in Radstone (ed.), *Memory and Methodology*), including her own *Family Secrets: acts of memory and imagination*, London, Verso 1995. Other influential examples are Ronald Fraser, *In Search of a Past*, London, Verso 1984, and Carolyn Steedman, *Landscape for a Good Woman: a story of two lives*, London, Virago 1986. For a recent example, see Parita Mukta, *Shards of Memory*, London, Weidenfeld and Nicholson 2001.

32 See works cited in n. 22 above.

33 Graham Dawson, ' "I remember ... And I wasn't even born." Reflections on second and third-generation nationalist/republican and loyalist postmemories in the Irish Troubles', paper given at Cultural Memory seminar, Institute of Romance Studies, London University, 27 April 2002. For an attempt to read political and personal memories and identities in tandem through psychoanalysis, see Anna Vidali, 'Political identity, identification and transmission of trauma', *New Formations: a journal of culture/theory/politics*, special issue 'Cultural memory' 30, Winter 1996–97.

34 It is striking, too, how often scholarly speculations about the current cultural prominence of memory discourses are framed as narratives of loss: of vertical (lineage) as opposed to horizontal (generational) identity groups, of oral as opposed to literate cultures, of collective as opposed to individual identity. These nostalgic narratives are part of a much wider modern framing of past/present relationships and the impact of modernity.

35 See Adrian Gregory, *The Silence of Memory: Armistice Day 1919–46*, Oxford and Providence, 1994. In 1994, with the shifting of the two-minute silence from 11 November itself to the nearest Sunday, it appeared that Armistice Day commemorations were withering away. Since then, however – associated with the events marking the fiftieth anniversary of the end of the Second World War – there has been a revival of enthusiasm, including an exhibition in Cambridge in the late 1990s, and calls in parliament for a public holiday to be attached to the day. 2001 saw the release of a CD by Jonty Semper which replayed recordings of seventy years of Armistice Day silences at the Cenotaph.

36 Alessandro Portelli, 'Memories of violence: Roman partisans and the experience of resistance', plenary paper delivered at conference 'Texts of testimony: autobiography, life-story narratives and the public sphere', Liverpool John Moores University, 23–25 August 2001.

37 Michael Lambek, 'Memory in a Maussian universe', *Regimes of Memory*.

38 Cf. Klein: 'The identification of memory with the psychological self has become so strong that despite the constant invocation of "public memory" or "cultural memory" it is difficult to find a sustained scholarly argument for the old-fashioned notion of "collective memory" as a set of recollections attributable to some overarching group mind that could recall past events in the (admittedly poorly understood) ways in which we believe that individuals recall past events'; 'On the emergence of *Memory*', p. 135.

39 Thomas L. Thompson, F. J. Goncalves, J. M. van Cangh, *Toponymie palestinienne*, Publications de l'Institut orientaliste de Louvain no. 37, Louvain-la-neuve, 1988.

40 See Simon Schama, *Landscape and Memory*, London, Harper Collins 1995, for a wide-ranging exploration of this theme.

41 Fredric Jameson, 'Postmodernism, or the cultural logic of late capitalism', *New Left Review* 146, 1984, pp. 53–92.
42 See Annette Kuhn's discussion of memory texts in her article 'A journey through memory', in Radstone (ed.), *Memory and Methodology*.
43 On the ways in which models of memory are framed and articulated by technological analogies, see Esther Leslie, 'Absent-minded professors: etch-a-sketching academic forgetting', in *Regimes of Memory*.
44 See *American History Review* 93 (5), 1988, special issue on film and history.

# Part I

# TRANSFORMING MEMORY

## Introduction

*Katharine Hodgkin and Susannah Radstone*

The past is not fixed, but is subject to change: both narratives of events and the meanings given to them are in a constant state of transformation. The essays in this first section engage with the ways in which memories of a given event or period change over time, as the event changes meaning; their focus is on memory as process, as something constantly being reworked. An event, an emotion remembered, inevitably cannot have the same meaning retrospectively as it had at the time, weighted as the memory must be with everything that has happened subsequently, with the changing needs and imperatives of times and peoples. These essays trace the ways in which memories of particular periods and events are differently articulated and represented in relation to those changing needs. At the same time the essays are confronting the problems of thinking through memory as at once individual and collective, public and private. The protean shapes of memory in this part emerge through many different media: individual consciousness and state institution, local legend and official memorial, family stories, newspapers, television. Memory in these discussions is visibly both an individual and a collective possession, so to speak; it is shared, transmitted, expressed, in various and complicated ways.

Thus on the one hand, the essays are very directly concerned with memory in culture; for the transformations under discussion are implicated in the processes of social and political change. But it is significant that in all these discussions personal memory, personal testimony even, occupies a central place; or perhaps that the two become increasingly hard to disentangle. The pooling of memory in Hirsch and Spitzer's account of 'postmemory' is one variant; the sense in Portelli's discussion that individual memories have become overlaid with an authorised social version is another. Rituals, memorials, folktales, television, all articulate versions of memory in which individuals may or may not recognise themselves, or find the story that fits their need. Shared memory, as it appears in several of these pieces, is something almost animate: it is a dynamic shaping force, which is capable of transforming both the narrative of what is remembered, and the individual subjects who do the remembering, as the meaning and content of their own memories change.

In Alessandro Portelli's account of the afterlife of a famous massacre in German-occupied Rome during the Second World War, memory is deeply but fascinatingly compromised. In the case he analyses, a firmly held and near-universal popular conviction about the course of events leading up to the massacre is wrong; and wrong in a way that specifically throws a greater burden of guilt for what happened onto the members of the Italian resistance movement, away from the German military who were the actual perpetrators. The question he asks, then, is how a memory so radically mistaken has come into being.

As Portelli explains, the dominant memory of the event in Rome flies in the face of the official documentary record. Working from a 'traditional' oral history standpoint, it might be assumed that popular memory serves to put documentary evidence into question; if the majority of the city's population tells a story that contradicts the historical record, that record should be subjected to scrutiny. In this instance, on the contrary, it is popular memory itself that appears compromised and problematic, since even those who were alive at the time and witnesses to the course of events regularly produce the 'wrong' account of what happened. But Portelli's argument also throws up complex questions about precisely the relation between social and individual memory. For if an individual's memory were simply the repository of the 'true' story, able to measure alternative accounts against experiential knowledge and find them wanting, then the reshapings and revisions of the story of the massacre could have gained no purchase in the minds of those who 'saw what happened'; whereas on the contrary, the secondary version has become rooted as firm conviction precisely because people who were there 'remember' it.

What makes this episode still more inexplicable is that at first sight not much seems to depend on it, politically speaking; on the contrary, indeed, this is a version that favours those who should be the enemy (Germans) against those who should be the heroes (partisans), and that seems to have gained currency without any particular agent visible behind it. There is no obvious political or state agenda behind the dissemination of the new version. Nonetheless, Portelli argues, this is not to say that there is no politics, broadly speaking, in the fact that the revisionary version gained the upper hand in popular memory. He reads this revision in relation to the complex political readjustments of the Italian state after the war, and how it went about making a new identity. In producing itself as a European liberal democracy in the post-war period, he suggests, Italy had to negotiate some peculiarly complex relationships with past and present political allegiances. Its own fascist past was one problem, of course; another was the prominence of communism in the resistance movement, at a time of cold war anti-communism. The changes in the meaning and the memory of the massacre in subsequent decades, he argues, are implicated in the social and political priorities of the newly reformed state, not at the level of government plot, but through a process of reinvention of national identity. 'Society' does not remake itself as an abstract entity; if social/political transformation is to succeed, there must be corresponding transformations at the level of individual consciousness – as revolutionaries have always known. Thus, presumably, the shifts and displacements going on in thousands of different Roman memories, the number of conversations reaching for the conclusion, 'of course, it must have been like that, somehow I'd forgotten', all adding up to a new popular knowledge.

In Anne Heimo and Ulla-Maija Peltonen's investigation of popular memory in Finland, what is in question is not the misremembering of a specific event, but rather contradictory ways of remembering a whole period: the Civil War of 1920 and the years after. Here again we see the construction of memory working on different levels. The inequity of the way in which the war was publicly remembered in its immediate aftermath, they suggest, as well as the general silencing of debate on the subject in subsequent decades, had a great deal to do with the persisting bitterness of those who lost. Public institutions, initially triumphalist, shifted towards a rhetoric of silence and amnesia in the name of national unity, which in its turn with difficulty gave way to an acceptance that there were stories still to be told, and memorials still to be erected, decades after the event. Working with archives of spoken and written words collected over a period between forty to seventy years after the war, Heimo and Peltonen examine the different stories told in relation to the changing emotional and political needs of the tellers. The meanings of the stories change as the 'rememberers' get further and further away, and start being rememberers for their families, say, or re-narrators of heard stories, even while for many the sense that they are at last bringing into the open unspoken and unchanged truths remains important.

Heimo and Peltonen's particular interest is in the forms memory takes, and the many different instances in which one can read the traces of these conflicting accounts. Their discussion is concerned with 'oral history' and 'folklore' simultaneously, seeing both as forms for the expression of popular memory. Folk stories and local legends demonstrate the villainy of one side or another through ghosts or through individual tragedies. The political content need not be explicit for them to work as statements about injustice or persecution or bloodthirstiness; on the other hand, their changing forms, and the disappearance of particular tales over the years, can be interpreted in relation to changing cultural needs. In effect, while Heimo and Peltonen describe a continuing and visible difference in the versions of tales ('Red' and 'White') told by each side, they also describe eventually a common changing emphasis, by which the stories are more concerned to locate the source of trouble 'elsewhere', rather than within the village. From being tales of the villainy of one's neighbour, these become tales of outsiders bringing disruption and distress. Thus they become as it were conciliatory: instead of perpetuating bitter memories of treachery near at hand, they project it outside. Over a few generations, it seems, memories can be transformed into shapes that are no longer internally damaging to the community. Like Portelli's, then, this essay poses the question of what oral history can deliver, and explores the ways in which memories may be read as narratives of meaning rather than event.

Graham Carr, also working with conflicts over the retrospective meanings of war, focuses not on changes over several decades, but on a particular upheaval in the public memory of the Second World War in Canada. The popular myth of the war, he suggests, has represented it as a time of national heroism, unity and mission, as well as a crucial moment in the history of Canadian national self-consciousness and self-confidence. The challenge to that consensual narrative by historians questioning the actual degree of unity, heroism and so forth in the armed forces (were relations between officers and men always happy? What about the bombing of civilians?) might have had little public impact if it had been simply a matter of historians writing obscure academic books. However, the fact that it had national exposure in the form of a TV series sparked off an angry national debate which effectively pitched the wounded and insulted memories of the old against the ignorant academicism of the young(ish).

This public row, Carr argues, was framed as an argument both about the memories of individuals and about the place of the war in Canada's national memory. As the debate proceeded, it became clear that it had peculiarly personalised and domestic resonances: the images appealed to were the anguish of veterans over how to speak to their grandchildren, and the contrast between Vietnam objector and Second World War soldier. To mobilise a rhetoric of memory here, once again, is antipathetic to critical inquiry: so long as the war exists in a register of memory rather than history then personal experience will be the touchstone. Precisely because the front man for the TV series had never fought in a war, by implication, he ought to show humility in front of those who had.

Carr's account of this contest continues with a more general examination of the ways in which Canada, as its old soldiers get older and start to die, has increasingly positioned its war experience as a baton to be passed from one generation to the next; the memory is almost reified, no longer purely attached to an individual and his experience, but transmitted as a national property. Looking at different instances of the way the war and its aftermath is represented in Canadian culture – from advertising to education to keeping of memorial days – Carr identifies this generational transmission and its attached generational bonding as a key element. Memory will outlive the survivors if it can be passed on whole to their descendants or to other young people; thus any lack of respect for the exact truth of that memory (of heroism) is a grievous national insult.

One might see it almost as a denial of generational difference and the passage of time: it is the middle generation, the sons of the soldiers, who are seen to reject the dominant accounts, but they are being sidelined by an attempt to recuperate the grandchildren and even great-grandchildren. To identify oneself with a generation, Pierre Nora suggests, is to think horizontally rather than vertically; it is an index of the relative weakening of the traditional vertical structures that worked to secure identity (families, in particular, but other cross-generational structures too), in favour of a relation to the past that is determined by identification with the present.[1] The struggle over the 'inheritance' of memory in such instances, however, suggests the possibility of rethinking generation as precisely the locus of transmission, rather than seeing generations as (self-)defined in opposition to their predecessors.

Marianne Hirsch and Leo Spitzer's chapter takes up the question of how memories are transmitted from one generation to the next, and what is at stake in that transmission, at a more intimate level: within a family, what is passed on, and what effect does it have? How does the next generation live with their parents' stories? The chapter thus stages a dialogue between generations about choices and chance; also about place and belonging. For Hirsch and Spitzer it has a particular application, in that the parental knowledge is of disaster and loss (as well as being the story of how the disaster was escaped). The concept of postmemory articulates the particular insistence of such memories of loss in the second generation. Escape may not be all it seems, and the children will carry that past forward into the future; their sense of belonging is partial, insecure; their sense of self is haunted by memories which are not quite their own. What is transmitted above all, it seems, is a sense of displacement, unrootedness ('Marianne doesn't have a home', her father declares). This could be seen as the failure of the *lieu de mémoire*, indeed; if identification with national myths is the patrimony through which identity is built up, then the absence of such identification might be held to transmit a wound to the next generation down as well, as their *lieux* are in fact located somewhere else, somewhere they have never been.

Memory, then, once again, is not tied to the individual who experienced a given event, but dispersed and transmitted to subsequent generations. But the process of transmission changes the rememberers too: the parents who share their memories find their memories changing. What emerges is a sense of sliding, elusive truths, which change shape and meaning as decades advance, as children take up and share and examine and revisit parental memories. The return to the original location – the crossroads, bringing together four people with different relationships to that liminal spot – highlights this sense of memory as process. The same place does not have the same meaning: simultaneously occupied by the young selves of the parents who could never have imagined such a future (or any future), the children of the parents (now mature themselves) who imagined that past differently, the parents themselves who remembered it over decades and find it other than their memories – in this shifting landscape, the notion of passing on truths down the generations is not only important (restorative, regenerative) but also problematic (what truth precisely is being passed down?). That memory is not exact, of course, does not make it untrue, a point which returns with particular urgency in Part II. Memory here is experienced intergenerationally: the exchange and sharing of memories is part of what makes them real and effective.

## Notes

1  Pierre Nora, 'La génération', in Nora (ed.), *Les lieux de mémoire*, III. *Les France* I, Paris, Gallimard 1993.

# 1

# THE MASSACRE AT THE FOSSE ARDEATINE

## History, myth, ritual, and symbol

*Alessandro Portelli*

This chapter is concerned with the interplay between what we can assume to have been fact, and what happens in the realm of memory, including imagined events and false memories. The specific event I shall discuss is the killing of 335 people – hostages, or just people randomly picked off the street – by the German occupying forces in Rome in 1944, as reprisal for a partisan attack which the British official record consistently calls a 'bomb outrage' the day before, in which 32 German soldiers had been killed.

This event, this massacre, resonates both backwards and forwards. It somehow illuminates the history of Rome and the country at large across the whole century, even though it lasted only about a day. It illuminates history through the people involved; at the same time it illuminates memory, having been the site of very fierce controversy not only in the historical record but amongst the population at large ever since the event.

I begin with two narratives. The first is a British official document, summing up the events on the occasion of the proceedings against the German commanders in 1946. According to this report, this was the course of events:

> At approximately 15.00 hours, on 23rd March, 1944, as a party of German police were marching along the Via Rasella, Rome, a bomb was thrown from a nearby house, causing the death of 32 German policemen, and injuries to others. As a result of this outrage, it was decided by the accused, von Mackensen, Commander of the 14th Army, and General Kurt Maeltzer, the Military Commander of Rome, to institute reprisals against the population of Rome. Ten Italians were to be shot for each German killed; the reprisals to be carried out within 24 hours of the bomb outrage.
>
> At 14.00 hours, 24th March, 1944, the persons to be shot were transported by lorries, in relays, to the Ardeatine Caves, in batches of five. They were taken inside the cave, and shot in the back of the head by SS men. At the termination of the massacre, it was found that 335

persons had been shot, which exceeded the original ratio of 10:1. The caves were then mined. No warning of the reprisal was given to the public, and enquiries by the German authorities to find the persons guilty of the bomb outrage were not completed until long after the massacre had taken place.[1]

Now this is quite an accurate account (actually, the bomb was not thrown from a window, but that need not concern us now). The point to be emphasised in this report is that no warning of the reprisal was given to the public. It was carried out immediately, within 24 hours, and the concern of the German authorities was not to punish the perpetrators, but to punish the city. So it had to be immediate and as stern as possible.

The other story is a personal anecdote. I had just been awarded a book prize for my book on the Fosse Ardeatine, and I called my wife who was at the hairdresser's. So she told the people in the hairdresser's the news, and the lady sitting next to her said, 'What was the book about?' 'The Fosse Ardeatine', my wife told her. 'Oh,' said the lady, 'I know all about it!' (This is what everybody always says. You mention this episode, and immediately, memories and emotions flare up.) 'I know all about it. It was the fault of those partisans who threw the bomb, and then went into hiding. And the Germans looked for them. I remember the bills that they posted all over the city. "If the perpetrators turn themselves in, we will not retaliate. But if they do not turn themselves in, we will kill ten Italians for each German."'

Now, this is not the way it happened. There was no warning to the population, no attempt to catch the partisans, no invitation to them to surrender themselves to avoid the retaliation. But this lady's version of the story is the prevalent one in public memory; it is the way people remember it. In claiming that she actually remembered seeing the bills, despite the fact that they never existed, this lady was one among many; the story as she reported it is completely pervasive. What I'd like to explore, then, is the meaning of this intensely remembered and dramatically misremembered event, asking how we are to understand the gap between what happened and the many ways in which it has been remembered.

It is particularly striking that although the facts have all been a matter of record for half a century, they have been consistently ignored; what people remember is the myth of the German search for the cowardly partisans who hid away and allowed the hostages to be killed. A space opens up between the historical and judicial record (not to mention the accurate memory of a number of first-hand witnesses, including the survivors, the families and the relatives of the victims) on one side, and the distorted, exaggerated, mythicised, common-sense memory on the other. In this space, there is all the complexity of national identity, of the foundations of Italian democracy, of the politics of memory, and of the interplay of institutional and personal memories.

The subtitle of this chapter summons up four terms: history, myth, ritual and symbol. These things of course cannot be wholly separated, but they will serve as angles from which to look at the question of the meaning of this tragedy.

History, first of all. When I began to be interested in this event, and started telling people that I thought of doing an oral history of the Fosse Ardeatine, many reacted with advice and suggestions for additional things to do. Many people told me I should do the deportation of the Roman Jews, for instance. And others said I should start with the 1938 Race Laws which instituted discriminations against the Italian Jewish population. I went one better: I began in 1870, when Rome became the capital of Italy. For the location of the massacre, in fact, is one reason why it is important. After all, it was not the worst Nazi war crime committed in Italy: there were much worse ones, with many more victims. It was not even the worst committed in Rome; over 1,500 deaths resulted from the deportation of the Jews. And it is not an isolated case. In the Public Record Office in London there are records of the investigations by British Forces of 145 massacres in Italy, and that list is not complete.

What makes the Fosse Ardeatine so resonant is that it happened in the country's capital. And, in fact, it's the only such massacre to have happened in a large metropolitan urban context, rather than a village or a rural area, in Europe. This is a metropolitan massacre, which creates an essential difference in the quality of the victims. In most other cases, the victims were relatively homogeneous, as homogeneous as a village population is. In this case, what makes it historically and symbolically powerful is the absolute heterogeneity of the victims. They were a cross-section of Italian society at large. Geographically, they came from all over Italy: I have travelled to Milan in the North and to Salento in the deep South to talk to the relatives of victims. They came from all over Italy, because people came from all over Italy to Rome: Rome was the magnet.

Also, because it was a big city, they came from all social classes. There were aristocrats from Piedmont, and pedlars from the Jewish ghetto, and all the social classes in between, from the professional middle classes – lawyers and doctors – to the urban working class – factory workers, construction workers. The victims' ages too ranged from 14 to 74. The whole spectrum of political opinion was represented, beginning with the basic distinction between those who were involved in politics and those who were not. Most of the victims were taken from among the political prisoners that the Germans had ready to hand at the moment of the attack; but as there were too few to make up the number they needed, they took people at random from off the street. When they still found a shortfall, they added the 'Jews awaiting shipment', as the British document quoted above has it, 'to Germany'. So the dead included both the political and the non-political. And amongst the politically committed too the political range is as broad as it can be, from the monarchist army officers, to the ultra-left Communists of Bandiera Rossa, a Left splinter group that lost 60 members to the massacre. There were Communists, Socialists, Liberals, Christian

Democrats. Even a former member of Mussolini's Cabinet was among the victims, a Jew who had become an anti-Fascist and worked with the Resistance. The people who died in the massacre were a cross-section of the city, and thus of the whole country.

Today, history has been replaced (effaced) by myth, and above all by the question: who do we blame? This is what feeds the myth, a myth that is functional to a historical debate about the nature of the Resistance in Italy. Italy is the only nation that, fifty years after the fact, is still arguing over whether its freedom fighters were criminals or heroes; where it could be a matter for debate whether it was a crime to attack a marching unit of uniformed police attached to the SS, belonging to a foreign occupying army.

In one sense, this could be seen as the flip side of a positive aspect of our national identity: Italians historically have not been a warlike people, and perhaps for this reason the attempt to construct the partisans as 'war heroes' never fully succeeded. But also very important in the way in which this event has been remembered is the fact that those who carried out the attack were Communists, and whatever the Communists do, especially from the perspective of the nineties, is a crime. Anti-Communism reinforces the idea that this was a criminal action, a new attack. And the myth is a very tenacious one. When my wife at the hairdresser's tried to persuade her neighbour that she was wrong, saying that her husband had just written a book about it, and the common account was not accurate, the response was, 'If he had talked to me, he wouldn't have written it!' It is a myth that is entirely resistant to historical information.

The action in via Rasella was a very well-organised military action, in which 18 partisans took part. Yet the myth has it that it was the act of a single person – which in itself turns a military action into a terrorist act – and that he felt so guilty after killing those poor SS that he subsequently committed suicide. (Fortunately, the person to whom this act is attributed is alive and kicking, and in fact he loves the book.)

A further aspect of the myth holds that the whole affair was not the fault of the Germans, on the basis of another myth, or a national stereotype: the Germans are stern, but just. They had their rules and they carried them out. And the ratio of 10:1 is so geometric, so perfect, that it really makes it make sense; it has a weird rationality. 'The poor Germans', the thinking thus goes, 'they had to do it, because this was the stern law of war, applied by a stern people. They were stern, but just.' Whereas the partisans, on the contrary, are represented as being underhanded, secret, cowardly; their act was furtive, they would not take responsibility. At the heart of this interpretation, I suggest, is the continuing struggle over the question of what kind of Italy emerged from the ruins of the Second World War. On the one hand, the founding narrative of the anti-Fascist Italian democracy was the idea of 'the Republic born out of the Resistance'; and however banal this phrase had become, it nonetheless had a certain truth. Many of the values of the Resistance are embodied in the Italian constitution. But if the idea of the Resistance, and of the heroism of the partisans, underpinned Italy's post-war democracy, then, of course, the anti-partisan version, the version which holds the partisans to blame for the massacre, is the counter-myth generated by the unfinished quality of our democracy. The democracy that came out of the Resistance was not the unanimous choice of the majority of the people, but rather a project, a plan, a dream, that not all shared; there was also a resistance to democracy itself.

So this is what is at stake in this story: is Italy an anti-Fascist democracy born out of resistance, or is it something else? A large section of the Italian population would not accept the anti-Fascist ethos that was, in theory, the inspiration of the Italian Republic. The most important institution in the country – the Church – was the first promoter of the wrong memory: the memory originates with an editorial in the *Osservatore Romano*, the official newspaper of the Catholic Church, on the front page of the issue of 26 March 1944, and of course, if the *Osservatore Romano* says something, it's repeated by parish priests all over the country. And why did the Church do this? Because the Church automatically refuses to take sides. It will, in theory, be neither for the Fascists, nor for the anti-Fascists, which means the Church will not be anti-Fascist; and this is equally the case with the Christian Democrat Party, which ruled Italy for 50 years.

One of the most fascinating reshapings that the mythical narrative offers has to do with the politics of time. Time is crucial in this episode. The retaliation was carried out within 24 hours (which is why I gave my book a title taken from the final words of the German press release: 'The order has already been carried out'), and the population was not informed of the partisan attack until after the massacre. However, if you ask anyone – and I have asked some 200 people, aged between 14 and 80 – how long it was between the partisan action and the massacre, the answers range from three days to six months. Why is that so? Basically, because they need to give the Germans time to look for the partisans and ask them to surrender – and thus they can blame the partisans for not responding to the summons. This example comes from an 18-year old high school student, Marco Maceroni:

> For a whole week the Germans went around taking prisoners, especially in the Jewish Quarter. And warning, warning, that if the perpetrators of the attack in the via Rasella had not come out, they would take, for each German who had been killed in the attack, 11 Italians, 11 or 13, I don't remember now.[2]

That is the basic myth, which you can collect at the hairdresser's in your neighbourhood or among the students in your school. On the other hand, since this myth has been challenged, at least in terms of public discourse, alternative narratives have emerged. There is a whole series of misunderstandings which are politically motivated, mythically motivated, humanly motivated and, of course, ideologically motivated. Myth, here, functions as an interchangeable set of stories that all support a preconceived conclusion: 'The Communist partisans are to blame.' So once it is clear that there never was a question of subordinating the massacre to the delivery of the partisans, the new version of the myth is: 'They should have turned themselves in anyway whether they were asked to or not, whether they knew of the retaliation or not.' Or, one especially popular these days: 'They should have known what the consequences would be. The Germans are like animals. They're like wild beasts. If you provoke them, they will react.'

Part of this myth, then, is the familiar anti-German stereotype: the Germans are beasts, the Germans are machines. But the Germans are human, and what they did was not a knee-jerk reaction, it was a carefully thought-through political decision. The myth that the partisans 'should have known' is based on another assumption: that this was the only armed action in Rome in which Germans were killed. This is absolutely not true. This was the forty-third attack that took place in Rome against the Germans. The belief that there really was no resistance in Rome, so via Rasella was an isolated event, a provocation in an otherwise tranquil city, is a myth with a meaning. It is both in harmony with the stereotype of the lazy fatalistic Roman, and functional to making Rome the Conservative capital of a Conservative government: since there was no resistance in Rome, the suggestion is, it was only a few madmen who planted a bomb. Actually, there was a great deal of resistance, both active and passive, armed and unarmed. According to the German commanders, Rome was 'not co-operating'; therefore, they needed to punish the city. The basic reason why retaliation had not taken place before was that previously the Germans had preferred to keep things quiet. They controlled communication; transportation had broken down in Rome, so the news of other partisan attacks did not circulate. The Germans relied on the myth of invulnerability and invincibility to keep the city quiet. But the attack in the via Rasella was too big. It happened in the middle of the day, in the centre of town. They couldn't hide it. (In fact, another aspect of the myth is that if you ask anyone from that generation, they'll tell you they were there, or were supposed to have been there, or a friend of theirs was there.) It couldn't be kept quiet: it was a visible crack in the armour of invulnerability of the occupying army, so something had to be done immediately. In fact, some versions of this narrative claim that the partisans carried out the attack precisely with the aim of ensuring retaliation: 'They did it on purpose. They did it so that the Germans would kill prisoners who belong to different parties, or so that the Germans would retaliate and it would start a rebellion.'

Turning now to consider the question of memorial rituals around this event, it is clear that there is a tension between what is both a collective massacre – 335 people killed – and at the same time 335 individual murders. These two different ways of looking at it have different consequences. The collective massacre generates public memory, monuments, ceremonies; the 335 single murders generate personal memory, personal loss. Since the only thing that the victims had in common was that they were all men, the bearers of the memory afterwards were mainly women: wives, mothers – a few fathers, but it is predominantly a women's story. And the tension between the monument and the personal memory emerged very quickly.

Rome was liberated in June 1944. The Allied Command proposed that since the victims of the massacre were already buried, there should be a monument built on top of the burial site in commemoration. But the relatives – the wives, mothers, daughters – protested. This is how Vera Simoni, the daughter of an Air Force General who was killed there, describes her mother's reaction:

> And so this is where my mother steps in. My mother said 'No', because otherwise we'd still be waiting for our father to come back. She said, 'No, I want each of them to be recognised.' So she talked to the officers, and they said, 'Madam, we'd like to do what all you ask, but it's impossible. It can't be done.' So mother and I, and my sister, we went to see General Pollock, who was the Head of the Allied Forces, and he received us right away. And my mother said, 'Look, we've come to ask for this. We know you're going to make this monument, and we refuse to accept it. We want recognition, body by body.' So the General looked at us, and he must have thought, 'My God, I'm looking at people who, perhaps, pain has deranged them a little bit.' So he says, 'Well, it's going to be difficult.' But my mother had already spoken with Dr Ascarelli, who was a pathologist, and Ascarelli had gone to the place and he said, 'It's a crazy idea, but it all can be done, and especially if the desire and the need is so strong.' So my mother said, 'No, it can be done, because we spoke to the Professor, it can be done.' So General Pollock said, 'Well, listen, let me think about it.' So he took us to the door and I said these words too, as well as my mother, 'Look, we don't give up. We don't want anything. We want nothing for ourselves. We just want them to be identified, because all the other families are in the same situation as us', and, in English, 'We don't give up.'[3]

Such a situation highlights the difference between putting someone under the earth and really burying them, having a ceremony where their death is recognised and somehow passes into value, as Ernesto de Martino says, it acquires a meaning. Before this, the families did not know what had happened; in a situation where many people were deported or disappeared, they could not be sure what had become of those they had lost. And it was the women who started going around and asking questions, trying to track down the missing; it seems that the men, the fathers, had such a crushing sense of failure in their role that they became useless. A colleague of mine, in my department, tells this story:

> I think my mother went with some friends of hers, that very day, to the caves. Of course, in the state they were in … and there are very physical impressions of smells, the smells, and this is distorted in time. But my mother always told me true things, without distortions. And she says

one of the things that ... wounded her most, and shocked her most, was these SS who were laughing. Maybe they were anxious. Who knows? And then the next day, they formed a sort of procession of women [which is a religious image]. She went, and I think Pilo Albertelli's wife went [Pilo Albertelli is one of the heroes of resistance; he was my mother's philosophy teacher in high school], and the other women. Lia Albertelli, Pilo Albertelli's wife, wrote a poem about this:

We're walking, groping, under the heavy roof.
The greasy air fills our mouth
and chokes our breath. And we support one another,
holding hands.
We are a few brides,
and with us is a sister and a mother.
And at the end of a cave, rises a tall heap.
We climb,
and the earth breaks under our feet.
And from the broken clods,
the heavy breath hits us stronger, stronger.
One picks up a strand of hair clotted with blood,
her desperate scream throws us to the ground.
They're underneath, and we're treading on our feet,
upon the fathers of our children.

These disintegrating bodies had to be unburied in order to bury them again; and they had to be identified. They had been there for months. They were killed in March; the disinterment began in July, and went on until the end of September. The bodies as they were uncovered were heaped on top of one another, because there wasn't enough room in the cave. The later victims had been made to climb on the bodies of those who had been killed before them, in order to be shot.

And the stories ... I have more gruesome stories than this one, but this is Giuseppe Bolgia's story. His mother was killed in an air raid by the American or British Air Force in Rome, and his father was killed at the Fosse Ardeatine. I asked him who he blamed, and he said, 'Well, I blame the Germans for my father, and the Allies for my mother. They did their share.' When he was 12, he told me, he had to identify his father's body.

And it's something I'd better not describe. No one can understand this, only those who. ... It was no easy thing, because this heap that they'd made, of two heaps of dead bodies, one on top of the other, a row of six, seven corpses, one on top of the other. And I went, and my sister, in the autumn, under those ugly caves. It was a negative experience to me. Now, fifty-three years later, it still stays in my mind as if it was yesterday, seeing all these slaughtered men. I remember a crate filled with skulls and skeletons everywhere, and those you couldn't recognise. So we

36

recognised Daddy's corpse. He was headless. Many of them were headless, because they were shot in the back of the head, you know. So we
recognised Dad through his clothes, and then he had a German watch
that they issued to railway workers ...

So the bodies were recognised through the clothes they wore, through details,
photographs, papers. This process of identification went on for months and
months. And meanwhile the memory was being appropriated by the public; it
was becoming a national memory.

Thus, two types of ritual arose. First there were the private responses: how
should the dead be mourned? Rome in 1944 was a very southern city, its population largely made of first-generation immigrants from the rural south. They
brought an extremely emotional way of mourning the dead, described in a
number of ethnographies in Southern Italy, involving crying, losing control, just
letting go. Carfla Capponi, a partisan who accompanied the wife of one of the
killed, recalls:

All her relatives were there, her son was there, and I realised this was a
hellish place, because all the parents had to recognise those pieces of
bodies. And it was a frightening scene. They were screaming as they
carried out these bodies. What can I say? It was a tragedy you didn't
know how to resist, to see the trembles.

I think tragedy has to be taken literally here, because the voices, the gestures,
are the voices of the ancient Mediterranean theatre – archaic Greek and
Southern Italian theatre. So there are scenes described in the papers of very
archaic forms of keening for the dead, like the image of an old woman with a
handkerchief; scenes such as used to be seen in Lucania in the far south of Italy,
with rhythmic movement and crying, until the crying and the screaming become
singing and poetry and rhythm, and it soothes.

At the same time, Rome was a middle-class city, and kept to the middle-class
type of mourning – control, and keeping it all inside. There are many stories of
repressed weeping, of people who were unable to weep until years later; and
then when eventually they wept, these middle-class children would stare at each
other, shocked at such a display of emotion – especially shocked to see their
parents fall victim to emotion.

Alongside the private mourning, however, there was the public monument.
The monument that was built is beautiful. In the ceremonies around it, the urge
was to spiritualise, and to make this appallingly concrete story abstract. How to
do this at the height of the Cold War, when suddenly the Communists were
enemies and the Germans allies, was an especially delicate question. The
Communists were closely identified with the Resistance, to the extent that for a
long time there was almost a suppression of the non-Communist element; and
while the post-war Communists were on the whole happy to go along with this,

because it gave them a monopoly of martyrdom, on the other hand it put the Resistance in a left-wing ghetto, and gave it a very ambivalent position in post-war politics. Meanwhile the armed forces – the carabinieri, the army, the air force – were active in patriotic resistance, and they had a number of victims at the Fosse Ardeatine; but these victims are hardly remembered. The institutions of the Italian state prefer not to remember the fact that they were involved in the anti-Fascist and the anti-Nazi war, for a number of reasons. In the event, the solution was to depoliticise the whole official ceremony. Public memory fell under the sway of religion on the one hand, and the military on the other hand – the institutions in charge of death. Now every year, on the commemoration date of 24 March, there is a Catholic ceremony, a Jewish prayer, and a couple of military manoeuvres. In the afternoon, the working-class organisations go, with red flags flying. And in the middle were the individuals who didn't know what to do, weeping for their fathers, their brothers, their sons, not for heroes. But there is no mention, in any of the official speeches, of who killed the people commemorated. They 'gave their lives'; they 'sacrificed themselves'.

They didn't; but their heterogeneity gives rise to further problems. If some of them put their lives at stake – the partisans – others did not; the Jews, or those picked at random off the street, never chose to risk their lives. So while all can be called martyrs, or indeed heroes, they cannot all be called innocent; many of them had done something. As one son said, 'My father was no innocent. He had tried to fight the Germans'. And a daughter similarly asserts, 'I don't want to be the daughter of an innocent victim'. There is no unifying category there, unless the very abstract and harmless category of the 'martyrs' of freedom, the 'martyrs' of liberty. Their actual options are barely mentioned.

Alongside the account of the Resistance that locates it as the property of the Communists, so to speak, there has been a different myth, of the Resistance as a united movement involving the majority of the Italian people. And the sense that everyone had to be represented in it caused a search for the lowest common denominator; in this case, patriotism and democracy. The Communists themselves went along with this drive to represent the Resistance as something harmless and uncontroversial, not least because in the middle of the Cold War they had to legitimise themselves as not just a legitimate, but actually a founding element, in the Italian democracy. So they underplayed the fact that the Resistance was a conflict. They underplayed the fact that partisans were armed fighters who had not only died, but also killed; all the monuments to the partisans are monuments to dying partisans. As a historian recently observed, the Resistance is the only war which is celebrated for the battles it has lost, rather than the ones it has won, because the ones that it has won would remind us that it was a war. Thus the partisans who took part in the attack in via Rasella have lived through the half-century with a sense that while the Party defended them and supported them, it never really owned their action. In fact, a number of anti-partisan versions, like the version, 'They should have turned themselves in', are widespread in the left as well, because it's common sense.

How did the survivors, the families, go on through life? This is the question that initially led me to work on this project. In 1994 one of the perpetrators, the SS Captain Erich Priebke, was located in Argentina, extradited to Italy, and tried; and the whole controversy flared up again. And as the relatives came forward, it appeared – in the media, the television, the press – as if the massacre were really a private matter. It had to do with the Nazis, the perpetrators, and the victims, the relatives and the Jewish community; but it was not something that concerned us good people any more, however we might sympathise with the victims, represented as frozen in time. Of course, they are, in a way. Guiseppe Bolgia, the 12-year-old who identified his father, says, 'It's like yesterday.' On the other hand, they have lived on since then for half a century. How did they go through life, with their mourning and their memories?

Following the massacre, the visibility of the widows, all dressed in black, throughout the city, was almost a disturbance to the citizens; their presence was disruptive to the consensus being constructed, although they might be sympa-thised with at a distance. Ada Pignotti was 23 years old. She had been married six months. She lost her husband and three other relatives, and she says:

> Well, back then, after it happened in '44, you couldn't really talk about it. You just couldn't talk. I worked for 40 years, so even in my office, sometimes when they asked me about it, I wouldn't talk because they … they respond arrogantly. They said, 'Oh well, blame the one who threw the bomb.' And I pretended that I didn't hear them, because they always answered that way. Or, 'It's not the Germans' fault, it's the fault of the one who put the bomb there, because if he had turned himself in, they would have killed him.' Well, who wrote the story? When did they ever say this? It never happened. They didn't warn us. They didn't post any bills. They put them up afterwards, after they'd already killed them.

This wrong memory, which is how the city chose to make sense of what happened, is also a way of exorcising her, of refusing to share her pain.

The visibility of the widows brought other troubles too. In 1944, women weren't supposed to go out to work; these women, going out into public space, were assumed to be defenceless. Having no man, they were fair game. Many were subjected to sexual harassment, something for which they didn't even have a name at the time, on top of what they had suffered. Several of the women have these kinds of stories, and it tells you a great deal about what male culture was at the time. There are also stories of mutual aid. For instance, a woman who had lost her brother tells how she would go to her sister-in-law's house, and secretly put a soothing pill in her sister-in-law's soup; later she realised that her sister-in-law was putting a pill in hers. And then there are the stories of children growing up in orphan homes, or growing up surrounded by the pain of their parents. 'It was a strange grief', a woman who lost her father says, over and over.

'It was a strange grief.' She describes calling her mother, in the mid-sixties, and asking, 'Mum, what are you doing?' Her mother replied, 'I'm weeping.' 'What are you weeping for?' 'I'm weeping for your father.' And the daughter said, 'Now?' Her mother answered, 'I didn't have time before, because I had to work. I had to keep three jobs, keep house, raise four daughters, now I'm retired, I can weep.' Some children grew up in orphanages; those who could stay at home were surrounded by this trauma, which has passed on through generations.

Finally, there is the question of symbols. One of the things I did was to inter-view young people. When you say you interview young people, older people's first response is always, 'Oh, they don't know anything. They don't have any historical memory.' In some cases this is true: they have as little historical memory as their parents and grandparents, that is to say, from whom they have learnt the wrong version of events, which they repeat. Others, fortunately, have no version at all. I say fortunately because they don't know the wrong version; there is nothing screening them from the knowledge of what really happened and its meaning. Thus many young people do not make that automatic connection between the attack and the massacre, as cause and effect. They do not shift their gaze away from the fact of the massacre. They may have a hard time historicising it, because they don't really know what was going on; but they symbolise it beautifully.

'The story, honestly, I don't really remember it', one young man told me. 'I don't remember it very well, to tell the truth. But the name makes me think. I know it makes me think. Fosse Ardeatine.' (The word 'fosse' is significant in this train of thought. The 'Fosse' were originally quarries, and the Italian for 'quar-ries' is *cave*, which is why they're known as 'caves' in English (as well as because they were underground). Soon after the war the name was changed to 'Fosse' which means 'graves', but also 'ditches'.) So he continued, 'Fosse Ardeatine. And I have this image of this huge ditch where they dumped people. What I imagine … this is what I imagine. A place where people are dumped, mutilated, massa-cred.' 'Like trash?' I asked him. And he said, 'Yes, exactly. Like trash. Taken and thrown away, as if they were sacks of potatoes or things. You know what it makes me think? It makes me think of the annihilation of the value of life. This is what it makes me think of. Man treated like a thing, like a piece … I don't know, like a rag.' This description is uncannily right: 'like a piece'. We all remember that the Nazis called 'Stücke', pieces, the prisoners that they deported to the extermina-tion camps. And in the Fosse Ardeatine they tried to cover the caves with trash, in order to hide the stench that was rising out of these bodies.

So what do young people see there? They see an image of absurd death, of sudden, casual death; death that is not the result of any natural process. And this ties in with their own experience of death. What I've realised, doing this book, is that my generation, that which grew up in the post-war boom years, was excep-tional, in the sense that it was a generation in which death was invisible. The death of young people was very rare; the middle-class ethic of hiding death from children prevailed. For today's young people things are different. There were three suicides in my older son's high school class. There are at least twelve markers made by young people, with flowers, photographs, soccer cards, of their contemporaries who died in accidents on the road where I live. And they know about death by drugs. So they are familiar with death. But since the older generation still believes that they know nothing about it and should not be exposed to it, nobody helps them deal with death; they have to come to terms with it on their own. The Fosse Ardeatine is one of the symbols. An outing to the Fosse Ardeatine is a typical school trip. Sometimes they make a joke of it; sometimes they're truly shocked and moved. But what is shocking and moving is no longer anti-Fascism, or any other political cause; it's the presence of death. The pioneering book on the Fosse Ardeatine massacre, by Robert Katz, was called *Death in Rome*.[4] I think it's a very appropriate title, but it's broader than he meant it. It's really about the meaning of death in a modern city, and the meaning of the memory of death.

So I'd like to close with a brief narrative on death, memories, ceremony, and the sense of history. The monument to the victims of the massacre is also a cemetery; there are three hundred and thirty-five concrete graves in one enormous room, raised from off the ground, and the concrete slab on top, a huge stone chest with a slight opening where it is lifted at the edge. This man – one of the few men – is a son, Modesto De Angelis:

> I was always somehow bothered in the ceremonies, even though I didn't have to stand out, I could be anonymous in the middle of the people. I didn't have to go up to the stage where the relatives were displayed, so somebody could look at me and say, 'He is the son of one of the victims.' But those ceremonial words, those words, they were so tired, and so tiresome. And so it happened one day – and after that this is what I always did – I happened, one day, to go to the monument on a springtime morning, at nine, when the monument opens to the public, and there's nobody. Now you've seen it. The shrine is covered with a huge stone. In the spring sometimes, there are a few birds that sit there and sing. So sometimes I went there, said a prayer, and I spoke … in a low voice, even though I was alone, to those dead, who I always called 'my boys'. And if there is something which still makes me bitter, after all these years, is that I was never able to go there one day and tell them, fully believing it, 'Well, we made it. *You* made it.'

## Notes

1   *Documenti della Resistenza a Roma e nel Lazio*, ed. Irsifar (Rome Institute for Italian History from Fascism to Resistance) and ANPI (National Association of Italian Partisans), Rome, Biblink 2001.

2   All interviews quoted were carried out by the author, chiefly in Rome in the late 1990s. For full details of sources, see Alessandro Portelli, *L'ordine è già stato eseguito. Roma, le Fosse Ardeatine, la memoria*, Rome, Donzelli 1999.

3   Vera Simoni, b. 1922, daughter of General Simone Simoni, killed at the Fosse Ardeatine; interviewed 5 April 1998.

4   Robert Katz, *Morte a Roma*, Rome, Editori Riuniti 1967.

2

# MEMORIES AND HISTORIES, PUBLIC AND PRIVATE

## After the Finnish Civil War

*Anne Heimo and Ulla-Maija Peltonen*

The purpose of this chapter is to examine the different ways the most traumatic event in the history of independent Finland, the 1918 Finnish Civil War, has been dealt with at different times in public and private forums. [1]The Civil War affected Finnish society at every level in a variety of deep and long-lasting ways, some of which can still be seen today.[2] In this chapter we will investigate the politics of memory in relation to the war. Our aim is to show that recollected narration, which includes folklore genres such as atrocity tales and belief legends, has played a major role in the social memory of the Civil War.

Social memory is a process rather than a fixed object; it is continually changing, part of the larger pattern of social change. Thus an examination of the ways death was dealt with during and after the Civil War can illuminate our understanding of the different phases in social memory. During the war atrocity tales – narratives describing particular violent events in the Civil War – were used as propaganda by both sides. Later such tales were used by the victors, the Whites, to justify the severity of their retaliations against the losers. The Reds, denied the right to mourn their losses and tell of their sufferings in public, were forced to develop new ways of handling their traumatic experiences. Belief legends, especially legends connected with the violation of a norm, proved to be a key location for accounts which both resisted and challenged the official versions of the Civil War. The later half of the chapter deals with the memory of the war at a local level, and shows how in the long run these memories may be used not only to preserve social memory, but to produce a common history to which all in the community may relate.

## Background

As a consequence of the Russian Revolution, Finland gained independence in December 1917. Within a month the nation was engaged in a civil war that was at once a class struggle over social conditions and a struggle for political power between the socialists and their opponents. The war divided the country and the people of Finland into two sides. Southern Finland was in the hands of the Reds, who were mainly industrial and agricultural workers and craftsmen; landowners, entrepreneurs and the intelligentsia, on the other hand, joined the Whites, who ruled the rest of Finland. The war lasted less than four months, from the end of January to the beginning of May. It led to the death of 35,000 people (of whom 28,000 were Red) during and after the war, in battle, acts of terror, or execution; or in prison of hunger or disease. About 82,000 people were accused of crimes against the state, condemned to imprisonment and deprived of their civil rights for years to come.[3]

The losing side, the Reds, suffered disproportionately in the aftermath of the war. High unemployment (exacerbated by grudges held by employers against known Reds) led to poverty and food shortages; children, especially war orphans, were fostered out when their families became unable to keep them. The nation was in mourning, and war memorials were built, but these official commemorations applied only to dead Whites; Red families were prevented from mourning and honouring the memory of their dead. The Whites never acknowledged the severity of the suffering that followed the war, and nor were they prosecuted for crimes committed during it. Unsurprisingly, bitter hatred and resentment among Reds were widespread.[4]

Since official accounts of the war were written by the Whites, the Reds were obliged to create their own historical interpretation of the war. Almost half a century had to pass before the perspective of those who had lost the war could even be expressed in public. Remembering, in such cases, is inevitably political: the question of what could or should be remembered was intimately tied to that of political allegiance. A vital part of remembering is the ability or the willingness to forget, select and disregard issues from a vast flood of things that could be remembered and told; but this is not a random process.[5] Memory's heterogeneity is manifested as a continuous dialogue between the old and the new, and between the different conceptions of the world of people of different sexes, classes, religions and ethnic groups.[6] After 1918, the Reds defended themselves against the victors by using their own narrative tradition, which could be designated a culture of contestation. These narratives conveyed values at odds with those endorsed by the official culture.[7]

At the beginning of the 1960s, however, the emergence of public debate about the Civil War produced a notable shift in attitudes. Writers were important in initiating the debate. The second part of Väinö Linna's trilogy *Under the North Star* (1960)[8] portrayed a Red version of the events of the war. The academic world also started to focus on the structural factors, economic and social, that had divided Finnish society during the years 1917 and 1918. Additionally and importantly, during the 1960s several oral history archives embarked on programmes to collect reminiscences and folklore. This inspired thousands of Finns to write tens of thousands of pages about their experiences of the Civil War, placing their accounts in their chosen archive when the opportunity arose.

## To remember or to forget?

The question of forgetting and remembering came into focus immediately after the Civil War. The victors insisted that 'unpleasant issues' should be forgotten, and emphasised that dwelling on them would only prolong antagonism. At the same time, however, they also wanted to portray the Civil War as a warning example. Meanwhile the losers emphasised the importance of remembering, because wrongdoings should not be forgotten and only remembering can heal the wounds. A political struggle over what to remember and what to forget has continued till this day; but the underlying question of *why* one should remember or forget has scarcely been discussed.

However, in their reminiscences, narrators take a stand on the issue of why. Those who identify with the losing party emphasise the importance of remembering for the sake of the truth; for them it is important that the wrongs committed should be publicly revealed. For example, a woman born in 1906 wrote in her memoirs, which she sent to the archive in the 1960s: 'Thank you for arranging this collection of memories. Now it will be possible to write the true history of the year 1918, when all the information and memories have been collected.'[9] At the same time a man born in 1910 wrote: 'I always hoped that finally the facts would be written for this side in the war as well; only after that can the wounds heal.'[10]

Those who identified with the victors, on the other hand, argued for the need to forget on the grounds that remembering will do no good to anybody, and indeed will only increase the suffering. A war veteran reacted to a doctoral dissertation on the subject of political violence with dismay:

> This is something that we old veterans think is wrong. When Marshall Mannerheim was still alive it was agreed that these issues would be forgotten by both sides; and this forgetting should continue, at least until we who suffered so much and who participated in the war are gone (male born in 1894).[11]

This comment, again recorded in the 1960s, reveals the writer's hostility towards a possible inquiry into the events of the war. It refers back to 1933, when the Civil War Commander-in-chief, General Mannerheim, speaking in a memorial service, declared that it was no longer important to ask what side a person fought on in 1918. Still in interviews at the end of the 1980s and even up to the present day, the same pattern persists: many of those who identified with the victors still want to forget, whereas those who identified with the losing party want to remember. As the writer of this letter to the 'War Victims in Finland 1914–1922' project put it in 1998:

> They ask if it is really necessary to start digging up old issues. I disagree; it is important just for history's sake to bring all this to light; it's not possible to just hide wrongdoings. As one old man once said:

'Even shit looks beautiful if it's covered with paper.' I am on the side of the truth in everything. I have carried [the memory of my father] like a burden for my entire life. My father was everything to me. I was seven years old and I still remember it like yesterday. That's the reason why I'm still here alive, so that I can testify to the truth.[12]

The writer, born in 1911, sees herself as a witness who will tell the truth about the death of her father. What one remembers and what one hears are closely linked; a narrative has significance as long as it meets with the awareness of the listener. The emotional charge of the war may change with time, but it remains powerful.

If the telling of the truth is of major importance for the narrators, for us the issues of origin are less significant: what is important is the fact that the narrators consider it to be true.[13] We are interested in all the ways the past is narrated, regardless of whether it is factually true or not. There are reasons for the shapes taken by people's memories, and for the ways in which they remember and speak those memories.[14] Moreover, collective concepts, describing what people believed to have happened during the war, are represented more clearly in stories than in eyewitness testimonies.[15] Many memories take the form of stories and local legends, cultural communications through which the beliefs, concepts, feelings and hopes of the community can be expressed. What is important is the interpretation of the tale, not the tale itself. The same narrative motifs will be reworked and applied to new circumstances and be re-interpreted. When meaning can no longer be found, the tale vanishes. Atrocity tales were and are a form of war propaganda, and also have clearly political aims. Another phase in the social memory of the Civil War can be seen in the belief legends and memoirs concerning school, church and law officers, who in most cases represented the Whites; in these belief legends the law of fate punished the perpetrator of the crime.

For the Reds, we have suggested, reminiscences were an important means to share a world of experiences that had been denied and forgotten by official culture.[16] In what follows, we will look at stories associated with violent death, and conflicts over mourning and memorials, before moving on to a local case-study of stories told in a particular town.

## Death in the Civil War

Death during the Civil War was both a personal and a public event. As a means of coping with the mental chaos of the war, those on the losing side turned to narration about their dead and about death in general, as well as to active participation in various organisations. The narrators who recounted and wrote about their experiences during the 1960s and later had all been involved in the Civil War, whether in person or through someone who, although absent, was 'one of us'. They played an important role in the upholding and handing down of social memory. Transforming death into narrative not only answered the wish to picture the war from the perspective of the losers, it was also a way of coming to terms with the burden of grief. It helped to fill the emptiness resulting from loss, and served as a means of paying respect to those who had died for a political cause.[17]

The death process can be divided into three phases: physical death, disposing of the body, and social death. Making death public is part of the death ritual, and informing the community affected by the death initiates the mourning rituals. Social death during the Civil War took on an added weight of meaning. In Finland, where the church plays a central role in the fulfilling of death rituals, both church and clergymen openly supported the White army. Inequality in death was concretely manifested in the different treatment of Whites and Reds in funeral services; many clergymen refused to perform funeral rites for Red victims. During the war itself, both Red and White supporters buried their dead equally according to proper burial rituals. Often in Red funerals a representative of the labour union rather than a member of the clergy conducted the funeral, and sometimes as well as a hymn, a labour-movement song was sung or played.

After the war, however, the situation changed radically. The church and its clergy received increasing criticism from the Reds, who could not understand why some clergymen denied them their right to mourn their deceased and to commemorate them.[18] Death's primary emotional meaning received political significance, and death rituals became a site for the assertion of power. The inequality in the commemoration of the dead was manifested most clearly by the memorial services conducted for White war heroes, while any attempts by the Reds to organise memorial services were considered the glorification of crime. The graves of the executed Reds were thus for a long time a very sensitive issue. Reds had been buried in cemeteries, but also in other places; some of the dead were buried at unknown execution sites. Information about these sites was passed on by word of mouth. The tending of Red graves was often forbidden, and mourners were not allowed to gather at them or to bring flowers, never mind erecting gravestones:

> In the spring of 1918, the bodies of the Reds who were shot were covered in the gravel pit on Tööri heath in Kuusankoski. In the summer the relatives brought flowers and name tags, even though it was forbidden. All sorts of ghost stories circulated, continuous crying and singing of hymns could be heard there.[19]
>
> (female born 1900)

To find new ways of mourning and honouring their dead the Red side drew on old beliefs and traditions that under new circumstances received a new meaning and created a new tradition.[20] Central to this new tradition was the urge to remember and reveal the crimes of the Whites. The crime of murder could only be reconciled if the fallen Red were allowed a decent burial in conse-crated soil. In the belief legends of the Reds, the 'law of destiny' often punished the wrongdoers because the judicial system, that is the law, failed to perform this function. Stories tell of clergymen who fell ill or committed suicide, executioners who became alcoholic, blind or insane:

> In those days they told how the legs of the parson of Jääski were covered with open sores, and nothing could cure them. So the people advised him to go to the old woman of Karisjärvi. Finally he gave in and went. The old woman said: you came to me seeking help, when you yourself caused this by kicking and cursing those corpses. Go and bless them and you will be cured, but if you don't go, your legs will never heal. No further medicine was needed than to go secretly and give his blessing.
>
> (female born 1896)[21]

In 1928, the Home Office announced that the remains of fallen and executed Reds were to be moved to cemeteries, and that fencing the gravesites would be allowed.[22] Official instructions and the reality did not, however, concur. The tending of Red graves was generally left to the Reds themselves, and in many places local labour organisations formed committees to take care of the graves. The authorities also opposed all attempts to erect memorials in honour of Red victims, considering such memorials to be the exclusive right of the Whites. In some cases this led to the demolishing of erected memorials.

Ten years after the war, in 1928, more than three hundred towns had erected memorials commemorating White victims. In the same year there were, according to present knowledge, twelve official statues in honour of the Red victims; however, in forests and on execution sites, there were hundreds of un-official ones. The exclusive right of the victors to erect memorials caused trouble as late as 1945, when the political climate in Finland started to become more liberal on this issue. An important moment in the official acknowledgement of Red victims was the charting of Red gravesites and memorials carried out in 1969 by the War Memorial Association formed by labour organisations. The official national memorial statue in honour of the Reds was erected in Helsinki in 1970 – fifty years after the official White memorial. A woman born in 1958 describes the importance of gravesites and of remembering:

> Finally after 70 years of waiting we got a grave memorial in Tammisaari, on which I found the name of my grandmother's father. All these years my grandmother has grieved over the fact that her father did not have a proper grave. Now he does. I visited the place on July 3rd, 1988, and took a photograph of the memorial. ... I also sent a photo to my grandfather and grandmother and their joy and surprise were great, they were proud of the fact that even one descendant will preserve the memory of her great-grandfather who starved to death. ... The legacy of 1918 is valuable and binding.
>
> (female born 1958)[23]

Unlike White memorials, which have had names engraved on them from the beginning, the naming of the Reds on memorials has only recently become a common practice. And despite the emotional and political significance of common grave memorials, many reminiscences emphasise the need for an individual grave, to acknowledge the particularity of the dead. The dead were not anonymous, but people of close personal importance to others.

## Case study in Sammatti

Sammatti is a small rural town of 1,000 inhabitants in Southern Finland. At the beginning of the war in Sammatti the Reds were in power; they confiscated arms and food for the Red troops, but otherwise everything remained quite peaceful. In late April, however, with the help of German and other alien troops, Sammatti was conquered by the Whites, and the executing of Reds began immediately. Numbers vary according to source, but local information suggests that of the fifty Reds killed in Sammatti as the result of the war over forty were executed, while only one White was murdered. The official figure for the number of Reds executed in Sammatti is twenty-six, which in proportion to the population of Sammatti still makes it the third highest war-time death toll in the whole of Finland.[24] The following discussion is based on interviews and written memoirs recorded between the 1960s and the 1990s, and on additional material from various archives.

Approximately two-thirds of the people interviewed had personal memories of the Civil War in Sammatti; the rest were either born later or had moved there after the war, in other words they had gained their knowledge from a range of different sources. Until 1992, when a local amateur historian published an article[25] on the war in Sammatti, information about the executions carried out there was sparse and scattered, to be found in official (for example clerical, parish, Social Democratic Party) statistics, in some random writings and on two memorial stones, on which the names of the victims are engraved. Thus, even in a modern and literate community like Sammatti, for more than seventy years most information about the war had to be communicated orally. Memories were passed on in many conversational contexts – on social occasions, at work, at meetings of the local labour organisation or White Civil Guard – but these conversations took place only within the group; Reds talked to Reds, and Whites to Whites. In addition many informants referred to books (both fiction and non-fiction) and magazines as sources of information about the war. Most had no reference to Sammatti, but could nonetheless serve several purposes: the gathering of information, the affirmation of the reader's view of events, and commemoration. References to books were also used to show solidarity. Stories about Sammatti could be verified by comparison with events elsewhere: 'Yes, the parish priest was White just like the one in *Under the North Star*',[26] or, 'The Reds did hideous things, in Vammala they tried to burn the whole town'.

Though most of the interview material from Sammatti seems at first to be autobiographical or non-traditional, in the interviews and written memoirs one may recognise familiar patterns and repetitive themes, of which some can be classified as tales, or local legends. Archive material from the 1940s and 1960s shows that belief legends used to be told in Sammatti, but they are no longer current. Most of the stories which are still told deal with peril and survival, and have in many cases become an important part of family memory, as they have all over Finland. The stories of survival tell of remarkable escapes, of rebellious women defending their kin, of kind masters and mistresses who saved their farm hands, and so on. The stories of peril tell of people who were sentenced to death for deeds of which they were innocent, of bad masters and mistresses who refused to help their workers and of unsuccessful escapes, etc.

The myth that the Second World War, particularly the Winter War of 1939–40, smoothed over the differences between the Reds and the Whites is powerful and persistent. In Sammatti, although the informants shared this common notion, they nearly all still showed signs of partiality towards either the Red or the White side. These attitudes were most apparent in their tellings of local legends, because story-telling requires a point of view. The tales are based on real incidents, but in the process of continuous retelling they have increasingly taken on the features of traditional tales: the plots have been simplified by discarding elements which no longer have meaning, while the repetition and emphasis of motifs central to the plot have increased. These local legends reveal the different views the informants have of the war, and especially the consequences of the war: the unjust punishing of the innocent, the escape of the guilty, righteous revenge, the innocence of 'us', the villagers, and the guilt of 'them', the outsiders. Though these stories can be told from two opposite points of view, they also have a common meaning: to point out that it was 'them', not 'us', who were responsible.

'The Death of Judge Nevalainen' is one of the most popular local legends. It tells the story of the only White who was killed in Sammatti during the Civil War. Lawyer Unto Nevalainen (born 1887) had moved to Sammatti in 1917. During the war family members, landowners, the local vicar and some other White sympathisers sought shelter at his remote villa. After the Whites occupied Sammatti with the help of German troops in the middle of April, Nevalainen's sister went to seek information, but was captured by the Reds. Nevalainen and his fiancée went looking for her, and they were also captured. The women were released the same day, but the Reds took Nevalainen with them when they fled to Nummi. He was released the next day, but was killed on the way home by unknown Reds:

> But yeah, that's fate. That winter, he was living here, he had his own villa: Judge Nevalainen. And he was the secretary in the committee that was promoting the Crofter's Land Redemption Law … well anyway, he was living here and when the Rebellion came he didn't go to Helsinki.

He came to the village on some business, and the Reds arrested him there and took him to Nummi, and in Nummi and in the evening two men said he'd be released, they went with him, and soon enough when they came to the road that branches off – the road to Sammatti – a narrow road, hard for the horses – when they reach that road, they start stabbing him with their bayonets, and even the next day – there's one neighbour there, a little croft farm and the children say mum, there's someone groaning there. She knew, but she didn't dare go, and she says to the children, it's a bird singing, can't you hear? That was Nevalainen's fate. He was completely uninvolved. Nothing to do with anything, nothing at all, he just happened to be there.

(male born in 1908)[27]

The Whites' versions of the story, like the one above, were usually much longer and more detailed than the versions told by Reds. The protagonist's innocence is described in many ways. At the same time all mention of his support for the Whites – the fact that he lodged White sympathisers, and that he was able to eavesdrop on the Reds' telephone calls – is left out. There is little mention of the events surrounding his actual capturing and release; instead, the focus is shifted to his death. His suffering is described through the detail of his multiple stab wounds, the fact that he was buried alive, and through reference to someone hearing his wailing, but not daring to help. For White narrators the story was just one more example of Red atrocity.

The shorter Red versions did not need to describe Nevalainen's background, the events that led to his capture or his death. The story was told as an example of how well-behaved the Reds were in Sammatti, that *only* one White was killed, and to be exact the murderers weren't even from Sammatti. Both sides use the story to explain, and in the case of the Whites also to justify, why so many Reds were executed after the war in Sammatti: 'For every stab wound they killed one Red' and 'Wasn't it that he had 47 bayonet stabs, when he was found'.[28] It is noteworthy that on neither side did anyone doubt the justness of the punishment, even though it was clearly excessive.[29]

Another Sammatti tale, 'The Murder of the Mistress of Löökulla', tells the story of the death of Hulda Vannas (born 1883), wife of Juho Vannas, who was leader of the White Civil Guard in Sammatti, and held responsible for the executions. Hulda Vannas died in a very unusual incident, an explosion at her home some months after the war; her husband received only minor wounds. An official enquiry was made, but no one was ever prosecuted. In the following years the unsolved murder gave rise to legends in which the dead wife was believed to be haunting the house.[30] Seventy years later, however, references to the haunting have disappeared, and most narrators on the Red side suggest that the husband himself planted the bomb so the Reds would be accused of the attack. In these stories the mistress is described as being a defender of the poor, and her husband as hostile to her activities (although in fact she backed her husband). Informants siding with the Whites, on the other hand, suggest that the attack was an act of revenge by the Reds.

The following version was told jointly by father and son. At the time of the murder the father was a 14-year-old boy living in the neighbouring house, and he was at the murder scene soon after the explosion. In the first half of the interview the father recalled the events, making it clear to the interviewer that he believed the Reds were responsible for the attack. Later on the son joined in, and the discussion continues:

SON  When you listen to him [father], well sure I believe him at that point – that he's – but then when I've talked to others and they say that the Reds – well I've thought that maybe Vannas himself – but they say – well, now at least – because there weren't such hostilities here and nobody really believes that they [the Reds] did it.

INTERVIEWER: But did this Vannas have any reason for doing something like that to his wife?

FATHER: I don't know, they were the kind of couple who were always fighting – but I don't know if that's what it was. So I almost – well there were some of them in the Red Guards even in August, hiding in the woods. So, maybe – well they could have come from there.

SON: So they would have hated him even more.

FATHER: Yeah, they hated people like that, he was the kind of man – he had so many people killed so they hated him for that, yeah.

SON: Yeah, well as for that – but I just assume, that maybe he threw it himself, what I've heard is they were sleeping in the same bed just like we [the narrator and his wife] do and the woman's brains are all over the lilac bush, and the guy gets a little scratch, so – so what the door was – it would have been Providence, if the fellow just happened to be outside pissing or somewhere else.

(father born in 1904, son born in 1950)[31]

The example is thought-provoking, because in spite of his father's eyewitness testimony, the son is ready to argue and believe that the Reds were innocent, that it was the husband who committed the murder. In a version told by another member of the family – the older man's nephew – the culprit once again is the husband himself; the nephew is sure of this, because his uncle was an eyewitness. The interesting thing is that though the nephew's presentation seems to follow his uncle's testimony in detail, his reasoning of what happened is the opposite of his uncle's. Has the nephew misunderstood his uncle's story, or has the uncle changed his version at some time? In a previous interview,[32] the man told a folklore interviewer that Vannas murdered his wife, without revealing his eyewitness role in the matter.

The story of the Murder of the Mistress of Löökulla cannot be understood out of its context, which in this case includes many other stories telling of Juho

Vannas and his oddities, all of which stress that ultimately he was to blame for all the executions carried out in Sammatti, and he was never a villager, not 'one of us'. No one seems to recall that Vannas, who had moved to Sammatti only some years before the war, had in a short time become a respected citizen with several positions of trust and was chosen without doubt to lead the White Guard. After the Civil War Vannas became a *persona non grata*, and it must have been a relief for the local inhabitants that he moved away from Sammatti a few years later. In a review concerning the White Guard in Sammatti published in 1926 Juho Vannas is only mentioned as the husband of the energetic mistress of Löökulla;[33] in a later review, published in 1938, there is no mention of him at all.[34]

These examples show the problems that may lie ahead if one regards oral history only as a source of empirical information, which may be used to corroborate the truth of other accounts. That oral accounts may be shown to be unreliable and inaccurate in relation to other sources does not mean they are not fruitful evidence in other ways. The central question here is about meaning, about how we are able to understand and interpret oral narratives. Subjectivity, and the narrator's interpretations of the stories he or she has to tell, are essential aspects of oral history, and of great interest to the researcher.[35]

## Conclusion

A dual and separate nurturing of Civil War memories was evident in Finland right up to the 1960s. The losers of the war were bitter, firstly, because the official truth did not admit to any of its own crimes or violence, but instead covered them up or concealed them. Furthermore it exaggerated and misrepresented the crimes and wrongdoings of the Reds, and even later this false information was not corrected. Important public officials, such as clergymen, judges and teachers, were biased against the Red side after the war. Thus the official interpretation of the war was one that Red supporters could not identify with; nor were they allowed to display their grief publicly by, for example, honouring their dead. Memory thus gives many different accounts of the war. Official versions are not the only factor that influences how people conceive fairness or injustice, goodness or harmfulness. 'Unofficial' common beliefs are important, and they are often passed on from generation to generation within families or among friends.

In reminiscing, narrators analyse the past from their own perspectives; they strive to control their pasts and to understand not only their experiences but also where they, as Reds, belong. The images of official authority revealed in recollected narratives refer to experiences with school, church and judicial system officials. Because the official administration of justice did not interfere with White terror tactics in 1918, the Reds developed belief legends which were based on the older folklore tradition, and which borrowed its forms. In these belief legends the law of fate punished the perpetrator of the crime.

They were a strong protest against the fact that someone could be killed for his opinions. At the same time, in their frequent emphasis on crying and hymn-singing – traditional forms for the expression of grief, especially among women – they could be a means to object to the official ban on mourning Red victims.[36] On the side of the losing party reminiscences were an important means to share a world of experiences that had been denied and forgotten by official culture. They have not only private but also wider social and political significance.

Recollected narration is a fundamental part of the micro-level processes associated with personal life histories. In narratives concerning the Finnish Civil War there are several different phases, linked to time and place, and also to the immediate political situation. One narrative phase after the war was that of atrocity tales, which were unambiguous reactions to the shocking events. By the retelling of atrocity tales, the narrator attempted to transform powerlessness and shame into organised hostility; the function of the narratives was also to indicate who was 'one of us' and who was 'one of them', that is one of the guilty, one of those to be held responsible. Both Reds and Whites told atrocity tales, but it is a key difference that the atrocity tales told by Whites concerning Reds were a visible part of official versions of history. In atrocity tales published in literature and newspaper articles of the period, the winning side constructed stereotypes of the Reds' immorality, brutality, and lack of patriotism, as well as their blasphemy against 'sacred values'. Atrocity tales were and are a form of war propaganda, with clearly political aims.

A later phase of social memory, however, organises the idea of 'us' and 'them' very differently. Even though the narrators in Sammatti still showed signs of ideological partiality, the war in the 1990s is no longer primarily remembered as a part of Finnish working-class history, nor that of the official victors, as it had been earlier. Rather, the function of the stories has changed: it is now to show that it was not 'us', the people of Sammatti, who were guilty of these crimes, but the Other: the outsiders, the non-locals, the Germans, the Swedish speakers, etc. Even in the case of the leader of the local White Civil Guard, who was held responsible for the executions, it was made clear that he was not originally from Sammatti; and all the other local people who held high positions were either forgotten or not mentioned. The only references to the possibility that 'we' might also have had something to do with the happenings were references to executions arising out of personal hate and revenge. The good and the innocent in the tales, the ones who had to suffer, were always 'us' the villagers. In addition to these distinctions between us and them, the time before the war has been mytholo-gised into a Golden Era, when masters and men worked together and there were no conflicts between the villagers. Few remembered the social differences between landowners, crofters and especially the landless and craftsmen, which existed before the war. As time has passed, the memories of the Civil War have been shaped to provide the local community with a past they can live with and a means to express outward unity.

# Notes

1 This chapter is based on Ulla-Maija Peltonen's and Anne Heimo's current studies, which are both part of a research project, 'Oral History and the Interpretations of History', funded by the Academy of Finland (1999–2001).

2 The public debate about the war is still in progress in Finland. There is not even agreement over what the war should be called; it is variously referred to as the 'National War', 'Civil War', 'War of Freedom', 'Class War', 'Rebellion' or 'Revolution'. The year 1918 is the most heavily researched moment in recent Finnish history; however, academic research has not yet seriously addressed the psychological impact of the war and its aftermath.

3 For more details see Risto Alapuro, 'Coping with the Civil War of 1918 in Twenty-first Century Finland', in Kenneth Christie and Robert Cribb (eds.), *Historical Justice and Democratic Transition in Eastern Asia and Northern Europe: Ghosts at the Table of Democracy* (London and New York: Routledge Curzon, 2002); Alapuro, *State and Revolution in Finland* (Berkeley, Los Angeles and London: University of California Press, 1988); Anthony F. Upton, *The Finnish Revolution 1917–1918* (Minneapolis: University of Minnesota Press, 1980); 'War Victims in Finland 1914–1922' project (URL: http://vesta.narc.fi/cgi-bin/db2www/sotasurmaetusivu/main).

4 Ulla-Maija Peltonen, '*Punakapinan muistot*': Summary: 'Memories of the Civil War. A Study of the Formation of the Finnish Working-class Narrative Tradition after 1918' (Helsinki: Finnish Literature Society, 1996a); Peltonen, 'Workers' Narrative Tradition in Finland after 1918', in Flemming Hemmersam (ed.), *To Work, to Life or to Death* (Copenhagen 1996b); Peltonen, 'Civil War Victims and the Ways of Mourning in Finland in 1918', in Christie and Cribb, *Historical Justice*. See also Mandy Hoogendoorn, 'Remembering the Finnish Civil War: Confronting a Harrowing Past', in *ibid*.

5 David Lowenthal, *The Past is a Foreign Country* (Cambridge: Cambridge University Press, 1990), 185–238; Alessandro Portelli, *The Death of Luigi Trastulli and Other Stories. Form and Meaning in Oral History* (Albany: State University Press of New York Press, 1991), 19–26; Luisa Passerini, Introduction, in Luisa Passerini (ed.), *Memory and Totalitarianism* (New York: Oxford University Press, 1992), 1–19.

6 James Fentress and Chris Wickham, *Social Memory* (Oxford: Blackwell, 1992), foreword; Popular Memory Group, 'Popular Memory: Theory, Politics, Method', in Richard Johnson, Gregor MacLennan, Bill Schwarz and David Sutton (eds), *Making Histories, Studies in History-writing and Politics* (London: Hutchinson, 1982), 207–209.

7 Ulla-Maija Peltonen, 'The Return of the Narrator', in Anne Ollila (ed.), *Historical Perspectives on Memory* (Helsinki: Suomen Historiallinen Seura, 1999b), 131.

8 Väinö Linna, *Under the North Star* (1960). Translation into English, part I in 2001 by Richard Impola, Aspasia Books. The second part is due in 2002, and the third in 2003.

9 Finnish Literature Society, Folklore Archives 1918 (1965), Vol. 35, 183.

10 Finnish Literature Society, Folklore Archives 1918 (1965), Vol. 3, 81.

11 Finnish Literature Society, Folklore Archives 1918 (1965), Vol. 42, 228. The dissertation in question was by Fil. Lic. [doctoral candidate] Jaakko Paavolainen: 'Poliittiset väkivaltaisuudet Suomessa 1918 I–II' (Political Violence in Finland in 1918 I–II), (Helsinki: Tammi, 1966).

12 Letter to 'War Victims in Finland 1914–1922' project.

13 Truth is a major issue in history-telling, and the interviewees used different techniques to assure their interlocutors that this was what they were doing. See Anne Heimo, 'Untold Stories, Twice Told Tales – How People Narrate Their Own History', in Ulrika Wolf-Knuts and Annikki Kaivola-Bregenhøj (eds), *Pathways: Approaches to the Study and Teaching of Folklore* (Turku: NNF, 2001).

14 Luisa Passerini, 'Women's Personal Narratives: Myths, Experiences and Emotions' in Personal Narratives Group (eds), *Interpreting Women's Lives. Feminist Theory and Personal Narratives* (Bloomington and Indianapolis: Indiana University Press, 1989), 187; Portelli, op. cit. 1991; Alessandro Portelli, *The Battle of Valle Guilia. Oral History and the Art of Dialogue* (Madison: The University of Wisconsin Press, 1997). See also Elizabeth Tonkin, *Narrating our Pasts. The Social Construction of Oral History* (Cambridge: Cambridge University Press, 1992), 113–115.

15 Fentress and Wickham, op. cit. 1992, xiii; Portelli, op. cit. 1991, 48–53.

16 Peltonen, op. cit. 1996a: 203–242; op. cit. 1996b: 172–195.

17 Jay Winter, *Sites of Memory, Sites of Mourning. The Great War in European cultural history* (Cambridge: Cambridge University Press, 1997), 223–226.

18 Peltonen, op. cit. 1996a, 223–231.

19 Finnish Literature Society, Folklore Archives 1918 (1965), Vol. 59, 183–184.

20 Peltonen, op. cit. 1996a, 223–231; op. cit. 1999a; (tale-type C 643); Marjatta Jauhiainen, *Suomalaiset uskomustarinat. Tyypit ja motiivit*. Revised and Enlarged Edition of Lauri Simonsuuri's *Typen- und Motivverzeichnis der finnischen mythischen Sagen*, FF Communications No. 182. Helsinki 1961 (Helsinki: SKS, 1999), 101.

21 Finnish Literature Society, Folklore Archives 1918 (1965), Vol. 37, 86.

22 Peltonen, op. cit. 1996a, 223–231.

23 Labour Archives (1988), Vol. 251/1125, 4.

24 Tauno Tukkinen, *Teloittajien edessä* (Karjalohja: Tuomo Tukkinen, 1999); Jaakko Paavolainen, *Poliittiset väkivaltaisuudet Suomessa 1918 II. Valkoinen Terrori* (Helsinki: Tammi, 1967), 166–167. The exact number differs from source to source. The interviewees, unlike historians or statistical experts, did not distinguish between the victims' official place of birth, their home, and whether they were actually killed in Sammatti or in a neighbouring commune.

25 Tauno Tukkinen, 'Sammatin ja Karjalohjan tapahtumia 1917–18', in *Kruuhu* 1991 (Lohja, 1992).

26 References to Linna's novel are common in reminiscences, especially in the 1960s. The Reds were grateful to Linna for revealing their side of the war, even though they considered that his portrayal of the events of the Civil War was too mild, whereas the Whites accused him of exaggerating.

27 Finnish Literature Society Sound Archive, SKSÄ 96: 17.1988.

28 The Archives of the Institute of Comparative Religion and Folkloristics, University of Turku, TKU/A/91/234: 5–6.

29 Alessandro Portelli, plenary talk 'The Massacre at Fosse Ardeatine: History, Myth, Ritual, Symbol', Frontiers of Memory Conference 17–19.9.1999. See his chapter of the same title in this volume.

30 Finnish Literature Society, SKS Kuujo 1949: 717 & 785; Jauhiainen 1999, 84. Tale-type C 122.

31 The Archives of the Institute of Comparative Religion and Folkloristics, University of Turku, TKU/A/91/235: 1.

32 Finnish Literature Society, Sound Archives SKSÄ 90: 5.1988.

33 *Sarkatakki* 11/1926.

34 *Länsi-Uusimaa* 3.5.1938.

35 Portelli, op cit. 1997, 64–67; Tonkin, op. cit. 1994, 39–41, passim. Cf. Jorma Kalela, 'The Challenge of Oral History – The Need to Rethink Source Criticism' in Anne Ollila (ed.), *Historical Perspectives on Memory* (Helsinki: Suomen Historiallinen Seura, 1999).

36 The third phase of social memory is that of the memories from a 'black time'. In the 1920s and the 1930s some Reds re-engaged in political activism, and memories of the Civil War played an important role in the rise of the illegal Communist Party. For more details: Ulla-Maija Peltonen, 'Red Memoirs from a "Black Time" in Finland –

Radical Working Class Reminiscences of the 1920s and 30s', in Tauno Saarela and Kimmo Rentola (eds), *Communism. National and International* (Helsinki: Suomen Historiallinen Seura, 1998), 273–298.

# 3

# WAR, HISTORY, AND THE EDUCATION OF (CANADIAN) MEMORY

*Graham Carr*

There is a secret agreement between past generations and the present one. Our coming was expected on earth. Like every generation that preceded us, we have been endowed with a weak Messianic power, a power to which the past has a claim. That claim cannot be settled cheaply.

(Walter Benjamin, 'Theses on the Philosophy of History')[1]

## Introduction

In the spring of 1985, the American president, Ronald Reagan, found himself embroiled in controversy when he visited a military cemetery in Bitburg, Germany, with Chancellor Helmut Kohl. Although the trip was designed to symbolize a spirit of international reconciliation four decades after the end of the Second World War, the political message foundered both on the revelation that dozens of *Waffen SS* were buried at Bitburg and on Reagan's stubborn insistence that German soldiers were 'victims just as surely as the victims in the concentration camps'.[2] Shortly after Reagan's misguided trip, the literary scholar and Holocaust specialist, Geoffrey Hartman, took up the 'question of memory and its educability'. Convinced that the ceremony at Bitburg exemplified a perverse 'mechanics of commemoration' which disburdened memory and constructed forgetfulness, Hartman argued that a 'crucial ... turning point' had been reached with respect to the Second World War. Notwithstanding the burgeoning monumentalization of the war, the gradual dying out of the witnesses themselves meant that memory was becoming 'increasingly alienated from personal and active recall' and that the 'living tie between generations' was being usurped. Concerned that this connection with the war was rapidly slipping away from the 'general public' and that '*in less than one more generation*' it would become the exclusive preserve of 'the historian', Hartman insisted on the need for 'education and ritual ... to carry the entire burden of sustaining the collective memory'.[3]

A recent Canadian debate about the Second World War recapitulates some of Hartman's anxieties about the education of memory. In January 1992, the

Canadian Broadcasting Corporation (CBC) triggered an unprecedented storm of controversy when it aired a three-part documentary on Canada's role in the war called *The Valour and the Horror*.[4] In Parliament and the media critics denounced as cynical and distorted the film's claims that Canadian troops had fought valiantly in the war only to be victimized by devious, incompetent leadership. The filmmakers were accused of distorting history and deliberately representing Canada's military in the worst possible light. Concerned about the negative effect of the series on 'impressionable Canadian children', some critics moved to censor it by pressing for revisions to the script or demanding that the videos be withdrawn from circulation. A group of Canadian RAF veterans tried to outlaw the series altogether, launching a $500-million-class action lawsuit which alleged that they had been defamed by the filmmakers' assertion that Bomber Command deliberately targeted German civilians.[5]

One retired air force officer typified the anxiety of many veterans when he wrote to the Prime Minister asking whether the programmes 'will be in our schools as a part of the curriculum?' Pointing out that 'in another decade most veterans will not be here to watch these tapes' or 'to dispute the case presented', he worried about the 'image' the documentary would 'leave' children 'of their fathers and grandfathers'. Although some veterans congratulated the filmmakers on 'bringing history to the newer generation that had no way of finding out what happened in those days', others were despondent that the series had 'insulted' the 'achievement of a whole generation'. 'When we ... are gone,' lamented one veteran, 'this biased and inaccurate series will still be shown and presented as the truth. I don't want my grandchildren and great-grandchildren thinking what I did was evil.' The 'tragedy of the whole matter', declared another veteran, is that 'these films will be shown in schools across Canada, giving a false message to this and succeeding generations.'[6]

These anxieties about death and the vanishing legacy of the past were hardly unique to the debate on the Second World War, for as Alison Landsberg points out, 'the problem of transgenerational memory is as old as the concept itself'.[7] In the early 1990s, however, unease about the precarious future of social memory was intensified by widespread cultural concerns – expressed by academic historians, through government commissions, and in the mainstream media – that Canadians were 'ignorant' about their 'history and evolution'. Much of the blame for this purported ignorance was laid on the education system which, rightly or wrongly, was faulted for having 'killed Canadian history', effectively 'burying the political memory of youth'.[8] Testifying before a Senate committee on the future of the Canadian War Museum, its Acting Director General spoke directly to these themes when he declared that the history of the Second World War was ignored and unknown by 'young people' in Canada. According to Donald Glenney, not only were the efforts of the veterans 'forgotten' when they 'came home and took their uniforms off', but subsequent generations of students also learned next to nothing about the war because 'the history is not being taught in the schools'. 'As the memory of war recedes,' he concluded somewhat wistfully, 'only by education can we ensure that commemoration remains alive.'[9]

This chapter explores 'the relationship between historical imagination and ... memorial consciousness' by examining the pervasive use of generational motifs as loose tropes of history and education in *The Valour and the Horror* controversy.[10] The fact that commentators on all sides of the issue habitually invoked the discourse of generations to give form and meaning to their arguments spoke both to the broad cultural power of generational identity as a social construct and to its sedimentation in the ecology of war remembrance. Emblematic of a biological and social continuum that imprints the character of the past onto the future, generational motifs served to activate the space between memory and history while simultaneously blurring the distinctions between them.[11] In one sense, the routine use of generational imagery in the debate about *The Valour and the Horror* fulfilled a broad civic obligation to affirm the war's contribution to national security and to uphold the social coherence of the Canadian community as its legacy. But the prevalence of these motifs also served to naturalize an epistemologically problematic perspective on history that was overdetermined by the logic of succession and neutralized by the pressures of commitment to familial affection.

Throughout the debate the idea of generation served two fundamental purposes. In the first instance it acted as a familiar marker of age, social identity and historical perspective. This was hardly surprising; the notions that people are products of their times and that each generation writes its own history are axiomatic in most theories of historiography. Indeed they are a core element of the widely held belief that 'each generation's inquiries about the past ... carry forward the implications of its predecessors' learning'.[12] During *The Valour and the Horror* controversy the director, Brian McKenna, routinely defended the series against critics in the veterans' community by maintaining that his interpretation of the war reflected his reality as someone 'of a different generation'. His detractors happily acknowledged the point by stigmatizing McKenna as a 'flower child' and scoffing at the opinions of the 'Vietnam ... generation'. One academic historian who was hostile to the series simply dismissed the director's perspective out of hand by insisting that there was 'no worse present for viewing the past of the 1940s than to have been a university student and a young man in the sixties and early seventies'.[13]

While age and generational identity are undoubtedly important variables in determining historical knowledge, the popularity of generational motifs tends to impair appreciation of social difference and encourage the perception that individuals share an 'automatic registering of events' by virtue of being part of a particular demographic cohort.[14] As Peter Novick points out, generations 'do not replace one another on cue' and individuals are 'shaped by very different experiences' and respond 'very differently to the same experiences'.[15] Although many participants in *The Valour and the Horror* controversy were loath to acknowledge the point, these subjectivities surfaced repeatedly in the debate. The most glaring examples occurred when veterans who believed that the series was 'a fairly accurate portrayal' of the war 'as I knew it' clashed with those who were adamant that the documentary's version of history 'was not the way it was'.[16]

Beyond the issue of experience, however, the utility of generational rhetoric as an explanatory tool was also over-extended with respect to education and the mechanics of historical knowledge acquisition. According to Peter Seixas, the cognitive issues surrounding teaching and historical understanding are among the 'least examined' topics in educational theory, with the result that there is relatively little informed scholarship about the developmental stages at which students acquire historical knowledge and begin to formulate an historical perspective.[17] Ironically, for all of its sound and fury about the dire state of contemporary history education, the furor over *The Valour and the Horror* did nothing to address this lacuna. Although participants in the controversy regularly invoked the image of young people as a constituency whose interests were most at stake, students and teachers were essentially an absent presence in the debate, conspicuous by their silence, or perhaps their inability to intervene.

In addition to serving the rhetorical demands of identity politics, a second way in which generational motifs were routinely manifested in the controversy was as a narrative device linking the transmission of historical understanding to the natural order of 'kinship lineage descent'.[18] Responding to one veteran's pleas that his government do something about *The Valour and the Horror*, a senior cabinet minister was reassuring about the genealogical relationship between history, kin and the cultural order of things. Notwithstanding the work of revisionists, he declared, 'this country will be handed down, unsullied and undiminished, to our children and grandchildren'. The historian Michael Bliss made a similar argument when he defended the series by proclaiming that 'my generation has a responsibility to uphold the values that an older generation went to war to defend'. Connecting knowledge of history to the bonds of filial affection, one media critic saluted the filmmakers' 'deep respect, admiration and even love for the generation of Canadians who went to war over fifty years ago'. The series, concluded Rick Salutin, was 'a credible way of passing on to future generations a crucial experience from the past'.[19]

My point in exploring how generational tropes of history and education are applied to debates about the war is not to deny the existence, or legitimacy, of shared experiences and memories, or to trivialize the meanings that commentators ascribe to them. Instead I am arguing that, as tools of social memory, these tropes have a 'hidden curriculum' that does additional cultural work.[20] In her book *Frames of Remembrance*, Iwona Irwin-Zarecka argues that social memory is 'a significant orienting force' in society, that it is 'imbued with moral imperatives'. Admittedly, the generational rhetoric that circulated in the debate over *The Valour and the Horror* tacitly acknowledged, and to some extent exploited, the reality of conflicting perspectives on the past. But in the main it functioned to subordinate conflict by accentuating the personal and familial on the one hand, and promoting intergenerational reconciliation on the other. By its affirmation of the 'normative order' of kinship and national identity, the discourse of generations subtly manoeuvred the controversy about the series away from the disciplinary realm of history which is 'objective in the coldest, hardest sense of the word', and toward the domain of memory which is 'subjective in the warmest, most inviting senses of that word'.[21]

## Touching gestures

In order to grasp the intrinsic role of generational rhetoric in *The Valour and the Horror* debate it is important to consider how deeply embedded these motifs have become in the 'ecology' of remembrance as a result of their 'repetition and recycling' in the half-century since 1945.[22] In Canada, the process of sedimentation began immediately following the war with the ritualization of generational motifs as a core element of official commemorative ceremonies. Linking up personal and family memories to the public history of the nation, images of 'the mothers and fathers, the children' who participated in these events, or merely gathered to witness them, were prominently inscribed in media narrations of Remembrance Day.[23]

One shorthand way to trace the cultural legacy of these motifs is through pictures. In July 1946 an official of the Canadian Embassy in Brussels sent a brief 'despatch' with enclosures to the Secretary of State for External Affairs in Ottawa regarding 'the commemorative ceremony' that had recently been held in the 'Canadian cemetery' at Edegem in Belgium. 'Sir,' the memo began, 'I have the honour to enclose herewith a small bag containing earth from the grave of D.142377 R.F.N. Rogers, H.W., which was handed to the Ambassador during the course of the ceremony. Perhaps you could see that this souvenir is transmitted to Rogers' next-of-kin. I also enclose pictures of some of the ladies of the Ghent Welfare Committee collecting earth from some of the graves in this cemetery' (Figure 3.1). Most of 'the ladies entrusted with this task', the official explained, 'had lost either a husband, brother or son in German concentration camps'.[24] Notwithstanding the formal tone of the despatch, the symbolism of a miniature body bag accompanied by poignant images of women digging the earth in a field of bleached wooden crosses is a stark point of departure for the sedimentation of memory.

Casting a gaze forward some fifty years to the front pages of various Canadian newspapers on Remembrance Day, 1997, we find a different figure squatting in a soldier's cemetery, surrounded by gravestones (Figure 3.2). Instead of a bereaved widow, mother, or sister, the figure this time is an eight-year-old boy, Kevin Paris – a 'Grade 3 student' at an elementary school, the newspaper caption was careful to point out – who 'is one of many Canadians taking time to commemorate the two world wars'. Instead of digging the earth with a trowel, however, the boy, the student, is planting a Canadian flag, the metaphorical flower of nation and citizenship germinated from the seed of D.142377 R.F.N. Rogers, H.W.'s noble sacrifice. With one arm reaching out to

*Figure 3.1* Untitled photograph. Woman in cemetry collecting earth.

*Source*: National Archives of Canada, C-036723

touch the gravestone of a soldier whose identity is not disclosed, the boy's, the student's, gesture fulfils the regenerative process begun in 1946 by connecting the private and public realms. But the caption accompanying the photo makes an additional point: 'After decades of silence,' it explains, 'there is renewed interest in making sure the past is not forgotten'. Before the approving eyes of the reading nation the education of social memory about the war is both enacted, and rendered somatic, by a child's patriotic embrace of a monument to the dead.[25]

Of course by capturing so vividly the image of the boy's outstretched arm the news photograph also points graphically to a familiar paraphrase of transgenerational continuity: the laying on of hands. In Canadian military culture the most famous inscription of this touching gesture is the couplet, 'To you, with failing hands we throw/The torch, be yours to hold it high', from John McRae's ubiquitous First World War poem, *In Flanders Fields* (1915). At once a benediction and a

*Figure 3.2* 'Kids Honour Veterans – Children from St Mary's Elementary School in Halifax took the time to lay Canadian flags on the graves of fallen comrades in a ceremony honouring them for their service in Halifax. Kevin Paris (8, grade 3) places a flag on one of the many graves.'

*Source:*Canadian Press. (CP Photo/Tony Caldwell). *Halifax Daily News,* 1997

call to civic duty, the stanza signals clearly the responsibility of future generations to carry forward the memory and achievements of the past. Significantly, a variation on this poetic impulse is alluded to by the establishing shot for *The Valour and the Horror,* which reworks a black and white photograph, entitled 'Wait for me, Daddy', that is something of an icon in the visual archive of the war (Figure 3.3).

Taken by Claude P. Dettloff in New Westminster, British Columbia, the photograph was chosen as a *Life* magazine 'picture of the week' in October 1940 and selected later as one of the magazine's top photos from its first decade. Although Dettloff's photograph is a remarkable study in movement in its own right, the documentary imposes its own rhythm on the image, with a slow camera pan across the chain of outstretched hands from a woman to a small boy to the line of marching soldiers. Here cinematography replicates *Life*'s captioning of the photo which merges the image of forward marching soldiers – 'a long, straight column … bound for points unknown' – with the inexorable passage of generations. 'Just before this picture was taken,' the *Life* caption reads, 'one little fair-haired boy had spotted his father and had broken away from his mother's hand. Without breaking step, the father holds out his hand. The other men smile and the column goes on.'[26]

*Figure 3.3* 'Wait for me, Daddy.' (Claude P. Dettloff)
*Source*: National Archives of Canada, C-038723.

But there is something else going on here too. For, as the opening frame of a documentary series that looks, retrospectively, back on the Second World War, the visual rhetoric of Dettloff's photograph is also made to draw viewers into the realm of 'prosthetic' memory by linking their 'sensuous' experience of the film with the tissue of bodies that is simultaneously archived and animated on the screen.[27] Here, an intergenerational template of the war's social context is literally extended into the present as contemporary viewers are urged to make a connection with the past that is both individualized and anonymous. In this context the experience of a woman who was born after the war and worked as a researcher on *The Valour and the Horror* seems especially revealing. During a pre-screening of one episode Susan Purcell was overcome by a sudden desire to gesture across the threshold of generations and touch the past. Moved by the emotional power of the documents with which she had worked and by the images now projected on the screen before her eyes, Purcell later recalled how she 'reached back to hold ... [the] hand' of a woman whose brother had been killed as a prisoner-of-war. There, in a convergence of memory with history, Purcell felt as though she was 'sharing with this brave woman the painful responsibility of helping tell a real Canadian story'.[28]

Yet while the intensity of Susan Purcell's epiphany attests to the cultural power of visual imagery as a source of prosthetic memory about the war, it is also important to acknowledge how susceptible such images of transgenerational reconciliation are to the cheapening banality of cliché. In the fall of 1997, for example, the corporate communications giant, Bell Canada, developed a television commercial to air around Remembrance Day. Keen to capitalize on the sacred aura of the war and eager to exploit the popular resource of family melodrama, Bell adapted its traditional slogan, 'Reach Out and Touch Someone', to a Generation X audience. In the virtualized equivalent of the outstretched hand, a young man is shown walking along a beach in Normandy. Seemingly moved by this experience he takes a cell phone out of his pocket and dials his grandfather with the message: 'I just called to say thanks.' According to the vice-president of marketing communications for Bell the spot was a runaway success. There had been 'nothing of this magnitude before', he explained, because 'this is a very strong part of Canadian history that we were able to [connect] to communications'.[29]

## Empathy for the life not lived

For all their differences as cultural constructions, the fundamental element that links the gestures of the boy at the gravestone to the women in the viewing room or the actor in the commercial is the desire to express, and elicit, empathy with the past, to identify both physically and emotionally with lives not lived. 'We "understand" someone's actions', Peter Seixas claims, 'if we believe that, facing similar circumstances, we would do the same'.[30] In the debate about *The Valour and the Horror*, a classic instance of this retrospective desire occurred during a televised exchange between Brian McKenna and two air force veterans who were offended by his representation of the allied bombing campaign against Germany. When one of the veterans tried to disqualify McKenna's opinion by asking if he was a 'war protester' during his 'college years', the director answered: 'Absolutely. The war in Vietnam was going on. That was a long time ago.' But then, referring to the veterans, McKenna went on to add that 'if I'd been alive in 1939 and sixteen years old or eighteen years old, however old these guys were, I'd have been in there, there's no question about it. I'm not a pacifist. I believe that that war needed to be fought.'[31]

While McKenna's reinvention of himself was an especially vivid performance of empathy it was hardly unique. Indeed, empathy for the past was the ideal outcome of the series as the director envisioned it. In order to overcome the cultural and demographic distance between people who experienced the events of wartime and younger viewers who had not, McKenna wrote into the documentary scenes in which actors were dressed in period costume and delivered lines from documents of the time. Justifying the use of docudrama as a narrative technique, McKenna insisted that it was 'extremely important that these stories be visualized for my kids in a way in which it's not a situation where their grandfather or their great-grandfather is telling them a story of the war, but it's like their brother is going through it'.[32] Here, too, the experience of Susan Purcell seems especially significant: in the course of doing research on the series she described 'how real' a soldier named John Payne 'had become to me through the letters and photos'. Later, during auditions for the dramatized portions of the series, she became so 'transfixed' by 'the boyish looks and delivery' of an actor who was reading from the soldier's letters that she 'just felt … this was John'.[33]

Although many critics of the series found McKenna's use of docudrama deeply problematic from the point of view of historical authenticity, his approach contrasted sharply with attempts to remind students about the history of the war through more traditional narrative forms.[34] More to the point, his desire to create empathy with the past seems consistent with a number of recent private and state-sponsored programmes that are designed to educate the memory of youth about the war. Like the docudrama segments of *The Valour and the Horror*, these programmes also work to create what Alison Landsberg calls 'transferential spaces' in which younger audiences are 'invited to enter into experiential relationships with events through which they themselves did not live'.[35] For example, the Department of Veterans' Affairs (DVA) recently prepared a kit for teachers which proposed that students 'in higher grade levels' who attended schools that existed in wartime 'could do research on previous students who served and outline what happened to them'. Citing the existing practice at one school, the DVA kit described how 'for each student lost, a present-day student gives a reading (poem, etc.) and talks a bit about the person's life'.[36]

While it is impossible to predict how different teachers might integrate these kits into their lesson plans, let alone how particular classes, or individual students, might respond to them, the exercise clearly seems intended to immerse students in an experiential relationship to the past. To be sure, there are valid reasons for employing pedagogical practices that go beyond a purely cognitive approach to history. Nevertheless, the orientation of these kits seems designed to educate memory by collapsing time and submerging the cultural differences between the dead and the living. The myriad social and political markers that might otherwise differentiate individuals and groups in and across time seem, in the framework of the kits, subordinate to the main agenda of recreating victims of the war as imaginary classmates. But the exercise is limited too by its selectivity, by the obvious point that only certain kinds of victims will do. The encounters that students are urged to have with the past are coded by a particular definition of commitment and sacrifice, one that precludes contact with the lives of conscientious objectors, for example, or civilians of Japanese descent who were forcibly relocated during the war.

The ease with which these various narrative agendas drift into transhistorical readings of the past is also underscored by the recent proliferation of adult-organized youth pilgrimages to commemorative sites. In June 1999, the government of France designated Juno Beach, a key landing site during the Normandy invasion, as a Canadian National Historic Site. To mark the occasion, the Department of Veterans' Affairs sent a number of 'youth delegates' overseas to accompany veterans and dignitaries on the 'Normandy Pilgrimage'. A 'Daily Report' posted on the Department's website described how 'the youth delegates' walked 'side-by-side with the veterans, gaining a unique perspective and insight into what these men and women lived through 55 years ago'. The reality of being there, on location as it were, is crucial to ratifying the immediacy of the past. But where, exactly, is there? The sanitized landscape of late 1990s Normandy – cleansed for tourist consumption of its mutilated bodies and other battle residue – is, at best, an ersatz experience of memory. It is the perfect analogue to a degraded image of history as a two-dimensional object, fixed permanently in time and space, as accessible and unmediated as a template.

But there is another issue here, too, for as Michel-Rolph Trouillot explains, there are 'two sides of historicity' which engage us 'both as actors and narrators'.[37] This is an important point, for while the youth pilgrims who accompanied Canadian veterans on these trips were, in a real sense actors – or perhaps re-enactors – in a great performance of historical imagining, they were not the narrators of the event. Instead their primary duty was to serve as transcribers of the past, who faithfully 'recorded the veterans' memories, thoughts and impressions'.[38]

Curiously, the desired cultural outcome of these field trips is best summarized not by one of the student tourists but by Terry Copp, an academic historian who has led battlefield study tours for The Canadian Battle of Normandy Foundation. Pitched to university-level students eighteen years of age or older, the tours are supposed to create an 'understanding' of 'the Canadian Army's role in the liberation of Northwest Europe'.[39] On a television programme bemoaning the 'burying [of] the past' in Canada, Copp described how the tours worked constructively to help recover the history of the war. His brow furrowed in earnest recollection, Copp described how 'the students and I stood on the beach on the 51st anniversary of D-Day and ... tried to imagine ourselves' plunged into the midst of battle. 'We all came away feeling humbled,' he remembered, 'feeling that ... it was important to try and understand the enormous challenges they [the soldiers] faced and how they'd ... overcome it.' Significant for its deeply-felt and very public performance of empathy with an imagined past, Copp's memoir of the Normandy visits is also revealing for its implicit attempt to intensify history by associating past and present through the re-enactment of experience. Predictably, the education of memory eventually comes full circle when Copp summons up a favorite homily of the good teacher:

professing to be regenerated by his students, he exclaims how gratified he was when he 'got to see it all through their eyes again'.[40]

## Family values

Beyond the seductions of battlefield tourism, however, the pedagogical ambition to promote memory of the war through retrospective identification is also accomplished by the practice of genealogy. As Fentress and Wickham point out, genealogy is a crucial element of social memory because it 'maps out the ideas of "succession"'.[41] The importance of genealogy to the memory of war is institutionalized at the National Archives of Canada, where one of the largest groups of researchers is made up of people inquiring about the military service records of their ancestors. In its Remembrance Day kit for Canadian schools the Department of Veterans' Affairs recommended that 'students prepare a family tree indicating those who have served in wartime'. The kit also suggests that teachers 'have students relate the veterans' experiences and describe how other family members were affected by the war'.[42] A similar impulse informs another government initiative by which the Department of Canadian Heritage joined forces with the Royal Canadian Legion – an organization for veterans and their families – to produce CD-ROMs for schools. According to the Minister of Canadian Heritage, the disks would feature 'grandchildren interviewing their grandparents about the war in order to get that sort of corporate memory'.[43]

Both of these exercises in the education of memory are transparent examples of the process by which education, under the aegis of the state, works to compose, articulate and schematize social memory. As Fentress and Wickham point out, social memory is more 'conceptualized' than individual memory because 'images can be transmitted socially only if they are conventionalized and simplified'.[44] The simple didacticism of these exercises works to fulfil that agenda partly by emphasizing the unbroken linearity of genealogy. But while one might argue that these programmes are useful in opening up a conversation about the past, they hardly seem designed to promote unfettered inquiry. Instead the larger social agenda seems intended to pay homage to history by binding children to the past deferentially through the ties of affection and family.

This is hardly surprising, for 'the ideology of the modern family' has always been intrinsic to the ecology of war remembrance.[45] On Remembrance Day in the nation's capital, for example, part of the official ceremony has always focused on relatives and descendents of war veterans. The figure of the Silver Cross Mother is emblematic of this as the representative of Canadian women who have lost one, or more, sons, to war. Many Remembrance Day ceremonies also feature the spectacle of government politicians – the Prime Minister or members of Cabinet – paying homage to the past with their children in tow (Figure 3.4). Although there are many components to the rituals of remembrance, it is remarkable how often these images of family dominate news photos and television coverage of the events. According to Marianne Hirsch 'the family photo

*Figure 3.4* Untitled photograph. 'Prime Minister Pierre Trudeau took along Mrs. Trudeau, Justin and Sacha yesterday as he placed a wreath at the National War Memorial in Ottawa. Hundreds of veterans attended the ceremony'.

*Source*: Canadian Press (CP Photo/Chuck Mitchell). *The Globe and Mail*, 12 November 1976, p.1.

both displays the cohesion of the family and is an instrument of its togetherness'. Because it 'gives the illusion of being a simple transcription of the real', the photograph helps to 'perpetuate familial myths' by 'naturalizing cultural practices and ... disguising their stereotyped and coded characteristics'.[46]

In the imagery of Remembrance Day the symbolic importance of the war as the guarantor of national security is inscribed in the visible link between government, official consciousness, and society's most cherished institution, the family. Astonishingly, the symbolism of that linkage became disturbingly conflated with reality in November 1970, when Remembrance Day was marked while the country was gripped by acts of terrorism that included bombings, hostage takings and the assassination of a provincial Cabinet Minister. In response, the government of Canada invoked the extreme emergency powers War Measures Act, suspending normal civil liberties. Despite, or more likely because of, the turmoil the federal Justice Minister attended the commemorative ceremonies at the national cenotaph in Ottawa with his wife and two young children, escorted by 'the family's personal armed guard'.[47]

Predictably the values of kinship and parental responsibility were also very much in the foreground of *The Valour and the Horror* controversy. When Brian McKenna testified before a Senate inquiry into the series he brought his teenage daughter along to observe the proceedings, but also to be observed observing. During his testimony the director recounted that his own education in the history of the war had begun inauspiciously when he had attended local Remembrance Day ceremonies with 'my children' several years earlier. Unable to tell his daughter whether or not the McKenna name etched onto the memorial was a relative of theirs, the director got launched on a genealogical quest that eventually prompted him to investigate the histories of the First and Second World Wars. Here, too, the historical became personal through the cultural influence of family values and the connecting tissue of generational succession. Invoking his patriarchal authority to defend his and his brother's work as filmmakers, McKenna emphasized his 'responsibility to my three children' and the responsibility of 'my brother ... to his four sons, all of whom could serve in the Canadian military in another war'.[48]

Of course, the parental burdens of remembrance have never fallen exclusively on men's shoulders, and no rituals of regeneration can succeed for long without a mother in the story. In the same Remembrance Day edition of *The Globe and Mail* that features the boy from the elementary school planting a flag of commemoration at a veteran's grave there is another photograph, two pages on but a lifetime away (Figure 3.5). It shows an elderly woman – Alice Taylor, aged 100 – and an elderly man – Tom Spear, aged 99. Improbably, he is a surviving veteran of both world wars. She, on the other hand, is a Silver Cross Mother. Literally from another century, Alice Taylor and Tom Spear are living, venerable emblems of age and personal sacrifice. Tom Spear's status as a veteran twice over authorizes his centrality to a Canadian political mythology that considers the rites of nationhood to have been conferred upon Canada by virtue of its participation in the world wars. Although not a veteran herself, Alice Taylor is no less a custodian of the past and has come to Ottawa on this occasion to represent 'the motherhood of Canada' in the ceremonies of remembrance at the nation's capital. The photograph shows them observing a ceremony. But reading the caption it is immediately clear that they are performers in this ceremony too, that they are its impresarios, if not its stars. Before the gaze of Alice Taylor and Tom Spear, and by their grace it is inferred, the right of citizenship is being bestowed on people who are known, colloquially, as 'new Canadians'. The process of regeneration, and its inextricable cultural link to generational identity and the memory of war, are here inscribed in the language of Canadian citizenship. The prior national identities of the new Canadians are not disclosed, nor

*Figure 3.5 War and Remembrance.* 'Silver Cross mother Alice Taylor, 100, and First and Second World War veteran Tom Spear 99, participate in the 50th anniversary citizenship ceremony in the House of Commons yesterday'.

*Source:* Canadian Press. (CP Photo/Fred Chartrand). *The Globe and Mail*, 11 November 1997, A4.

are their reasons for emigrating. Theirs is an immaculate conception. The ceremony is a rite of passage in the re-education of their memories.

## Epiphanies of reconciliation

If the symbolism of Remembrance Day speaks to a desire for a socially coherent, and culturally unified, relationship to the past, the controversy over *The Valour and the Horror* attests to the point that reality does not fulfil this ideal. Indeed, for many participants the most troubling aspect of the debates is precisely their provocation, or exposure, of family tensions along generational lines. When the CBC Ombudsman criticized the Bomber Command segment of *The Valour and the Horror* one lobbyist declared that air force veterans were 'going to feel a lot more comfortable ... because they have had to answer to their children and their wives'. Similarly, a former Supreme Court justice and veteran of Bomber Command, recounted his horror when his 'grandchild, a little boy of five', came to him 'very upset' because one of his teachers had said the grandfather 'dropped bombs on people'. While this incident was disturbing in part because it subverted expectations about the role of the school system in the education of memory, it nevertheless typified similar complaints by veterans who

71

positioned themselves in the debate as fathers, uncles and grandfathers. On a nationally broadcast radio talk show about the series another veteran of the bombing campaign over German cities broke down as he recounted 'last night's question from my thirty-eight-year-old son. "How'd you feel dad,"' the son had asked, 'about going to kill civilians?' For this veteran the double jeopardy of the series was not simply that it ruptured the stability of his own familial relations, but that it called into question his status as a man by blaming him and his colleagues for 'being children and women killers'.[49]

While these examples speak to the realities of inter-generational tension in debates about the war, their public impact as discourse on the education of memory is invariably muted by media enthusiasm for epiphanies of inter-generational reconciliation. Despite ample evidence of the devastating psychological and social effects of the war on returning veterans, one thing that is strikingly absent from the social memory of the war is the explicit reference to domestic strife or family dysfunction.[50] To the extent that such problems do surface they are likely to be hastily swept aside by narratives of closure or by sympathetic attempts to explain away the difficulties that many veterans have in talking about the war.

Here too part of the explanation for the lack of discussion about veterans' dysfunction is attributable to the media's broader agenda to foster 'social consensus', particularly about issues such as commemoration of the war. Although media representations of the *Valour and the Horror* debate played up the entertainment value of opposing points of view about the series, the 'implied dynamics' of these confrontations ultimately affirmed 'the ideology of public discourse' by demonstrating that 'communication is always possible'.[51] This ideal was dramatized in the closing moments of a bitter television debate between Brian McKenna and two veterans of Bomber Command. The moderator, who seemed particularly uncomfortable with the gulf in age and experience separating him from the veterans, tried to bring the discussion to a satisfactory resolution. In an awkward formulation he shifted onto the common ground of masculinity to thank 'you guys' for participating in the debate even though 'a lot of your buddies disapproved of your coming in here'.[52]

Predictably, this desire to reflect cross-generational consensus is a stock element in both the visual repertoire of war commemoration and news reporting of such events. Group shots of veterans and young people – such as the students on tours of battlefields in Europe – are a staple of this iconography. Typical too was the upbeat, page-one article that *The Toronto Star* ran as part of its Remembrance Day coverage in 1997. Under the headline 'This Remembrance Day, It's "Cool" to be a Vet', the paper described 'a gaggle of exuberant high school students' who 'threw their arms around' Second World War veteran Sam Macdonald 'and clamoured for group photos as if he happened to be a rock star or other celebrity'.[53]

Another variation on this theme that has become increasingly fashionable in recent years is the minor confessional genre of middle-aged, male journalists revisiting relationships with their veteran fathers. Addressing the outcry over *The Valour and the Horror*, syndicated columnist Ken MacQueen recalled that he, like many other children 'born in the 1950s', was the child of a veteran. As a 'boy' and a 'son', the columnist recalled, he eventually 'began to suspect that his father's war was different than the war on television and in the comics' and so 'put away his war toys and went on to other things'. Reacting to the documentary, radio host Peter Gzowski told a national audience that he wished his 'dad', who 'did make it through' the war, 'could have seen this film' but he died 'about ten years ago'. Yet perhaps the most self-conscious attempt to achieve closure was a column by Claire Hoy, a nationally syndicated writer who described how, as a 5-year-old boy, he met his father for the first time when the war finally ended. Explaining that his father 'is dead now', Hoy acknowledged that, 'in life, sadly, we were never close. Whether it's because we missed sharing those early years, I can't say', he confessed. 'But whatever else our lives brought, I did come to understand and appreciate the sacrifices he and millions of Canadians just like him made to keep us free. Each Remembrance Day I remember him.' Then, switching briefly, but symbolically, to the patriarchal mode, Hoy reaffirmed the ideal of generational succession – albeit with a gender twist – when he proudly recounted that his '12-year-old daughter', who was an Air Cadet, had 'joined some veterans selling poppies in an east Toronto mall'.[54]

## Conclusion

When CBC Television first aired *The Valour and the Horror* in January 1992 it showed the documentary in prime time on successive Sunday evenings, during the slot in the North American broadcast week that is most traditionally associated with family viewing. This was no accident, but was instead the product of a deliberate choice that spoke both to specific institutional assumptions about the nature of television audiences, and to more general cultural assumptions about history and the social memory of the Second World War. Although the link between Sunday evening television and the family may seem quaint in light of contemporary social realities and the proliferation of alternative forms of entertainment, media organizations continue to assume that 'the family, or familial life-world, is … the predominant context of viewing'.[55]

The assumption was doubly significant in the case of *The Valour and the Horror* because, as a social text, the public history of the Second World War in Canada is commonly narrated through the prism of the family. From the outset, the filmmakers consciously played on, and to, the theme of family values. They spoke eloquently about their desire to produce a history that paid homage to the men and women who had experienced the war but which would also appeal to their own children. Even when the controversy about the series reached fever pitch, the films' defenders claimed that the debate was therapeutic in giving veterans the opportunity 'to discuss with their families their contribution to the war and to making Canada the free country it is today'.[56]

Regardless of whether such assertions were accurate, or merely self-serving, they were given some anecdotal credence by the testimony of audience members. Several viewers wrote letters or made calls to radio talk shows in which they described watching the programmes with other family members including, most often, 'with my father', a veteran of the war. Self-identified both as adults and as children, these viewers inevitably went on to pass judgment on the documentary based on their privileged access to the private testimony of their father-veterans.[57] Similarly, one woman recalled how, as a child, she visited her grandmother's house and saw pictures of her uncle, a bomber pilot who was killed in the war. Referring back to those images and memories she went on to describe how she 'had my own fourteen year old daughter sit with me to watch these shows, and as we watched I talked about her own great-uncle, far too young at nineteen to have been involved in the things he was'.[58]

Motivated in part by the perception that the history of the war is no longer known in Canada, the cultural imperative of films like *The Valour and the Horror*, as well as recent school programmes sponsored by the state or private organizations, is dominated by the desire to educate the collective memory of youth about the meaning of the war. But whereas the history of the war was once understood, narrowly, to comprise a body of cognitive knowledge that had to be learned and memorized by successive generations, the emphasis of contemporary narratives is on activating memories and passing on experiences over time.

The point of this distinction is not to encourage some false choice between memory and history as an avenue for encountering the past. Instead it is to try to focus attention on the ways in which the desire and ability to educate memory about the past are shaped by the cultural power of generational tropes of history. In many respects, the motif of generational identity has become the default position for viewing and transmitting the history of the war. This did not happen overnight, for the construct of generational identity and the reification of transgenerational links have always been essential elements in commemorating the war. Nevertheless, in the current rush to recuperate and refresh the education of memory about the past, it is important to recognize what the limitations of a generational perspective on history are. While it is obviously the case that recent debates in Canada about the Second World War have consciously worked to strengthen the 'living tie between generations', some of these ties bind collective memory less to the interpretation of history than to an idealized narrative of the family in society.

## Acknowledgement

I want to thank Katharine Hodgkin both for her perceptive comments on earlier versions of this chapter and for her constructive editorial suggestions.

# Notes

1 Walter Benjamin, 'Theses on the Philosophy of History', (1940), trans. Harry Zohn in *Illuminations* (New York: Schocken Books,1969), 254.

2 Remarks of President Reagan to Regional Editors, White House, 18 April 1985, in *Bitburg in Moral and Political Perspective*, (ed.) Geoffrey H. Hartman (Bloomington: Indiana University Press/5 1986), 239.

3 Geoffrey H. Hartman, 'Acknowledgments' and 'Introduction: 1985', to *Bitburg in Moral and Political Perspective*, pp. xi, 1 – 3; and 'Public Memory and Its Discontents', *Raritan* 13:4 (Spring 1994), 34–35.

4 National Film Board of Canada, *The Valour and the Horror* (video), 1992. This was written by Brian and Terence McKenna, directed by Brian McKenna, and co-produced by Galafilm, Inc., the Canadian Broadcasting Corporation, and the National Film Board of Canada (NFB), in association with *Société Radio Canada* and Telefilm Canada. The series is available on three videocassettes from the National Film Board of Canada. The first episode of the series examined the horrific battle of Hong Kong at which a small contingent of Canadian troops was completely over-whelmed by superior Japanese forces. The second episode focused on Canadian participation in RAF bombing campaigns over Germany, while the final segment dealt with a disastrous infantry attack in the Battle of Normandy.

5 Donald M. McVicar, letter to *The Montreal Gazette*, 11 April 1993. Although the public attacks on the series were widely disseminated in the media, the main points of criticism are summarized in 'The Valour and the Horror', *Report of the Standing Senate Committee on Social Affairs, Science and Technology* (Ottawa: Queen's Printer, 1993). The Ontario General Court rejected the claim of defamation in January 1994 and the Ontario Court of Appeal upheld the decision in June 1995. In March 1996 the Supreme Court of Canada declined to hear a further appeal.

6 George S. Hogg, letter to the Right Honourable Brian Mulroney 28 April 1994. Copy in Canadian Radio-television and Telecommunications (CRTC) file #7240, v. 121 (CRTC Archives, Hull, QC); Johnny Fontaine, *Cross-Country Checkup*, CBC Radio, 15 Nov. 1992; John Thompson, Letter to the Editor, *Globe and Mail*, 18 Nov. 1992; Jack McIntosh, quoted in Lorne Gunter, 'Defending History Against the CBC', *Alberta Report*, 11 May 1992, 41; and John Bourne, Letter to the Editor, *The Gazette* (Montreal), 27 Nov. 1992. One woman, the wife of a former bomber pilot who was taken prisoner-of-war, worried the 'children will revile their grandparents' war effort instead of honouring their tremendous struggle'. Joan Hoad, letter to Bill Scott, MP, 26 Jan. 1993, CRTC, v. 147.

7 Alison Landsberg, 'America, the Holocaust, and the Mass Culture of Memory: Toward a Radical Politics of Empathy', *New German Critique*, 71 (1997), 64.

8 *Citizen's Forum on Canada's Future: Report to the People and Government of Canada* (Ottawa: Minister of Supply and Services, 1991), 38–39; and Bob Davis, *Whatever Happened to High School History? Burying the Political Memory of Youth: Ontario, 1945–1995* (Toronto: Lorimer, 1995). See also Michael Bliss, 'Privatizing the Mind: The Sundering of Canadian History, the Sundering of Canada', *Journal of Canadian Studies* 36:4 (Winter 1991–92), 6–12; and J.L. Granatstein, *Who Killed Canadian History?* (Toronto: HarperCollins, 1998). For a critique of these arguments, see Graham Carr, 'Harsh Sentences: Appealing the Strange Verdict of *Who Killed Canadian History?*' *American Review of Canadian Studies* 28 (Spring/Summer 1998), 167–176.

9 Daniel Glenney, Testimony, Senate of Canada, Standing Senate Committee on Social Affairs, Science and Technology, *Proceedings of the Subcommittee on Veterans Affairs*, 2 February 1998, Ottawa: Queen's Printer 1998.

10 Kerwin Lee Klein, 'On the Emergence of *Memory* in Historical Discourse', *Representations* 69 (Winter 2000), 129.

11  On the ambiguous space between memory and history see for example, Pierre Nora, 'Between Memory and History: *Les Lieux de Mémoire*', *Representations* 26 (Spring 1989), 7–25; Barbie Zelizer, 'Reading Against the Grain: The Shape of Memory Studies', *Critical Studies in Mass Communication*, 12 (1995), 214–239; and Klein, 'Emergence of Memory'.

12  Joyce Appleby, Lynn Hunt, and Margaret Jacob, *Telling the Truth about History* (New York: W. W. Norton, 1994), 270.

13  Brian McKenna, interviewed on *Right to Reply Special* [moderator Roger Bolton], Channel 4 TV (United Kingdom), August 1994; John English, quoted in Anne Collins, 'The Battle over *The Valour and the Horror*', *Saturday Night* (May 1993), 74; and Terry Copp, interviewed by Neil Bissoondath, *Burying the Past*, SIM Video Productions (1996), broadcast on Vision TV, 10 March 1996.

14  Howard Schuman, Robert F. Belli and Katherine Bischoping, 'The Generational Basis of Historical Knowledge', in *Collective Memory of Political Events: Social Psychological Perspectives*, eds James W. Pennebaker, Dario Paez and Bernard Rimé. (Mahwah, N. J.: Lawrence Erlbaum, 1997), 75. See also Martin Conway, 'The Inventory of Experience: Memory and Identity', and Roy F. Baumeister and Stephen Hastings, 'Distortions of Collective Memory: How Groups Flatter and Deceive Themselves', in *ibid.*, 21–45; 277–293.

15  Peter Novick, *That Noble Dream: The 'Objectivity Question' and the American Historical Profession* (Cambridge: Cambridge University Press, 1988), 16.

16  Frank Tripp, interviewed by Peter Gzowski, *Morningside*, CBC Radio, 1 May 1992; and Lionel Hastings, interviewed by Brian Johnson, Post-screening debate on 'Death by Moonlight', Episode 2 of *The Valour and the Horror*, CBC Newsworld, 28 March 1992. (Audio tapes of CBC Radio broadcasts are available at the CBC Archives, Toronto; Video tapes of CBC Newsworld broadcasts are available at the CBC Newsworld Archive, McOdrum Library, Carleton University.)

17  Peter Seixas, 'Beyond "Content" and "Pedagogy": In Search of a Way to Talk about History Education', *Journal of Curriculum Studies* 31: 3 (May/June 1999); and 'Conceptualizing Growth in Historical Understanding', in *The Handbook of Education and Human Development*, eds David Olson and Nancy Torrance (1996), 765–783.

18  Vern L. Bengston, 'Is the Contract Across Generations Changing? Effects of Population Aging on Obligations and Expectations Across Age Groups', in *The Changing Contract Across Generations*, eds Vern L. Bengston and W. Andrew Achenbaum (New York: A. de. Gruyter, 1993), 11.

19  The Rt.-Hon. Joe Clark, Letter to Mr. M. Arnold Todd, 16 June 1992, CRTC file #7240, vol. 125; Michael Bliss, Testimony, Senate of Canada, Standing Senate Committee on Social Affairs, Science and Technology, *Proceedings of the Subcommittee on Veterans' Affairs*, 5 Nov. 1992; and Rick Salutin, 'Let's Not Lose Sight of the Power of *The Valour and the Horror*', *The Globe and Mail* (Toronto), 20 Nov. 1992, A12.

20  Henry Giroux and David Purpel, eds, *The Hidden Curriculum and Moral Education: Deception or Discovery?* (Berkeley: MCutchan, 1983).

21  Iwona Irwin-Zarecka, *Frames of Remembrance: The Dynamics of Collective Memory* (New Brunswick, NJ: Transaction 1994), 9; Kerwin Lee Klein, 'On the Emergence of Memory', 130.

22  Patricia Mellencamp's concept of ecology is discussed by Mimi White, *Tele-Advising: Therapeutic Discourse in American Television* (Chapel Hill: Univeristy of North Carolina Press, 1992), 14.

23  'Millions Pay Respects To War Dead of Two World Wars', *The Globe and Mail* 12 Nov. 1946, 9. On the legacy of First World War commemorative practices, see Denise Thomson, 'National Sorrow, National Pride: Commemoration of War in Canada', *Journal of Canadian Studies*, 30: 4 (Winter 1995–96), 5–27; Jonathan Vance, *Death So Noble. Memory, Meaning and the First World War* (Vancouver: UBC Press, 1997).

24 Despatch #353, Canadian Embassy, Brussels to The Right Honourable, the Secretary of State for External Affairs, Ottawa. RG 25, vol. 3824, File 8768–40, Pt. 1: 'Liberation of Belgium – Commemoration Day – Proposals Re.' The memo refers to 'some' photographs but there are only two in the file.

25 Photo caption, *The Globe and Mail*, 11 November 1997, A1. The picture was widely syndicated in Canadian newspapers.

26 *Life*, 21 October 1940, pp. 36–37. The photograph was also reproduced in the 10th Anniversary issue of *Life*, 25 Nov. 1946, p. 118. A variation on this theme occurs in Donald Brittain's 1964 documentary, *Fields of Sacrifice*. In a section dealing with the Canada's role in liberating Sicily, the camera focuses on the face of an elderly woman then pans to reveal an infant in the woman's arms and a young girl and boy nearby. Meanwhile the narrator explains: 'the old people remember. And they will tell the children. An episode passed down.' National Film Board of Canada, *Fields of Sacrifice*, Donald Brittain, producer (1964; re-released, 1989).

27 Landsberg defines prosthetic memories as 'memories that circulate publicly, are not organically based, but are nevertheless experienced with one's own body – by means of a wide range of cultural technologies – and as such, become part of one's personal archive of experience, informing not only one's subjectivity, but one's relationship to the present and future tenses'. Such memories, she argues, are prosthetic 'because, like an artificial limb, they are actually worn by the body; these are sensuous memories produced by experience' Landsberg, *Mass Culture of Memory*, 66

28 Susan Purcell, 'Canadian Soldier's Drama Unearthed by TV Researcher', *The Montreal Gazette*, 11 January 1992.

29 Bruce Barr, quoted in Graham Fraser, 'Remembrance of Past Wars Resonates with Canadians', *The Globe and Mail*, 11 November 1997, A9.

30 Seixas, 'Conceptualizing the Growth of Historical Understanding', 775–776.

31 Post-screening Debate, *Death by Moonlight*, CBC-TV Newsworld, 28 March 1992.

32 Brian McKenna, quoted in Ted Shaw, 'Canada at War: Repentant Reporter Seeks Terrible Truth', *Windsor Star*, 10 January 1992.

33 Purcell, 'Canadian Soldier's Drama'.

34 For example, each Remembrance Day at the national cenotaph 'the youth of Canada' are symbolically represented by the laying, in their name, of a wreath to the war dead. The perceived importance of these rituals was underscored in the mid-1960s when the Province of Ontario's plan to make Remembrance Day a school holiday was brought down by parents who wanted their children to participate in organized school ceremonies 'to help them realize what we were doing on that day'. Mrs Norman Allen, quoted in 'H & S Disapproves of Remembrance Day Holiday', *The Globe and Mail*, 25 March 1964.

35 Landsberg, 66.

36 Veterans' Affairs Canada, 'Getting the Most Out of Veterans' Week', http://www.vacacc.gc.ca/week/1998/genguide.htm.

37 Michel-Rolph Trouillot, *Silencing the Past: Power and the Production of History* (Boston: Beacon Press, 1995), 150.

38 'June 1999 Normandy Pilgrimage – The Daily Report', http://www.vacacc.gc.ca/feature/normandy/daily_jun6.htm.

39 Canadian Battle of Normandy Foundation, Poster for the 1998 Study Tour.

40 Terry Copp, interviewed in *Burying the Past*, [Neil Bissoondath, host] SIM Video Productions (1996), broadcast on *Markings: An Anthology of Ideas*, Vision TV, 10 March 1996.

41 James Fentress and Chris Wickham, *Social Memory* (Oxford: Blackwell, 1992), 80.

42 Veterans' Affairs Canada, 'Getting the Most Out of Veterans' Week'.

43 The Hon. Sheila Copps, Testimony, Senate of Canada, Standing Senate Committee on Social Affairs, Science and Technology, *Proceedings of the Subcommittee on Veterans Affairs*, 11 February 1998.

44 Fentress and Wickham, *Social Memory*, 47.

45 Marianne Hirsch, *Family Frames: Photography, Narrative and Postmodernity* (Cambridge, MA: Harvard University Press, 1997), 8.

46 Hirsch, *Family Frames*, 8–9.

47 Photo caption, 'A Family Engagement with Armed Guard', *The Globe and Mail*, 12 Nov. 1970.

48 Brian McKenna, Testimony, Senate of Canada, Standing Senate Committee on Social Affairs, Science and Technology, *Proceedings of the Subcommittee on Veterans' Affairs*, 6 November 1992. *Right to Reply Special* (moderator Roger Bolton), Channel 4 TV (United Kingdom), August 1994.

49 Cliff Chadderton, quoted on *News* with Sheldon Turcotte, CBC-TV Newsworld, 10 November 1992, 16:00h; J.R. Barr, letter to Canadian Radio & Television Commission [*sic*], 15 May 1992, CRTC file #7240, v. 123; and Paul Bourdage, interviewed on *Cross-Country Checkup*, Host: Dale Goldhawk, CBC-Radio, 15 November 1992.

50 See Terry Copp and Bill McAndrew, *Battle Exhaustion: Soldiers and Psychiatrists in the Canadian Army, 1939–1945* (Montreal: McGill-Queen's University Press, 1995), and Terry Copp, 'From Neurasthenia to Post-Traumatic Stress Disorder: Canadian Veterans and the Problem of Persistent Emotional Disabilities', in *The Veterans' Charter and Post-World War II Canada*, eds Peter Neary and J.L. Granatstein (Montreal: McGill-Queen's University Press, 1998), 149–159. The frankest accounts of domestic problems encountered by demobilized veterans are included in the oral history by Barry Broadfoot, *The Veterans' Years: Coming Home from the War* (Vancouver: Douglas & McIntyre, 1985).

51 Paolo Carpignano, Robin Anderson, Stanley Aronowitz, and William DiFazio, 'Chatter in the Age of Electronic Reproduction: Talk Television and the Public Mind', in *The Phantom Public Sphere*, ed. Bruce Robbins (Minneapolis: University of Minnesota Press, 1993), p. 115.

52 Brian Johnson, Post-screening Debate, *Death by Moonlight*.

53 Allan Thompson, 'Thoughts of War Bridge Generations', *The Toronto Star*, 12 November 1997, A1.

54 Ken MacQueen, 'Senators Cheapen True Glory', *The Vancouver Sun*, 5 November 1992; Peter Gzowski, Interview with Brian McKenna, 'Morningside', CBC Radio, 10 January 1992; and Claire Hoy, 'A Nation Estranged from Its Warrior Class', *The Toronto Star*, 11 November 1998, A21.

55 Tony Wilson, *Watching Television: Hermeneutics, Reception and Popular Culture* (Cambridge: Polity Press, 1993). Bruce Cummings makes a similar point about industry assumptions that families are 'modal viewers' in *War and Television* (London: Verso Press, 1992), 33.

56 Joan Pennefather, letter to Sen. Jack Marshall, 17 June 1992, copy in Brian McKenna Papers, Concordia University Archives, HA 1154.

57 Colin and Samuel, callers to the radio talk-show *Cross-Country Checkup*, CBC Radio, 15 Nov. 1992.

58 Corette Oseen, letter to Hon. Perrin Beatty, 11 Nov. 1992, CRTC, v. 140.

# 'WE WOULD NOT HAVE COME WITHOUT YOU'

## Generations of nostalgia

*Marianne Hirsch and Leo Spitzer*

Czernovitz expelled its Jews, and so did Vienna, Prague, Budapest, and Lemberg. Now these cities live without Jews, and their few descendants, scattered through the world, carry memory like a wonderful gift and a relentless curse. For me, too, the childhood home is that 'black milk' – to use the expression of Paul Celan – which nourishes me morning and evening while at the same time it drugs me.

(Aharon Appelfeld)

In der Luft, da bleibt deine Wurzel, da,/in der Luft
(In the air your root stays on, there/in the air)

(Paul Celan)

### Resistant nostalgia: 'Where are you from?'

On our first walk through the city once called Czernowitz, a woman stopped us on the street. In a mixture of Russian and Yiddish, she asked Marianne's mother, Lotte: 'Where are you from?' With our cameras and maps, we were obvious tourists and she no doubt wondered whether we were from Germany, Israel, or the United States. In response, Lotte pointed, emphatically, to the ground: 'From here, Czernowitzer.' It was the first time in our memory that this simple question, 'Where are you from?' evoked such a brief, clear-cut response. Three words. 'From here, Czernowitzer.' Usually, it has required a long-winded, complicated narrative, if not a short history and geography lesson.

In present political reality, of course, Czernowitz is nowhere – a place that cannot be found in any contemporary atlas. It ceased to exist as a political entity long ago, in 1918 (the year Lotte Hirsch was born), with the collapse of the Austro-Hungarian Habsburg Empire. Nowadays, its name is Chernivtsi, and it is located in the southwestern region of the Republic of the Ukraine, on the river Prut, some fifty kilometres north of the present-day border of Romania. After the First World War, when it fell under the rule of Greater Romania, it was

79

called Cernăuţi, and subsequently, under Soviet rule after the Second World War, Chernovtsy.

For Lotte and Carl Hirsch, however, and for all those surviving Jews of their generation who were born there but who are now largely dispersed throughout the world, the place has forever remained Czernowitz – the capital of the Bukowina, an outlying province of the Habsburg Empire, the 'Vienna of the East', the city in which (in the words of its most famous poet Paul Celan) 'human beings and books used to live'.[1] For them, the long imperial connection of Czernowitz with Vienna, and their own whole-hearted embrace of the German language, its literature, and the social and cultural standards of the Austro-Germanic world, are intimately connected – a core constituent of their identity. They, like their parents and grandparents, had accepted the premise inherent in the century-long process of Jewish emancipation and acculturation to Germanic culture that had taken place in lands once ruled by the Habsburgs. One could remain a Jew in religious belief, was the basis of this premise, while also becoming culturally, economically, and politically integrated within the dominant social order. Karl-Emil Franzos, the Bukowina's first internationally famed German-language writer, best characterizes the complicated cultural identity of most assimilated Czernowitz Jews at the end of the nineteenth century: 'I wasn't yet three feet tall, when my father told me: "Your nationality is neither Polish, nor Ruthenian, nor Jewish – you are German." But equally often he said, even then: "According to your faith you are a Jew."'[2] Indeed, even after the annexation of Czernowitz and the Bukowina by greater Romania in 1918 and the institution of a policy of 'Romanianization', a predominant segment of the Jewish population of the city and region remained devoted to the German language and its culture. Czernowitz, the city, with its Vienna look-alike centre, its Viennese-inspired architecture, avenues, parks, and cafés, remained a physical manifestation of this continuing allegiance to a bygone Austrian imperial past.

The continuing vitality and strength of this identification is not surprising. It attests to the positive connection so many of Czernowitz's Jews had drawn between Jewish emancipation and assimilation in the imperial Habsburg/ German realms, and the significant social, political, and cultural rewards that this process had yielded. For the majority of Jews in the Bukowina, Romanian rule and Romanianization had closed doors to rights and opportunities that they had enjoyed for decades under the Austrians. Despite anti-Semitic eruptions and the rise of Nazism in German-speaking Central Europe, it was after all in pre-war Romania, and not Austria or Germany, that anti-Semitic legal restrictions remained active and discrimination flourished after the end of the First World War and throughout the 1920s.[3] For several years after Romania gained control of the area – until 1924 – Jews in the Bukowina were denied the full citizenship rights they had long enjoyed under Austrian rule, and their legal definition and exclusion as 'foreigners' greatly inhibited, if not prevented, their cultural integration and social advancement. In this context, the German language through which they communicated with each other, and the Austro-German/Jewish cultural background they shared, provided them with an alternative basis of continuing group identity. 'In spirit,' during this period, the poet Rose Ausländer maintains, 'we remained Austrians; our capital was Vienna and not Bucharest.'[4]

It is perhaps this point that is startling and in need of emphasis: the fact that even when political reality indicated otherwise, Jews here *kept alive an idea* of a pre-First World War city and culture in which German literature, music, art and philosophy flourished among its Jewish intelligentsia. Instead of the Cernăuţi in which they now lived, they continued to nourish and perpetuate the notion of 'Czernowitz' as it had been transmitted to them physically and in cultural memory. The world in which Lotte and Carl Hirsch and their contemporaries grew up was thus already shaped by a 'postmemory' – by a mediated memory of a lost 'world of yesterday' that they themselves had inherited from parents and grandparents who had enjoyed the benefits of Jewish life under the Habsburgs.[5] If, in their youth, they held on to that world nostalgically, it was not simply to reconstitute or to mourn what they posited as a 'better' imperial past. It was also one of the ways in which they resisted Romanianization and its increasing social, political and intellectual restrictions.[6] In this sense their 'resistant nostalgia' reflected what Svetlana Boym has characterized as inherent in all nostalgic constructions: the longing 'for a home that no longer exists or *has never existed'*.[7]

At the same time, however, Czernowitz/Cernăuţi was also that place in which Carl and Lotte, like their contemporaries, had suffered anti-Semitic persecution, Soviet occupation, internment in a Nazi ghetto, the yellow 'Jew' star – and where the two of them, managing to escape deportation, survived the Holocaust. Of the more than 120,000 Jews who had inhabited the Bukowina at the start of the Second World War, fewer than 40,000 were alive at its conclusion. When Lotte and Carl moved away in 1945 from the, by then, Soviet-ruled Chernovtsy they thought it was forever. They also knew that the place they had considered their homeland had now definitively been taken from them. Czernowitz and the Bukowina, now twice lost, came to persist only as a cultural landscape, deterritorialized, diasporic – an idea of a city and place, less and less connected to its geographical location and tenuously dependent on the vicissitudes of personal, familial and cultural memory.

And yet, in September of 1998, Lotte and Carl Hirsch and the two of us – parents accompanied by daughter and son-in-law – made a 'return' journey to the place itself. But why return? Why go to this place that for Carl and Lotte had been, in Eva Hoffman's words, 'home in a way, but … also hostile territory?'[8] Survivors transmit to their children layered memories of 'home' – nostalgic longing, negative and critical recollections. 'My feelings about returning to Czernowitz are ambivalent', Carl said to us shortly before setting off on our journey. 'Is Czernowitz our *Heimat*? The events that took place there – that we lived through especially in the war years – call that into question. … The truth of the matter is, we would not have decided to go back there now if it were not for Marianne – because Marianne doesn't have a home, and we want to show her ours because ours is also in some ways hers. We didn't have money there, but we had a very happy childhood. … The friendships we made were powerful. They stayed strong through life. We shared experiences and culture. We were like brothers, my Czernowitz friends and I. … There are probably not many places in the world that have produced such close fellow feelings among its émigrés. I am curious to see what has become of all of this.'[9]

Recorded on the eve of return – at the moment of anticipation – these remarks suggest some of the complex factors that motivate the exile-refugee's return to the place that was once home. They blend ambivalence, self-affirmation, nostalgia, and curiosity with the desire to pass on a sense of *Heimat* to a daughter born and raised elsewhere, in emigration. But what happens during the return journey itself, at the site? What narratives are generated when the present intrudes upon the past? What can these narratives tell us about the persistent and shifting shapes of nostalgia in the face of trauma? And what of the children of exiles/refugees who 'return' to a 'home' where they have never been before? How do they receive and in turn transmit the conflicting memories generated through their act of witness?

## Ambivalent nostalgia / negative memory

Nowadays it strikes us as no more than curious that nostalgia (from the Greek *nostos*, to return home, and *algia*, a painful feeling) was considered a debilitating, sometimes fatal, medical affliction for almost two centuries after first being named and described in a 1688 Swiss medical thesis. Initially identified in exiles and displaced soldiers languishing for home, physicians had observed that the symptoms of nostalgia could be triggered in its victims through sights, sounds, smells, tastes – any of a number of associations that might influence them to recall the homes and environments they had unwillingly left behind. Returning the 'homesick', the 'nostalgic', to their origins, it was believed, was the potential cure for the 'disease'– its restorative ending.[10]

Although interest in nostalgia as a medical problem waned considerably by the mid-nineteenth century, its link with absence or removal from home or homeland has continued to remain one of its definitional components. But the meaning of nostalgia also broadened over the years to encompass 'loss' of a more general and abstract type, including the yearning for a 'lost childhood', for 'irretrievable youth', for a vanished 'world of yesterday'. Since no *actual* turning-back and return in time is possible in this latter sense of the term, nostalgia became an incurable state of mind, a signifier of 'absence' and 'loss' that could in effect never be made 'presence' and 'gain' except through memory and the creativity of reconstruction.[11]

In much of the literature on nostalgia, however, the feelings associated with 'looking back' to a place or time in the past generally reflect a bitter-sweet, affectionate, positive relationship to the 'lost'. They express a contrast between 'there' and 'here', 'then' and 'now', in which the absent/gone is valued as somehow better, simpler, less fragmented, more comprehensible, than its existent alternative in the present. Indeed, it is this indiscriminate idealization of past time and lost place that has angered nostalgia's critics, and engendered vitriolic denunciations of nostalgic memory as 'reactionary', 'sentimental', 'elitist', 'escapist', 'inauthentic' – as a 'retrospective mirage' that 'greatly simplifies, if not falsifies, the past'.[12] But nostalgic memory has also been seen more positively, as a resistant relationship to the present, a 'critical utopianism' that envisions a better future. A past reconstructed through the animating vision of nostalgia can serve as a creative inspiration and possible emulation within the present, 'called upon to provide what the present lacks'.[13] This is precisely the role it played in the Romanian Cernăuţi of the interwar years.

It would no doubt be correct to assert that Lotte and Carl Hirsch, and other survivors of deportation or displacement from Czernowitz, were and are to some degree afflicted by affectionate longings for earlier stages and scenes in their own lives, as well as for pleasurable experiences in familiar places and settings in this city of their birth. The disappointment that Carl and Lotte expressed during our first walk in the city after our arrival, that things had changed – that, 'yes, this is the Rathaus, or the Jewish high school for girls, or the Herrengasse, or the Café Europa' but that each is also 'different', renamed (in Cyrillic script), no longer as beautiful, or elegant, as it had once been, and certainly not as animated – all this attests to the fact that their nostalgic memories of the past had been replete with positive images which present-day viewing challenged. Certainly, a prime motivation for Carl and Lotte's return visit to Czernowitz was their desire to reconnect an idea of the city which they had continued to keep alive in their minds to the sites which they had once held so dear: to view these and touch them again in a material sense, even though they were also sure that, after more than fifty years and the intervention of fascism and communism, the past would certainly have become a foreign country. Life experience had taught them what Czernowitz's internationally best-known non-Jewish German author, Gregor von Rezzori, had expressed so insightfully in an autobiographical work: 'You must never undertake the search for time lost in the spirit of nostalgic tourism.'[14]

But it is also crucial to indicate that the layered nostalgia for Czernowitz/ Cernăuţi, as positive remembrance of the past, was only one aspect of their recall. Like others who had been displaced from their homes and native lands and become refugees or exiles, Carl and Lotte Hirsch also carried very negative and bitter memories of the past with them – traumatic memories of bad times when they had suffered discrimination and oppression. Our walks through 'old' Czernowitz reflected the centrality of these negative and traumatic recollections – the emphasis that Carl and Lotte placed on the late 1930s and on the war years in their on-site narratives to us, and their (at times frustrated) determination to find, revisit, and to show us the different apartments and houses where they had found refuge during their confinement in Czernowitz's Jewish ghetto in October of 1941. For them, as for other refugees and exiles, negative and traumatic memories such as these were nostalgia's complicating other side.

This ambivalent desire to recall negative experiences at their place of happening, and to transmit them to sympathetic listeners and co-witnesses, is a significant motivation for return journeys such as the one we took to Czernowitz. In the act of recall, traumatic events are inevitably linked to the place of their occurrence, and thus physical return can facilitate the process of working through. Associated with the largely positive recollections of childhood and youth, and the traumatic events that precipitated their departure, these sites, and the city itself, survive in their ambivalent remembrance through what we might define as a psychic mechanism of 'splitting'. Like the small child who endows parental images alternately with good and bad qualities, the survivor needs to split off nostalgic memory from negative and traumatic memory in order to sustain nostalgia's positive aspects. Geographical and temporal distance, and the trauma of exile or expulsion, make it difficult to develop an integrated memory of a lost home. Conflicting memories thus co-exist unreconciled: the place called 'Heimat' contains both 'what we lived through, especially in the war years' and the 'experiences and culture' that Carl so fondly recalled on the eve of our journey. Memory is fragmented, and the fragments are shaded with clashing emotional colourings. Traumatic dissociation – the process by which traumatic fragments survive and remain vividly present without being integrated or mastered by the traumatized person – is an extreme form of the splitting that characterizes ambivalent nostalgia / negative memory.[15]

In reconnecting with both the *positive* and the *negative* in the past at the site, journeys of return require a renegotiation of the conflicting memories that constitute the returnees' ideas of 'home'. Once they make the journey back to the places they had left, their recognition of change generates corrective anecdotes and narratives. 'Let me tell you *how it was* … '. Svetlana Boym calls this narrative type of nostalgia 'reflective' rather than 'restorative': 'Reflective nostalgics are aware of the gap between identity and resemblance. … This defamiliarization and sense of distance drives them to tell their story, to narrate the relationship between past, present, and future.' 'If restorative nostalgia ends up reconstructing emblems and rituals of home and homeland in an attempt to conquer and spatialize time, reflective nostalgia cherishes shattered fragments of memory and temporalizes space.'[16]

But, for returnees to the sites that had contained Jewish life in Nazi-occupied Europe, the useful notion of *reflective nostalgia* requires some further elaboration. For them, the recognition of change – of the inevitable disappointments and ironic incongruities in all attempts at homecoming – is not the only disturbing factor. At each moment of their journeys, the past-*positive* is also overlaid by the past-*negative*. *Nostalgic* memory clashes with *negative* and *traumatic* memory, and produces *ambivalence*. In the act of return, that ambivalence is generative not so much of corrective narrative as of a kind of performance, the creation of a scenario that can hold both sides of the past simultaneously in view, without necessarily reconciling them, or 'healing' the rift.

## Rootless nostalgia/negative postmemory

In a profound sense, nostalgic yearning in combination with negative and traumatic memory – pleasure and affection, layered with bitterness, anger and aversion – are internalized by the children of the exiles and refugees: by us, members of the 'second generation'. We of that generation have very peculiar relationships to the places from which our families originated and from which they had been removed or displaced. For Marianne and her contemporaries, children of exiled 'Czernowitzers', Czernowitz has always been a kind of primordial site of origin. Although none of them had ever been there or seen it (or even thought they might be *able* to see it), it was the source of their 'native' German linguistic and cultural background, with which they closely identified and – although now living in the United States, Canada, Australia, Israel, France, Germany, Austria – still identify. For Marianne, the streets, buildings and natural surroundings of Czernowitz – its theatres, restaurants, parks, rivers and domestic settings, none of which she herself had ever seen, heard, or smelled – figured more strongly in her childhood memories and imagination than the sites and scenes of Timisoara in Romania, where she was born, or Bucharest, where she had spent her childhood. Some of these same places, however, were also the sites of her childhood nightmares of persecution, deportation, fear and terror. Her memory of Czernowitz (like Leo's of Vienna, from which his parents had fled to South America – where he was born) is a postmemory, a secondary, belated memory mediated by stories, images and behaviours among which she grew up, but which never added up to a complete picture or linear tale. Its power derives precisely from the layers – both positive and negative – that have been passed down to her, un-integrated, conflicting, fragmented, dispersed. As Eva Hoffman writes: 'I come from the war, it is my true origin. But as with all our origins, I cannot grasp it. Perhaps we never know where we come from; in a way we are all created *ex nihilo*.'[17]

Marianne's desire to visit Czernowitz was not exactly a nostalgic longing for a lost or abandoned 'home': how could a place she had never 'touched', and which her parents left under extreme duress, really be 'home'? Nor was it a yearning to recall some better past time in that city, for she had experienced no actual time there at all. Children of survivors who 'return' to former homes need to soften overwhelmingly negative postmemories of coming 'from the war' by making a material connection with a 'before' – a time (and a place) in which their parents had not yet suffered the threat of genocide. They need to bring to the surface what the trauma of expulsion has submerged, to witness the sites of resistance and survival, and thus to construct a deeper and more nuanced understanding of history and of memory.

In a complex way, Marianne's nostalgia for Czernowitz incorporated the ambivalence of her parents' generation with a *need* to repair the ruptured fabric of a painfully discontinuous, fragmentary, history. Unlike that of her parents, however, her nostalgia was *rootless* – a longing driven by the layered postmemories she carried, and the conflict between 'home' and 'hostile territory' that they, in turn, generated. Carl's notion of 'not [being] from anywhere', identifies a dynamic element motivating the *rootless* nostalgia of the children of exiles and refugees. 'Our roots are "diasporic"', writes the French–Polish writer Henri Raczymow. 'They do not go underground. They are not attached to any particular land or soil. … Rather they creep up along the many roads of dispersion that the Jewish writer explores, or discovers, as he puts his lines down on paper. Such roads are endless.'[18]

Citing Kafka, Raczymow goes on to say that, like Moses, the Jewish writer will never reach Canaan. If our parents hoped to find at least some traces of their past by returning to Czernowitz, for us, in the postmemorial generation, 'returning to the place' could not serve as a means of *reparation* or *recovery*. Having inherited shards of memory, positive and negative, we could not hope to reunite the fragments. Instead, our journey remained a process of searching – a creative vehicle of contact and transmission enabling an encounter between nostalgic and negative memory. Its force derived precisely from its irresolution, the simultaneity of promise and disappointment. Returning to the site *with* our parents enabled us to bear witness to and participate in their transitory acts of memory, acts that allowed – for some moments, at least – conflicting recollections to coexist.

## The crossroads

If there is one story from Carl and Lotte's wartime experiences that would illuminate these negotiations between nostalgia and negative memory, thus staging the workings of ambivalence, it is the story of the fateful moment in which they evaded deportation to Transnistria, the region where two-thirds of the Jews of Czernowitz were forcibly relocated and where more than half of those met their death. We had both heard that story repeatedly, and, in fact, Marianne had always seen that place – where they turned right instead of left – as the life source from which she sprang: it led directly to her parents' marriage in the Czernowitz ghetto, to their survival during the years of war, and eventually to their emigration to Romania where she was born. For us, it was a story of survival and hope in the face of extreme persecution, suffering and fear. It thus promised to offer us what we most wanted from the trip itself: a thicker version of the past, modulating expulsion and humiliation with resistance, defiance and hope. Carl and Lotte had always described it as located at a corner, a corner where they turned back (into the ghetto) instead of following deportees towards the train station. As soon as our trip to Czernowitz was in the plans, we knew we had to see that corner.

We began our walk in front of Lotte's family apartment on what used to be Dreifaltigkeitsgasse – only one block from where Carl had lived with his mother, brother and sisters. We had visited Lotte's apartment yesterday, but now we were back, facing the entrance to the house, and it seemed the appropriate place to start the story of 11 October 1941, the day that the ghetto was formed in Czernowitz, and of the first few days of their internment.

'In those days', Carl began, 'I worked at the railroad administration office from eight to one and from four to seven. Before work, on that Saturday the 11th of October, I stopped at Lotte's house to say hello. As I was walking along, a neighbour stopped me and said 'read this', and showed me an ordinance that was posted on a near-by building. It said: 'Anyone who harbours Jews or other undesirables, anyone who owns firearms, etc. will immediately be put to death.' I told her I didn't think that that concerns us, and I went to work, what was I supposed to do? At one when I come home, I see that everyone is carrying knapsacks and bundles. What's that, I thought? When I came home to my mother's they were all packed to go. Lotte's family had arranged for us all to go to their cousin Blanka Engler's apartment in the Steingasse within the newly established ghetto. We were eleven, my mother, two sisters, my brother, Lotte and I, her father and mother, her sister, her sister's fiancé and his mother.'

We were still in front of the house in Dreifaltigkeitsgasse, the home where Lotte had spent her first 27 years. Lotte gestured, 'The ghetto was formed and our street was not a part of it, and we had to be inside the area that would be closed off as the ghetto by six in the afternoon.'

We were standing there, trying to understand, to remember other tellings of this story, to imagine it at the very site where it happened. The tree-lined street looked peaceful, a little run down, though the houses have maintained their turn-of-the-century elegance. Leo was videotaping, some passers-by stared. A few trucks drove by and we worried about the noise on the tape. 'How did you know to go – was there any order in writing, any ordinance?' Marianne asked.

'The members of the Jewish Council went from house to house and said, by 6:00 pm you have to be within this perimeter. Nothing was posted. I said, "we're leaving – we must set the house on fire." Do you remember, Lotte?'

'My father said, "This could not be true!"' Lotte had quoted this on many occasions, always with a smile that indicated her pleasurable memories of her father's incongruous sense of justice. '"This violates the European rights of man." He was a lawyer.'

We had been walking a few blocks now. 'Marianne, Leo, come here, look,' Carl called us, pointing. 'Here they made a fence and soldiers stood here. Here was the edge of the ghetto. And here, now we are inside the ghetto.' He stepped inside the boundary he had drawn for us in the air. 'And here we moved into Blanka's apartment, there on the second floor. The next morning we went out to talk to everyone. We could move around freely inside the ghetto; everyone was dressed casually, for the trip. And we knew, now start the 'Forty days of Musa Dagh' (you know, that novel by Franz Werfel about the Armenians chased out of their homes and into the desert by the Turks in World War I). We're on a Sunday. We're here Monday, Tuesday. On Wednesday everyone living here on this and the surrounding streets was supposed to go to the train station for deportation. We went outside and saw a lot of peasants with horse-drawn carts waiting for customers to transport to the depot, and Lotte's father said, 'It's a sunny day, a good day for travelling.' So we loaded all our things, for eleven people, on one of these carts and waited our turn to go.'

Lotte was gesturing; she wanted to say something. 'May I add something here? This is something, Carl, which you don't totally admit. They said, now the Steingasse is on, and we put everything on that wagon. Everything. We had pillows, bedding, pots, all our sick relatives on foot, everyone carrying something. What you won't admit is that a soldier came to our door and said, "Ok, now you have to go."'

Carl was impatient, 'There's no point. Everyone was already outside, we all knew. We have to tell the same story. The soldier is beside the point. The Jewish council said, get ready.'

'Yes, the Jewish council worked with them, they hoped perhaps to save at least a few people.' She was ready to agree, 'Yes, we knew we had to leave.'

We were on the very street where they stood with hundreds of others, with carts and belongings. Did a soldier come to the door or were they resigned to leaving? Does it matter? These are the things we would have to sort out later. But this detail, about the soldier, and the discrepancy between the two versions of the story, emerged there on site: we had never heard it before.

There was barely time for some of these thoughts, as Carl continued his narrative. 'As we were standing there on the street, a neighbour came by and said, 'I hear that some professionals will be allowed to stay in Czernowitz.' About a half hour later – we were still on that street, there were lots of carts ahead of us and everything was moving really slowly – a Romanian major walked by and I said to him, 'Sir, I hear that professionals will be allowed to stay. I am an engineer.' He said to me, 'Stay.' That's all. Imagine, I was on my way to the station with eleven people: my old mother, Lotte's old parents, her sick sister, the old mother of my brother-in-law. All were scared. Lotte and I had to act. So we took the carriage and ...'

Leo spoke from behind the camera, 'But wait, you had nothing in writing, and that Romanian major was gone. How could you ... ?'

'He had said only three words,' Lotte pointed to the ground. '"Rămâi pe loc, stay right here!"'

As we left the former Steingasse, we came to a small memorial plaque mounted on a building, which, we were told, commemorates the Czernowitz ghetto. It was illegible; only a menorah could be made out on it with any clarity. But across the street a new, more legible commemorative plaque had recently been installed. In Ukrainian and Yiddish it read: '*Here, in this place in 1941, was the Czernowitz ghetto where 50,000 Jews were incarcerated.*' That plaque was on a wall of a building on a busy crossing of five streets; two led down a steep hill toward the railroad station, and three were on level ground going in the opposite direction. Here was the corner we had heard so much about. But it was not at all as we had imagined it. It was not merely a corner, the intersection of two streets: it was a major crossroads, one of the city's largest hubs, the former Springbrunnenplatz or the site of the city's ancient well.

It was noisy and hard to talk there. But we stopped, and Carl's narrative continued. There was now a small crowd of onlookers as Carl and Lotte pointed in different directions. '*Here* were the carriages in a row on their way to the train. *Here* there was a chain of soldiers and here, on this side, was only a single soldier. So I brought the carriage over here to the single soldier, and I gave him 100 lei. I said nothing.'

Although we had heard all this before, it seemed more difficult to believe now. 'You went this way while everyone else was going that way, and he let you through?'

Carl nodded, 'Yes. On the Schulgasse, only two blocks from here, lived the Lehr family, distant cousins, and we knew that their street had not yet been evacuated.'

Leo handed over the camera and started pointing himself. 'That way is to the train station?'

'Yes, and this way was back inside the ghetto. We thought, where to go? Maybe the Lehrs will take us in?'

'You paid to get back inside the ghetto?'

'We went on to the Lehrs. There were already about thirty to thirty-five people there, but they took us in, eleven more. My siblings slept in the laundry room behind the house and for the rest of us they found some floor space somewhere. This was on a Wednesday. On that evening, in the Jewish Hospital, which was the seat of the Jewish Council, the Romanian mayor came and said ... '

Lotte added an explanation, 'The mayor was Traian Popovici and he was very friendly to the Jews.'

'He spoke in Yiddish,' Carl added. 'He said, "I have good news for you. You are staying here." You see, he had to arrange for professionals with technical skills to stay. He couldn't run the city otherwise. Only later, he changed it to say that only part of the Jewish population will be able to stay.'

'So Lehr, the man we were staying with, said, "Mazel Tov" and he went to the basement and got out some champagne and we all drank champagne and celebrated.' They had recalled these details in previous tellings, but now we were there. We turned into the street that was the Schulgasse and we were looking at the house that belonged to the Lehrs.

'That was on a Wednesday,' Carl continued. 'On Thursday morning, another piece of news. The ghetto will be expanded. Some streets had already been evacuated and were closed down, but new streets were opened for this purpose. In that new part on the Wojnarowiczgasse, an uncle of Lotte's lived in a new villa, so on that Thursday the eleven of us moved again to that uncle Rubel.'

'We were also over sixty people there. We slept all over the house. You can imagine the long lines for the bathroom.' Lotte started laughing. 'One day, my aunt really had to go, so she pushed to the front and announced: "I am still the owner of this house!"'

'We all settled in. We played cards and we waited. Traian Popovici had promised, but we began to have some doubts and worries. So it was Thursday, on Friday I said to Lotte, "Whatever happens, whether we stay or go, let's get married." So around two pm on Friday, I look out the window and there's a rabbi standing outside. So I say to him, can you marry us? And he says that after two pm on a Friday it's too late to get married under Jewish law, because of the Sabbath. On Saturday morning, the 18th of October, we go to the commander of the ghetto, a Romanian major, and we say, "Sir, we want to get married." '

'This was complicated because by law you have to post an official "intention" for two weeks preceding a civil wedding, so we had to get a dispensation from the court.'

Carl continued: 'But the major gave us a soldier to escort us and we went to the courthouse to get the dispensation.'

Lotte was eager to clarify, 'That major actually called the soldier aside and told him to walk on the other side of the street so it wouldn't be so obvious. But when we got to the courthouse and told the official what we wanted, he said, curtly, "But how did you leave the ghetto?" So I opened the door and pointed to the soldier and I said, "Under military escort." '

'We got the dispensation and went back to the ghetto. At five we were supposed to be back at the registry in the city hall. So we got the soldier at three.'

'My sister and her fiancé were allowed to come with us as witnesses,' Lotte added.

Carl continued, more animated, 'We had an extra hour so first we went right to the railway administration where I worked. I went in and they said, we have your official authorization to stay here. When we went to city hall, the registrar, who was a professor, received us very warmly and he said to me, "*Domnule inginer*, I hope that we will be able to celebrate many other happy occasions with your people here in Romania." '

The irony in this statement became apparent to us as we listened. The act of marriage might have been one of the last acts they could undertake as legal subjects of the Romanian state, their last link to citizenship. Yet their military escort – even if outside the door – served as the clear indicator of their status as prisoners of the very state that consented to marry them at the same time as it was in the process of expelling them. From their narrative, it seems that the registrar was equally uncomfortable with his role, trying to find an unofficial and thereby resistant connection to them at this moment. Calling Carl '*Domnule inginer*' was a mark of respect, and a gesture of continuity with saner social conventions.

'Well, we celebrated as best we could under the circumstances, we stayed there a few more days and then we got our authorizations and were able to return home,' Lotte added. 'Many thousands had been deported by this time. And many more were deported before they dissolved the ghetto in mid-November.'

'My brother had his authorization, and my sisters and mother could be added to mine, and each one of the others got one somehow. And I never forgot this – even more than fifty years later. The next day I went back to work and the boss, not the real boss but my immediate supervisor, a Romanian, kissed me. Some of them were very nice to us', Carl concluded.

Lotte contributed an important final detail: 'We were lucky to have the official authorizations, because Popovici, the mayor, also gave out some other so-called "Popovici authorizations" and later, when the mayor was fired, those were declared invalid and most of those people were deported in the next wave of deportations.'

## Memory and place

As Lotte and Carl repeated their walk of that day, and as we walked along with them from the houses they had to evacuate, to the house to which they first moved, to the crossroads where they turned back into the ghetto instead of going to the train station and deportation, they propelled themselves back into that moment in 1941 when their future was so uncertain. They re-lived the days of waiting, their wedding at the city hall under military escort, their relief at obtaining authorization to remain in Czernowitz, the frightening insecurities of the subsequent months. But, owing to our presence perhaps, and through the experience of telling the story to us in all its details and nuances, they could also gain a retrospective distance from that past. They could look back on it with the child who might not have been born had they taken a different turn.

On site, their memories gained relief, dimensionality, texture and colour. We had visited Terezín, Lvov, and other Nazi-created ghettos; we had seen films and photos, and maps of the ghettos in Warsaw, Lodz, Cracow. But walking through Czernowitz with our parents, seeing the houses in which they had been children and grown into adulthood, and having them identify the houses where their various friends and acquaintances lived, we finally internalized, in a way we never could before, the reality of what we now euphemistically refer to as 'ethnic cleansing': the brutality involved in forcing people to abandon their homes, gathering them into one small area, and then, systematically, clearing the city of their presence. We could sense the strange resignation, the compliance with which they must have packed their belongings and lined up for the train station, but also the anger and bitterness that would make Carl want to set the house on fire as he left. We could more than visualize their journey: we could smell and touch that crisp October day, hear the commotion on the street, the rumours that were flying, participate in the split second decision that they re-enacted at the cross-roads with their bodies as they pointed and turned in the one direction over the other. Suddenly, as we talked and listened, the barricades and rows of soldiers became visible. And as we walked about this landscape of memory, the streets became animated with the presence of people from that past: long-lost relatives, friends, neighbours, Lotte and Carl, young, in their twenties – ghosts emerging

91

from the shadows between the buildings, conjured up by recall and narration, by our being there, by our presence and witness.

When Toni Morrison describes the aura that attaches itself to a place in her novel *Beloved* she uses the language of traumatic re-enactment: ' "Some things you forget. Other things you never do. ... Places, places are still there. If a house burns down, it's gone, but the place – the picture of it – stays, and not just in my rememory but out there, in the world ... if you go there – you who never was there – if you go there and stand in the place where it was, it will happen again; it will be there for you, waiting for you." '[19]

This was indeed the risk of our journey. The location authenticates the narrative, embodies it, makes it real, to the point where it threatens to re-engulf those who come to tell and to listen. Our presence there, together, gave a substance and concreteness to that October day in 1941 that no stone plaque memorial could possibly evoke. And yet, at the same time, the traffic noises and the people around us, many of them watching as we videotaped our parents' testimony, propelled us back into the present. Here we found the retrospective vantage point that powerfully confirmed their spur-of-the-moment decision to 'turn a corner and change direction'. But, looking back, we could also see something else that Lotte and Carl had not until that moment conveyed to us: that this 'corner', as they had characterized it, was also a 'crossing' of *many* roads that symbolically reflected the many different turns that their lives *could have* taken – and that the lives of others among their contemporaries took. Emigration ... Exile ... Flight into the Soviet Union ... Deportation ... Transnistria ... Bucharest ... Paris ... Vienna ... Tel Aviv ... New York ... As literal as that intersection was, it acquired additional symbolic significance through our contemplation and interpretation – meaning we were able to find in our parents' narrative. And through this insight, which took our journey *out* of the past into a symbolic – *timeless* – significance, retrospective witnessing became prospective.

'No one/ bears witness for the/ witness' wrote Paul Celan in the late 1960s shortly before he committed suicide in Paris, feeling isolated, displaced, and misunderstood.[20] The 'listening' he yearned for, he describes in another poem as the kind in which you 'hear deep in/ with your mouth' (*'hör dich ein/ mit dem Mund'*).[21] For Carl and Lotte, our interest confirmed something about their past, its importance, its narrative and its dramatic quality, the need to pass it on. Our challenge was to receive the story from them, and to receive it as active, collaborative listeners, who could encourage the emergence of the more painful, the more tentative, the more fragmentary, ambiguous, and vulnerable aspects of that past experience, alongside the more positive reminiscences of good fortune and community.[22]

This is how we tried to listen, and our retelling, here, is the measure of that effort. But there was so much that we still don't know and did not get. We never found the Wojnarowiczgasse where the villa in the ghetto was where they took refuge: though we walked and searched, no street corresponded to the old map and, surprisingly, neither Lotte nor Carl was able to identify the house in the general neighbourhood. We never went back to the courthouse where Lotte and Carl received their dispensation, permitting them to marry: at the last minute we were too tired to make one more detour. And, during the next week, when we visited Carl's sister Lilly in Germany and went over the same moments with her, she remembered them somewhat differently, detracting again from the solidity the narrative had acquired during our visit.

Mostly, we wonder, given our presence as an audience, how much was the narrative ruled by the desire for sequence, drama and closure, the elements that make a good story? We became sensitive to the story's multiple happy endings: they were able to marry, they received their authorizations, the boss was very nice, their authorizations were not rescinded. To what degree were the loose ends tied up, the i's dotted, for our benefit? We found that, on site, their previously more triumphalist narrative of courage, ingenuity and survival was interrupted by other conflicting memories – a soldier standing by the door, the burden of having to care for eleven people, their fear and ill health. And yet there were also community, humour, small moments of celebration. The scene of narration allowed the enactment of contradiction and the emergence of disagreement in ways that we had not witnessed before.

## Generations of memory

We have come to see this intersection in Czernowitz, and the vicissitudes of telling and listening we enacted there, as a figure describing the different dimensions of nostalgia that we have been evoking in this chapter. For Lotte and Carl – the first generation – the crossroads is a site of nostalgic return because it confirms their good fortune while highlighting their decisiveness and agency. It grounds the enabling moment that set a direction for their subsequent lives in a physical space. It enables them to hold on to their positive memories of Czernowitz. Simultaneously, it also concretizes traumatic memory – memorializing (in the very physical sense of that concept) their immeasurable loss and their mourning for those thousands of others who were forced to take the other turn.

And for us, in the postmemorial generation, this crossroads is – paradoxically – an index for our ambivalent and rootless nostalgia. It is less location than transitional space where the encounter between generations, between past and present, between nostalgic and traumatic memory, can momentarily, effervescently, be staged.

Children of refugees inherit their parents' knowledge of the fragility of place, their suspicion of the notion of home. The site of our encounter, where the fracture between eras was briefly bridged, could not provide the soil where roots of belonging could ever again take hold. Still, at the crossroads in Czernowitz, telling and listening became a collaborative endeavour. 'It would not have made sense to return except in this constellation', Lotte and Carl repeated again and again. 'We would not have come without you.'[23]

# Notes

1 Paul Celan, 'Speech on the Occasion of Receiving the Literature Prize of the Free Hanseatic City of Bremen', *Selected Poems and Prose of Paul Celan*, trans. John Felstiner (New York: W.W. Norton, 2001), 395. For historical and cultural background on Czernowitz see: Andrei Corbea-Hoisie, ed., *Jüdisches Städtebild Czernowitz* (Frankfurt am Main: Jüdischer Verlag im Suhrkamp, 1998); Hugo Gold, *Geschichte der Juden in der Bukowina*, (Tel Aviv: Olamenu 1962); Hermann Sternberg, *Zur Geschichte der Juden in Czernowitz* (Tel Aviv: Olamenu, 1962).

2 Handwritten document in the Franzos archive at the Wiener Stadt- und Landesbibliothek, cited in Ernest Wichner and Herbert Wiesner, eds, *In der Sprache der Mörder: Eine Literatur aus Czernowitz, Bukowina* (Berlin: Literaturhaus Berlin, 1993), 31.

3 Radu Ioanid, *The Holocaust in Romania: the Destruction of Jews and Gypsies under the Antonescu Regime, 1940–1944* (Chicago: Ivan Dee, 2000), ch. 1.

4 Cited in Carola Gottzmann, ed., *Unerkannt und (un)bekannt: Deutsche Literatur in Mittel- und Osteuropa* (Tübingen: Francke Verlag, 1991), 209.

5 On postmemory see Marianne Hirsch, *Family Frames: Photography, Narrative and Postmemory* (Cambridge: Harvard University Press, 1997) and 'Projected Memory: Holocaust Photographs in Personal and Public Fantasy', in Mieke Bal, Jonathan Crewe and Leo Spitzer, eds, *Acts of Memory: Cultural Recall in the Present* (Hanover: University Press of New England, 1998).

6 The flourishing socialist and Zionist movements and the revival of Yiddish culture constituted other utopian alternatives to a political culture that discriminated against them.

7 Svetlana Boym, *The Future of Nostalgia* (New York: Basic Books, 2001), xiii.

8 Eva Hoffmann, *Lost in Translation: A Life in a New Language* (New York: Penguin Books, 1989), 84.

9 Carl Hirsch, videotaped interview with the authors, Frankfurt-am-Main, September 1998.

10 See Johannes Hofer, 'Medical Dissertation on Nostalgia', first published in 1688 in Latin and translated into English by Carolyn K. Anspach, *Bulletin of the History of Medicine* (1934), 2: 376–391; Jean Starobinski, 'The Idea of Nostalgia', *Diogenes* (1966) 54: 81–103; David Lowenthal, 'Past Time, Present Place: Landscape and Memory', *The Geographical Review* (1975), 65: 1; Fred Davis, *Yearning for Yesterday* (New York: Free Press, 1979); Suzanne Vromen, 'The Ambiguity of Nostalgia', in *YIVO Annual*, 21, 'Going Home', edited by Jack Kugelmass (Evanston: Northwestern University Press, 1993), 69–86. Also see Leo Spitzer, *Hotel Bolivia* (New York: Hill and Wang, 1998), ch. 5, and Boym, *Future of Nostalgia*, Introduction and ch. 1.

11 Spitzer, *Hotel Bolivia*, 144; Boym, *Future of Nostalgia*, 13–14.

12 Spitzer, *Hotel Bolivia*, 145; Robert Hewison, quoted in David Lowenthal, 'Nostalgia Tells It Like It Wasn't,' in *The Imagined Past: History and Nostalgia*, eds Christopher Shaw and Malcolm Chase (Manchester: Manchester University Press, 1989), 20; Raymond Williams, *The Country and the City* (New York: OUP, 1974). Our discussion here is informed by the work of Vromen, 'The Ambiguity of Nostalgia', 71–74, and Lowenthal, 'Past Time', 20–21. Also see Suzanne Vromen, 'Maurice Halbwachs and the Concept of Nostalgia', in *Knowledge and Society: Studies in the Sociology of Culture Past and Present: A Research Annual*, vol. 6, ed. by H. Kuklick and E. Long (Greenwich, Conn.: JAI, 1986), 55–66.

13 Mieke Bal, *Quoting Caravaggio: Contemporary Art, Preposterous History* (Chicago: University of Chicago Press, 1999.), 72. For the concept of 'critical memory' see Spitzer, *Hotel Bolivia*, 145–6.

14 Gregor von Rezzori, *The Snows of Yesteryear: Portraits for an Autobiography* (New York: Vintage, 1989), 290.

15 On 'splitting' see Sigmund Freud, 'The Splitting of the Ego in the Process of Defense' (1940), *The Standard Edition of the Complete Psychological Works of Sigmund Freud* (London: Hogarth Press, 1953), vol. 23, 271–8; Melanie Klein, 'Notes on Some Schizoid Mechanisms' (1946), *International Journal of Psycho-Analysis*, vol. XXVII, 99–110. On the mechanism of doubling in perpetrators, also see Robert Jay Lifton, *The Nazi Doctors: Medical Killing and the Psychology of Genocide* (New York: Basic Books, 1985). On traumatic dissociation see Bessel A. Van der Kolk and Onno van der Hart, 'The Intrusive Past: the Flexibility of Memory and the Engraving of Trauma', in Cathy Caruth, ed. *Trauma: Explorations in Memory* (Baltimore: Johns Hopkins University Press), 158–182; Cathy Caruth, *Unclaimed Experience: Trauma, Narrative and History* (Baltimore: Johns Hopkins University Press, 1996), and Mieke Bal, *Acts of Memory*, Introduction. See also the critiques of the notion of traumatic dissociation by Ruth Leys *Trauma: A Genealogy* (Chicago: University of Chicago Press, 2000) and Susan Brison, *Aftermath: Violence and the Remaking of a Self* (Princeton: Princeton University Press, 2002).
16 Boym, *Future of Nostalgia*, 49–50.
17 Hoffman, *Lost in Translation*, 23.
18 Henri Raczymow, 'Memory Shot Through with Holes', trans. Alan Astro, *Yale French Studies* (1994), 85: 103–4.
19 Toni Morrison, *Beloved* (New York: Alfred A. Knopf, 1987), 36.
20 Celan, *Selected Poems and Prose*, 260.
21 Celan, 'The Shofar Place', *Selected Poems and Prose*, 361.
22 On 'active listening', see Roland Barthes, 'Listening', in *The Responsibility of Forms: Critical Essays on Music, Art, and Interpretation*, trans. Richard Howard (Berkeley: University of California Press, 1991), 245–260.
23 We dedicate this chapter to the memory of Rosa Roth Zuckermann whose lessons about courage and survival have deeply enriched our lives. Her hospitality, along with that of Felix and Marina Zuckermann, and Matthias Zwilling, during our 1998 visit to Chernivtsi embodied its continuity with the lost Czernowitz. We would also like to thank Lotte, Carl and Lilly Hirsch for their intense and always helpful conversations about a painful past.

Earlier versions of this chapter were presented at the 1998 Modern Language Association Conference, the 1999 American Comparative Literature Association Conference, and the 1999 conference on 'Frontiers of Memory' at the University of East London. It is reprinted by permission from a special issue of *American Imago* vol. 59, no.3 (Fall 2002) on 'Postmemories of the Holocaust'.

# Part II

# REMEMBERING SUFFERING: TRAUMA AND HISTORY

## Introduction

*Katharine Hodgkin and Susannah Radstone*

Trauma, as the introduction to this volume suggested, has become a central term within the field of memory studies; but it is at the same time an intensely problematic concept, both in its applications and its implications. If one set of questions touches on the issue of what is classed as a traumatic experience, and under what circumstances theories of traumatic memory can usefully be appealed to or applied, another more fundamental problem relates to the model of memory and the psyche implicit in much work on trauma. The cluster of ideas that may be identified as trauma theory works within a specific causal framework, in which a given event (a catastrophe) produces a given effect.[1] Trauma theory thus explains the origins of particular types of psychic distress in relation to happenings in the real world. For some, however, this emphasis on the traumatic event as origin is misleading; what is absent from this teleological narrative, in effect, is precisely the way in which the mind makes its own meanings. Trauma from this point of view is a response not so much to an event as to the meaning given to that event. And even the event itself is not a precondition: trauma may be the product of fantasy, of things that did not happen as well as of things that did (as in the case of Binjamin Wilkomirski, discussed by Stephan Feuchtwang in our companion volume).[2] The event itself, if there is one, is thus fortuitous; trauma may be seen as a product of the inner workings of the mind, rather than the outcome of a happening.

Similarly, the characteristic features of 'traumatic memory' – its elisions, interruptions and reinventions – need bear no specific relation to an event, but rather can be seen to characterise the workings of memory in general. These insights into how memory works have been central both in the work of oral historians, as discussed in our introduction to this volume, and perhaps more visibly and influentially in psychoanalytic accounts of memory. Thus Paul Antze in our companion volume discusses memory as a metaphorical system, rather than a direct record of events.[3] Memory here is characterised precisely as non-identical with the happened; meaning is always part of a system of symbol and metaphor, and in the absence of such a system, memories cannot acquire meaning.

Thus while debates about the concept of traumatic memory have been very significant in thinking about the place and workings of memory both at the level of the individual and the social (as for example in Marianne Hirsch and Leo Spitzer's discussion of postmemory in the preceding part), the chapters in this part of the book address the question of the relation between suffering and memory in a wider perspective. The question of how suffering may be remembered has several different layers of meaning. Firstly, it asks about the very possibility of memory under certain circumstances. How can catastrophe be remembered? Does memory delete the unendurable? What are the capacities of memory to represent and recall suffering? But it also refers to the political – how should such events be memorialised? – and the therapeutic – what needs to happen to bring about healing? And finally, it is a question about the workings of memory and forgetting, and what memory does with wounds.

Debates over all these points are particularly associated with, on the one hand, the issue of childhood sexual abuse, and the ways in which the adult does or does not retain memories of such experiences; and on the other, with the aftermath of the Holocaust, both in the memories of survivors and in the cultural memory of the West as a whole. In both these instances the concept of trauma has been central, and much work has been done on the specificities of traumatic memory, as a way of thinking about the distortions and silences of memory in the wake of terrible things. The concept of post-traumatic stress disorder (PTSD) has allowed for a very wide extension of the idea – as the list of potential triggers quoted by Janet Walker in her chapter reminds us. But it is in relation to sexual abuse initially that it became necessary to elaborate the theory of trauma as one of measurable and determinable psychic consequences; and there is a direct relationship between the growth of the diagnosis of PTSD and the arguments around the nature and possibility of recovered or false memories.

The legal system, necessarily, works with the measurable and demonstrable. The memory of long-ago events is problematic from this point of view – and more so once the possibility that memories may be mislaid, recovered, false, implanted, and so on, arrives to muddy the waters. Symptoms, on the other hand, are in principle empirical evidence, presupposing a clear chain of cause and effect: the presence of a given effect allows us to deduce a given cause. Thus in preference to the slipperiness of memory, and its tendency to get things wrong – to collapse different events, to misremember important details, to change from one telling to the next – the definite teleology of the symptom, signalling an originary event and a psychic consequence, has come to be increasingly important. And, in a curious twist back to memory, the symptoms are concerned especially with disruptions of memory: memory that has gone missing, blanked something out; or conversely memory that repeats obsessively, that suffers flashbacks, dreams, hallucinations.

Trauma theory, whether in relation to an individual or a larger social phenomenon, thus has at its heart the problem of witness testimony, and of memory. As the theory came to be elaborated in relation to the 'false memory debates' of the 1990s, it focused on the individual who 'forgot' and then 'remembered' something too terrible to belong to a normal register of memory. The individual who speaks of the suffering s/he has experienced is the iconic figure, and the moment of disclosure, in which the unspeakable tries to find representation in speech, is the central and shattering instance. The relation between silence and speech is figured as one of liberation, both politically and personally: to reveal truths which have been denied and to remind the world of its responsibilities to those who have suffered, on the one hand; to heal the self by the very act of speaking and being heard, on the other. The injunction to remember, and the corresponding language of forgetting and denial, are directed equally at individuals and at groups.

There is a sliding scale here, though, which negotiates with difficulty the question of the relation between the psychic and the social. At one end, trauma is the suffering of an individual child, and the repercussions of that suffering in after life. At the other, it is the collective suffering of millions in the concentration camps: those who died, those who survived; and then arguably by association those who identify with them, those who narrowly escaped, those who saw it happen, those who fear its recurrence – the question of where to draw the line is not a straightforward one. In between there are those who encounter terrible things in the course of normal life, and arguments in court over who may or may not be considered traumatised (reidentified as 'suffering from PTSD'): if you were in a plane crash, if you were on the rescue team and saw horrors even though not personally injured, if you were waiting at home for a loved one who never returned and saw it on TV ... The question of trauma has become deeply politicised in all its aspects, and its association with literal reparation and repayment is not the least important aspect of this politicisation. The very concept of damages, and the economy of guilt, is a fascinating side of this debate which there is no space to enter into here.

In the chapters in this part of the book, then, all of which could be said to engage with the aftermath of trauma, we hope to highlight some of the questions about memory which arise in relation to this material. We were anxious not to replicate existing debates, but rather to reposition the question of trauma and its political and therapeutic dimensions. How might trauma theory be extended to address the problem of suffering in other contexts than those with which it has come to be most closely associated? And more fundamentally, how useful is such an extension? Is trauma theory necessarily the best language in which to address the problem of suffering, whether individual or social?

Janet Walker's chapter, which opens this part, is concerned with the ways in which memory, and specifically traumatic memory, can operate in different registers of truth at the same time. In a series of readings of autobiographical film documentaries, of which some address childhood sexual abuse and others war trauma, she emphasises the central problem of the relation between individual and collective memory. The theory of traumatic memory, she suggests, is a means of bridging the gap between the two: the making public of private trauma relocates individual suffering in historical and social context, while also foregrounding the problem of historical truth itself. The traumatic event, in her account, wounds the psyche; unable to engage with or represent the trauma, memory constructs an alternative story, which may at points coincide with the original, but at others will produce a different – sometimes falsifiable – narrative of what happened. It is however, she suggests, *because* of the wound that memory makes these mistakes. Thus the ways in which memory distorts and misrepresents events can actually be evidence for the truth of the memory, rather than its error, if what we are dealing with is trauma. This for Walker is the 'traumatic paradox'.

This argument thus has at its heart the problem of representation. On the one hand, there is the issue of how memory as a system of representation may fail: faced with a 'world-shattering event', the process of symbolisation is cut off, and proves incapable of dealing with 'the breakage of the frame' in literal terms. Memories correspond to the experience, but not literally; amnesias, exaggerations, mistakes, bear witness to the enormity of the attempted resistance. Alongside this problem of representation internal to the individual psyche, however, is the problem of how such experiences may be externally represented. Walker is also deeply concerned with ways of telling, and specifically with how film allows for non-realist representation of world-shattering events; this is in contrast to historiography, which is, she suggests, unable to acknowledge its own 'imaginary' components. The autobiographical documentaries she discusses are 'exemplary' because of their ability to disrupt narrative closure, their 'simultaneous insistence on irrevocable truth and refusal of the realist mode'. For Walker, then, the problem of the relation between fantasy, trauma and the event can perhaps be resolved through a narrative medium which allows for the coexistence of incompatible truths.

Something in certain respects very similar to the disruptions of memory in the films described by Walker is going on in Carrie Hamilton's exploration of the memories of Basque nationalist women, and in particular their memories of violence and loss. In their accounts, Hamilton comments, 'the details are in disarray, but the key elements are stressed and repeated' (p. 125). Once again, what is significant is not so much the historical accuracy with which 'events' are recollected, as the 'exploration into their complex relation to identity, memory and history' (p. 120). In attempting to negotiate these relations, the memories produced by her informants collapse and telescope different stories into one another, confuse different historical moments, and elide material too distressing to confront. While such processes might be considered characteristic of traumatic memory, Hamilton's analysis is not conducted in relation to trauma theory. Rather, drawing on the work of oral historians such as Portelli and Passerini, her account positions these disruptions of memory as typical of the workings of memory in general, with its dynamic reconstruction and renarration of the past.

The importance of memory in nationalist struggle is often emphasised, and will be taken up in more detail in the final part of the book. In this chapter, Carrie Hamilton is particularly concerned with the relation between the individual and the collective narrative of national struggle, and in particular with how gender inflects the experience of being directly involved in such struggle, and its subsequent narration. Memory, in a sense, has a great deal of work to do in the community, producing an agreed narrative that gives meaning and value to collective struggle, but simultaneously allowing for the expression of moments of disaffection and suffering within that community. A similar tension arises in the erasure of historical change in the name of memory – it is the memory of the martyrs that binds the present (loyalty to their memory, they should not have died in vain, etc.), and it is the memory of the immemorial past of oppression that drives the struggle. In her discussion of the repeated phrase '*igual, igual*', Carrie Hamilton reminds us that memory's focus on making the past work in the present can in the long run be deeply anti-historical.

The next chapter in this part, by Paula Hamilton, focuses on the encounter between memorial and historical discourses as they articulate the relation to the past in contemporary Australia. Commenting on the Eurocentric tendencies of much work in memory studies, and in particular on the iconic position of the Holocaust as both origin and object of the 'memory boom', she argues for an outside perspective, and an extension of the analysis of the memory of cataclysmic events to a wider field. The 'memory struggles of indigenous peoples', she suggests, 'have something to offer' those who see memory exclusively through the lens of the Second World War (p. 142). In particular she is concerned with the experience of the 'lost generation', a generation of Aboriginal children who were taken from their homes during the middle decades of the twentieth century to be fostered by white parents, and on how the loss and dislocation inflicted on these children has been articulated and responded to subsequently. Like other instances in which authorities are called to make reparation for a wrong done to a large group as a matter of policy, this process has been complex, manifesting itself in many different contexts, from government inquiries to the visual arts. The call for 'public expiation of wrongs' (p. 143) has not been fully met by a government which prefers to regard the past as past, unless military heroism is involved; conversely a counter-memory to the heroic narrative of the Australian nation has grown up around the figures of the lost children, both in themselves and for their resonance as symbols of the dispossession, displacement and violence committed against the Aboriginal population. Thus within the context of a majority non-indigenous narrative of the past, the subordinate Aboriginal account can function as a counter-memory.

Paula Hamilton's argument, however, is not in any simple sense that the model of traumatic memory should be applied more widely than it has been hitherto, so as to interpret the experiences of the lost generation in the light of trauma theory (and compensate them accordingly). Rather, she suggests, the problems of 'memorial culture' in general, and of the theory of traumatic memory in particular, that have emerged in the debates over the lost generation are problems more generally associated with it elsewhere. Counterposing memorial and historical consciousness as ways of engaging with the past, Hamilton identifies in Australian society a generalised memorial culture, closely tied to ideas about trauma, guilt and redemption, in which particular authority is accorded to the eyewitness. Without the development of this memorial culture, she suggests, the debate about the lost generation could not have been articulated or disseminated in the forms it has taken. But memorial culture is not necessarily something to be celebrated; it raises, among other things, the problems implicit in laying claim to the status of the victim, the difficult notion of authenticity in guaranteeing the truth of the witness, and the assumption that a therapeutic language, with the healing strategies it entails, can appropriately be applied to a group or a nation. If recent decades have, as she argues, seen an often fruitful shift in how the relation between history and memory is constituted, it is nonetheless important to keep a critical and questioning perspective on the turn to memory.

This point is at the heart of the last paper in this part, by Chris Colvin, which investigates the historical and therapeutic models underpinning the work of the South African Truth and Reconciliation Committee, and in post-apartheid South Africa more generally. The TRC is often taken as a model for the possibility of coming to terms with an embittered and violent past, with its injunction to confront and testify and move on. But, Colvin asks, is the therapeutic discourse associated with trauma – of the liberating and healing potential of speech – perhaps a problem in itself? Whether because it incorporates cultural assumptions about 'speaking out' that may not be universally applicable, or because it can attempt to institute a language of amelioration and reconciliation in situations where the material or political conditions do not in fact justify such a move – storytelling as a substitute for material aid. There may be, in effect, a wish to transform something into 'memory' by converting it into narrative, at a point where the story has not attained closure and the suffering is not yet a memory. For members of the 'survivors' group' interviewed by Colvin, testifying is not enough, and moving on cannot happen, without a change in objective conditions.

Other post-apartheid memorial settings are also characterised by this combination of institutional and therapeutic imperatives. The Robben Island prison museum is organised around a move to consensus: it simultaneously insists on the terrible things that happened there and fixes them in the past, as something no longer to be feared. This is as it were the institutional moment; but also arguably the therapeutic moment for those tour guides who now make a living out of reliving their pasts. Against this, what might be called the popular memory of the long-term white residents of the island is detached from the prison narrative, harking back nostalgically to earlier times, and evoking an alternative history which sidelines the prison – not so much 'it never happened' as 'it wasn't really the main thing about the island'. These memories assert a depoliticised and sanitised version of the past, which puts into question the consensus towards which the museum strives. The problem of who takes the position of victim in these memorial contexts, and how non-victims may best respond, remains unresolved.

In the continuing attempts to think through and reconceptualise the relations between memory and history, then, discourses of suffering have a particular significance. To think about history, suffering and memory implies the need to move between public and private, psychic and social, therapeutic and political, for all these have a bearing on the complex relations between the three terms. The prominence of trauma theory perhaps owes something to the sense that it may provide a resolution to these tensions, offering a theoretical framework within which the opposing terms may all be finally accommodated, and suggesting a tidy theorisation of the relation between memory and suffering. But as the very divergent approaches taken by the chapters in this part indicate, as a way of thinking about these complex questions trauma theory remains problematic.

## Notes

1   On 'trauma theory' see Thomas Elsaesser, 'Postmodernism as mourning work', *Screen* 42.2, Summer 2001.
2   Stephan Feuchtwang, 'Loss: transmissions, recognitions, authorisations', in Radstone and Hodgkin, eds, *Regimes of Memory*.
3   Paul Antze, 'The other inside: memory as metaphor in psychoanalysis', in Radstone and Hodgkin, eds, *Regimes of Memory*.

# 5

# THE TRAUMATIC PARADOX

Autobiographical documentary and the psychology
of memory

*Janet Walker*

Lynn Hershman is a San Francisco-based performance and multi-media artist
who, over the course of a career spanning more than thirty years, has explored
the construction of self and identity. In her video works, particularly the autobiographical *Electronic Diary* series begun in the mid-1980s, these explorations of
selfhood have adopted the technique of documentary direct address, but direct
address pushed to its most radical ends, complemented with other forms of
expression that irrupt strategically into the text, and used so as to foreground the
specificity of the video medium.[1] In *Binge* (1987) she confides to the camera,
ironically, 'I would never ever talk this way if someone were in the room'. And
what she confides in particular are almost unbearable (her word) truths (her
word) about her personal history of physical and sexual abuse and about how
that history forms a link in a worldwide chain of human rights abuses. What
makes Hershman's work radical, suggests the critic Julia Lesage, is its specifically
feminist endeavor to bring to light the relationships among psychic fragmentation, the physical and sexual abuse of children, and patterns of men's
domination and women's masochism under patriarchy.[2]

For me, the additional element of great interest in Hershman's tapes is their
concentration on revealing the naked truth of her abuse while at the same time
calling into question the memory processes through which that abuse is remembered *and* forgotten, communicated *and* denied. In other words, while one
self-avowed purpose of the diaries is to speak aloud dirty family and social
secrets, their actual work is to make connections that are elusive and abstract
rather than bald and technical. I begin with the work of Hershman, therefore, in
order to broach the vicissitudes of traumatic memory. These I will pursue
through contemporary psychological theories into a realm where mistaken
memory and historical truth make strange bedfellows, but bedfellows nonetheless.

At the end of *First Person Plural* (1988), Hershman makes it perfectly clear that
her history is one involving childhood abuse. 'I showed this tape to friends,' she
states, 'but they didn't get it. I'll just have to come right out and say that when I

was very young I was physically abused and sexually abused'. And in fact *First Person Plural* begins with a monologue repeated from an earlier tape,[3] *Confessions of a Chameleon* (1986): 'When I was ... uh ... small. I mean, when I was little, there would be these ... uh ... kinds of episodes of battering. And I would go up into my attic and almost retreat into myself'. In *Binge* she says bluntly, 'I will acknowledge the incest'. Equally important to disclosing a history of abuse is the exploration of how the events that took place were at one time cloaked in secrecy. Hershman also includes passages about the prohibition against admission. Several times throughout *First Person Plural* we see a shot of her in the dark whispering 'you're not supposed to talk about it' and we see several times a giant close-up of her lips mouthing 'don't tell'. That revelation and the prohibition against it go hand in hand is further illustrated by the 'talking head' shot of Hershman standing in front of a wall covered with the words 'Do not say it' and 'Don't talk'. She does talk, speaking of how she was harmed and how as a later result she would tend to be attracted to abusive men; ultimately the prohibitive graffiti is wiped out by her image grown large.

And yet, as I have indicated, Hershman interjects doubt about the statements she makes to the camera/to us and about how perfectly or imperfectly the past may be preserved in her memory. She 'toys with her own credibility ... she drops us in an abyss between belief and denial', as David James astutely observes.[4] This point bears elaboration. For one thing, some of the autobiographical facts Hershman reports sound improbable. In *Confessions of a Chameleon* she states that she started college when she was going into the third grade. In point of fact, this was the case. Hershman had been part of a pilot educational programme in which a handful of elementary school-age children were selected to attend college. But the tape offers only the bold, incredible statement, leaving the viewer to grapple with it, believing or disbelieving. Hershman also casts doubt on her own statements by revealing that she has lied to others in the past. For example, she states that when her husband left her she didn't tell anybody for years. 'I kept saying that he was on vacation', she explains.

The major way in which Hershman calls into question the same facts that she is also asserting is through reference to personality dissociation. When she was small, Hershman says, she would react to episodes of battering by creating other 'characters':

> I would create these characters, each of which had their own life. Very completely. And sometimes it was hard to tell who was who or what the real truth of the ... uh ... incidents were. And ... uh ... what was fantasy.
>
> (*Confessions of a Chameleon*)

In *First Person Plural* Hershman suggests further that memory can be a matter of perspective: 'I always told the truth ... for the person I was. But the personas kept fluctuating. They would see things from all sides ... And be afraid from all sides.' On the one hand, the suggestion that 'it was hard to tell who was who or what the real truth of the [past] incidents were' might make her sound like a woman completely out of touch with reality. But, on the other hand, this admission allows Hershman to illustrate what is also a central argument of contemporary psychological literature on trauma and memory: namely, that one possible effect of real trauma is the reconstruction of fantasy material.

Contemporary American psychological definitions of trauma borrow Freud's initial, economic conception of the phenomenon as being related to an exogenous matter, the result of an actual external shock to the psyche. Trauma, wrote Freud, is 'an experience which within a short period of time presents the mind with an increase of stimulus too powerful to be dealt with or worked off in the normal way'.[5] The *Diagnostic and Statistical Manual for Mental Disorders* includes a list of possible precipitating experiences, harrowing to contemplate:

> Traumatic events that are experienced directly include, but are not limited to, military combat, violent personal assault (sexual assault, physical attack, robbery, mugging), being kidnapped, being taken hostage, terrorist attack, torture, incarceration as a prisoner of war or in a concentration camp, natural or manmade disasters, severe automobile accidents, or being diagnosed with a life-threatening illness. For children, sexually traumatic events may include developmentally inappropriate sexual experiences without threatened or actual violence or injury.[6]

A person who is traumatized will re-experience such events as 'recurrent and intrusive distressing recollections of the event, including images, thoughts, or perceptions', that may take the form of memories, dreams, flashbacks, hallucinations, recurrences, and/or dissociation.[7] While such imaginary scenes assuredly take place in the mind, they are connected to traumatic events with a historical dimension, and they are known to be quite veridical in their particular form of psychic expression.[8]

Nevertheless, the relationship between memories and real events is significatory rather than indexical, and, according to both Freudian and recent findings, memories can be disturbed by or become abstracted from the very catastrophic events to which they refer. Feminist psychologists, notably Judith Herman in her groundbreaking work *Trauma and Recovery*, along with Elizabeth Waites and Lenore Terr,[9] have developed this idea under the pressure of having to respond to a special challenge: the need to explain cases where it does seem that women's memories of childhood sexual abuse have departed from literal truth, without *explaining away* the social reality in which such assaults continue to be perpetrated in epidemic proportions. Such theories of traumatic memory suggest that, whereas popular and legal discourses tend to reject reports of traumatic experiences that contain mistakes or amnesiac elements, these very mistakes and amnesiac elements are actually a feature of traumatic experience itself. Far from belying the truth of an event, an imagined scene that seems untrue may be inextricably, but obliquely, connected to and catalyzed by real events of the past. This is the inherent contradiction of traumatic memory – what I term the 'traumatic paradox': traumatic events can and do result in the very amnesias and mistakes in memory that are generally considered, outside the theory of traumatic memory, to undermine their claim to veracity.

The case of Eileen Franklin-Lipsker and her father, George Franklin, is illustrative. On November 30 1990 a jury found George Franklin guilty in the first degree of the murder of 8-year-old Susan Nason. According to the jury's finding and to Dr. Lenore Terr's account in *Unchained Memories*, Eileen had been present and had witnessed the crime, which began with Susan's rape. Terr, who was an expert witness for the prosecution, describes in her book how Franklin-Lipsker repressed the memory of her father's actions only to recall them twenty years later, the recall triggered by the tilt of her own daughter's head and her daughter's similarity in appearance to the murdered girl. Memory researcher and False Memory Syndrome Board Member Dr. Elizabeth Loftus argued forcefully against the possibility of repressed memory. Franklin-Lipsker could not have *lost* such a memory, she maintained, and therefore it could not have been a true memory at all. Loftus also used the content of the memories themselves to undermine their validity. Eileen Franklin-Lipsker's memories were in fact mistaken in several details. The murdered girl did not wear a sweater or jacket, she was not buried where she was killed, nor covered with a mattress from the murderer's van. This, for Loftus was additional evidence that the memories were false. Remarkably, however, the finding in favor of the prosecution suggests that this jury interpreted memory as being capable of encompassing repression, recovery, and variability.

But Franklin's conviction was subsequently overturned.[10] Although the reasons for this ultimate reversal were constitutional, defense attorneys refuted the validity of recovered memories in general and they asserted that Eileen Franklin-Lipsker's memory, in particular, is 'an unstable machine that generates wildly contradictory images'.[11] With a similar logic, Holocaust deniers seize upon inconsistencies within and between the testimonies of Holocaust survivors and Holocaust historians to argue that Jewish genocide never really took place. One may point, therefore, to a 'politics of denial' that pertains both to the recovered memory/false memory debates and to Holocaust revisionism. In both cases naysayers rely on a true/false binarism in which memory is regarded as an infallible entity or flawless record (to use a mechanical or digital metaphor), and apparent mistakes in memory are therefore construed as evidence of dissembling or of the absence of memory rather than of its inherent vicissitudes.

All of this suggests that there are political as well as theoretical reasons to take cognizance of contemporary psychological theories of memory, and also of the writing of those cultural/trauma studies scholars and historians who describe witness testimony as having a more intricate – that is, a sufficiently intricate – relationship to historical reality.[12] Inconsistencies in testimony do exist, affirm

Deborah Lipstadt and Pierre Vidal-Naquet, but it simply does not follow that the central events of the Holocaust may be denied on that basis. In fact, total consistency rather than differing subjective memories would be the more suggestive of confabulation.[13]

A large portion of *Testimony: Crises of Witnessing in Literature, Psychoanalysis, and History*, by Dori Laub and Shoshana Felman, is concerned precisely with exploring the *mechanisms* through which eyewitnesses to real historical events entertain memories and deliver testimonies that are divergent often to the point of incommensurability. The contention that a fallible memory may speak to a historical truth is made through Laub's description of an experience with oral testimony and the Holocaust. A woman in her late sixties testified to researchers from what is now the Fortunoff Video Archive for Holocaust Testimonies at Yale that she had seen four chimneys explode as a result of actions during the Auschwitz uprising. 'The flames shot into the sky,' she recounted, 'people were running. It was unbelievable'.[14] Apparently, it *was* unbelievable. At a subsequent gathering of historians watching the videotape of this testimony, the accuracy of the woman's account was questioned. In reality only one chimney and not all four had been destroyed. Thus, as Laub explains, the historians discredited the woman's account: '[s]ince the memory of the testifying woman turned out to be, in this way, fallible, one could not accept – nor give credence to – her whole account of the events'. But Laub disagreed:

> She was testifying not simply to empirical historical facts, but to the very secret of survival and to resistance to extermination. ... She saw four chimneys blowing up in Auschwitz: she saw, in other words, the unimaginable. ... And she came to testify to the unbelievability, precisely, of what she had eyewitnessed – this bursting open of the frame of Auschwitz. ... Because the testifier did not know the number of the chimneys that blew up ... the historians said that she knew nothing. I thought that she knew more, since she knew about the breakage of the frame, that her very testimony was now reenacting.[15]

Laub's unconventional point is that the register of reality testified to here is not just empirical but abstract. Mistaken memories also testify, here to the 'breakage of the frame'. For Laub, and also for Felman, as the latter illustrates through the example of the documentary film *Shoah*, a catastrophic event such as the Holocaust is an 'unprecedented, inconceivable historical advent of *an event without a witness* ... an accidenting of perception ... a *splitting of eyewitnessing*' that 'radically annihilates the recourse (the appeal) to visual corroboration'.[16]

These examples illustrate the value of reading ostensible memories over and against the historical events to which they refer. True events may produce veridical, abstract, or mistaken memories. Alternatively, the mind may produce an impression of memory, even an incredibly veridical one, where none is actually warranted.[17] We come to 'know more' about memory process itself and about the impact of traumatic events on human psychology, I submit, when we differentiate among these various cases instead of assuming that they are identical for all practical purposes just because memory is an internal psychic phenomenon. Ignorant of the three-chimney-large exaggeration, we have access only to the textual qualities of the woman's reportage. Cognizant of the difference between the true memory (one chimney did blow up) and the mistaken memory (the other three chimneys didn't blow up), we can read the exaggeration itself: hyperbole expresses that resistance at Auschwitz was resistance against all odds.[18]

In this memoro-historiography, evidence must be 'triangulated', as an anthropologist might say, drawn from multiple epistemological realms. For example, physical symptoms can 'bear witness to the actualities of traumatic events' of which a person has no active memory.[19] Lenore Terr writes that Eileen Franklin-Lipsker developed the habit of 'pulling out the hair on one side of her head, creating a big, bleeding bald spot near the crown', and that this hair-pulling predated Franklin-Lipsker's recovered memory of seeing her father crush the skull of her best friend with a rock.[20] Is it a coincidence that Eileen Franklin-Lipsker's 'bleeding bald spot' and Susan Nason's mortal wound were located in the same relative position on the head? Or is it evidence, as Terr argues, that while habitually pulling the hair from her head, Eileen Franklin-Lipsker forgot on a conscious level the rape and killing she had witnessed?

Traumatic memories are highly fraught 'imaginary scenes' that are constructed with regard to reality rather than reincarnating it; a traumatic memory both weaves itself around and substitutes for an event too terrible to acknowledge non-traumatically. The definition of Freudian fantasy provided by Jean Laplanche and J.-B. Pontalis is a useful point of reference. 'Phantasy (or Fantasy)', they state, is *both* 'a distorted derivative of the memory of actual fortuitous events' *and* 'an imaginary expression designed to conceal the reality of the instinctual dynamic'.[21] Fantasy refers to a non-veridical construction that is 'propped on' reality in the sense that a fantasy scenario (even if its existence precedes the introduction of a 'fortuitous event') nevertheless interacts with and is not independent of the memory of a given real event.[22] This suggests something of the complications that can ensue when the memory itself – that which the fantasy will embellish – is traumatic and therefore already recurrent, intrusive, and/or distressing.

Hershman's work fits into and helps define a 'trauma cinema'[23] of the 1980s and 1990s in which unconventional filmic strategies raise epistemological questions about history, memory, and representation. By 'trauma cinema' I mean a group of films, drawn from various genres, modes, and national cinemas, each of which deals with world-shattering events (DSM-IV's list of traumatic events is a veritable subject catalogue of trauma cinema) in a non-realist style that figures the traumatic past as meaningful, fragmentary, virtually unspeakable, and striated with fantasy constructions.

In 'Mirrors without Memories – Truth, History and the New Documentary', Linda Williams identifies a group of 'new' or 'postmodern' documentaries based on the premise that catastrophic histories are *difficult* but not *impossible* to know. Focusing on *The Thin Blue Line* (Errol Morris, 1987), *Shoah* (Claude Lanzmann, 1985), and with additional reference to *Who Killed Vincent Chin?* (Christine Choy and Renee Tajima, 1988), Williams reasons as follows:

> What interests me particularly is the way a special few of these docu-
> mentaries handle the problem of figuring traumatic historical truths
> inaccessible to representation by any simple or single 'mirror with a
> memory', and how this mirror nevertheless operates in complicated and
> indirect refractions.[24]

Williams' 'indirect refractions' are perhaps the filmic equivalent of Saul Friedlander's 'disruptive commentary'. In the idiom of documentary aesthetics these films and videos tend to adopt a historiographic language analogous to that which Friedlander advocates for historical writing about cataclysmic events. That is, either overtly or implicitly these documentaries 'disrupt the facile linear progression of the narration, introduce alternate interpretations, question any partial conclusion, [and] withstand the need for closure'.[25] Friedlander is certainly not proposing the absolute relativity of historical truth. Rather, he is suggesting that the words and experiences of any given interview subject or protagonist be qualified and correlated to other evidence and commentary, so that their partial misperceptions *and* partial truths might emerge in the place of a reductive true/false regime.[26]

Experimental feminist autobiographical documentaries tend to emphasize the jointly personal and political dimensions of filmic epistemologies, just as theories and practices of women's autobiographical writing have emphasized the social, psychic, and representational constructedness of the unified 'self' upon which traditional male autobiographical writing was conventionally based.[27] For example, in *The Ties That Bind*, handwritten titles on a black background spell out the phrase 'so you did know', thereby disrupting a woman's (the filmmaker's mother's!) oral testimony that as a young woman in Germany she didn't know about the genocidal mission of the concentration camps. Likewise, *History and Memory* (Rea Tajiri, 1991) locates the filmmaker's familial past in the context of cataclysmic public history, for the film's subject is the U.S. internment of Japanese-Americans during World War II, and specifically, the internment of the filmmaker's mother before her birth. 'I began searching for a history,' we hear Rea Tajiri say in voice-over, 'my own history. Because I had known all along that the stories I had heard were not true and parts had been left out.' Like *The Thin Blue Line*, this text is made up of snippets of film conveying impressions not fully registered and footage of different modalities on the continuum between docu-mentary and fiction. A mere thirty-two minutes in length, the film includes the following elements: rare archival footage of the Poston, Arizona relocation camp (shot with a contraband movie camera); scenes from period newsreels selling internment to the American public and from the few Hollywood films to treat anti-Japanese racism; archival and personally collected photographs; voice-over narration or written text displayed as crawls over black backgrounds or superimposed as commentary over images from various sources; scenes of present-day Poston and of the Salinas/Rodeo Grounds barracks where Tajiri's mother was initially held; and several re-enactments to which I'll return in a moment. The film exists, as the filmmaker explains in voice-over, as an answer to her mother's silence, forgetting, sadness, and shame, as an image given to her mother to stand where she had none. It calls attention to the 'unspeakable', here both spoken and shied away from by the elliptical style employed.

What strikes me, though, about both this film and the ones Williams discusses is their simultaneous *insistence* on an irrevocable truth and *refusal* of the realist mode: in *The Thin Blue Line* we see a number of different re-enactments of the crime, but the truth is that somebody – David Harris – killed the Dallas police officer; and, in Tajiri's film, the fact is that Japanese and Japanese-Americans were interned in camps during World War II. Both films complicate the reliability of historical memory and material documentation by way of other qualities of memory, including repression, silence, ellipsis, and elaboration. If, as the psychological literature on trauma argues, 'severe trauma explodes the cohesion of consciousness',[28] then these texts are traumatized. Their components exist in an 'altered and exaggerated state';[29] chronological linearity has been broken; the texts are fragmented, marked by repetition, and centered on events that they simultaneously call attention to and deflect attention from.

Physical artifacts may validate Tajiri's history. Consider the passage concerning a little wooden bird. Tajiri speaks of having discovered it as a child in her mother's jewelry box. Her mother said it was a gift from Tajiri's grandmother. We see the bird floating in a black background and Tajiri provides us with the story of its origin.[30] While doing research at the National Archives in Washington, she narrates, she came across an archival photograph that included her grandmother seated at a long table with other Japanese men and women. Turning the picture over, Tajiri read, 'Bird carving class. Poston, Arizona'. Thus autobiography, in the form of her own memory of a coveted trinket, is connected to collective history. This is made visually apparent in a video special effect in which the grandmother's image, isolated at first against a blank background, is 'joined' by the images of her fellow bird-carving classmates as the rest of the whole photograph is faded in. Thus a wooden bird leaves a trail of historical shavings which may be followed in reverse, back to its place of origin; objects testify to the reality of the events from which they were carved out.

But consider, in addition, a recurring image from the film: a woman catching water in a canteen and bathing her face with the cooling liquid. We see the woman initially from behind (in a high angle shot reminiscent of the kind of oblique approach found in dream images) and later from the front in close-up. In each of the many occurrences the image is slowed and accompanied by the disembodied sound of running water, adding to the dreamlike effect. As Tajiri recounts,

> I don't know where this came from, but I just had this fragment, this picture that's always been in my mind. My mother, she's standing at the faucet and it's really hot outside. And she's filling this canteen and the water's really cold and it feels really good. And outside the sun's just so hot, it's just beating down.

But, as we learn, this is not an image she actually could have seen, since her mother was released from the camp before Tajiri's birth. It may have come from an overheard conversation or perhaps from a dream; in this sense it is false. And yet, it too testifies to an historical truth: an actual mother who was interned, and it was hot, and the Japanese people in the camps really did bring water to an arid land. 'For years I've been living with this picture without the story,' says Tajiri about the fragment from her mother's past, 'but now I found I could connect the picture to the story and could make this image for her'.

The filmmaker-daughter's impression that her mother lacks and/or needs an image of the past is perhaps a response to the gaps in her mother's memory of the events of her forced relocation and internment. 'I don't remember how we … I don't remember how we got there because we had to sell our car and everything and I'm not … All I know is just a brief train ride as we got to Poston, you know, and the blinds were down and all that. But that's all I remember', explains Tajiri's mother in voice-over accompanied by a blurred view of desert scenery taken from the window of a moving vehicle. But as Tajiri's written commentary notes in a slightly earlier passage about her mother's faulty memory:

She tells
the story of
what she does
not remember
But remembers
one thing:
why she
forgot to
remember

'I don't remember any of this stuff', says the mother in simultaneous voice-over. 'All I remember is if you … ah … when I saw this woman who had lost her mind you know … a beautiful woman … beautiful young girl … how did this happen? You can even go out of your mind, so you just put those things out of your mind, you know'. As Tajiri indicates, what her mother testifies to is *why* she has forgotten: because 'you can even go out of your mind'; or because your memories might be denied, as in the case of an acquaintance who apparently refused to believe the truth of Tajiri's mother's experience; or, because your personal memories might be cast in a different light by others, as in the War Department films designed to sell relocation to Americans as a public necessity and harmless defensive measure. Thus *History and Memory*, like *Shoah* in Felman's description, 'is a film about silence: the paradoxical articulation of a *loss of voice* – and of remembrance, but for the self-negating, contradictory, conflictual remembrance of – precisely – an amnesia'.[31] The image of the woman with the canteen testifies to an 'inconceivable historical advent', the memory of which is, very precisely, to be avoided.

Of course the woman is not really Tajiri's mother at all, but a younger woman playing her as she was many years before at camp. In this sense too the image is that of an absence, or of the absence of memory. In fact, although she speaks on the film's audio track, on the image track Tajiri's mother exists only partially, here and there, as a small figure in a old family photograph, or just off-screen, her voice coming from the back seat of the car as she is conducted past the Salinas Rodeo Grounds where she was initially held for relocation.

But although we don't see her, in a passage reminiscent of the colour footage in Alain Resnais' *Night and Fog* (1955), we do see the places she inhabited: the Rodeo Grounds; Parker Station, where the train deposited her at camp; a floor-plan of the barracks where she was housed; the muted desertscape of the present. But this is no realist recreation of what the mother couldn't see because 'the blinds were down'. Instead the passage is constructed to reveal the centrality of forgetting and interpretation in the historical process. The mother's line, 'All I know is just a brief train ride as we got to Poston, you know, and the blinds were down and all that … ', is repeated a second time over footage of a train from the 1954 Hollywood feature *Bad Day at Black Rock*, a film about a western town's cover-up of the murder of a Japanese-American who had made money by bringing water to the land. A graphic reads 'On July 5, 1942 my mother went on a train to Poston. She didn't see the view. On April 12, 1988 I went to Poston in a rental car and filmed the view for her'. We hear an audio description by Tajiri's mother of how they were prevented from looking out the train windows during relocation. This is followed by a passage from the 1990 Alan Parker film *Come See the Paradise* about Japanese-American internment. 'Why are the blinds down?' a woman queries as she boards the train for relocation. 'So we won't know where we're going', answers her companion. In this complicated passage, *History and Memory* is concerned to constitute a forgotten or denied history, but to constitute it not through realist assertions of past events, but through a fragmented structure that acknowledges as well the gaps and resistances to history and memory. 'I could identify with the search for an ever absent image,' Tajiri says, 'and the desire to *create* an image where there are so few'. And speaking of identification, Rea Tajiri herself is the young woman who plays her mother in the re-enacted scene with the canteen.

Thus, while *History and Memory* asserts that the mother's memories are historically valid, and true in some of their details (she remembers, for example, that there was no canteen at the Salinas Rodeo Grounds where she was first held and that her camp address in Poston was Block 213, Unit 11a), it simultaneously writes into history what could not be grasped at the time, not even by the very participants of the events as they unfolded.

This aspect of the film gives it the status of what Cathy Caruth would call a 'history of trauma': a history of events that are forgotten in their very experiencing:

> The historical power of the trauma is not just that the experience is repeated after its forgetting, but that it is only in and through its inherent forgetting that it is first experienced at all. ... For history to be the history of trauma means that it is referential precisely to the extent that it is not fully perceived as it occurs.[32]

The pattern of the film, then, in response to a traumatic past, is to constitute itself as a work of double 'delayed historical understanding'[33] through the acknowledgment of the mother's forgetting as well as through the use of recurring and reconstructed images from the past and thoughts about it. In this respect the film is perhaps more aligned with later Freudian notions of trauma – and with Cathy Caruth's particular reading of Freud – than with early Freudian or contemporary psychological formulations. For, as Freud's ideas about trauma developed, internal excitations came to be emphasized over external shock:

> Although Freud calls the first scene [the scene of seduction] traumatic, it is plain that ... this quality is only ascribed to it after the fact ... it is only *as a memory* that the first scene becomes pathogenic by deferred action, in so far as it sparks off an influx of internal excitation.[34]

*History and Memory* prioritizes not so much the internment itself, but the mother's distracted experience and imperfect memory of it. Also foregrounded is the daughter's non-realist attempt to 'create an image'. One might say that the daughter's memory of her mother's partially conveyed story 'sparks off' the deferred excitement of the daughter's traumatic text. Rea Tajiri fabricates a memory of her mother at camp; this memory is expressed both internally ('this picture that's always been in my mind') and on film.

If Lynn Hershman's *First Person Plural* seems at first glance a world apart from the historical project of *History and Memory* to rethink Japanese-American internment, this impression is refuted by the tape itself. *First Person Plural* is deeply concerned with the realm of the 'plural' – with the social psychology as well as the personal psychology of abuse. And, like *History and Memory* and *The Thin Blue Line*, Hershman's piece is concerned with history as much as it is concerned with memory, fantasy, and the fluid boundaries among all three.

One of the connective metaphors for this reading of the personal through the social and the mythic realm invoked by Hershman is that of approaching footsteps, first heard in the pre-title sequence. 'The story of Dracula has always had a special meaning for me', Hershman says in direct address to the camera. As she continues to speak ('It's always been kinda close to my heart ... the story of a diabolical craving in which you give up your vital fluids through seduction') the image shifts to that of Nina Harker writhing in her bed in F.W. Murnau's *Nosferatu*. We then begin to hear the sound effect of footsteps and Hershman's account, 'when I was small I would feel that he was coming down the hall into my room ... I mean often I would hear the footsteps', while visually we are given the unforgettable image of Nosferatu's silent approach up the stairs to Nina's room. Hershman finishes with Murnau's Nina superimposed over live-action highly diffused footage of Hershman's Dracula, 'and I would be both excited and repelled. He's always been there and I've always felt his presence'.

But whose footsteps do we hear? Those of the shadowed father of the dark nights of Hershman's childhood, or those of the vampire, Dracula? The point of the sequence, I believe, is that the two are intimately connected; that the popularity and longevity of the Dracula legend may be explained by its covert representation of the simultaneous excitations and repulsions inherent in sexual violation.

And the footsteps have still a further resonance. Just before a passage in which Hershman discusses how the abuses Hitler suffered at the hands of his family were similar to the atrocities inflicted in the concentration camps, she alludes to the footsteps of history. Of her Jewish grandparents who fled Austria and Germany during Hitler's rise, Hershman says, 'They heard the footsteps that were not quite on the ground'. This commentary is illustrated by the boxed and slowed image of Hitler's march from *Triumph of the Will* followed by a boxed and supered image of the sea rising in an upward wipe to blot out the background as Hershman discusses the number of European family members exterminated during World War II.

In *First Person Plural* the material cosmos and the realm of fantasy together explain incest and the silencing of testimony about incest as political acts of social domination. 'The blood won't clot', says Hershman, to evoke the generational march of a 'dominant force' which overtakes 'the weaker parts' in a connective history of political and domestic violation and abuse.

Part of what makes *First Person Plural* so effective is its liberation from the burden of proof. Childhood sexual abuse is accepted categorically as a crime all too real. The points Hershman is interested to investigate are the denial of the abuse and its underground residual effects on memory, psychology, and history.

By elaborating such associations and by bringing a subject generally regarded as individual (childhood sexual abuse) together with one generally regarded as public (war trauma), I have tried to echo the attention paid in these exemplary autobiographical documentaries to personal *and* collective memory, and to the imaginary components of history.[35] Certainly not all claims of memory are true. But, at the same time, not all false details signify pure invention. Fallible memory components can attest to as well as belie the existence of traumatic events.

The work of these autobiographical documentaries is to reintroduce individual memory to the sphere of rational history, acknowledging the different relationship of each term to the real historical event, but allowing them to be mutually corroborative. As Saul Friedlander advocates with regard to traumatic historiography, 'the so called "mythic memory" of the victims' is integrated, in these films, 'within the overall representation of this past without its becoming an "obstacle" to "rational historiography" '.[36]

If Michael Frisch is correct, and I think he is, the issue of historical understanding in contemporary society 'has come to seem a threat, even *the* threat to the authority of traditional political culture'.[37] The prevalent and heated debates over the legitimacy of repressed and recovered memories are an aspect of this. To the extent that they are remembered and believed, women's accusations of childhood incest and abuse have the ability to threaten male dominance and the subordination of women and children. And to the extent that they are remembered and believed, the memories of Holocaust and U.S. internment survivors help secure our toehold against the 'ethnic cleansing' model of fascism. But, since one response to trauma is non-veridical memory, the grievances of the traumatized cannot be redressed as long as fantasy is held to mean the absence of truth. This is the very formulation that the traumatic documentaries discussed here are structured to combat.

## Acknowledgements

I would like to thank Susannah Radstone and Katharine Hodgkin for their astute comments on this chapter, which is a substantially revised version of 'The Traumatic Paradox: Documentary Films, Historical Fictions, and Cataclysmic Past Events', *Signs* 22, no. 4 (Summer 1997).

## Notes

1 See David James, 'Lynn Hershman: The Subject of Autobiography', in *Resolutions: Contemporary Video Practices*, Michael Renov and Erika Suderburg, eds. (Minneapolis: Minnesota University Press, 1996), p. 124. James refers to the specificity of video as opposed to cinema when he writes, 'Only in the multiple, dispersed, yet interconnected practices that constitute television as a whole can an adequately extensive, flexible, and nuanced metaphor for the self now be found' (p. 124). But this is not to say that film excludes such investigations, and in fact James mentions avant-garde films of the late sixties and early seventies as a filmic mode where similar explorations historically have taken place. To his historicization of self-reflexivity, I would add the rich tradition of specifically feminist autobiographical documentary, as will be discussed in the body of the chapter.
2 Julia Lesage, 'Women's Fragmented Consciousness in Feminist Experimental Autobiographical Video', in *Feminism and Documentary*, Diane Waldman and Janet Walker, eds. (Minneapolis: Minnesota University Press, 1999). I am grateful to Julia Lesage not only for her insightful essay on Hershman's videotapes, but for sending me an entire, thick clippings file on Hershman's life and works.

3 This recycling of material relates to another of Hershman's practices mentioned by Julia Lesage and David James, which is to re-edit the tapes after they have been finished and shown (Lesage, p. 336, note 8; James, p. 126).

4 James, p. 126.

5 Jean Laplanche and J.-B. Pontalis, *The Language of Psycho-Analysis*, trans. Donald Nicholson-Smith (New York: W.W. Norton, 1973), p. 466. Quoted from Freud, *The Introductory Lectures on Psycho-Analysis* (1916–17) in *The Standard Edition of the Complete Psychological Works of Sigmund Freud*, ed. and trans. James Strachey (London: Hogarth Press and Institute of Psychoanalysis, 1953–1974) 16, p. 275.

6 *Diagnostic and Statistical Manual of Mental Disorders*, fourth edition (DSM-IV) (Washington, DC: American Psychiatric Association, 1994), p. 424. According to the DSM, as a summary of accepted psychological theories, one may also be traumatized by witnessing or even 'learning about' an event experienced by another.

7 These are the diagnostic criteria for Posttraumatic Stress Disorder as defined in DSM-IV, pp. 424–25.

8 Lenore Terr, 'True Memories of Childhood Trauma: Flaws, Absences, and Returns', in *The Recovered Memory/False Memory Debate*, Kathy Pezdek and William P. Banks, eds. (San Diego: Academic Press, 1996). See also Elizabeth Waites, *Trauma and Survival: Post-Traumatic and Dissociative Disorders in Women* (New York: W.W. Norton, 1993), p.28. Waites cites Lenore Terr, *Too Scared To Cry: Psychic Trauma in Childhood* (New York: HarperCollins, 1990) and C.M. Fair, *Memory and Central Nervous Organization* (New York: Paragon House, 1988).

9 Judith Herman, *Trauma and Recovery* (New York: Basic Books, 1992); Lenore Terr, M.D., *Unchained Memories: True Stories of Traumatic Memories, Lost and Found* (New York: Basic Books, 1994).

10 Tamar Lewin, *Los Angeles Times*, April 5, 1995, p. A18.

11 Quoted by Maura Dolan in 'Credibility Under Attack in Repressed Memory Case', *Los Angeles Times*, February 21, 1996, p. A3. Franklin-Lipsker is particularly vulnerable to this attack because she has made it public that she has recovered memories of two other murders perpetrated by her father, but the validity of these memories has not been borne out by investigators.

12 See for example, Paul Antze and Michael Lambek, eds. *Tense Past: Cultural Essays in Trauma and Memory* (New York: Routledge, 1996), Ruth Leys, *Trauma: A Genealogy* (Chicago: University of Chicago Press, 2000), and Kirby Farrell, *Post-traumatic Culture: Injury and Interpretation in the Nineties* (Baltimore: Johns Hopkins University Press, 1998).

13 Deborah Lipstadt, *Denying the Holocaust: The Growing Assault on Truth and Memory* (New York: Plume, 1993), especially pp. 58–61, and Pierre Vidal-Naquet, *Assassins of Memory: Essays on the Denial of the Holocaust*, trans. Jeffrey Mehlman (New York: Columbia UP, 1992).

14 Dori Laub, M.D., 'Bearing Witness, or The Vicissitudes of Listening', in Shoshana Felman and Dori Laub, M.D., *Testimony: Crises of Witnessing in Literature, Psychoanalysis, and History* (New York: Routledge, 1992), p. 59.

15 Felman and Laub, *Testimony*, pp. 59–63.

16 Shoshana Felman, 'The Return of the Voice', in Felman and Laub, *Testimony*, p. 211.

17 John F. Kihlstrom, 'Exhumed Memory', in *Truth in Memory*, eds. Steven Jay Lynn and Kevin M. McConkey (New York: The Guilford Press, 1998), p. 18.

18 This is the distinction that is lost in text-based studies such as those of James Young and Lawrence Langer. Young's and Langer's works are undeniably brilliant in many respects, but limited, I believe, from an historiographic perspective. See James Young, *Writing and Rewriting the Holocaust: Narrative and the Consequences of Interpretation* (Bloomington: Indiana University Press, 1990); Lawrence L. Langer, *Holocaust Testimonies: The Ruins of Memory* (New Haven, NJ: Yale University Press, 1991).

19 Waites, *Trauma and Survival*, p. 36.

20  Terr, *Unchained Memories*, p. 35.

21  Laplanche and Pontalis, *The Language of Psychoanalysis*, p. 315. The relationship between fantasy and always-reconstructive memory is not thoroughly discussed by feminist psychologists of memory, who generally understand fantasy in the vernacular or as a term Freud developed to dismiss the importance of real events. But Elizabeth Waites (see n.8) does observe that 'Actual trauma does affect fantasy', thereby emphasizing the internally reconstructive response to, and nature of, exogenous trauma.

22  The concept of a fantasy being 'propped on' reality is derived from Jean Laplanche's discussion in *Life and Death in Psychoanalysis*, trans. and intro. Jeffrey Mehlman (Baltimore: Johns Hopkins University Press, 1976).

23  My current project is a book entitled *Trauma Cinema: Disremembering Incest and the Holocaust*.

24  Linda Williams, 'Mirrors Without Memories – Truth, History, and the New Documentary', *Film Quarterly* 46, no. 3 (Spring 1993), p. 12.

25  Saul Friedlander, 'Trauma, Transference and "Working Through" in Writing the History of the *Shoah*', *History and Memory* 4 (1992), p. 53.

26  Indeed, such theorizing by Williams and Friedlander, while carried out with reference to catastrophic subjects, is also applicable to the historiography of events along the whole continuum from more to less upsetting. Would that the vagaries of history and memory were more explicitly acknowledged in the discipline of history.

27  Laura Marcus, *Auto/biographical Discourses: Theory, Criticism, Practice* (Manchester and New York: Manchester University Press, 1995); Shari Benstock, ed., *The Private Self: Theory and Practice of Women's Autobiographical Writings* (Chapel Hill: The University of North Carolina Press, 1988); Sidonie Smith and Julia Watson, eds., *Women, Autobiography, Theory: A Reader* (Madison: University of Wisconsin Press, 1998); Estelle C. Jelinek, ed., *Women's Autobiography: Essays in Criticism* (Bloomington: Indiana University Press, 1980); Bella Brodzki and Celeste Schenck, eds., *Life/Lines: Theorizing Women's Autobiography* (Ithaca: Cornell University Press, 1988); Françoise Lionnet, *Autobiographical Voice: Race, Gender, Self-Portraiture* (Ithaca: Cornell University Press, 1989); Valerie Smith, *Self-Discovery and Authority in African-American Narratives* (Urbana: University of Illinois Press, 1979); Hertha Dawn Wong, *Sending My Heart Back Across the Years: Tradition and Innovation in Native American Autobiography* (New York: Oxford University Press, 1992).

28  Jonathan Shay, M.D., Ph.D, *Achilles in Vietnam: Combat Trauma and the Undoing of Character* (New York: Atheneum, 1994), p. 188.

29  Herman, *Trauma and Recovery*, p. 34.

30  See the reference to the carved bird passage in *History and Memory* in Laura Marks, 'Transnational Objects: Commodities in Postcolonial Displacement', presented at Visible Evidence II, University of Southern California, 19 August 1994. On *History and Memory* see also Michael Renov, 'Warring Images: Stereotype and American Representations of the Japanese, 1941–1991', *The Japan/American Film Wars: WWII Propaganda and Its Cultural Contexts*, eds Abe Mark Nornes and Fukushima Yukio (Chur, Switzerland: Harwood Publishers, 1994); and Bill Nichols, *Blurred Boundaries: Questions of Meaning in Contemporary Culture* (Bloomington and Indianapolis: Indiana University Press, 1994).

31  Felman and Laub, *Testimony*, p. 224.

32  Cathy Caruth, 'Unclaimed Experience: Trauma and the Possibility of History', *Yale French Studies*, no. 79 (1991), p. 187.

33  Friedlander, 'Trauma, Transference and "Working Through"', p. 43.

34  Laplanche and Pontalis, entry on 'Trauma (Psychical)', p. 467.

35  It is telling that Freud's investigation of war neurosis after World War I led him back to an economic model of trauma as an impressive external force. The importance of external factors seems to rise and fall according to the extent to which they are

believed to be extant. Having disavowed his original idea that the etiology of hysteria is childhood sexual abuse ('sexual seduction'), Freud concentrated on the internal excitations of trauma. In the face of public cataclysms in a time of war, he returned to the external model.

36 Friedlander, 'Trauma, Transference, and "Working Through" ', p. 53.

37 Michael Frisch, *A Shared Authority: Essays on the Craft and Meaning of Oral History* (Albany, New York: SUNY Press, 1990), p. xxii.

# 6

# MEMORIES OF VIOLENCE IN INTERVIEWS WITH BASQUE NATIONALIST WOMEN

*Carrie Hamilton*

Recent discussions about the uses of oral sources have added new dimensions to old debates over what constitutes historical truth. Early practitioners of oral history tended to use their sources as historians have traditionally used written documents, as factual evidence about specific historical events. Over the past two decades, however, oral historians have suggested that interviews can tell us about the construction of social subjectivity, myth and memory.[1] Oral history, in the words of Alessandro Portelli, 'may ... be viewed as an event in itself'.[2]

This chapter draws on two interviews with women active in radical Basque nationalist politics in the 1970s and 1980s.[3] The sections of the interviews examined here are centrally concerned with memories of 'anti-terrorist' violence, and in particular with the deaths of the informants' partners, male members of the armed organization ETA, at the hands of 'anti-terrorist' squads. The debate over historical truth, which is always a highly charged one, takes on a special emotional currency when it involves the history and memories of war and violence. In this chapter, then, these interviews become the focus not of an attempt to discover more about historical events, but of an exploration into their complex relation to identity, memory and history.

Each informant's memories of this violence form part of her unique life story. Yet they also have their place in the wider collective memories of the Basque conflict. By collective memories I mean those memories handed down through generations, via private and public story-telling,[4] which form an integral part of a community's narrative about its identity and its history. I define the community in question here – the radical Basque nationalist community – as comprised of those people who support ETA and its aim of Basque independence. Since there is ongoing debate within this community over ETA's armed actions, I understand support for ETA not strictly as support for its strategy, but more broadly as sympathy for its aims, as well as political and personal identification with its members.[5] The collective memory of this radical nationalist community has been selected and shaped historically in opposition to what is considered an 'enemy memory', a collective 'Spanish' memory seen as distorting the historical 'truth' about ETA and its supporters. This has not been a one-sided process;

among the most vivid of contemporary Spanish collective memories are those of ETA's terrorist actions – meticulously summarized in the Spanish press after each new attack.

This chapter, then, is concerned with various sets of memories, personal and collective. It aims to show how certain personal memories highlight, when read against collective memories, the selections and silences of the latter. In the first place, the interviews point to the gendered nature of the collective memories of ETA as constructed within the radical nationalist community. These informants' memories are gendered not just because they are women's memories (men's memories are, of course, also gendered), but because they emerge in the interviews in the context of discussions about gender roles in the radical nationalist community. The memories should therefore be read in relation to these historical gender roles, while also being read against collective memories (and historical studies) which tend to disregard women's experiences of political activism and violence.

Second, through their repetitions and silences, the individual interviews suggest some new ways of interpreting the collective amnesia around certain forms of violence in Spain's recent past. In the interview excerpts we find the frequent repetition of expressions of 'sameness' in reference to 'anti-terrorist' violence across time, a 'sameness' which defies historical change. This claim of unchanging violence against ETA and its supporters from the time of Franco to the present is common to radical nationalist collective memory as well. Importantly, however, in these interviews – and in others conducted with female ETA supporters – the motif of sameness appears precisely in those passages where the informant is remembering her role in protecting her own family/community against outside attack. 'Sameness', then, is another strategy in the memories, another form of 'wrong' memory, that resists the exclusion of women's memories from collective memories of ETA.

Furthermore, the theme of 'sameness' in the interviews has important parallels with collective memories of Spain's recent past. In the final part of this chapter I argue that in collective memories of the Basque conflict, across national and political lines, political violence often appears 'outside history', something whose origins are obscure, and which threatens to stretch endlessly into the future. Looking at memories of 'sameness' in relation to different forms of political violence helps to locate memories of ETA violence within a context of the wider process of remembering – and forgetting – other forms of political violence in Spain over the past forty years. An analysis of the memories of these female ETA supporters therefore opens the way for a reassessment of competing collective memories of the Basque conflict. The women's interviews, through their own 'wrong' memories, point to the gendered gaps common to the collective memories, and also to their shared strategies of remembering certain violences while forgetting others.

## Personal memories of political violence

Although personal memories of the Basque conflict cannot be reduced to micro versions of collective memories, they do contain similar elements. Both tend to rely on a stark division between 'us' and 'them', for example, and typically privilege moments of struggle and sacrifice. But if the main themes of both personal and collective memories are similar, their expression may differ. Collective memories, as expressed for instance in political speeches or popular literature on the history of ETA, are likely to be constituted as a series of coherent and chronological events.[6] Conversely, the personal memories of anti-terrorist violence expressed in these interviews with female ETA supporters rarely respect chronological order, and are often characterized by rupture and pause, one set of memories sometimes collapsing into another.[7] This last – an effect known as 'telescoping' – is a common feature of oral history interviews (and of memory in general), with informants confusing one incident in the past with another. While potentially a source of frustration for the historian seeking factual and chronological accuracy, telescoping arguably gives access to the emotional and political associations of an interviewee's memories.

In his interviewing of Italian Communists from the resistance and post-war periods, Portelli has analyzed different forms of what he calls the ' "imaginary", "wrong", "hypothetical" motif' in interviews[8] – memories which are factually inaccurate, but which tell their own history of political fantasies and frustrations. In an article entitled 'Uchronic dreams', Portelli argues that 'these stories are not about how history went, but about how it could have gone: their realm is not reality, but possibility'.[9] In particular, he notes that precisely because of their divergence from historical facts, the memories often offer astute political analysis by revealing the disappointments and disillusionments of workers and rank-and-file activists with the Party leadership.

Keeping in mind these insights, I will turn now to one woman's story of 'anti-terrorist' action against ETA in the French Basque country from the mid 1970s to mid 1980s. This woman's memories collapse separate incidents of death and violence into one another, creating an impression that all repression is identical and never-ending (i.e. that it is somehow outside history). Using Portelli's notion of the 'wrong' motif in interviews, I will first look at these memories in relation to gender discourses in the collective memory of radical nationalism. Second, I will suggest that this woman's memories of political activism and violence, while clearly individual, are nonetheless related to the complex set of 'collective memories' of the Basque conflict in the post-Franco period.

The informant discussed here joined ETA in the late 1960s. After a brief period in prison she went into exile in the French Basque country, where a community of ETA members lived with their families. There she met and married a prominent ETA leader who was subsequently killed by the 'GAL', a far-right 'anti-terrorist' paramilitary force with connections to Spain's Socialist administration.[10] Memories of 'anti-terrorist' violence emerge in two separate moments in the interview, in both cases as part of a wider discussion of the role of female partners of male ETA members, and the support provided by the exile community.

*So activism, his activism, or the activism of someone who was very involved, had a huge influence on family life.*[11]

Yes, of course, yes, yes, yes. Well, just look how much it influenced. One time, well, he said to me, 'Well, be careful they don't pick you up, to ask you for, or the children' [mumbled words]. Because the situation in Iparralde (the French Basque country) was also very dangerous, and it was really, really, really awful, wasn't it. So, maybe you were walking in the street one day and they picked you up or maybe that happened, or things like that. And, 'So well be wide awake, because here, the children, you and the children, you can't be replaced. I mean, be careful.' Because it was very hard.

*And in fact, you did have an attack, didn't you? By the BVE or …*

Yes, yes, I don't know if it was the Batallón Vasco Español[12] or – Yes. I mean, it's the same. It's the same as the GAL, we know they're the same. And, and, well, I mean it was, a responsibility that made you – That for us was also vital, that, I mean, that had repercussions for us. Yes, and all of us, all of us, any activist. Any activist, and any family. Because in fact there have been, well many children who have gone to their father's car, and just at the last minute have been separated, and well, a rifle over here, a rifle over there. I mean, there have been many cases, yes [mumbled words]. Etxabe's wife was also killed, wasn't she. I mean.

*Yes, in a very similar situation, wasn't it.*

Yes, the same, the same. The poor woman went to the car, she went to take the car out to leave first, to go home, and well, it exploded. Yes, yes …

(#1; b. 1946)[13]

It is unclear in these last sentences what the informant means by 'the same' (*igual, igual*). Which two paramilitary attacks are being compared? This confusion arises from an inconsistency in the material details of the attack described: what the informant remembered as an explosion involving one person ('Etxabe's wife') is recorded in written documents as a rifle attack in July 1978 which killed Agurtzane Arregi and seriously wounded her husband, Juan Etxabe.[14] This attack was indeed very similar to the one directed against the informant, her husband and their children a few years earlier, leaving the informant with serious injuries. However, the reference to a car explosion suggests another event: the car bomb which killed the informant's husband in the mid 1980s.[15] In the above excerpt, then, three separate events (two rifle attacks and one car bomb) appear to be compressed or 'telescoped' into one memory, so that memories of violence against the informant and her family are recounted from a distance, in the third person.

These memories are not 'false' – they do not invent events that never occurred. Rather, they get the details wrong, confusing one event with another.

These telescoped memories are indicative neither of 'poor memory' nor of deliberate distortion of the past. For while the material facts of the memory may be wrong, they convey an important emotional truth. By collapsing the memories of different events into one, the informant communicates not only the pain of remembering those deaths closest to her, but also a sense of years lived at an accelerated pace, events speeding by too quickly to be remembered separately. The emotional immediacy of these particular memories is characteristic of this interview as a whole. The events recounted at moments seem reminiscent of a dream. But this is not one of Portelli's 'uchronic dreams', which he likens to daydreams or fantasies of an alternative past and future.[16] This informant's memories seem more like night dreams as Freud described them: a series of memory fragments whose order rarely makes 'sense', but which always has something to say about the dreamer's psychological history.

The emotional immediacy and dreamlike-quality of memories of violence appear in another excerpt from the same interview, where we find a second example of 'telescoped memory':

> what I want to make clear is for instance, at the level of, like you said, between the refugees, and between the women and that, I think there's been a level of community and friendship well, wonderful. And well, great, great. A pleasure, a pleasure. Wonderful, wonderful. And in fact, well, sometimes I've called her and that, but that one [informant #2], well her husband is in prison. It's been I don't know, well it would be ten, nine years. Around that I think. And she's with two girls, she's been left with two tiny little girls. And she has also had trouble with the police and that. They're very kind people, totally – So, well.
> *This is a woman you knew in –*
> In Iparralde (the French Basque country).
> *Iparralde. And her husband is still in –*
> Yes, he is, he is, he is. They say maybe they'll bring the husband back now.[17] So she was left with two little girls, and they didn't let her go and visit her husband either. Well. A disaster. In terms of her family, a disaster. But later, in terms of, her circumstances, the poor thing, a disaster. But on the other hand, well. But she has friends with, well, wonderful. I mean it's, and the same when it happened to me. Well she got involved and great, great. I mean a, lots of help, great, great.
> (#1; b. 1946)

Here the informant has collapsed a recent memory of the imprisonment of the current husband of her friend (informant #2) with an earlier memory of the same woman, whose first husband had been killed in another 'anti-terrorist' attack in the mid 1980s.[18] Thus the two 'tiny little girls' remembered by the informant were, by the time of the interview, teenagers, with a younger sister whose father was in prison. Again, these memories are not so much 'wrong' as collapsed; the details are in disarray, but the key elements are stressed and repeated, giving the impression that the point of the story is not to be found in the factual details, but in the emotional atmosphere around them, i.e. the strong sense of community and friendship among women in exile ('wonderful', 'great', 'a pleasure') in the face of perpetual threat to their families ('a disaster').

It is interesting to compare the above memories with those of the friend in question, informant #2, of the same events. In this interview, memories of the first husband's death came in response to questions about how he and the informant had managed their relationship in the face of the constant danger of his death:

> *Well, in the end the moment arrived. ... Was it like you, was it something you had expected but was nonetheless unexpected? Or, or, how did you experience it?*
>
> I, the thing is it's very difficult to say. I think, in spite, that it's a good thing I knew. Or that I had considered it a few times. [Interruption as informant speaks to her young daughter.] I don't know how to tell you. Let's see. It was very hard. Even though, though you've, thought about it and all that. But good thing, because everything else I think, I think I would've, that my life would've been. I wouldn't have been able to, to live my life and I wouldn't have gone on and, and, that my children were well and that, well to take in this death and all that. I think I would live – But it's very hard. I don't know, I mean, I'm trying to tell you that many times I thought about it. Because well, they killed him when he was coming home with me. One night. I thought, I wished I had died there too. I thought about it many times. It was much easier. You don't have to face anything. Understand? But more than anything, I remember [interruption as informant calls out to her older daughter] that at the time [mumbled words] someone said to me [younger daughter again], 'The most important isn't, isn't the one who's left behind. It's that that person can't live anymore.' And, and later, with time, I've realized that the great pain is that he's gone. At the time you suffer but later you realize that the most serious is that that person is no longer there. And with time you say, it's true that's something serious. Because everything else goes on, but that person is no longer there.
>
> (#2, b. 1958)

In this case the informant's memories of witnessing her husband's death are not confused with others, nor are they stated as simple fact. Instead, the words are carefully chosen and spoken with hesitation; expressions such as 'I don't know' and 'I don't know how to tell you' are repeated throughout this passage and the longer discussion around it of the informant's relationship to her husband before his death, accenting the distance between informant and interviewer. In other words, even if the memory is more accurate in factual terms than those of informant #1, there is no suggestion that informant #2 is 'telling all'. The slow pace of the account and the lengthy pauses suggest that the silences may be deliberate, but also that the informant is conscious of the impossibility of adequately putting these memories into words, and is considering how best to express complex, painful issues.

Another striking feature of this interview, however, is that these painful memories do not obliterate pleasurable memories of the same period of time. In fact, the two sets of memories, painful and pleasurable, are inextricably connected in this interview, as evidenced here by the emphatic 'but' which interrupts the previously recounted memories of violence:

> But you're not envious of other people. I at least have never felt envious. Because I think I've had the great fortune to be very happy. That's the issue. You live by bits. In bits, in strokes. But it's much more intense, life, everything. I don't know. I consider myself privileged, because I've been very happy in life. I know a lot of people who live everyday with their partner, with their children and all that. I don't know, you're stripped of everything. But happiness is in yourself and in the other person. There aren't, aren't any materialisms, there's nothing. It's another way.
> *You live more intensely because you don't know if the next day or …*
> Not just because of that. Because you don't have anything either. Because, tomorrow, it worries you but it doesn't worry you. It's here, now, you know?
>
> (#2, b. 1958)

Two of the themes in the above excerpt are found in many of the interviews with female radical nationalists, including interview #1: struggle as life, and struggle as sacrifice. These themes are also common to radical nationalist discourse generally, and indeed can be found in men's personal memories of activism as well.[19] But they have a specific, gendered meaning in these women's interviews. If men's memories of military activity are often characterized by nostalgia for male comradeship and bonding, memories which draw on myths of the masculine soldier as national hero,[20] women's memories of war and conflict can likewise be traced to popular representations of women in Basque culture. For example, in interviews with women who were directly involved in ETA, the rebel woman who rejects dichotomous gender roles appears as a recurring motif. For these female ETA militants participation in armed actions constituted, among other things, an expression of gender equality.[21] In contrast, for women such as the ones discussed in this chapter, who were involved primarily 'behind the lines', memories of their roles in the conflict tend to affirm sexual difference (even if in other areas of their lives – such as work and education – the informants assert their equality with men).

We can see this affirmation of difference, and its attendant gendered role division, in the first excerpt from interview #1 above, when the informant remembers a discussion with her husband in which she accepts the responsibility for protecting their children from the threat of violence against the family. At another point in the same interview the informant claims her husband knew that regardless of the demands of his activism – including possible arrest or death – she and the children would 'go on with their lives'. Likewise, informant #2 recalls that when she asked her husband what she would do after his death, he responded: 'Don't worry, you'll go on ahead. If not, I wouldn't be with you. If not, if I knew you were someone who was going to collapse, I wouldn't be with you' (#2, b. 1958).

Here the informant's husband seems to be evoking the image of the strong Basque mother as a figure into which his future widow can imagine herself after his death. This image – an example of what Luisa Passerini calls 'recurrent narrative forms' in oral life stories[22] – appears in many of the interviews, even in those with women who rejected motherhood for themselves.[23] The strong maternal figure who holds together the community, and is instrumental in passing the nationalist tradition from one generation to the next, is of course central to many nationalist discourses.[24] In the Basque case, the myth of the strong mother can be traced to popular mythology and folktales, as well as a long tradition of Marian worship.[25] This 'maternal myth' plays a contradictory role in the interviews, as in Basque popular culture generally. On one hand, by portraying women as historical heads of the Basque household, it masks the significant evidence of men's power and prestige in both the private and public spheres;[26] but on the other hand, it provides a powerful point of identification, both personal and political, for many women.

Thus the memories of the conflict expressed in the interviews above resonate not only with a broader discourse in which state violence against ETA is at the centre of radical nationalist identity, but also with a sense of women's unique historical roles as the guardians of the community in the face of this violence. Such memories connect these informants to a wider 'imagined community'[27] of women – past, present and future. Women's nostalgia for their days of activism, which stresses female friendship and solidarity, is therefore an alternative memory to that of the male warrior.

In theory, women's traditional roles as mothers are most highly valued in the radical nationalist community, and in Basque society as a whole.[28] In practice, however, several of the women interviewed noted that women's roles were often eclipsed by the figure of the male militant. Informant #2, for instance, recalls that following the death of her husband:

> everyone said to me, 'Hey, well one day your daughters will be really proud of their father.' And I said to them, 'But I think they also have to be proud of their mother.' That's a mistake, to think proud of their father. Yes. And their mother? I don't know [mumbled words]. I think maybe at one time yes, women, but in reality the woman has supported the home economically, I think emotionally and all that she's supported him, as well as the children, that. She was the one who brought balance,

the one who managed the situation, I mean every day, in some way. I
don't know. I think without women there wouldn't have been this kind
of movement, things wouldn't have been managed in, such a way ... I
remember a poem he wrote, I remember that, I think it says, 'You help
me hold up the gun. But you don't touch any guns.' But you help that
person at a certain point. Understand? I don't know. I don't think it's ...
I don't know. And for me one thing is just as, well, just as important as
the other. And one thing is just as good as the other.

(#2, b. 1958)

This excerpt is exceptional among the interviews, in that it contains one of
the few direct references to the arms used by an individual ETA militant. In most
of the interviews, as in radical nationalist discourse generally, ETA's actions are
referred to collectively as 'the armed struggle' or 'political violence', while little
explicit mention is made of the practical roles of individual militants in carrying
out armed actions (i.e. in killing and/or injuring people). In the above memory
the gun symbolizes both the masculinity of military action, and the separate but
complementary roles of husband and wife in war. The informant upholds this
principle of sexual difference, validating the gendered division of roles, and the
nationalist tradition of celebrating women as mothers. At the same time,
however, she challenges what she perceives as a double standard behind the ideal
of the separate roles model, manifested in the public honouring of men's armed
activism in a way which obscures women's roles in supporting the nationalist
movement both materially and emotionally. Her identification with a wider
community of women – historically and in the present – contests, even as it
conforms to, the wider discourse of women's position in radical nationalism.

Read in this way, these women's memories of 'anti-terrorism' are doubly resistant. They are counter-memories formed by and in resistance to different
collective memories – both a dominant Spanish memory of ETA members and
supporters as 'terrorists', and a more local radical nationalist memory of the
male militant as the hero of the movement. But even as they challenge the
restrictions of these dominant collective memories, they draw on another, that of
the Basque matriarch, affirming their identities as active protectors and
guardians of their own families and the wider radical nationalist community, as
well as Basque cultural memory itself.

## Political violence in memory and history

The remainder of this chapter will be concerned with another motif in the first
interview above: the repetition of the expression 'the same' (alternately in
Spanish, *igual* and *Lo mismo/los mismos*) in reference to 'anti-terrorist' violence.
This theme of violence as 'never-ending', committed incessantly by 'the same'
people over the years, is common to many of the interviews. Sometimes it can be
detected in similarly direct language (political 'repression', as well as the Spanish

'ruling class', are described as 'never changing', 'always the same'); at other times the 'same' motif appears in the form of anecdotes which compare the practice of police violence or the situation of political prisoners in the past with the present situation, creating the impression that 'repression' is suffered endlessly by the same people ('us') at the hands of the same enemy ('them').

The claim that violence against ETA and its supporters is always 'the same' is doubly striking: first, in its repetition within and across the interviews; second, in its stark contrast to the myriad memories of social, political and personal change in the same interviews. For instance, when asked about what differences she had noticed in the Basque country between her exile in 1971 and her return in 1985, informant #1 responds:

> A lot, a lot. I mean, in the place, the place, I mean in, in *el pueblo*.[29] *El pueblo* changed a lot, a lot, a lot, a lot.
> *When you say, 'el pueblo', which? Bilbao, the people? or –*
> Yes. Well, yes. The rank and file, well that. Well. I mean the work and those things, and later, I also saw – that the thing about unemployment, that had also had an effect, had had a lot of influence. There wasn't any. And then later there was. But, at the level of, of *el pueblo* and that, there were also changes. But more than anything I discovered that I had changed. I had changed an awful lot. I, and my age. I mean. And my situation. I had left, well, at 22, 23, about 23 I think I was, and I came back older, with a bad arm, with – [change of tape] I mean, because you leave at a certain point and, and later, I mean, you come back to this society, but it's very different. And you're very different.
>
> (#1; b. 1946)

This sense of enormous personal change is again found in most of the interviews, as is a recognition of the major social, economic and political developments in the Basque country, in Spain, and internationally from the 1960s onwards. In particular, many of the interviews emphasize – and celebrate – the changes in women's lives in all areas (politics, work, sexuality) from the Franco period when they first became politically active, to the present day.

This contrast in the interviews between memories of wider change, on one hand, and the relentless, unchanging violence of the Spanish state, on the other, gives the impression that such violence is stuck in a separate, static time zone, outside history itself. Another excerpt from interview #1 suggests memories of 'repression' stretching backwards in time prior to personal memory:

> *Optimistic. You're optimistic.*
> Yes. Well, optimistic, I think it's going to be hard. I think it's going to be hard. On that side I don't know if I'm optimistic or not. I don't know, I think it's going to be really hard. But, it will go on being hard. But, if not, if we don't get self-determination, I don't think it will get

anywhere. It won't get anywhere. Go on, well, go on for centuries. Because I don't think this comes from '36,[30] or anything, it comes *much* before. I mean, the repression and all that, it comes much before. I think it's many centuries old, and many.

(#1; b. 1946)

In politically pragmatic terms, of course, this popular memory of perpetual repression serves to justify ETA's ongoing violence, which has taken hundreds of lives over the past three decades, while failing to attain the aim of independence for the Basque country. Likewise the promotion – by mainstream political parties and Spanish media – of a collective memory of ETA members as 'terrorists' with no legitimate political agenda has helped to justify the heavy-handed police tactics with which the state has responded to ETA violence, and the 'hardline against terrorism' stance adopted by successive administrations. Thus it is not only the supporters of ETA who have constructed a memory of endless, unchanging repression. Increasingly over the past twenty years, the violence of ETA itself has been represented by Spanish politicians and media as a force outside history. Such representations typically ignore the organization's roots in the Franco regime and its evolution through the 1970s, reducing its 'history' to a litany of horror.[31]

But memories – including collective memories – cannot be explained purely in terms of political pragmatism, or dismissed as deliberately 'false' by a historian seeking the 'truth'. Instead, the task of the historian of memory should be to analyze the relationship between history and memory. Memory, argues Raphael Samuel in *Theatres of Memory*:

> is dialectically related to historical thought, rather than being in some kind of negative other to it … memory is historically conditioned, changing in colour and shape according to the emergencies of the moment; that so far from being handed down in the timeless form of 'tradition' it is progressively altered from generation to generation. It bears the impress of experience, in however mediated a way. It is stamped with the ruling passions of its time. Like history, memory is inherently revisionist and never more chameleon than when it appears to stay the same.[32]

What are the historical changes obscured by the almost ritualistic claim of sameness in the interviews and in reports of ETA violence in the Spanish media? What 'emergencies of the moment' have conditioned such memories? In other words, how have these memories of unchanging repression been constructed historically?

There has been much discussion in recent years of the 'collective memory' of the civil war and Francoism in Spain, and in particular the tacit agreement between former Francoists and the democratic opposition to 'forget' the past in an endeavour to forge a new democracy following Franco's death in 1975.[33] In relation to this, other observers of contemporary Spain have noted that there is a general urge in the country to forsake public discussion of the past in favour of collective plans for the future. The 'celebrations' of 1992, which focused on Spain's place in the new Europe – the symbol of the country's 'arrival' as a modern, democratic state – at the expense of analyses of less palatable aspects of Spain's history, are indicative of this attitude.[34]

In many of these discussions, it is not very clear how memory is being measured. Most of these analyses rely on the policies or public statements of political regimes, parties and politicians, on media representations, or on other cultural forms such as architecture, department stores, museums, film and television.[35] While all of these offer fascinating examples of how historical memory is constructed and projected by certain individuals and groups, it is much more difficult to assess the ways in which the Spanish public have received, rejected or negotiated such public promotions and displays of memory, both individually and collectively. Such a project would require an analysis of the relationship between these public forms of memory, and the circulation of more local and personal memories, through the kinds of sources suggested by the Birmingham Popular Memory Group, including oral history.[36]

In the conclusion of this chapter, I will propose a framework for further analysis of the relationship between 'public' and 'popular' memories of ETA. The public memories here are taken from readings of the Spanish press over the past twenty years; the popular memories from the oral history interviews with female ETA supporters. The set of examples is small, and what follows should not be taken as definitive findings, but rather suggestions for further research.

There is important evidence that over the past twenty years mainstream Spanish political parties and media have selected a memory of the late Franco and transition years in which ETA figures as the single greatest threat to Spanish democracy. This prominent memory of ETA violence stands in stark contrast to the collective 'amnesia' with regard to the atrocities and violations committed under the four-decade dictatorship. This contrast takes on new meaning when we note the extent to which many of these 'forgotten' characteristics of the Franco regime – authoritarianism, indiscriminate violence, fascism – have been projected onto ETA.[37] From the late 1970s onwards, for instance, the terms 'fascist' and 'nazi' were often applied to ETA and its supporters. At the same time, ETA came increasingly to be held responsible for all the ills of the transition process, an analysis summarized in an editorial in the leading weekly news magazine *Cambio 16* in 1978:

> Without ETA there would be no military plotting, without ETA the forces of Public Order would not be on the verge of losing their nerves, without ETA [far-right leader] Blas Piñar would not have been able to get to Parliament, without ETA democracy would be firm.[38]

Two months earlier another editorial in the same magazine had called on all supporters of the new democracy actively 'to forget' any sense of solidarity they may have felt with ETA during the Franco years, because the organization had metamorphosed from an enemy of dictatorship into a force which threatened to drag the country back to its authoritarian past.[39] This projection of the traits of Francoism onto ETA reached a culmination during the public outcry over ETA's murder of the young town councillor Miguel Angel Blanco in July 1997, when an editorial in the national daily *El País* declared that 'ETA members are worse than Franco.'[40]

While this statement was made during what amounted to a national emergency, what is of interest is the frequency with which the Franco regime (as well as other fascist regimes, including the Third Reich) is used as the measure of ETA's barbarity. The labelling of any movement as 'fascist' is clearly highly effective in polemical terms; but in the case of Spain, and especially in the context of the lack of public discussion of the atrocities of Francoism, the comparison seems to say as much about the Spanish memory (or 'amnesia') of Franco as it does about the memory of ETA itself. This admittedly limited example of public memories, and the language used to describe ETA, suggest a connection to be traced between the obsessive repetition of memories of ETA violence and a highly selective, and sanitized, memory of Francoism. Collective Spanish memories of ETA violence and of state-sponsored 'anti-terrorism' are inversely proportionate to memories of violence in interviews with female ETA supporters. In both cases, the theme of 'sameness' may compensate for the silences of others' memories. But the repetitions of 'sameness', like the perpetuation of certain silences, also have the dual effect of de-historicizing (in the sense of denying or at least ignoring material context) the violences of the Franco regime *and* of ETA.

To return to Samuel's argument, '(l)ike history, memory is inherently revisionist and never more chameleon than when it appears to stay the same'. There is a need for further historical analysis of the relationship between the individual and collective memories of the Basque conflict – memories in which both ETA and anti-ETA violence are placed outside history, and silences surround other violences in Spain's recent past. This does not mean that these memories of the Basque conflict are 'wrong' memories that should be 'put right' by historians. Nor should it be claimed that because there is no single truth, one version of history is as good as the next. Rather, historical analysis of the Basque conflict should take popular memory seriously as part of the historical process itself. In other words, we should treat these memories as Portelli has suggested we treat oral history, as 'events in themselves'. For if individual and collective memories are often 'wrong' in that they conflate different violent events while they silence others, they nonetheless carry the weight of 'truth effects'. They are stories which, as Begoña Aretxaga has written, 'constitute an immediate, affective, charged political reality.'[41] As such, they are testimony to the power of popular memory in helping to sustain a conflict whose complex historical roots often seem to be forgotten.

## Acknowledgements

I would like to thank Kate Hodgkin, Susannah Radstone and Anny Brooksbank Jones for their helpful comments on earlier drafts of this chapter.

## Notes

1 Raphael Samuel and Paul Thompson, eds, *The Myths We Live By* (London: Routledge, 1990).
2 Alessandro Portelli, 'Uchronic Dreams: Working-class memory and possible worlds', in Samuel and Thompson, p. 143.
3 The interviews form part of a larger oral history project on women in radical Basque nationalism, including ETA, during the late Franco and transition periods. Carrie Hamilton, 'The Gender Politics of Radical Basque Nationalism, 1959–1982' (Ph.D. Thesis, University of London, 1999).
4 Not only written and oral stories, but also other forms of communication, such as photographs, graffiti, demonstrations, political speeches, media representations, etc.
5 This broader definition is necessary for an understanding of the complexity of the conflict, because it takes into account the intense emotional identification with ETA members – in particular prisoners – among a significant proportion of the Basque population, even those who publicly denounce ETA's actions, often at the expense of being labelled 'traitors'.
6 The best and biggest example of this is the multi-volume history of ETA published by the radical nationalist press Txalaparta, which contains a strictly chronological history of ETA, including a day-by-day record of ETA actions, arrests and deaths at the back of each volume. Editorial Txalaparta, *Euskadi ta Askatasuna/Euskal Herria y la Libertad* (Tafalla, 1993).
7 This is especially the case with those informants (such as informant #1 here) who had not held a prominent political position, and/or had rarely if ever been asked to express their memories or opinions in public. Those informants more versed at giving interviews did sometimes recount their personal memories of activism in a manner reminiscent of the coherent collective memory cited above.
8 Portelli, 'Uchronic Dreams', p. 143.
9 *Ibid.*, p. 150.
10 For a brief history of the GAL, and an analysis of its impact on the radical nationalist community, Begoña Aretxaga, 'Playing Terrorist: ghostly plots and the ghostly state' *Journal of Spanish Cultural Studies* 1, 1 (March 2000): 43–58.
11 Interviewer's comments and questions in italics.
12 The Batallón Vasco Español (BVE) was one of several far-right paramilitary organizations which attacked supporters of ETA in the 1970s. Most of these were made up of members or former members of the Spanish security forces.
13 Interview excerpts will be identified by number and date of birth, as here. Interviews were conducted in Castilian Spanish in 1996–97, and translations from the original transcripts are my own.
14 *Enbata* 516, 13 July 1978; Editorial Txalaparta, *Euskadi* vol. 5, 56: 137.
15 According to written sources, the original rifle attack on the informant and her family was claimed by the BVE, while the bomb that caused her husband's fatal injuries several years later was attributed to the GAL. Editorial Txalaparta, *Euskadi* vol. 6, 141.
16 Portelli, 'Uchronic dreams', pp. 145, 150.
17 The informant is referring to the fact that at the time of the interview (1996) the husband was in prison in France, and could be transferred to a Spanish prison.
18 Editorial Txalaparta, *Euskadi* vol. 6, 105.

19 See the interviews with former ETA members in Miren Alcedo, *Militar en ETA: historias de vida y muerte* (San Sebastián: Haranburu, 1996).

20 Of course, men's memories, like women's, also contain many other motifs – including regret and re-evaluation – in addition to nostalgia. See Alcedo, *ibid.*

21 See Carrie Hamilton, 'Changing Subjects: gendered identities in ETA and radical Basque nationalism' in Barry Jordan and Rikki Morgan-Tamosunas, eds, *Contemporary Spanish Cultural Studies* (London: Arnold, 2000), pp. 223–32.

22 Luisa Passerini, *Fascism in Popular Memory* (Cambridge: Cambridge University Press, 1987), p. 19.

23 For a lengthier discussion of this motif in the interviews, as well as in radical nationalist discourse and Basque popular culture generally, see Hamilton, 'Changing Subjects' and 'Re-membering the Basque Nationalist Family: daughters, fathers and the reproduction of the radical nationalist community', *Journal of Spanish Cultural Studies* 1, 2 (2000): 153–71.

24 Nira Yuval-Davis and Floya Anthias, eds, *Woman-Nation-State* (London: Methuen, 1989); Valentine Moghadam, ed., *Gender and National Identity* (London: Zed Books, 1994).

25 For a critique of the matriarchy theory, Teresa del Valle, *et al.*, *Mujer Vasca: Imagen y realidad* (Barcelona: Antropos, 1985).

26 Ibid., p. 141.

27 This community of women who may not have met in life, but who imagine themselves as part of the same collective, can be understood as a sub-set of Benedict Anderson's national 'imagined community'. Anderson, *Imagined Communities: Reflections on the Origins and Spread of Nationalism* (London: Verso, 1983).

28 Del Valle, *et al.*, *Mujer Vasca*, p. 53.

29 *El pueblo* can be translated as 'the village', 'the people' or 'the nation'. In this context, the informant seems to be using it in the sense of *el pueblo vasco* – 'the Basque people', the collective which radical nationalism as a movement claims to represent.

30 1936 – the start of the Spanish civil war, in which the Basque nationalists supported the Republican government against Franco's forces.

31 Today, press reports of ETA killings are invariably accompanied by a chronological list (often including photographs) of the organization's past actions. See for instance *El Pais*, *El Mundo*, *ABC*, 22 September 2000.

32 Raphael Samuel, *Theatres of Memory*, vol. 1, *Past and Present in Contemporary Culture* (London: Verso, 1994), p. x.

33 Elías Díaz, 'The Left and the Legacy of Francoism: political culture in opposition and transition', in Helen Graham and Jo Labanyi, eds, *Spanish Cultural Studies* (Oxford: Oxford University Press), p. 288; Paloma Aguilar Fernández, *Memoria y olvido de la Guerra Civil española* (Madrid: Alianza Editorial 1996).

34 Helen Graham and Antonio Sánchez, 'The Politics of 1992' in Graham and Labanyi, *op. cit*, pp. 406–18l; Michael Richards, 'Collective memory, the nation state and post-Franco society' in Jordan and Morgan-Tamasunas, *op. cit.*, pp. 38–47; Tony Morgan '1992: Memories and Modernities' in Jordan and Morgan-Tamasunas, *op. cit.*, 58–67.

35 The various articles on the themes of memory, nostalgia and heritage in Jordan and Morgan-Tamasunas, *op. cit.* contain examples of all of these cultural forms.

36 Popular Memory Group, 'Popular memory: theory, politics, method', in Robert Perks and Alistair Thomson, eds, *The Oral History Reader* (London: Routledge, 1997), pp. 81–2.

37 The Basque historian Francisco Letamendia has argued that during Spain's transition to democracy, ETA and its supporters began to replace Franco as the enemy against which the new democrats measured their own political credentials. Letamendia, 'La Transición en Euskadi', *Viento Sur* 24 (November–December 1995): 94–5.

38  *Cambio 16* #365, 3 December 1978. As part of the negotiated pact of the transition, Franco's security forces and military were never demobilized.

39  *Cambio 16* #363, 19 November 1978.

40  *El Pais* 14 July 1997.

41  Aretxaga, 'Playing terrorist', p. 52.

# 7

# SALE OF THE CENTURY?

## Memory and historical consciousness in Australia

*Paula Hamilton*

Like other postcolonial countries Australia has witnessed profound changes to understanding of the national past over the last twenty years, particularly in relation to events which have occurred within the 'living memory' of the twentieth century. This chapter explores some of the issues relating to history and memory that have emerged in a range of public forums. I argue that historical understanding is now shaped by an overall shift to a memorial framework as the principal mode of interpreting the past. This memorial culture is characterised by a shifting range of historical sensibilities, so that the past, its meaning and relationship to the present, has been a central factor in the politics of memory played out in parliaments and the press, particularly in relation to the experience of indigenous people over the past century. I also explore the limits to this memorial framework and the tangled relationship between memory and history currently evident in public discourse.

The contradictions of memory in multicultural societies and the more participatory nature of commemoration in the late twentieth century are evident across a range of sites in contemporary Australia, both public and private. In 1998, for instance, the New South Wales parliament passed a motion to erect a plaque commemorating the massacre of Armenians by the Turks, 1915–1921.[1] Turks from around the world choked the parliament's email system with over 70,000 messages of protest, crashing it (as well as the federal parliament's internet system when they were diverted there). The government nevertheless unveiled the memorial plaque in March 1999 in time to condemn all genocides carried out during the twentieth century.

The date chosen for commemoration was April 24. A day later, ironically enough, April 25 presents a very different version of Turkey: it is a 'sacred' national day in Australia that commemorates several thousand Australians who lost their lives on the shores of Gallipoli in Turkey in 1915. Though a loss for the Allies, in Australia this day is 'celebrated' as our baptism of fire, marking the emergence of a nation, and the Turks have been correspondingly elevated to the status of a truly worthy enemy. The Friendship Gate at Anzac Cove in Turkey testifies to the strength of a relationship forged in the years after the war. In an Australian memory, Turkey would thus emerge as both a noble enemy and a

136

nation carrying out genocide at the same time, illustrating some of the tensions evident in the attempts to reconcile group memories in a single account of the national past.

The sense of disjuncture that characterises the experience of migration and the remaking of family and community through memories that reach across space and time is also apparent in an example from the domestic sphere. Last year a reward was offered in a Sydney local newspaper for the return of family videos and film stolen in the course of a household burglary. Mr Henry Lee, an Australian born in Malaysia and now living in Sydney, was distraught that thieves had stolen the recording of his three-year-old daughter's birthday party, her first steps, and unprocessed photographic film of his wife's grandmother in Malaysia, which were for them irreplaceable. Mr Lee not only offered a reward for anyone finding the videos, but was also willing to pay the thieves for their return. 'We just want our memories back' he said, 'whatever the cost.'[2]

This is at first sight a sad story about late-twentieth-century loss, a consequence of our increasingly externalised modes of remembering. We pay thieves who stole our memories in the first place to get them back. Our memories are for sale, for barter and exchange. But like the example of the commemorative plaque, this latter story also highlights other aspects of historical culture, or ways of living historically, in Australia today.

Both stories reveal a historical consciousness, that is, a sense of living in time or being a subject of history, which expresses itself through artefacts of memory. With the globalising of identity politics, contesting the memory of events which took place in Europe eighty-five years ago is possible in the Australia of today; and so is recreating family identities that can transcend a Malaysian place of origin. Both are examples of an expanding memorial culture, a historical sensibility where temporal continuities are strengthened and sustained through communication with others. The widespread availability of and access to new technologies of memory contributes to the dissemination of this historical sensibility, although little is known as yet about how the use of these most recent electronic forms is shaping memorial expression.[3]

The meaning of the twentieth century is in the grip of memory, Eric Hobsbawm declared, towards that century's end. While many scholars might agree, we as yet know little about how people individually or collectively understand the past in their everyday lives, how the memories of their experiences shape choices for the future. Nor has the relationship between the act of remembering and a sense of historical consciousness been the subject of much investigation. With my colleagues at the University of Technology, Sydney, I am currently conducting a national survey, based on an American study by David Thelen and Roy Rosenzwieg, investigating how Australians think about, evaluate and use the past.[4] When completed, this study may be able to help us connect the work of professional historians with the historical understanding of people in general, linking history as a professional study with history as a form of social knowledge and activity. The context for this research is a much publicised retreat

from formal learning of history in classrooms and lecture theatres – the so-called
'crisis in history' shared by other countries. Yet at the same time there is an
increasing obsession with the past both personally and in a range of public
forums, especially within political debate and in an increasing number of arenas
in popular culture. Newspapers, for example, have become intensely concerned
with marking anniversaries of historical events, and some scholars have written
about the struggle between journalists and historians to tell stories about the past
in their columns.[5] This growing preoccupation with the past for public consumption has been matched by a proliferation of sites (such as memorials, national
parks, museums, television, film) and practices (for example re-enactments,
genealogy, local history, autobiography, oral histories) which are all now viewed
as constituting our cultural memory and its social expression.

But in Australian society, it is the public debates that have caused most intense
division about the nature and meaning of the past. Since 1992/3, indigenous
people have made claims to native title within the context of national reconciliation and revelations of a 'dark history' of violence, separation and massacres.
These claims have been deeply unsettling to those who want to cling to a cele-
bratory concept of nation, and have had a profound impact on both indigenous
and non-indigenous historical consciousness. One commentator remarks:

> This really is a major change, from an Australia that defined itself as a
> nation primarily in terms of its relationship to an outside power, to an
> Australia that defines itself primarily in terms of a set of internal rela-
> tions and an internal dynamic. We are not used to thinking of our
> history as contentious, morally compromised or volatile, as dangerous,
> as say, Japanese or South African history, American Civil War history,
> or recent Russian history.[6]

These complex political and cultural changes have been the stimulus for our
study, and in the first part of this chapter I now want to explore the shifting
ground between memory and history that is a consequence of these shifts. The
second part of the chapter takes up the question of that relationship through the
particular case of the 'stolen children' in Australia, where the issues relating to a
unified national past have been most clearly illuminated.

## Between memory and history

Many have argued that the impact of new technologies of remembering, consequent changes to the forms of historical representation and an increasing shift to
sites in popular culture (film, television etc.), have contributed to the changing
relationship between the past and present in our societies. The effects of playing
with time, its use as a marker in our lives, the collapse of the distance between an
event occurring and its representation; and the endless recycling of the past all
help to provide what some have defined as 'prosthetic memory': a mediated

access to a past that individuals have not themselves experienced creating 'memories' that transcend space and time.[7] According to Vivian Sobchack these new technologies have effected the creation of 'a new and pervasive self-consciousness about individual and social existence as an "historical subject"'.[8] There are also those who argue that gradually we have lost faith in time itself. It is certainly evident that in Australia today there are many different understandings of temporality, and these co-exist in considerable tension.

While there is as yet no history of historical consciousness in Australia, it is still possible to discern some trends over time. Across generations many will have different levels of knowledge and understanding about the past. Those over sixty, for example, have had very little of their historical knowledge informed by school learning, since only 17% of Australians before 1945 completed high school. For those born after the Second World War in an era of mass secondary schooling and increased tertiary education, a larger number will have been exposed to formal history classes at school, especially since in some states it is a compulsory area of study. The rapid expansion of historical sites since the 1960s, alongside a proliferation of historical organizations, has also no doubt had a considerable impact on inter-generational knowledge and attitudes. The number of people growing older and surviving longer and the growth of cultural diversity in Australia's population have created a very different context for the transmission of historical knowledge in Australian society. Certainly these changes have meant that more people become historical 'monuments' (or 'living treasures') in their own lifetime, as the society increasingly values those who remain to tell the stories of their past experiences.

The tumultuous social change of the last four decades has seen up to four different generations shaped by quite divergent understandings about 'race' and 'empire'. Some still living remember a time when their sense of belonging rested with England, which they called 'home'. Others, now middle-aged, grew up identifying with the 'pink bits on the world map' that signified the British Commonwealth, rather than with a strong sense of Australia as sacred territory and nation. What we may be currently experiencing in the traditional Anglophone population, then, is the final death of a consciousness justifying the national and colonial projects of European powers.

But such change also encourages a desire for temporal anchoring, for continuities not necessarily satisfied by the existing modes of writing Australian history. There's a game they play in the 'eccentric' news column of the main Sydney newspaper about the extent of 'living memory' through the generations. Thus, we can still find the grandchildren of transported convicts. Rev Colin Dyster, 92, grandson of Thomas Dyster, transported in 1827 at 14, who opened a skin-and-hide store in Adelaide when he completed his sentence. Mrs Doris Schrader, 89, and Mrs Lorna Havill, 86, granddaughters of John Woolbank, transported at 15 in 1836 for stealing 24 necklaces and 4 pairs of shoes (although the ladies don't know about the news item because they are ashamed of the family skeleton). These popular lineages suggest that the past can still be linked through the generations even though the meaning of that lineage has altered: for some, it is now acceptable (even desirable) to acknowledge convicts as ancestors, though others of venerable years still hold to a different historical sensibility.[9]

Not all of those involved in history-making desire continuity with the past. Many are attracted by exoticism and difference in historical representation or activities. Moreover, sometimes these contradictory attitudes are evident in the same practice. In re-enactments, for instance, the desire to link with the past and make it familiar juggles with the pleasure of difference and estrangement. To be a re-enactor requires great dedication and intimate knowledge of a certain kind of history – dressing up in 'authentic' costumes, imagining the past as closely as possible to our knowledge of the original, wanting to connect and relive it. At the same time there is the relishing of mystery, the thrill of the performance, the costume which in another sense is totally removed from one's own humdrum daily existence. In less participatory modes, such as historical sites, museums or memorials, the past is more usually sealed off and exoticised, impeding a dialogue between the audience and the past they see before them.[10]

## The authority of the witness

On June 23rd, 2001 the national newspapers mourned the death of Roy Longmore, which leaves only 102-year-old Alec Campbell as 'the Last Anzac'. 'Australia has now only one living link to the battlefield that forged a national identity,' the journalist said. (Longmore did not see active service. He was 16 when he arrived in Gallipoli. He carried water from the beach to the trenches and was evacuated when he became ill several weeks later.) Kate, Campbell's 80-year-old second wife, says she has been 'dreading this day' because 'she knows that her husband will slip away a little from her, that he has become a living national treasure, the property of the nation'. Like many others before him whose lives came into the media spotlight, Campbell eschews his status as a 'hero' simply because of his longevity and is wary of glorifying war. 'We just did what we were told', he said.[11]

This valorising of the 'last' witness to Australia's most powerful myth of nationhood is an indication of the extent to which a memorial culture has come to dominate the national consciousness, that these old men are left to attest to the 'truth' of a collective experience which over the last few years has come to mean much more than war service in an overseas battle. The myth of brave white masculinity forged in Anzac is almost impossible to challenge, despite attempts by activist feminist groups since the 1970s to do so. Indeed, the Anzac legend has been 'rediscovered' by a different younger generation making pilgrimages to the sites of battle in Turkey and seeking almost a religious reliving of the event. Unease about that moment when the 'living memory' will be lost seems to imply fears about the loss of continuity with the experience, or mistrust of the ways in which it will be retold in the future through different forms such as film or novels. Pierre Nora writes of the time in societies 'when memory passes from the generations that are its bearers to the historians who reconstitute a past they have not experienced'. He argues that these positions can co-exist in one generation or overlap, as they do in contemporary Australia, since there are many historical accounts and analyses of Australian participation at Gallipoli. Yet Nora identifies another process which accompanies this transition from first-hand account to abstract historical narrative: the inevitable loss of a detailed specificity of events as memory passes from one generation to another.[12]

The rising obsession with individual remembering as 'authentic' or the individual as eyewitness to what becomes a 'collective memory' owes much to the shifts in modernity, including increasing affluence and education, as well as the democratisation of many western societies after the 1950s. The importance of the individual's life, the altered sense of entitlement, what one critic has called 'egocentric' histories, have been linked with equally profound shifts in what it means to think historically in these societies, a shift evidenced by the growth of a massive industry in published life histories, memoirs etc.[13] In these circumstances, historical consciousness entails seeing oneself as an individual subject of history. As a consequence, the decreasing gap between present and past encourages us all to be 'historical subjects' in the same or immediately succeeding generations. It also signifies important changes to our understanding of a public and private self that witnessing, confession or disclosure entails. 'Testimony has become the crucial mode of our relation to events of the times', remarks one commentator.[14] This newly acquired authority is in tension with an enduring modesty by some of those in an older generation who feel the story of their lives is unimportant in the wider scheme of things; or gendered shifts whereby women see their life stories as not worthy of a public audience compared to the 'real work' of men's lives. Historians often claim that an individual witness to events does not constitute a 'history' in the sense of an abstracted account, and there are a great many perceptual limits to a single point of view. Nonetheless, argues Saul Friedlander, 'the altogether disruptive voices of the historians and victims must be heard, despite their unsettling dissonance'.[15]

## Historians and memory

Changes to our understanding of the nature of history as a discipline reflect how closely memory and history have become intertwined over the last few years. Some scholars claim that the formal discipline of history posits a separation of past and present not evident in forms of remembering which have captured the public imagination in many countries. For Michel de Certeau all writing of history 'institutes a reality by establishing a division between past and present such that the past functions as the other to the time of writing and is made intelligible by this writing'. 'This division', he says, 'organises its production and is concealed as much as possible'.[16] He does not suggest, however, that there is a simple division between memory and history, nor that history functions as the 'bad boy' in the relationship, or as memory's other. It is rather that the changing relations between memory and history are central to an understanding of shifts in historical consciousness. When I was training as a historian in the 1970s, only specialists studied what was called 'contemporary history', and tertiary history courses at universities all stopped about fifty years before the current generation.

The recent emergence of an interdisciplinary field of memory studies constitutes one of the contemporary points of convergence between memory and history. Most of the writing in this field tends to be Eurocentric, often claiming the Holocaust of the Second World War as the origin and rationale for the 'memory boom'.[17] Much of this focus on the Holocaust has been useful for my analysis of the Australian case below, while Truth and Reconciliation Commissions in South Africa and Chile provide evidence of a broader phenomenon involving major state-sanctioned public debates about remembering the past. Perhaps the memory struggles of indigenous peoples in post-colonial countries within the dominant framework of non-indigenous memory and history have something to offer those who have explored the field only from the viewpoint of those affected by the 1939–45 war.[18] These struggles focus more specifically, for example on the relationship of memory to place, and the strongly localised nature of some group memories, which may or may not act as countermemory to national mythologies.

Several recent surveys of the field of memory studies have questioned the ubiquitous use of 'memory' and have been critical of the indiscriminate reference to associated terms, particularly 'collective memory', questioning its validity as either a descriptive or analytical tool. However, when utilised in the Australian case, 'collective memory' helps us to understand the 'continual presence of the past' in public debates, as Susan Crane puts it, as well as the 'politics of time' that has become evident in the contest over the meaning of past events.[19]

'Collective memory' can be variously defined, though the term usually refers to the making of a group memory so that it becomes an expression of identity, and accepted by that group as the 'truth' of experience. Collective memory can be set in stone as an unquestioned myth or it can be continually renegotiated across time in accordance with external circumstance and generational shifts. James Young distinguishes between a memory of an experience which is shared by all who participated, with the meaning negotiated afterwards (such as a war reunion, for example); and memory of an event which has affected only some members, but comes to represent the traumatic experience of the whole. Thus the experience of indigenous children in Australia who were taken from their parents by the Australian state governments between the 1920s and the 1960s comes to stand in for the traumatic experience of everyone who is indigenous of that generation.[20]

## The Australian case

In 1995–6 the Human Rights and Equal Opportunity Commission's National Inquiry (HREOC) into the Separation of Aboriginal and Torres Strait Island Children from their Families heard oral submissions from 535 indigenous people about the effects of separation and institutionalisation by the state. The life stories told in the report, titled 'Bringing Them Home', trace the impact of government policy on individuals, families and communities. Most express profound loss and dislocation, 'one by one by one', as Judith Miller said of Jewish experiences during the Holocaust, or 'like a tragic dirge', according to Anna Haebich, a historian who has written about the history of indigenous child removal in Australia.[21]

Released in 1997, the report provided a focus of considerable emotive power for the politics of memory in contemporary Australia, and brought issues of responsibility for past wrongs to centre stage. One of its major recommendations was for an apology from the state for its past actions towards Aboriginal people – a recommendation that the federal conservative government has yet to accept. In all likelihood the inquiry was influenced by previous models for public expiation of wrongs such as those of the Truth and Reconciliation Commissions in South Africa, Holland and Chile. These models shaped the type of evidence heard and its subsequent harnessing to the cause of reconciliation. One might argue, however, that the HREOC Report had more in common with Holocaust remembrances by 'victims', since there were no memories of those involved in carrying out past government policies gathered at that time. But the factors already identified, such as the dominance of a memorial culture and the authority accorded eyewitnesses in Australian society, provided a context for the nature of the response and the subsequent debates in Australia.

In his report, Ronald Wilson, president of the HREOC inquiry, made a statement that expressed his understanding of the relationship between the present and the past:

> For individuals, their removal as children and the abuse they experienced at the hands of the authorities or their delegates have permanently scarred their lives. The harm continues in later generations, affecting their children and grandchildren. In no sense has the inquiry been 'raking over the past for its own sake'. The truth is that the past is very much with us today in the continuing devastation of the lives of indigenous Australians.[22]

As the public clamour from a broad section of the population for an apology from government increased, the Prime Minister, John Howard, emphasised the distance between the present and the past. In one of his speeches to parliament on this issue he declared:

> Australians know that mistakes were made in the past; know that injustices occurred and that wrongs were committed. But for the overwhelming majority of the current generations, there was no personal involvement of them or of their parents.[23]

There is a clear political struggle here between two very different understandings of the relationship between the past and the present. For indigenous people and those non-indigenous participants in the HREOC Report who heard the many stories of lives destroyed by separation and its effects across the years, past and present are blurred. For the Prime Minister and his government, the past is at a distance and quite separate from any continuing responsibility in the present – although since on other occasions Howard has taken the opportunity to capitalise on the mobilising power of memorials, particularly in relation to the commemoration of prisoners of war in Japan during the Second World War, there is an obvious element of political expediency in his rhetoric. Military commemorations are designed to strengthen connections between past experience and present conservative understandings of masculinist nationhood.

Some commentators have argued that the emergence of indigenous testimonies has brought about a sense of 'bad conscience' in Australia, an awareness that the well of the past from which a nation drew strength has been poisoned, underlying the pressure for an apology: repentance will be followed by forgiveness, and the past will be cleansed. Though Gooder and Jacobs are aware of the strong undertone of an almost religious 'seeking of absolution' in the public anxiety, they argue that the quest for an apology gained momentum because it 'becomes a lifeline for a legitimate sense of belonging'. [24]

In this time of intensive national memory work much of the public discourse was expressed in the rhetoric of 'forgetting'. *Why weren't we told?* is the title of Henry Reynolds' book on the issues, repeating a question asked frequently of him at public speaking engagements by non-indigenous people. One of the problems with a confessional model of public testimonies is that it obscures the transformation of a national consciousness which has already taken place to allow their articulation. The idea of 'forgetting' encourages an empiricist explanation, as if memories were waiting under a rock to be found rather than constituted at a time of different questions. Historians and commentators alike drew on this rhetoric of a 'forgotten' history, which at its extreme blamed historians and journalists for keeping knowledge from the public. Bernard Smith, for example, refers to Aborigines as 'the locked cupboard of our history': not only have we dispossessed them but we have then 'forgotten' what we have done. Equally damaging is the assumption that Aboriginal people have collectively always 'known' about these events, while the non-indigenous population was kept in the dark. In practice, of course, the interplay between memory and the public knowledge of our history is much more complex. We should be worried, says Klein, 'about the tendency to employ memory as the mode of discourse natural to the people without history'.[25]

For some years both before and after the HREOC report, indigenous narratives about life under colonialism circulated through various public arenas as an insistent counterpoint to the powerful myths of white nationhood. Through published autobiographies, novels, songs, films and other cultural forms, individual stories gradually gained greater currency with non-indigenous and indigenous audiences alike. With few exceptions the majority did not adopt historiography as an avenue, yet these accounts of personal experience that spoke on behalf of a group helped to redefine what constitutes historical knowledge and its transmission. Gordon Bennett, for example, uses the visual to make interventions into western modes of historical understanding: 'I see much of my recent work as history painting, not as documentary history painting, but rather as painting that investigates the way history is constructed after the event', he said.[26] Often the lines between personal and collective stories are obscured through these forms of memory work, just as there is no clear division between public and private, family and community. Because many of the chosen modes of communicating the Aboriginal past rely on less formal ways of educating a non-indigenous public about indigenous 'histories', they not only question traditional epistemologies of history as a writing practice, they also encourage a historical sensibility which collapses the past and the present because it is largely grounded in collective memory.

In latter years the almost compulsive telling of stories, particularly involving removal from indigenous families, can be explained by the previous 'absence' of memory, not simply of the events themselves, but of the pain associated with them. Apart from some localised instances, much of the knowledge had been lost within Aboriginal families, who were often themselves split from traditional communities and moved around as a result of government policies. Michael Roth argues that 'when communal memory is fractured and no longer able to provide the continuity essential to community life, storytelling, narrative memory, which transfigures and transforms the past, is a condition of retaining it'.[27] Like others who have examined the stories of painful experiences, Roth sees that they are usually of a fragmented nature. Thus it is 'narrative integration' that produces the memory of the event, and it is when these memories are told as stories that guilt and blame are attributed.[28] Many have explored how memory operates in this way to recreate traditions, but once the bonds of community are broken only names remain, rescued from oblivion perhaps in the storytelling process. More importantly, what is also lost through community disruption is the communicating of the memory to a subsequent generation, a story of transmission that provides continuity through 'vicarious witnessing'.

From the 1970s, a number of non-indigenous historians researching the field began to be influenced by questions of memory, particularly if they drew on the new oral history methods that changed the relationship between past and present in historical research. Many found it impossible, or undesirable, to separate their historical practice from their role as public advocates and activists. Peter Read was one of the founding members of Link-up, an organisation set up in the 1980s to bring together indigenous parents and children who had been separated by the practice of child removal. In a recent reflection on that work he says:

> Those of us who have worked in Aboriginal history for some years are astounded by the transformation in the self-perception of the separated children, and of the communities from which they were removed. In

1980, the only writer who had described the experiences of a removed Aboriginal child was Margaret Tucker. Today there are at least a dozen books on the subject. Hundreds of former wards and adoptees have been interviewed for a dozen television and radio documentaries ... no removed Aborigine now writes of his or her separation without linking personal experience to general Aboriginal removals, and that phenomenon to the wider policy of assimilation.[29]

Many academics working in the field of Aboriginal history have been vitally involved in identifying and nourishing the 'stolen generation' memories. They have added the weight of their activism within Aboriginal communities and their historical research to the general understanding of the 'stolen generations' as a countermemory that subverts the traditional assumption of an unproblematic national history. Among those who have made a major contribution to our understanding of these events few scholars have taken a more dispassionate approach than Bain Attwood. Attwood has recently traced the process by which the 'stolen generations narrative' has come to assume centre stage in the national consciousness and its emergence as a 'collective memory' for indigenous people. In doing so, he argues that the story of children being taken away moves from highly specific localised knowledge amongst the Wiradjuri and the Yorta Yorta groups about a particular level of government practice, to a national narrative which has 'slipped its moorings' in historical research and become a 'metanarrative' or myth. Attwood's work reveals in some depth how the creation of memory about the 'stolen generations' has been mutually constituted by both indigenous and non-indigenous people; and argues that its mobilisation by indigenous people has become an important element in their collective identity.[30] His argument is particularly useful in this context for its explication of the complex strengths and weaknesses of interpreting an Aboriginal past within a memorial framework, and the role of historian advocates in that process.

The gradually increasing force of the 'stolen generations narrative' which Attwood analyses has of course led to its contestation by the federal government. 'A generation was not stolen', Minister for Aboriginal Affairs, John Herron claimed in the Sydney Morning Herald last year:

> HREOC's conclusion as to the size of the 'stolen generation' has been treated as a finding. The available evidence clearly suggests that it is an inflated estimate which has led to the assumption of vast numbers having been affected and whole generations of trauma across the entire indigenous community ... at most it might be inferred that up to 10% of children were separated for a variety of reasons.[31]

Attwood himself has been an outspoken contributor to the public arguments between commentators about the significance of the HREOC inquiry testimonies. He is wary about the critical understandings that he has derived from historical analysis being utilised by conservatives to undermine Aboriginal community claims, particularly in relation to compensation. But there are many voices from across the political spectrum speaking against the dominance of memory in public forums for quite different purposes. Ironically they share some of the same anxieties.

Other historians have been more concerned about the previous 'absence' of knowledge in relation to government policies and their destructive effects on indigenous people. Anna Haebich's new work documents extensive evidence in the public domain of child removals during the twentieth century, and even brings to light public opposition that was both vocal and influenced government policies. Underpinning her historical inquiry is the worrying question, 'how could we not have known?' a question which has resonances for those who lived through the Holocaust. She terms it 'A Twilight of Knowing'.[32] However, as Irwin-Zarecka argued, 'something that does not fit within the established structures of thinking and feeling is likely to be excluded from remembrance'.[33] This is also the case with the writing of history or what is constituted as 'history'. There is an epistemological gap between what we 'know' at the time and what we understand later. Haebich's research was financed by Bill and Pauline Johnson, who commissioned her to write a history in memory of their adopted indigenous son, murdered in 1991 in Perth 'because he was black'. These tragic circumstances of the book's generation shaped Haebich's project; they also illustrate starkly how the past weighs on the writing of history in contemporary Australia.

## Against memory

There have been few voices to date that speak against the dominance of memory in public debates about the past, particularly its effects on the historical imagination in contemporary society. But there are troubling aspects of its use that need closer analysis. Some of these issues have been addressed in more general terms with other countries in mind by scholars such as Klein and Winter, who are concerned about the unquestioned assumptions not only in the academic discourse relating to memory studies but also about the way public discussion of memories is framed.[34] They apply equally to the Australian case.

The first issue addresses the tendency of indigenous peoples to adopt a 'strategic victimhood' as a result of their experience in the past, and the memories now made public, or to be ascribed the identity of 'victims' by non-indigenous people; so that increasingly over time the moral identification of being a victim and the 'heritage of suffering' becomes a feature of this group's identity. Within this discourse, Aboriginal people are left only the category of 'survivors' if they want to transcend the past. The solidarity provided by remembered victimhood is especially attractive, suggests Ian Buruma, to those whose communal identity is already under threat.[35] Thus Michael Jackson, an indigenous writer, speaks of 'a kinship born of identification with others', an 'empowering sense of being part of a collective tragedy, a shared trauma'.[36] Some years ago, Charles Maier warned against this trend in the USA, calling it a 'surfeit of memory'. Under these circumstances, 'confessional memory is seen as the only valid reparation, and as a claim upon official memory, the victim's anguish comes to be seen as a valuable possession. Other peoples also want the status of victimhood'.[37]

This problem leads to a second issue emerging from the collection and representation of many individual stories about the indigenous past, particularly their collection within the framework of the HREOC Inquiry – the question of 'authenticity' in remembering. This is a common problem with oral or life histories as an historical practice, but where feelings can only be expressed, rather than discussed or debated, then they cannot be readily challenged.

The third issue refers to the widespread use of psychoanalytic terms to explain the cause and effect of bringing to light stories involving personal hardship and pain. Thus it is a small conceptual step from individuals to national and indigenous groups who suffer 'trauma' that needs to be 'healed' through the psychiatric terms of a 'talking cure'. 'There is a persistent assumption in current discourses of reconciliation that encountering the "truth" and apologising will function palliatively', say Gooder and Jacobs, 'and that from these two interlinked processes will emerge a healed nation'.[38]

The title of commentator Robert Manne's recent essay, for example, a salvo fired against conservatives who refuse to accept the legitimacy of the HREOC Inquiry report, was 'In Denial: The Stolen Generations and the Right'. However well-meaning his rhetoric, the problem with using such psychoanalytic terms, argues historian James Young,

> is the consequent tendency to see all the different kinds of memory in terms of memory-conflict and strategies for denial. If memory of an event is repressed by an individual who lacks the context – either emotional or epistemological – to assimilate it, that is one thing. But to suggest that a society "represses" memory because it is not in its interest to remember, or because it is ashamed of this memory, is to lose sight of the many other social and political forces underpinning national memory.[39]

Others note that this language reduces complex events and experiences to a simplistic notion of 'trauma' and the need to exorcise pain caused by denial or displacement of their memory. Not only has the 'cure' proved problematic in almost every country where testimony has been collected for this purpose, but as others have noted some time ago, even the speaking out is a double-edged sword. In relation to the Holocaust, Lawrence Langer argued that 'there are different types of representation embedded within the same narrative: one which seeks transcendence and one which enmeshes the witness in the events of the past'.

Telling the story can bring relief, he says, but the unfolding plot often brings nothing but pain and anguish.[40]

'The inquiry has just fucked all our heads', a friend told the Murri [Queensland indigenous] novelist Melissa Lucashenko. 'They just won't shut up about it, will they?' she asked Melissa, referring to the mainstream commentators. 'I don't want an apology from that prick [the Prime Minister], I don't want to hear them going on and on and on about it. ... I just want them to shut up'.[41] This woman spoke of indigenous people who were very disturbed by continued revelations about Australia's troubled past, indicating the problematic nature of strategic victimhood, the sense of being haunted by a now public past.

This Australian case study has traced the increasing influence of memory on public opinion, as a factor in public debates; and on some areas of the historical discipline itself. I have argued that the emergence of an indigenous national past which functions as a countermemory can challenge the traditional narrative of nation, but also has major effects that impede rather than enhance historical understanding. Central to the constant shadow play, sometimes collaborative, sometimes confrontational, between memory and history have been equally important shifts in historical consciousness characterised by a strengthening of temporal continuities and the continual presence of the past in contemporary discourse. The consequence of such profound shifts is a changed attitude to the meaning of the past and its role in Australian cultural life: the past *matters* to people now more than ever before.

## Acknowledgements

An initial version of this chapter was presented to the Frontiers of Memory Conference, London 1999. I am grateful to several people who have helped with discussions along the way including Paul Ashton, Denis Byrne, Joy Damousi, Anna Haebich, Peter Read. Special thanks to Louella McCarthy for assistance with some of the research and editing; and Bain Attwood, Tony Taylor and Chris Jackson for their valuable comments on the draft.

## Notes

1 In this instance, 1.5 million Christian Armenians were killed by Muslim Turks. Turkish peoples claim the conflict was a Civil War, not a genocide. The weight of western historical scholarship, however, regards it as genocidal.

2 *Inner Western Suburbs Courier*, 9 March 1998, p. 25.

3 The 'relationship between the modern media and the contemporary politics of memory' is a central theme of Nancy Woods' book *Vectors of Memory. Legacies of Trauma in Postwar Europe*, Berg, Oxford, 1999. See also Chris Locke, 'Digital memory and the Problem of Forgetting' in Susannah Radstone (ed.) *Memory and Methodology*, Berg, Oxford, 2000, and Radstone's introduction to this volume.

4 This project is being carried out at University of Technology, Sydney, by Jane Connors from the Australian Broadcasting Corporation, Paul Ashton, Heather

Goodall and myself with assistance from Australian Research Council grants. Louella McCarthy is the project's senior researcher. The website is <http://www.austpast.uts. edu.au>. Roy Rosenzweig and David Thelen published their findings as a book: *The Presence of the Past. Popular Uses of History in American Life*, Columbia University Press, New York, 1998.

5 Barbie Zelizer, *Covering the Body. The Kennedy Assassination, the Media and the Shaping of Collective Memory*, University of Chicago Press, Chigaco, 1992.

6 David Carter, 'Working on the past, working on the future' in Richard Nile and Michael Peterson (eds), *Becoming Australia. The Woodford Forum*, University of Queensland Press, Queensland, 1998, p. 10.

7 See Celia Lurie, *Prosthetic Culture. Photography, Memory and Identity*, Routledge, London, 1998.

8 Vivian Sobchack (ed.), *The Persistence of History. Cinema, Television and the Modern Event*, AFI Film Reader, Routledge, London, 1996, Introduction, p. 3.

9 'Column 8' in *Sydney Morning Herald*, 13 and 20 May 1999, Front page. The 'First Fleeters' are an Australian historical society, membership of which is confined to those who can document their descent from those aboard this first convict fleet to Australia. Among members, descent from a convict is considered preferable to descent from the 'brutal' guards who brought them out.

10 See Graeme Davison, *The Use and Abuse of Australian History*, Allen & Unwin, Australia, 2000, esp. chapter 6. Chris Healy recently argued that 'we are in the middle of a mundane heritage crisis' as national cultural institutions try to come to grips with historical shifts. See his ' "Race Portraits" and Vernacular Possibilities: Heritage and Culture', Chapter 13 in Tony Bennett and David Carter (eds), *Culture in Australia. Policies, Publics and Programs*, Cambridge University Press, Cambridge, 2001. There is no space here to address the possibilities of cultural tourism, an increasing factor in the experience of the past.

11 Front page, *Weekend Australian*, 23–4 June 2001. For a thoughtful discussion of the impact of indigenous issues on war commemoration see Ann Curthoys, 'National narratives, war commemoration and racial exclusion in a settler society. The Australian case' in T.G. Ashplant, Graham Dawson and Michael Roper (eds), *The Politics of War Memory and Commemoration*, Routledge, London, 2000, pp. 128–144.

12 Pierre Nora 'Generations' in Vol. 1: Conflicts and Division, *Realms of Memory. The Construction of the French Past*, 3 Vols, under the direction of Pierre Nora, 1992 (translated from French) Columbia University Press, New York, 1996, p. 530.

13 Kerwin Lee Klein, 'On the emergence of *Memory* in historical discourse' *Representations*, Vol. 69, Winter 2000, uses this term, pp. 127–150.

14 Shoshana Felman 'Education and crisis, or the vicissitudes of teaching' in Cathy Caruth (ed.), *Trauma: Explorations in Memory*, Johns Hopkins University Press, Baltimore, 1995, p. 16. See also Shoshana Feldman and Dori Laub (eds), *Testimony: Crises of Witnessing in Literature, Psychoanalysis and History*, Routledge, New York, 1992.

15 Saul Friedlander 'History, memory and the historian: facing the Shoah' in Michael S. Roth and Charles G. Salas (eds), *Disturbing Remains: Memory, History and Crisis in the Twentieth Century*, Getty Research Institute, Los Angeles, 2001. Friedlander says, 'The historian cannot and should not be the guardian of memory. The historian's gaze is analytic, critical, attuned to complexity, wary about generalizations', pp. 278–279.

16 Michel de Certeau, *The Practice of Everyday Life*, trans. Steve Rendell, Berkeley, University of California Press, 1984, p. 10.

17 Jay Winter, 'The memory boom in contemporary historical studies', *Raritan*, Vol. 21, No. 1, 2001, p. 52.

18 Some recent work in anthropology has begun to explore this field. See Jeannette Marie Mageo (ed.), *Cultural Memory. Reconfiguring History and Identity in the Postcolonial Pacific*, University of Hawai'i Press, Hawaii, 2001.

19  Susan Crane, 'Writing the individual back into collective memory' and Alon Confino, 'Collective memory and cultural history: problems of method' in *American Historical Review*, 'Forum on History and Memory', December 1997, Vol. 102, No. 5, pp. 1,372–1,385 and pp. 1,386–1,403 respectively.

20  James Young, *The Texture of Memory. Holocaust Memorials and Meaning*, Yale University Press, New Haven and London, 1993, p. xii.

21  Anna Haebich, *Broken Circles. Fragmenting Indigenous Families, 1800–2000*, Fremantle Arts Centre Press, Fremantle, 2000.

22  'Bringing Them Home', Report of the Human Rights and Equal Opportunity Commission National Inquiry into the Separation of Aborigines and Torres Strait Islanders from their Families (afterwards HREOC) Commonwealth of Australia, 1997, Introduction, p. 3.

23  *The Australian*, 27 August 1999.

24  Haydie Gooder and Jane M Jacobs, 'On the borders of the unsayable. The apology in postcolonising Australia', *Interventions*, Vol. 2 no.2 pp. 230–247. See also Robert R. Weyeneth, 'The power of apology and the process of historical reconciliation', *The Public Historian*, Vol. 23, No. 3, Summer 2001, pp. 9–38 and Elazar Barkan, *The Guilt of Nations. Restitution and Negotiating Historical Injustices*, W.W. Norton & Co., New York, 2000, Chapter 10 on Australian Aborigines.

25  Klein, op. cit., p. 144.

26  Ian McClean and Gordon Bennett, *The Art of Gordon Bennett*, Craftsman House. G & B Arts International, 1996.

27  Michael S. Roth, *The Ironists' Cage. Memory, Trauma and the Construction of History*, Columbia University Press, New York, 1995, Introduction, p. 9.

28  This is a point made by Efrain Sicher in 'The future of the past. Countermemory and postmemory in contemporary American post-Holocaust narratives', *History & Memory*, Vol. 12, No. 2, Fall/Winter 2000, pp. 56–91, and Susan J. Brison, 'Trauma narratives and the remaking of self', in Mieke Bal, Jonathan Crewe and Leo Spitzer (eds), *Acts of Memory. Cultural Recall in the Present*, University Press of New England, Dartmouth College, 1999, pp. 39–54.

29  Peter Read, *A Rape of the Soul So Profound: The Return of the Stolen Generations*, Allen & Unwin, Sydney, 1999, p. 49.

30  Bain Attwood, ' "Learning about the truth": the Stolen Generations narrative', in Bain Attwood and Fiona Magowan (eds), *Telling Stories: Indigenous History and Memory in Australia and New Zealand*, Allen & Unwin, Crows Nest NSW, 2001, pp. 183–212. For more general points about historians' role in memory scholarship, see George G. Iggers, 'The role of professional historical scholarship in the creation and distortion of memory' in Anne Ollila (ed.), *Historical Perspectives on Memory*, SHS Helsinki, 1999, pp. 49–67; and particularly Saul Friedlander, 'History, memory and the historian: facing the Shoah', op. cit.

31  *Sydney Morning Herald*, 4 April 2000, p. 15.

32  Haebich, *op. cit.*, Chapter 9, 'A twilight of knowing', pp. 563–570.

33  Iwona Irwin-Zarecka, *Frames of Remembrance. The Dynamics of Collective Memory*, Transaction Publishers, New Brunswick, 1994, pp. 52–53.

34  Klein, op. cit. and Winter, op. cit., *passim*.

35  Ian Buruma, 'The joys and perils of victimhood', *New York Review of Books*, 8 April 1990. Elazar Barkan, *The Guilt of Nations. Restitution and Negotiating Historical Injustices*, W.W. Norton & Co., New York, 2000, p. xvii, argues that Buruma does not deal with the 'perpetrators' and 'leaves the guilt component unexplored'.

36  Michael Jackson, *At Home in the World*, Sydney 1995, cited in Haebich, op. cit., pp. 568–569.

37  Charles S Maier, 'A surfeit of memory? Reflections on history, melancholy and denial', *History & Memory*, Vol. 5, No. 2, Fall/Winter, 1993, p. 149. Maier argued that

the dominance of memory in public discourse signified a retreat from transformative politics, p. 150.

38 Gooder and Jacobs, op. cit., pp. 238–239.

39 Young, op. cit., p. xi.

40 Lawrence Langer, *Holocaust Testimonies. The Ruins of Memory*, Yale University Press, New Haven, 1991, and *Preempting the Holocaust*, Yale University Press, New Haven, 1998. For a discussion of these issues see Chapter 3, 'Holocaust testimonies. Attending to the victim's voice' of Dominick LaCapra's book *Writing History, Writing Trauma*, The Johns Hopkins University Press, Baltimore, 2001.

41 'Three responses to Robert Manne's In Denial – More Migaloo words?', Melissa Lucashenko, *Overland*, 163, Winter 2001, p. 16.

# 8

# 'BROTHERS AND SISTERS, DO NOT BE AFRAID OF ME'

Trauma, history and the therapeutic imagination
in the new South Africa

*Christopher J. Colvin*

## Introduction

In recent years, South Africa has been busy with the historiographical work of producing, interpreting and circulating traumatic memories of apartheid. With the inception of the Truth and Reconciliation Commission (TRC), 'storytelling' arrived as a privileged mode of publicly communicating painful experiences of apartheid. Part psychotherapy, part legal testimony and part historiography, 'telling your story' has become a powerful, if ambivalent, way to contribute to a new history of the old South Africa.[1] South Africa since the TRC has been a space infused with an attention to trauma. Trauma is what the TRC commissioners wanted to hear about, what the media wanted to portray, what researchers wanted to document and understand, what the government wanted to harness and what some, though not all, victims wanted to talk about. As Paul Antze and Michael Lambek have recently noted of the contemporary moment more generally, in South Africa, 'increasingly, memory worth talking about – worth remembering – is memory of trauma'.[2]

In this chapter I explore this recent emphasis on traumatic memories, and the psychotherapeutic discourse that frames and accounts for this emphasis. By looking at several attempts to begin writing the history(s) of apartheid, I argue that the twin concepts of trauma and therapy offer an alternative and contested way of writing the history of South Africa. I use the terms 'history' and 'historiography' broadly. In this chapter I examine formal, written historical accounts as well as more generalized cultural strategies for representing the past, through storytelling sessions, museum tours and interviews with individual South Africans.

## Performing trauma and recovery on Robben Island

The Robben Island Museum has been a key site for the production of public discourses of trauma, memory and recovery. It is the most prominent and public memorial space in South Africa, and continues to host not only daily tours, but foreign dignitaries, conferences, press briefings, concerts and art exhibits as well. This first fieldwork scene opens in July 1998 in the middle of my first tour of the Robben Island prison, the island prison that held those anti-apartheid activists considered by the government to be the most dangerous. The members of the tour group were mostly white tourists from Europe and the United States. Our guide, Thembile Mzola,[3] was sitting on the dusty floor of the prison workyard lifting an imaginary hammer high into the air and bringing it home on the large piece of gravel he told us to picture in front of him.

'Every day we would come out here and beat the rocks', he yelled. He pointed to a picture next to him of ANC and PAC prisoners sitting in rows, beating piles of gravel into dust. 'Together, they are loving one another', he admonished us, asserting that at Robben Island, partisan politics between the black liberation groups were mercifully suspended, allowing him and the other prisoners a space of shared and redemptive suffering.

Thembile was on Robben Island for 18 years, held for all of that time with Mandela and others in the section for the leaders of political parties. When he finished his demonstration, he lowered his invisible hammer beside him and, spinning around, flashed a big grin, saying, 'We were not suffering for family or country, but for the humanity of God! Our loving visitors, my brothers and sisters, I love you all ... do not be afraid of me, I love you ... welcome.'

We continued into the main hallway of Section B, where Mandela's former cell waited for us to visit. Once we had gathered around the small iron-barred door of the cell, Thembile walked in, and after waiting for us to quieten down, began: 'Brothers and sisters, my name is Thembile Mzola. Brothers and sisters, I tell you again, my name is Thembile Mzola, arrested in 1962, sentenced in 1963, dying for you all on Robben Island, dying for you all ... I am not joking.' The point of this invocation became clear as he began to describe the conditions he and others lived under while at the prison. He did not want his stories of the suffocating heat in the summers and the rats in the winters to be taken for exaggeration. He did not want the tortures of the lime quarries to seem any less dramatic or the cunning of the censors at the prison to seem any less sinister. Throughout his description of harsh prison life, he repeated 'I love you all ... do not be afraid of me ... '.

Soon we were at the end of the hallway and making our way to the showers. Thembile stood under the shower spigot and announced to us loudly, 'Be happy! I am not afraid of you, because we are brothers and sisters.' He finished the last part of the tour here, miming the coldness of the ocean water used for showers and pulling at his grey hair and holding his thick glasses high as proof of the salt water's harsh effects on the prisoners' bodies.

When I asked some of the other guides to explain to me the motivation behind Thembile's particular style of presentation, I was told that Thembile's part of the tour is the most important of all, that it is the prison cells and the experiences there that are the key to understanding both Robben Island and apartheid itself. Since the nation does not know (or some have chosen not to know) the 'dark secrets' of Section B, Thembile's job is to expose those secrets, using both his traumatic memories of his time there and his own body as evidence of the suffering he had experienced. When I asked for whose benefit this was, the other two guides told me that it was both for Thembile and for the visitors. They said that Thembile, like many of the other guides, was drawn back to Robben Island after it was closed, as if he had 'unfinished business' there. Coming back, giving tours, and walking their way through their own stories of suffering is a way for these ex-prisoners to find some release from the island. This work is also meant, though, for the visitor, who does not or has refused to know the story of Robben Island. Confronting them as Thembile does with the re-enactment of his own pain is intended to allow (or force) visitors to confront their own hidden participation in apartheid.

## Stories of trouble, 'traumatic' memories and the therapeutic ethic

One cannot talk about 'trauma' for long without engaging with the languages and practices of psychiatry and psychotherapy. Stories framed as stories of 'trauma' are always already implicated in some way in a specific perspective on psychological suffering and recovery. This first scene highlights what I describe below as a 'therapeutic ethic' that frames and justifies the work of telling stories of trouble. In the broadest sense, stories of trouble can take on any number of narrative forms and purposes. They can involve spiritual, individual or communal pain and redemption. They can emphasize either the value or the uselessness of that suffering. They can be deployed as moral claims and condemnations or as absurdist tales of a cold, violent and senseless world. Some reveal the transformations the sufferer has undergone or continues to undergo, while others do not. Some implicate the listener/reader in the suffering of the victims while others maintain a safe distance between the two. However a narrative of suffering is configured, though, if it is cast as a story about 'trauma', its telling can be interpreted as (also) a therapeutic process. This therapeutic framework both defines what (psychological) trauma is and outlines the steps necessary to overcome its debilitating effects.

In the numerous recountings of the traumatic memories of apartheid in newspapers, in academic writing, in magazine interviews and in the TRC's work, examples of the therapeutic ethic abound. The TRC has spoken of its mission to 'open the wounds only in order to cleanse them, to deal with the past effectively, and close the door on that dark and horrendous past forever'.[4] Lloyd Vogelman, of the Centre for the Study of Violence and Reconciliation, has written that only through the work of the TRC can the 'secrecy of evil [be] unlocked and society begin to come to terms with itself'. He argues that the 'undemocratic system' of apartheid was 'imprinted on the public conscience'.[5] One theologian refers to the TRC commissioners as 'psychological archaeologists'.[6] And Robert Brand, a journalist, wrote, 'if the primary purpose of the [TRC] is, as its members insist, to bring about catharsis and healing, the first weeks ... have been a resounding success'.[7] The *vocabularies* of trauma and therapy have become widespread features of the public and professional discourse surrounding the TRC and post-apartheid South Africa in general.

Therapy, however, is not merely a popular *representation* of the proper or obvious framework for dealing with a painful past; the *practice* of therapy in public rituals has figured prominently as well. Part of the TRC's work included holding hearings where victims could come and testify to the details of their specific suffering and apply for the chance to be officially classified as victims of gross human rights violations. Many of these emotional hearings were televized and included an audience as witnesses of these stories of apartheid-era violence. The TRC made visible use of an array of largely volunteer psychological counsellors before, during and after the hearings to deal with the entire range of TRC particip-ipants: the victims and their families and lawyers, the perpetrators, their families and lawyers, the TRC commissioners themselves, the TRC staff, the media covering the TRC and even the data-entry temps hired to transcribe victim testi-monies. The TRC even extended this therapeutic ethic to those whom the TRC did not identify as official victims of gross human rights violations, since failing to qualify for victim status was understood in itself to be a traumatizing event.

The particular therapeutic ethos that emerges here draws from standard psychodynamic psychology,[8] but incorporates elements of a newer therapeutic discourse on trauma important in the United States and Europe. A number of recent writers have argued that the concept of 'traumatic memory', as it is deployed in psychological practice and beyond, is especially important to new understandings of the relationships between suffering, the self, the social and the past in the US, Canada and Europe.[9] As they explain, trauma discourse is typi-cally centred on a definition of 'trauma' as a singular and extraordinary event that leaves a deep and uninterpretable wound on the individual psyche. The suffering inflicted by a trauma stands outside everyday experience and outside an individual's ability to make cognitive or emotional sense of the experience. As a result, the traumatized person shuts him- or herself off from the memory of a violation that cannot be accounted for. The trauma, however, doesn't go away; instead it festers and continues to cause physical and psychological sickness. The therapeutic solution involves forcing the sufferer to confront the repeating, painful memory, relive the moment of violation in difficult, painstaking detail and come to understand that the trauma is actually over, a past event that need not continue to cause harm in the present.[10]

In a similar vein, Kirby Farrell has identified the 1990s as a period of 'post-traumatic culture' wherein the trope of 'trauma' has become a powerful interpretative framework for making sense not only of specific past injuries, but of the past itself more generally.[11] These references to the dangers of a haunted past destructively repeating itself, like a festering physical wound, until it is lanced and cleansed, draw from a set of therapeutic narratives and images of trauma grounded in twentieth-century psychological knowledge and practice.

One of the unique features of this recent emphasis on trauma, traumatic memory and the various therapeutic strategies for recovery is that the ground of the newly healed self – of the patient or of the nation – is understood to be constituted out of the *mastering of a painful past.*

Having sketched the outlines of this therapeutic interpretation of and response to traumatic memories, I turn to a consideration of how this therapeutic ethic is related to a new, therapeutically inspired mode of historiography that seems to be developing in post-apartheid South Africa. I will outline how 'history borrows from psychotherapy' by integrating key aspects of the therapeutic narratives of trauma, memory and recovery into the historical narrative.[12] I continue by illustrating how this particular historiographical mode is encountering resistance not only from those who would defend apartheid but also from those most intimately involved in narrating its ruinous effects – the victims of apartheid-era violence.

## Transforming traumatic memory into therapeutic history

Where history is a history of trauma, then perhaps a traumatic historiography, the writing of that history of trauma, might be thought of as a form of therapy both for the individual and for the nation writing its history. If the act of writing history is considered to be therapeutic, then perhaps the history-writing project has a place in reconstructing the social, political and psychological constitution of a nation. This certainly has been a prominent justification for the necessity of reliving the traumatic memories of apartheid through processes like the TRC. The following passage from the preface of the African National Congress's submission to the TRC illustrates this ambition as well as the ANC's acceptance of the therapeutic understanding of the TRC:

> The ANC campaigned actively for the TRC ... because we believe that such a Commission can play an important role in ensuring the psychological, intellectual and political well-being of the new democracy. Only by unveiling and acknowledging as far as possible the truth, ... can the millions whose basic human rights were legally trampled upon ... be accorded the kind of respect which they deserve, and the reparations which are possible. Only by confronting the past can there be genuine reconciliation, nation-building and unity in our country. Creating an official record of what happened could help in a cathartic way to heal South Africans psychologically. By knowing what happened and why, South Africa will be better placed to ensure that the evil deeds of the past are never repeated.[13]

There are a number of other institutions and processes that embrace this approach to nation-building through history-cum-therapy. Cape Town's Institute for the Healing of Memories runs weekend workshops for South Africans of all social, racial and political affiliations, 'based on the premise that telling one's experiences of the apartheid years can lead to a process of healing, provide relief for the individual and at the same time initiate a more collective healing process among South Africans'.[14] Khulumani, the victim support group described below, participates in some ways in this therapeutic mode of storytelling for the nation. The storytelling sections of their monthly meetings bear a striking resemblance to the public hearings the TRC held for victims. The Trauma Centre counsellors who facilitate this part of the meeting emphasize the individual, social and national benefits to peace- and nation-building that 'getting these stories out there' should have.

One principal feature of many of these historiographical enterprises is the emphasis on a 'traumatic secret' – an event or series of events so violent and disruptive that it upsets the 'fabric and flow' of history, becoming the key event to unlock all subsequent, and sometimes even prior, events. This is what Allan Young calls the 'pathogenic secret' or Richard Wilson, in a slightly different vein, the 'constitutive violence': an event of such extreme disruption that it acts as the central organizing principle for a relationship to the past.[15] Apartheid, in the South African incarnation of a traumatic history, supplies and organizes the key categories and symbols of South Africa's past. The interesting twist that develops then is that the trauma of apartheid is cast as the source at once of South Africa's current problems (its pathogenic secret) and of its cure (a sort of 'like cures like' model for historiography). This homeopathic metaphor is at the centre of most theories of trauma therapy. Just as an immune system might be trained to fight off invading pathogens through the use of weakened and diluted inoculations of the pathogen itself, individuals are encouraged to tame the traumatic memories that haunt them by re-exposing themselves to these very memories.

This therapeutic model of history also differs in its choice of the memories and memorial styles it brings to bear on history. Traumatic memory is, of course, the most appropriate source of memory for a history defined by its traumatic secrets. This memory is 'emotional' (that is, not bound by burdens of proof or 'reasonableness'), often accompanied by a strong political consciousness, and is not interested in maintaining a neat and progressive distancing of the present from the past. The therapeutic model of history seeks redemption from the past for the present. It does not do this through 'rational' debate, open and apolitical dialogue or a careful sifting of the documentary and anecdotal 'evidence'; rather, it tries to create an encounter between the past and the present that, like psychotherapy, creates a space that is both safe ('brothers and sisters, do not be afraid of me') and discomforting ('dying for you all ... I am not joking') at the same time.

What emerges then is a model of history where the principal subject of history is the long-suffering but now-recovered victim of violation. The suffering of victims acquires historical meaning by highlighting the ways in which their suffering became part of the overall movement from oppression to freedom. The transformation of the dangerous, injured victim into the reconciled 'survivor' is effected through an encounter with traumatic memories, a reliving and taming of these painful experiences. The audience for this history, like the audience of the tour group in the first scene, is largely composed of 'bystanders' and/or those who would seek to be witnesses to suffering. In a therapeutic historiography, the key events of history are portrayed as a series of traumatic events, tempered by moments of relative, unimportant calm. Trauma, here, is the central mode and consequence of power; it is the hidden hand that moves history and creates new kinds of people with new forms of historical experience. Fortunately, though, this history moves towards an enlightened peace, and the final moral of the story is the triumph of love, tolerance, understanding and reason. It is a story that redeems victim, perpetrator and witness through the grace of the victim.

This is a history centred on the primacy of traumatic memory, a history whose narrative is organized in terms of the generic conventions of the psychotherapy of traumatized individuals, and a history that places the memories of its victims at the centre of its imagination. Most importantly, it uses a language of individual suffering and recovery to tell the story of the struggle and redemption of a nation.

## Calls for 'context': resistances to trauma-centred history

There are, of course, resistances to this mode of history making. The first, and perhaps least surprising, critique of this historiographic style comes from individuals and groups invested for one reason or another in the normalization of apartheid, casting its programme of 'social engineering' as a mistake, made with good intentions, and as part of a process that eventually and logically led to the current configuration of non-racial, democratic power. These individuals and groups critique a notion of history centred on trauma. Instead, from their historical perspective, trauma becomes an unfortunate and sometimes mysterious by-product of well-intentioned government policies. In the National Party submission to the TRC, former President F.W. de Klerk argued that:

> Many of those who took part in the struggle from the side of the Government, especially most of the Afrikaners, believed, to start with, that they were defending the right of their people to national self-determination in their own state within a territorially partitioned South Africa. They believed that their actions were in line, not only with the traditions of their forefathers, but also with the universally accepted principle that nations were entitled to defend their right to self-determination in a country of their own.[16]

He continued:

> I retain my deep respect for our former leaders. Within the context of their time, circumstances and convictions they were good and

honourable men – although history has subsequently shown that, as far as the policy of apartheid was concerned, they were deeply mistaken in the course upon which they embarked.[17]

Complicating the theme of progressively enlightened policies, he added a structural explanation for change, arguing that 'much of history has been the story of how changing economic relationships have led to changed social relationships'.[18] Because of the reasonable, progressive and structural nature of government policy, the submission asserted that the TRC process 'must be scrupulously impartial in dealing with transgressions by all parties. It must also ensure that people who may be innocent of any wrong-doing are not publicly humiliated or subjected to trial by the media on the basis of untested allegations.'[19] It also argued that 'the Commission should ... consider the elusive nature of "truth" in an historical or political context. Perceptions of what is true vary from time to time, from place to place and from party to party according to the affiliations and convictions of those involved'.[20]

The idea that multiple causes must be factored into any historical analysis is developed in the submission's statement that 'there is a tendency now for some parties to claim a monopoly of the credit for the transformation process. There were, in fact, many different forces at play'.[21] The submission goes on to list the reformation of the National Party, the role of reformers who worked against apartheid within the system, the collapse of global communism, the importance of the international community, and 'socioeconomic forces'.[22]

Good intentions gone wrong, a reasoned and progressive enlightenment through time, the importance of relating multiple economic, macropolitical and social causes for historical change and an emphasis on impartiality and 'context' – all characterize an historiographical ethic organized very differently to the therapeutic one outlined above. This is a history where trauma is an unintended side-effect of the development of a modern state rather than the central instrumentality and consequence of that state's power.

This resistance to letting the traumas of apartheid stand as the centre of gravity for historiography can also be seen in interviews I conducted with staff at the Robben Island Museum. The first person I spoke with, Eva, had lived on the island since 1982, when her husband began work at the prison. Almost her entire account of Robben Island consisted of trying to downplay the role of the prison on the island, saying she and her husband worked on Robben Island 'because they liked the island ... not because of the prisoners'. She recounted how telling new acquaintants that she lived on Robben Island used to disrupt conversation. But now, she said, Robben Island is a 'popular neighborhood address'. She attributes this problem of Robben Island's lack of social status to a lack of *complete* knowledge about the island during apartheid; for example, 'its natural beauty'. For those who did visit, 'the prison wasn't the main focus of the island, it was just a visitor island', most commonly a place to see the thousands of penguins that cover the island's beaches.

Her account of domestic life on Robben Island reveals similar perspectives. She told me that every Friday there used to be a dance and people could get together and talk. She says life is more hectic now, not as communal as before. Now there are too many people who leave on weekends and have no real ties to the island. Eva's account of an apartheid-era communalism passing into a kind of anomic individualism seeks to de-pathologize Robben Island, changing it from a symbol of the sickness and brutality of the apartheid regime to simply another island getaway that happened to have a prison on it. For her, the history of Robben Island is long and varied, and though it certainly includes the prison, it also includes the mental hospital that was once there, the shipwrecks and even, or perhaps especially, the penguins.

Helen, another long-time employee on Robben Island, expressed a similar concern with the revival of the deep history of the island. She argued that Robben Island needs to recover its archaeological heritage because 'so much history might be lost'. One of the island's chief preservation officials echoed this sentiment when he said that he was interested in integrating all of the historical and ecological aspects of the island's history into the presentation at Robben Island. Both of these residents of Robben Island shared a view of the island that sought to place the prison period of Robben Island, especially the period from the 1960s to the early 90s, firmly in the 'context' of history, and sought out many different kinds of memory of the island's past for that purpose: deep ecology, the native peoples, colonial, military, medical as well as prison histories.

Portraits of the prison were also a source of contention, with several of the people I interviewed expressing scepticism at the idea that Robben Island was any different from any other prison. Helen claimed that it was 'luxurious compared to other prisons'. She approvingly told a story about a Russian visitor to the island who had been sent to a Siberian prison and had said that he wished he had had a place like this [Robben Island] to spend his time. She continued, 'Some guides focus on despair, pain, and the visitors leave depressed. Others are more balanced and when they [the visitors] leave, they feel elated, like something good has come out of this. Something should be done to preserve this balance ... people should leave feeling good, not depressed.'

Her concerns about balance and fairness in the overall picture carried over into a conversation we had about the TRC: 'Causing people to sit down there and repeat or confess' she said, 'the more comes out, the less chance for reconcil-iation. The truth perhaps, but not reconciliation. In this country, everyone was a victim, to focus on certain people is not going to work. Wrong things were done by everyone. Both should be forgiven. It must not be a one-sided thing, it must be very well-balanced.' To anyone who has followed the TRC these are familiar arguments, expressing an anxiety about historical representations that, in this view, sacrifice the long-term, the objective and the contextual to the dramatic, the political and the overly specific.

In these interviews and political party documents, the proper approach to the past is presented as multifaceted and contextual. It must contain all of the known facts and must seek to link these facts together into a complex but balanced picture of various actors, events and constraining conditions. It is a project to be undertaken outside of politics, outside of emotion, and at a safe enough distance from the past that the varied and contradictory 'memories' that compete with history's telling of the past can be effectively incorporated into or discarded from the narrative progression being crafted, according to the prevailing standards of evidence. It argues that the way to remember properly, the way to assemble private memories into a coherent public narrative, is to be as objective, thorough and unemotional as possible, finding out all that happened, putting everything into 'context' and trying to understand the 'development' of the past, how each 'period' flowed from the previous period and into the next. It is equally important to understand the 'reasons' behind history's steady movement into the future, the causes and effects of each event and its attending actors. The preferred source of data for this kind of history is documentary. If people must be used, they are taken to be most reliable when they have the least invested in the story they are telling.

## Unfinished business: resistances to history-writing as therapy

It is not only those who find themselves at odds with the moral message of a therapeutic history, however, who object to history as therapy. The victims themselves have increasingly had something to say about being part of this national historiographical project. What follows is another brief vignette from my fieldwork to illustrate ways of writing trauma into history that resist the therapeutic framework.

This second scene is also about telling stories of painful pasts, but the message and effect are quite different. About a year and a half after the Robben Island interviews, I went to the April 2000 monthly meeting of a victim support group known at the time as the Ex-Political Prisoners and Survivors Group (now known as the Western Cape branch of the Khulumani Victim Support Group). These meetings of victims of apartheid-era gross human rights violations are held in coordination with a psychological support clinic. It was the first time I, a white American researcher, had attended a monthly meeting. There were about sixty people in attendance (including three counsellors, a translator and myself) and we were just about to start the 'storytelling' section of the meeting where individual members volunteer to come before the group and tell their 'story' of their experiences during apartheid.

Mbuyiselo Noqorha, who was sitting across the circle from me, was the first person to raise his hand to speak. I had met Mbuyiselo just before the meeting began, and as the room grew quiet for Mbuyiselo's story, his eyes focused on me. He opted to speak exclusively in English, not waiting for the Xhosa translation. He said:

My name is Mbuyiselo Noqorha and I am a psychiatric patient. I go to see a psychiatrist every week because I have been traumatized. My psychiatrist's name is Dr. Erica Mills and she gave me a brain scan and I get medicine from her every week. I am suffering because I was a black under apartheid and that meant that I was no one.

The whole time, Mbuyiselo locked his eyes on me, and I uneasily met his gaze. The rest of the room seemed to have disappeared; it was as if there were only Mbuyiselo and I, with his struggle to communicate to me his pain and ongoing trials with his memories, and my attempt to figure out what was expected of me at that moment. As he continued, he never took his eyes off me; he spoke very slowly and clearly, and frequently paused for me to nod my under-standing. He continued,

I have post-traumatic stress disorder because I was tortured in prison. They took me and put me in solitary confinement for three months. I had no one to talk to ... that was the worst part, it was a kind of psychological torture. And the food they gave us was shit, it was not something they would give to their dogs. And it was dark for ninety days and I suffered, man did I ever suffer.

At this point, he stood up and raised his shirt and said, 'Look at me, I am skin and bones, I am nothing but skin and bones ... this is what they have done to me. I am not healthy anymore, I cannot eat properly because of the torture.' He finished but kept his shirt raised and continued staring at me, shaking his head. I nodded my comprehension and empathy, but he remained in this position and continued, 'This is what they have done to me, and I still cannot eat, I am still sick. What will happen to me? I ask you, what will become of me?'

To my relief, he sat again and said,

Now I am out of prison and I go to Dr. Mills, ... I had a brain scan and she told me I have PTSD. And I get counselling at the Trauma Centre. The Trauma Centre has helped me, but I am still suffering. I still have to live in the township and it is very dangerous. Last week, I was attacked by some skollies [criminals] and they took my money and I was hurt and it made me very angry. So I am suffering. I am telling you this story because you are new to this group and maybe you can help us, but I do not want to tell it again. It is not good for me.

The main point Mbuyiselo seemed to be trying to drive home to me was that things have not changed, that the historical moment is not, for him, a new one in any tangible way. He still suffers physically and psychologically from his torture. He still lives in poverty and fears for his life. He still has not been able to recover from a past (and a present) that keeps him too thin, too medicated, too hungry

163

and too vulnerable. Storytelling here is not a redemptive exercise. It is a means to an end, addressed to a new visitor who might have some way to help. Therapy perhaps has had some benefit for him personally, but even in his private life, it fails to address or have an impact on the structural and historical problem of what group members often refer to as 'real change'.

Mbuyiselo is now a member of the local executive committee of Khulumani, and since this first meeting I attended, he and the group have developed a deep scepticism of the idea that telling your story has any lasting or significant historical or therapeutic effect.[23] In fact, several group members have asserted that telling their story has actually been harmful. Most group members, however, continue to come to monthly meetings and report that they value the storytelling process; but not for the expected reasons. Their stories of the past are framed by a very different historiographic ethic, one that is still centred on traumatic memories, but that puts those tales of trauma to different historical and political uses.

One of the group's major critiques is that storytelling about trouble carries with it an implication that the suffering is over and the narrator is now in a position to reflect on and speak out about it. For the members of the group, their key assertion is that things have not changed and that to ask victims to tell their stories of (and thus recover from) *prior* suffering for the good of the nation is premature, insulting and politically suspect. For these members, writing South African history as a history only of traumatic events misses the social, political and economic structures that made apartheid in the first case a condition of chronic suffering rather than of acute, traumatic suffering. The traumatic suffering they experienced was real and makes up the content of many of their stories, but it is not the centrepiece of their story about the past.

In addition, many group members resist the idea of a memorial imperative implicit in a therapeutic historiography. They are often sceptical of the culturally alien idea that talk therapy with a stranger should be the privileged mode of recovering from traumatic events. Because they feel their suffering is not over, the idea that they should be narrating their trouble is rendered doubly strange. For these reasons, the proposition that storytelling is an important, necessary means of crossing boundaries and facilitating interracial understanding in a post-conflict context is generally not paid much attention. Instead, the group members often describe the usefulness of storytelling in terms of the solidarity it builds among those who have suffered and continue to suffer the violences of apartheid.

> We come to tell our stories because it makes us strong in our hearts to know there are other people like us, and it helps us to work together and not fight amongst ourselves, because, you know, the victims, the victims have been forgotten and so we can come together like this and remember that we are all suffering.[24]

So history-writing, rather than being an exercise that redeems and reconciles former antagonists, is a means of strengthening intra-group bonds in the face of continued trouble.[25] Storytelling for this group also serves as a way to highlight to the media and the government their moral claim that their suffering has not ended and that they have been forgotten. Historiography-as-therapy assumes, as trauma therapy does, that the trauma is over and that it is the task of the therapist, or historian, to convince the patient or the nation that the trauma is over. For Khulumani, however, crafting the history of the struggle means writing a history about a struggle that is not over. Time has passed but the suffering and the struggling continues.

Another major critique of the history-writing as therapy model is that it has been, in South Africa, a victim-centred, but not a victim-driven process. Instead, the group feels that the victims are asked to do the difficult work of uncovering and struggling with painful memories for the benefit of others, whether those others are the Trauma Centre staff, outside observers or the South African nation.

> It does no good. ... I tell my story to the TRC, I tell it to the Trauma Centre and still I have nothing. I am so frustrated. Why do they want to know my story if they don't do anything for me, they give me nothing except, oh, we are so sorry, Mrs. H ... no, I will not tell my story again. They are just laughing at me.[26]

And the same person reiterated at a later interview:

> They [Trauma Centre facilitators] just want us to be victims and tell our stories so they can help us. I am sick of telling my story. It makes them feel good to show that they are helping us, that things are really OK. They don't really want to change things and what good does telling our stories over and over and over do?[27]

Khulumani's history may be framed as a traumatic history, but the group objects to participating in a history-writing effort that is supposed to heal and reconcile the entire nation on the backs of the memorial/therapeutic work of its victims. They want to make traumatic memories, both chronic and acute, the centre of the history of South Africa and of apartheid, but they want to deploy these memories, control them and put them to use in different ways, ways that aren't modelled primarily as 'therapeutic' or reconciliatory.

## Conclusion

What emerges in this group, in contrast to the therapeutic mode of historiography, is a story of the past centred on a long-suffering, but not yet recovered victim. In this story, the suffering of victims acquires meaning not through moral victory in the abstract sense, but through improvement in specific conditions and qualities of life. For these victims, the idea that the past was a period of oppression and the present is a new and redeemed moment of freedom is an illusion, a premature verdict on a not yet finished phase of history's unfolding. Traumatic memories remain the central focus of the historical narrative, but confronting these memories through stories is not enough to redeem the victim. Furthermore, these traumatic memories belong to those who experienced the suffering, and not to others (the nation, researchers, therapists, etc.) who would ask victims to produce and distribute these memories for some greater good. This history is a story that could redeem all involved, not through the grace of the forgiving victim, but through a moral balancing of payments, through practical, tangible means of redress, whether the mode is confession and forgiveness, retribution, reparation or prosecution. Psychotherapy is embraced privately by many as a means of individual recovery, but not as a guide for how the history of apartheid should be written.

## Acknowledgements

None of this would have been possible without the support and trust of the members and staff of Khulumani, the Trauma Centre and the Robben Island Museum. This research was funded by grants from the Academy for Educational Development and the Institute for the Study of World Politics as well as the Anthropology Department of the University of Virginia.

## Notes

1 R. Handler, *New History in an Old Museum: Creating the Past at Colonial Williamsburg*, Durham, N.C., Duke University Press, 1997.
2 P. Antze and M. Lambek (eds), *Tense Past: Cultural Essays in Trauma and Memory*, London, Routledge, 1996, p. xii.
3 All names have been changed to maintain confidentiality.
4 Truth and Reconciliation Commission, *Interim Report*, Cape Town, Truth and Reconciliation Commission, 1996, p. 1.
5 L. Vogelman, 'It's hard to forgive – even harder to forget', *Work in Progress*, 1993, Vol. 9, pp. 14–16.
6 R. Botman and R. Petersen (eds), *To Remember and Heal: Theological and Psychological Reflections on Truth and Reconciliation*, Cape Town, Human and Rousseau, 1996, p. 120.
7 Quoted in I. Liebenberg, 'The Truth and Reconciliation Commission in South Africa: context, future and some imponderables', *SA Public Law*, 1996, Vol. 2, No. 1, pp. 123–159.
8 By psychodynamic psychology, I am referring to the model of psychological form and process rooted in, but extending beyond, Freudian notions of the unconscious, ego and superego, the effects of trauma, the mechanics of emotional and cognitive repression and the techniques of 'working though' and cathartic release.
9 Antze and Lambek, op. cit., and A. Young, *The Harmony of Illusions: Inventing Post-traumatic Stress Disorder*, Princeton, Princeton University Press, 1995.
10 This account is a generalization of a complex field of psychological knowledge and practice. I intend here only to outline those elements of trauma theory that have currency in the broader popular conception of trauma and its effects.
11 K. Farrell, *Post-traumatic Culture: Injury and Interpretation in the Nineties*, Baltimore, MD, The Johns Hopkins University Press, 1998.

12  Antze and Lambek, op. cit., p. xii.
13  African National Congress, *Preface to the Statement to the Truth and Reconciliation Commission*, Cape Town, African National Congress, 1996.
14  U. Kayser, *Creating a Space for Encounter and Remembrance: The Healing of Memories Process*, Johannesburg: Centre for the Study of Violence and Reconciliation, 2001.
15  Young, op. cit., p. 142, and R. Wilson, 'The *sizwe* will not go away: The Truth and Reconciliation Commission, human rights and nation-building in South Africa', *African Studies*, 1996, Vol. 55, No. 2, p. 16.
16  New National Party, *Submission to the Truth and Reconciliation Commission*, Cape Town, New National Party, 1996, p. 7.
17  Ibid., p. 8.
18  Ibid., p. 9.
19  Ibid.
20  Ibid., p. 15.
21  Ibid., p. 16.
22  Ibid.
23  I explore many of the group's critiques of the storytelling process in a report on Khulumani in C. Colvin, *'We Are Still Struggling': Storytelling, Reparations and Reconciliation after the TRC*, Johannesburg, Centre for the Study of Violence and Reconciliation, 2001.
24  From a Khulumani member at the February 2001 monthly meeting.
25  In a related vein, some group members object to the individual-centred focus of the TRC's historiographic approach and insist, instead, that 'the struggle' was the struggle of groups and not of individuals.
26  From an interview with O.H., a Khulumani member, on 18 October 2000.
27  From an interview with the same person on 22 January 2001.

# Part III

# PATTERNING THE NATIONAL PAST

## Introduction

*Katharine Hodgkin and Susannah Radstone*

The intimate relation between nationalism and history has been reiterated in practically every text on the subject since Ernest Renan in 1882,[1] though its complex dynamics are often taken for granted. 'No ideology needs history so much as nationalism', writes Abbas Vali. 'History is indispensable to its romantic narrative, essentialist conceptual structure and apocalyptic claim to truth.'[2] But despite this apparent privileging of history, Vali goes on to argue, nationalism is primarily not so much a 'discourse of origin' as 'a discourse of identity ... constituted in a relationship of otherness'.[3] Rather than being a politics deriving from a certain idea of the past, it arises out of a conception of identity in the present, in which notions of self and other, the sovereign and the non-sovereign, are constitutive. Memory, then, with its particular purchase on the construction of subjectivity, and its insistent bearing on the present, must equally be central in constituting the historical narrative of identity within which the nationalist subject is produced. In nationalist movements and in achieved nation states alike, the appeal to memory articulates the narrative of the nationalist past, and enjoins its subject to recognise and own it.

Memory is thus at the heart of nationalist struggles, transmitted from one generation to the next as a sacred injunction, as Carrie Hamilton's chapter on Basque nationalist families earlier in this volume reminds us; it is also one of the major mobilising forces in the modern nation state, as Pierre Nora's *Lieux de mémoire* effectively demonstrates.[4] That it is precisely *lieux* at stake for Nora – sites, even if abstract and conceptual ones – also reiterates a further bond between memory and nationalism, that of place. Nationalist memory describes a geography of belonging, an identity forged in a specified landscape, inseparable from it. To study memory in the context of the nation, then, is to engage very directly with the relations between individual and collective memory, between the subject and the state, between time and space, that have been recurrent themes in this volume. Public memory – memory in the public sphere – is insep-arable from discourses of national identity, as the chapters in this part of the book will show.

Nationalism is also, notoriously, particularly associated with the notion of contestation. To construct a narrative of the nation implies a large task of suppression and denial of incongruous or undesirable elements – a task Renan described as forgetting its history, placing the failings of memory at the heart of the new nation state.[5] Memory, then, both underpins and undermines the national narrative. The materials available must be constantly reworked to cope with changing priorities, changing national boundaries, changing social or ethnic compositions. The (very widespread) claim to antiquity is in tension with the claim to modernity. Moreover, national narratives are constructed from very different positions. A new postcolonial nation does not tell its story in the same way as an old empire. A stateless nation remembers a very different past to the history taught in the schools of the state which impedes their access to national realisation (and presents a complex set of theoretical issues for concepts of the nation, which cannot be explored here). Nations which have undergone dramatic changes of regime need to establish a way of remembering that will bridge the gap between past and present, asserting continuity and identity at the same time as difference. The public expression and articulation of memory in a national context is thus both problematic and highly charged.

The question of how people remember their own stories, then, is intimately entwined with how they remember the national story. The chapters in this part explore the ways in which shared narratives of the national past work with and work against individual memories, and analyse discourses of memory in the public sphere. Two are concerned with the remaking of societies after dramatic change. Both Nadkarni and Hughes identify the problem faced in the countries under discussion – Hungary and Cambodia – as a problem of continuity: when the regime has been radically transformed, how do people who live through such changes articulate the relationship, bridge the gap, between past and present selves? The day-by-day narrative of events, or the physical landscape, may appear the same, but the meanings assigned to events and landscapes have changed, and as both chapters show, the new regimes are anxious about how that change is signalled and acknowledged in public. In the other two chapters in the part, by Robert Burgoyne and Chris Healy, the problem is not so much continuity as consensus. Both these chapters address specific instances of public memory in the United States. In both, the triumphalist narrative of the rise of America is potentially threatened from the inside by counter-memories, versions of the national past which see conflict and repression rather than liberty and historic destiny; and the question is how different media – museums, memorials, films – may contrive either to mask or to reveal such conflicts.

The problem confronted in Rachel Hughes's chapter is how to come to terms with the memory of civil war – if civil war is the right way to describe genocide perpetrated within a society. The scale and horror of the Cambodian genocide are indeed well up on the scale of the unthinkable, and in trying to explain what happened in Cambodia, to find a narrative structure within which the unthinkable can be accounted for, the post-Khmer Rouge state draws on European models – Pol Pot as the Asian Hitler, the genocide as holocaust. But what Hughes describes is not the irreparable wound of trauma, so much as the problem of how a state can both publicly acknowledge a horrific past and distance itself from it, while the places and people remain the same. 'The killing fields', the name given to the sites of massacre, is a reminder of the normality of the places in which the mass murders took place: the territory which had been the scene of business-like butchery had to be retransformed into the shared land of the population of Cambodia. Hence the dense symbolism of Tuol Sleng, a site that began life as a school, became one of the most feared prisons of the Khmer Rouge, and now serves as museum and memorial to those who died there (and elsewhere). It is, as she describes it, a production of 'post-genocide nationalism' – a particularly difficult and fraught variation on the nationalist theme.

The Tuol Sleng museum, in Hughes's account, is a point of intersection: it must address national and international politics (not to mention international tourism); it must engage with the past while addressing the perceived needs of present and future; it must try to provide something that will do justice to the victims of atrocities, and recognise (authorise) the grief of the survivors; and it must accommodate different religious attitudes. The museum, indeed, could be seen as an institution that combines both recognition and authorisation of catastrophic memories, in the sense suggested by Stephan Feuchtwang in his chapter in our companion volume,[6] and Tuol Sleng exemplifies the tensions implicit in such a programme. To cremate or preserve the remains of the dead; to direct the memorial towards visitors from home or abroad; how to assign guilt, when many of those who died there and are commemorated as victims were themselves members of the Khmer Rouge – all these decisions have implications beyond the immediate questions of curatorial practice. Memory of the killings is localised in the museum, a site in which names, faces, skulls can be gathered together, to make anonymous through their anonymity the killers as well as the dead. The collective memory will be shaped by such sites; it needs them to find a focus, in order to be articulated; but it will also be critical and suspicious, and put them to unexpected use. Thus to talk about public, or indeed national, memory in such a context conceals the divisions and tensions within each category.

Nadkarni's account of the Statue Park in Budapest also reflects on the complex and shifting meanings assigned to the monuments of past regimes. The toppling of the massive statues of the heroes of communism remains one of the most vivid images of the fall of the communist regimes at the end of the 1980s, a clear and straightforward symbol of the overthrow of oppression; but it was not the only response to the presence of these markers of the old regimes. In deciding neither to destroy the statues of Budapest nor to leave them standing, the new Hungarian state is making a series of statements about its relation to the past. On the one hand it attempts to assert a more sophisticated appreciation of Hungary and its history than the simple act of demolishing them would imply. If the destruction of a statue announces that what the statue represents was not 'really' part of the national past but merely an alien imposition, their preservation implies that Hungary is capable of a moderated and analytical approach to its period of Communist rule. This in itself, of course, is also intended to differentiate the new regime from the old: if rewriting history and refabricating the physical environment in the name of ideology are associated with communism, then it is clearly necessary to do the opposite in the name of liberal democracy and toleration.

On the other hand the acceptance of continuity could hardly extend so far as to leave the statues in place, dominating the squares of the city. Hence the ingenious compromise of the Statue Park, relocating the statues to what is effectively a cemetery for dead monuments, and inviting visitors to view them in a new physical – and thus political – environment. This solution, however, produces its own nostalgia and its own narrative of loss, alongside a new identity of tourist kitsch. The question of what the statues meant to the population of Budapest who lived alongside them, or what statues ever mean – to what extent they do indeed act as preservers of memory – is not addressed by the decision to relocate them. The ambiguities and tensions implicit in any attempt to map changing politics onto the city's public spaces remain, summoning up once again the image of Freud's imagined city: what difference might it make to the city as the symbol of memory, if its buildings and monuments were repeatedly moved out to the margins rather than built over?

Robert Burgoyne too engages with the complex ambivalences of public memory, and how it changes over time; here not in the context of a new regime, but of the changing position of rock and roll in the narrative of American identity. The museum is a site of public memory, defined as what is produced out of the interplay between official, commercial and vernacular memory; and if each of these has a different stake in the representation of the past, public memory mediates between their differing accounts to produce a version of the past that may be, as he puts it, 'simultaneously multivocal and hegemonic' (p. 210). The account given by the museum is accordingly complex and multi-layered, insisting on the local, domestic and spontaneous roots of rock music, and at the same time presenting its history as a triumph of American international influence and technological know-how. The central symbolic value of the American flag similarly crosses boundaries between different versions of the American past, summoning up both patriotism and protest, the working class and the nation state.

In the way that the museum strives to produce 'a shared vision of the past that is useful to the present and future' (p. 209), Burgoyne identifies a consensual imperative characteristic of the US's narrative of nationhood: even when the museum presents to the spectator an account of rock and roll as springing out of cultural conflict and upheaval, the narrative drive is to produce an account of how that conflict was overcome. In this way the racism of the music industry, or the anti-authoritarianism of 1960s pop groups, can be contained: the history of rock and roll is recuperated as part of American adolescence, and maturity will approve some aspects and shake its head fondly over others. Rebelliousness becomes part of the authorised past; illegal drugs, on the other hand, have to be sidelined. Protest and dissent are located at the origin of rock and roll, and continue to be at its heart, but at the same time they are recuperated into the mythically American virtues of energy and individualism.

Like Burgoyne, Chris Healy reminds us how the national myths inscribed in cultural forms are driven by a desire either to conceal, or at least to assign safely to the past, the marks of injustice and inequality, of tensions between oppressors and oppressed. But if the rock and roll museum in Burgoyne's account is in the end complicit with hegemonic national narratives, Healy suggests by contrast that film at least potentially may offer a medium in which this wilful forgetting of the nation's history can be challenged. Film, of course, is one of the central sites through which we encounter and re-imagine the past and its relation to the present; and the Western has a particular significance for the United States, Healy suggests, as 'a mythic space which has been crucial to how America's past has been remembered' (p. 226). In his analysis of *Dead Man*, he explores the ways in which film may offer a radical critique of memory practices, and specifically of the Western as fantasy, on many levels beyond that of content (such as editing techniques and music, for example).

Healy's primary concern is with the way in which American history has been misremembered, its colonialist character bypassed or obliterated in order to produce the narrative of the heroic pioneer. By foregrounding the relationship between indigenous and non-indigenous Americans, he suggests, the film simultaneously remembers the Western as genre, and reminds the viewer of the silence at the heart of that genre, its inability to acknowledge its own complicity in the construction of the white American hero. At the same time, however, he also suggests that film can itself offer a critique of conventional ways of thinking about the relation between memory and forgetting in history. If identity politics posits an opposition between the colonised subject who remembers (and claims justice) and the coloniser who forgets (and denies), then the ambiguities and paradoxes of film, and the way it works through sense and affect, can move us beyond this 'positivist' (however politically important) model of history, to 'remind us of the anti-historical qualities of memory' (p. 233). In this sense it is precisely the fact that film does not need to produce a finished narrative or a common version of the past that for Healy makes it particularly fruitful; like memory, indeed, it allows us to rethink the question of historical truth, by way of an awareness of uncertainty, partiality, and constant reinvention.

The complex interweaving of different registers of memory explored in these chapters – individual, popular, public – cannot be reduced simply to the agenda of the politically hegemonic; at the same time, what appear to be counter-

KATHARINE HODGKIN & SUSANNAH RADSTONE

memories and narratives of resistance may be themselves entangled in national mythologies. Political projects more or less explicitly determine the representations of the past in these public memory sites. Museums, films, and other such media are places not only of memory but of intervention: the national subject is to identify with and remember these stories of the national past. If memory is, as Bill Schwarz puts it, the subjective dimension of history,[7] then nationalism, as a discourse of both history and identity, of origin and of subjectivity, is perhaps key in coming to an understanding of the articulation of individual and social in memory.

## Notes

1   See Ernest Renan, 'What is a Nation?' (1882), in Homi Bhabha, ed., *Nation and Narration*, London, Routledge, 1990.
2   Abbas Vali, 'Nationalism and Kurdish Historical Writing', in *New Perspectives on Turkey*, no. 14, spring 1996, p. 23.
3   Ibid. p. 28.
4   Pierre Nora, ed., *Les lieux de mémoire*, 7 vols, Paris, Gallimard 1984–1993.
5   Renan, 'What is a Nation?', op. cit.
6   Stephan Feuchtwang, 'Loss: transmissions, recognitions, authorisations', in Radstone and Hodgkin, eds, *Regimes of Memory*, London, Routledge 2003.
7   Bill Schwarz, 'Memory and Historical Time', in *ibid*.

9

# NATIONALISM AND MEMORY AT THE TUOL SLENG MUSEUM OF GENOCIDE CRIMES, PHNOM PENH, CAMBODIA

*Rachel Hughes*

## Introduction

This chapter interrogates a principal memorial site of the mass political violence of Cambodia under the Khmer Rouge[1] – the state of Democratic Kampuchea. The site of the most significant Khmer Rouge secret police institution, located in Phnom Penh, Cambodia's capital city, is now the Tuol Sleng Museum of Genocide Crimes. The Museum is a place of national traumatic history that has also been taken up in significant international political discourses, and film and tourism literature representations of Cambodia. To discuss Tuol Sleng Museum, it is necessary to examine the local and international discourses that have conspired to produce the symbolic spaces and memorial declarations of a post-genocide nationalism in contemporary Cambodia.

I begin with a discussion of the national, regional and international politics brought to bear upon the Museum during the People's Republic of Kampuchea period (1979–1989). The People's Republic of Kampuchea (PRK) immediately followed the genocidal years of Democratic Kampuchea (1975–1979). I trace the politics of memory in the People's Republic of Kampuchea through to recent years by examining two highly affective sections of the Museum's display. The first of these sections involves photographs of the victims of the genocidal regime – images that have become centrepieces of international representations of modern Cambodia. The second section is built around human remains which are arranged in the shape of a 'map' of Cambodia. Public declarations by Cambodia's King Sihanouk and by prominent government figures have long contested the religious, political and curated role of these remains.

## Site

Tuol Sleng Museum is a renovation of the 'S-21' Khmer Rouge secret police facility – the largest interrogation centre of Democratic Kampuchea.[2] David

175

Chandler, who has extensively examined the institutional role and logic of the S-21 facility, notes that between 1976 and the first days of 1979, S-21 functioned as a place of incarceration, as well as supporting investigative, judicial and counter-espionage activities. Strictly speaking S-21 was an interrogation and torture facility rather than a prison; although people were confined and punished there, no one was ever released.[3] By late 1978 Democratic Kampuchea was under fire from Vietnamese and allied anti-Khmer Rouge *Renakse* (Cambodian) forces advancing from the eastern zones of the country. These armies took Phnom Penh on 7 January 1979, liberating the city from almost four years under Khmer Rouge rule. The gruesome discovery of S-21 was made some hours after the victory.

Tuol Sleng Museum retains a strangely quotidian, unmonumental appearance – a legacy of its origin as an inner-city high school of 1960s Cambodia. The Museum, as a collection of curated objects and spaces, opened to the general public in July 1980. Despite its unremarkable appearance, Tuol Sleng Museum is a highly significant national monument which seeks to educate visitors about the period 1975–1979 and to honour the near-to-two million victims of Cambodia's genocide, especially those 14,000 to 16,000 victims who passed through S-21. The victims of S-21, the Museum's official brochure states, 'were taken from all parts of the country and from all walks of life. They were of different nationalities ... but the vast majority were Cambodians.'[4] Tuol Sleng Museum seeks to preserve the artefacts and extensive secret police files of S-21 'for future Cambodian generations'.[5] As a symbol of the traumatic past at the (urban) centre of the modern nation, the Museum seeks both individual, inter-generational and national renewals. However, as I will detail, the Museum envisaged in 1979 by the PRK government was already vexed by political and popular demands within Cambodia and other nations.

## Nation, memory, landscape

Immediately following the January 1979 defeat of the forces of Democratic Kampuchea in Phnom Penh, Vietnamese and Cambodian administrators faced the reconstitution of a country on the brink of famine, without currency, communications, transport or health systems, and purged of educated and artisan classes. Grant Evans and Kelvin Rowley note that there were few people with knowledge or experience of the bureaucratic functioning of a government, and that by July 1979 warnings arose of an impending famine in Cambodia.[6] Hunger and malnutrition were widespread and medical facilities were to all practical purposes non-existent. Evans and Rowley also observe that, even a year later, the machinery of the new government 'had to do without almost all the usual paraphernalia of a modern bureaucracy'.[7] Yet, despite the country-wide demand for emergency welfare, administration and infrastructure at this time, the new authorities pursued a detailed investigation of the S-21 facility, and readied the site for visitors. The first group of visitors to the S-21 site arrived within three months of liberation, in March 1979. It would seem that a most pressing concern of the new authorities was to have the S-21 site represent to international delegations and foreign journalists the violence and suffering of Cambodians under Pol Pot.[8]

The further development of S-21 as a national museum took place within a wider state objective of exposing the mass political violence of Democratic Kampuchea. The national and international legitimacy of the People's Republic hinged on this exposure and the subsequent production of a coherent memory of the recent past. In addition to S-21, four major initiatives were implemented: a 1979 trial *in absentia* of Khmer Rouge leaders Pol Pot and Ieng Sary; a 'Genocide Research Committee' investigation into Khmer Rouge crimes, involving exhumations of a number of provincial mass graves (1981–1983); the establishment of local memorials into which people were encouraged to place victims' remains; the initiation of an annual day of national public remembrance known as *tivea chang kamheng* (the 'Day of Anger') on May 20; and the 1988 construction of a large memorial *stupa* (shrine) at the Choeung Ek 'killing field' on Phnom Penh's outskirts. Significant personal memorialisation in the form of Buddhist observances undoubtedly occurred alongside the government's initiatives during this period. However, Khmer Buddhist religious influence and practice, though tolerated, were not strongly supported during the greater part of the PRK decade.[9] In contrast, genocide museums, memorials and the May 20 commemorations were facilitated by all levels of government of the PRK. As a result, both the *tivea chang kamheng* commemoration and the physical structures of local-level *stupa* continue to mark scores of prisons, burial and killing sites throughout the country.[10]

Throughout the PRK period ministerial conferences were convened at the Museum, and schoolchildren and army cadres were regularly chaperoned through the Museum's halls.[11] Many such visits and conferences coincided with May 20 observances. After 1984, these solemn gatherings were centred around a small *stupa* erected in the north quadrangle of the Museum. Buddhist rites and political oration were fused into a single ceremony involving song, speech, prayer and offerings. Survivors like Ung Pech, the Museum's first Director, and painter Vann Nath[12] played a key role in such events through their re-telling of personal experiences of incarceration in S-21.

## Tuol Sleng Museum, regional politics and international legitimacy

Tuol Sleng Museum draws primarily on visual material (without explanatory text) to foreground the calculated violence of S-21. Distributed between the Museum's four main buildings are thousands of photographic portraits of prisoners[13] produced by the S-21 authority in the course of the facility's meticulous self-documentation (see below). Also displayed are torture implements used at S-21. By way of secondary sources the Museum displays S-21

177

survivor Vann Nath's paintings of incarceration, torture and execution at S-21, alongside wall-mounted, hand-painted maps of Cambodia. One map represents the demographic scale of forced urban–rural migration under Democratic Kampuchea. Another map details Democratic Kampuchea's 'acts of aggression' toward Vietnam on the Democratic Kampuchea–Vietnam border during 1975–1978. Also shown are photographs of exhumed remains in various locations (most numerous are those of the 'killing field' of Choeung Ek, which serviced S-21) and other images of the general desecration inherited by post-1979 Cambodia. The largest single exhibit of the Museum is a wall arrangement of skulls in the shape of the Cambodian territory, with rivers and lakes painted in 'blood' red. Numbers of persons killed under Democratic Kampuchea, tallied by province, are posted on an adjacent wall. The 'map of skulls', located in the eastern end of Building D, is the final section of the exhibition for visitors who perform a clockwise circumambulation of the Museum (through Buildings A, B, C and D), as encouraged by Museum signs and staff. Issues pertaining specifically to the 'map of skulls' exhibit are addressed below.

The map, which depicts the locations and escalation of Democratic Kampuchea's 'acts of aggression' toward Vietnam, is one of the most important and polemic of all the displays in the Museum. This map presents Vietnam's invasion of Democratic Kampuchea as an act of self-defence by Vietnam. The Museum's photographs and artefacts recount the horrors of S-21 (and, by extension, of Democratic Kampuchea) so forcefully that Vietnam's incursion appears as a humanitarian intervention, providing the salvation of the Cambodian people from further suffering under Pol Pot. According to the Museum, liberation of Cambodia was enacted by a regional ally. Legitimacy was thus afforded to the government of the PRK, which in turn retained Vietnamese (and Soviet-bloc) aid and advisors throughout the following decade.

William Shawcross attests to the shock experienced by foreign correspondents in Cambodia in spring and summer of 1979. At this time, reports from Tuol Sleng prison in particular, as well as photographs of collections of human remains and mass graves elsewhere in the country, 'had an enormous impact as they flashed around the world'.[14] Having successfully initiated the development of S-21, the governing apparatus of the PRK drew widely on museum spaces as zones of 'evidence' and authoritative explanation, capable of fostering both popular national unity and international sympathy and assistance.[15] Long after the first wave of foreign media and local visitors, Tuol Sleng Museum continued to seek national and international audiences. While the United Nations continued to support the exiled Khmer Rouge as the legitimate governing body of Cambodia over the PRK government in Phnom Penh, foreign diplomats, journalists and working visitors to Phnom Penh were escorted on compulsory visits to Tuol Sleng Museum and the Choeung Ek 'killing field'. In such moments of global exposure, the S-21 site came to function as the archetype of prison and killing sites reported throughout the country. Printed texts for foreign consumption and radio broadcasts of the PRK state made careful mention of the horrors of S-21. These publications explicitly narrated a rekindling of Vietnamese and Cambodian solidarity against the China-backed Khmer Rouge. One such text declares:

> At least two million and perhaps three out of Kampuchea's seven million people died. Kampuchea was drained of blood. The cities and villages were utterly devastated. ... Such was the Pol Pot–Ieng Sary regime, installed with the aid of Chinese advisers and Chinese weapons. As a tool of Peking policy, Kampuchea got involved in an atrocious war against Vietnam.[16]

The text – written in English, French and Spanish – also features images of the battered bodies of the last victims found in S-21 'when revolutionary forces arrived'. But the motivations of Vietnam's incursion into Cambodia in 1978, and the value of the resulting changes wrought in Cambodia's reemergence as the People's Republic of Kampuchea, remain grounds for bitter contention, dividing Cambodian commentators and political parties to the present day.

This contention has generated a range of accusations directed at Tuol Sleng Museum. Andreas Huyssen suggests that 'a modern society's memory is shaped by such public sites as the museum and, thus employed, museums are spaces in which the social and symbolic order is produced and affirmed'.[17] While this is true in the Cambodian context, Tuol Sleng also demonstrates that the chaos of the past is, in Milan Kundera's words, 'eager to irritate us, provoke and insult us, tempt us to destroy or repaint it'. Here we find a public site at which 'masters of the future' have accessed the 'laboratories where photographs are retouched and biographies and histories rewritten'.[18] Tuol Sleng's exhibited photographs and material 'evidences' have been consistently and motivatedly misrecognised by international observers. The United States of America and its geopolitical allies – vehemently anti-Vietnamese, and driving what was to be the final decade of Cold War antagonisms – were generally sceptical of Tuol Sleng's graphic portrayals. Official responses from these and other western administrations denounced the Museum as an exaggeration or a fabrication. Such scepticism was fuelled by the assumption that Vietnam's invasion of Democratic Kampuchea was the first in a series of imperialist annexations that Vietnam was planning for the Indochina region. Such sentiments were, unsurprisingly, echoed by remnant Khmer Rouge as they enjoyed the support of the US, China and ASEAN[19] on the Thai–Cambodia border. The Tuol Sleng site, seen as 'Vietnamese trickery', furthered the Khmer Rouge contention that Democratic Kampuchea had been illegally invaded by Vietnam. Extreme versions of this story accused Vietnamese curators of bringing human remains from Vietnam to display at the Museum. The Vietnamese were held to have entirely fabricated S-21 and exaggerated the extent of the killings. Shortly before his death, Pol Pot himself dismissed Tuol Sleng Museum as simply 'a Vietnamese exhibition'. He added: 'People talk about Tuol Sleng, Tuol Sleng, Tuol Sleng ... When I first heard about Tuol Sleng it was on the Voice of America [radio]. I listened twice.'[20]

## Internationalised memory? The application of Holocaust discourses

One of the most notable aspects of the Vietnamese-inflected memorialisation of Cambodia's genocide sites was the deployment of an internationally recognised discourse of genocide – consistently aligning Cambodia's genocide with the European Holocaust of the Second World War. Shawcross traces this phenomenon to 1978, when, following border disputes, Khmer Rouge and Vietnamese officials engaged in 'public warfare and violent recrimination'.

> Vietnam and its allies in the Soviet bloc now directed their own considerable propaganda resources towards blackening of the reputation of the Khmer Rouge. Vietnamese propaganda began what was to be a long campaign to equate Pol Pot with Hitler.[21]

There can be no doubt that such comparisons sought purchase within international political and humanitarian forums. While official representations of 1975–1979 as the 'Cambodian Holocaust' persist in Cambodia to the present day, issues of the political genealogy, i.e. the *communist* basis and Maoist influences of Khmer Rouge ideology, are elided. Instead, Democratic Kampuchea is represented in two (seemingly incompatible) ways. First, that the genocide was an aberration of humanity, *unimaginable* in any experiential sense and in its true effects. Alternatively, the genocide is traced to the obscene misdeeds and malevolent temperaments of the top Khmer Rouge leaders. In fact, these two explanations – the 'inexplicable aberration' and 'a few bad men' theses – are mutually supportive. That the few bad men had their orders carried out clearly indicates that an aberration had indeed gripped the populace, while the unimaginable consequences of the aberration are neatly localised as having originated in the specific psychologies of the *kbal masin* (literally the 'leading apparatus').[22] The complexity of the political, military and socio-cultural circumstances which fostered the Khmer Rouge, the unique concatenation of ideological, isolationist and nationalist desires pursued by an educated party centre, and the various horrific acts carried out by the middle hierarchy under the threat of their own death, are not part of the past memorialised by the new Cambodian state.

But external commentators, in their shock at what was revealed to them in 1979, also drew premature comparisons. John Pilger's report for the British *Daily Mirror* in September 1979 was among the first to expose (to a mass Western audience) Pol Pot's Kampuchea.[23] As Shawcross notes, Pilger described the political and intellectual basis of the Khmer Rouge as 'anarchist' rather than communist, and on a centre spread depicting Tuol Sleng and a killing field, his account invoked the spectre of fascism with the words: 'Murder, Nazi style'. Tuol Sleng prison, Pilger wrote, 'might have been copied from the original [Auschwitz]'. Evans and Rowley recall that Pilger was later criticised for being simplistic and sensationalist and that Shawcross made a specific objection to Pilger's denunciation of Pol Pot as 'an Asian Hitler'.[24] However, Evans and Rowley also comment that: 'The images of starvation and suffering Pilger presented to television audiences may have been overdrawn. But they did much to alert the western public to a disaster that was indisputably real.' They continue by arguing that Pilger 'had also compared Pol Pot's rule to Stalin's rule of terror and Mao's Cultural Revolution' and, moreover, pointed to the fact that 'Shawcross had no objections to those who compared the *Vietnamese* with the Nazis'.[25]

Although the new wording of the Tuol Sleng Museum visitor brochure makes no comparison between Democratic Kampuchea and other states of mass political violence, the connection is still drawn on the English-language signboards at Choeung Ek:

> the most tragic thing is that: – even in this 20th century, on Kampuchean soil, the clique of Pol Pot criminals had committed a heinous genocidal act, they massacred the population with atrocity in a large scale, it was more cruel than the genocidal act committed by the Hitler fascists, which the world has never met [*sic*].

Courtesy of the fraternal relationship between the PRK and East Germany, curators from Tuol Sleng did visit European Holocaust museum and memorial sites. Exactly which European sites were visited, when and by whom, remains unclear. On this question, Judy Ledgerwood draws on an interview conducted by Sara Colm with Mai Lam, a Vietnamese curator who provided significant expertise to Tuol Sleng Museum. Ledgerwood notes that Mai Lam 'traveled to Germany, Russia, France and Czechoslovakia to research other museums' and also notes help from specialists in East Germany where 'death camps were memorialised as monuments to socialism and Soviet liberation'.[26] Serge Thion suggests that Vietnamese working at Tuol Sleng Museum in 1979 'had been trained in Poland' and that an effort had been made to 'attract part of the sinister character of Auschwitz' to Tuol Sleng.[27] The current Director of the Museum, Chey Sophera, reports that he visited East Germany with the then Director Ung Pech by official invitation in 1982.[28]

The 'Tuol Sleng = Cambodian Auschwitz' and 'Pol Pot = Asian Hitler' equations, and their continuing and often confused reformulation in mass media and popular discourses, demonstrate the multiple, internationalised, ideological investments in representations of Cambodia's recent past.

# The improper place of objects: affective and sovereign objects in interstices

## *A memory for faces*

The Museum's Building B displays thousands of photographic portraits of individuals incarcerated at S-21. The portraits were taken by Khmer Rouge cadres assigned to the prison's photography sub-unit. The photographs were proof of each prisoner's entry into S-21. The cadres in S-21's photography sub-unit were also responsible for photographing those prisoners who died during incarceration and important prisoners after they had been killed.[29] Prisoner portraits were proof of extermination, as death was the only possible 'exit' for individuals from the institution. Photography thus also confirmed the efficacy of the institution; through photography the regime enjoyed total recall, a memory for faces. Photo prints and negatives were part of the extensive documentation discovered at S-21 in January 1979.[30] The prisoner 'mug-shot' photographs now occupy the entire ground floor of Building B – exhibited in banks of hundreds of faces. Some portraits of well-known individuals of pre-1975 Cambodia have been enlarged and hung individually, other portraits are grouped in 'family' series to illustrate the commitment of the Khmer Rouge to the total liquidation of the bourgeoisie, including their potentially vengeful progeny.

The prisoner portrait photographs have long been a focus for Cambodian and non-Cambodian engagement with the Museum. Visitor and curatorial interest in the photographs has resulted in the photos being dislocated both physically and semiotically from the physical and representational confines of Tuol Sleng Museum. They are now promoted in multiple international domains and, in this sense, operate as undisciplined envoys of the Museum. Particularly in non-Cambodian contexts, the images are a synecdoche for *all* victims of Pol Pot. For Khmer survivors, the great majority of whom knew only *rural* life and death under Khmer Rouge cadres, the portraits signify a familiar brutality in an unfamiliar setting of urban, highly institutionalised incarceration.

An East German film group assisted in the initial printing from negatives for display at Tuol Sleng.[31] The resulting prisoner portrait photographs and other images of S-21 appeared in early films produced by the PRK government for domestic consumption, such as *Kampuchea: 3 + 4*. Further cleaning, archiving and printing from negatives took place in 1994 with assistance from the Photo Archive Group, a non-governmental organization set up by American photojournalists Douglas Niven and Chris Riley. In 1996, Niven and Riley facilitated the publication of a selection of the S-21 prisoner portraits in a photographic book titled *The Killing Fields*.[32] Innumerable news reports, documentaries and films about Cambodia have featured the Museum's prisoner portraits display. Through these and other media – including local and international tourism literatures – the prisoner portrait photographs have attained wide exposure[33]. However, for reasons of space it is necessary to limit further discussion of these striking images to their role as objects within the Museum exhibition.

Many Khmer, particularly in the first two years of the Museum's operation, came to view the photos in their search for missing relatives.[34] During this period, a number of individual photographs in the prisoner portrait display were recognised by visitors. When recognised, relatives or friends wrote the name of the individual on the displayed photograph in an act of personal and public remembrance. To name and thereby individuate one of the anonymous mass of S-21 victims was also to symbolically reject the inhumane treatment perpetrated *en masse* by the S-21 authorities. But such permanent, public memorial inscriptions were not unproblematic. The practice of inscribing the photographs with names was subsequently disallowed by the Museum, and a sign to this effect remains in place in Building B. For the Museum, the photographs are evidential materials that ought not to be tampered with. Once 'damaged' they are expensive or impossible to replace (they must be reprinted from the negative, where it exists). The current Museum Director's alternative course of action is to offer family or friends a copy of a recognised individual's photograph.[35] What this circumvents is the permanent, public recognition of a victim as a named individual. Also implicit in the alternative offered is an official determination that the proper place of memorialisation and mourning for an individual victim is the private, non-institutional space of the home – not the Museum. The most obvious explanation for the prohibition on naming 'ordinary' victims is that the setting apart of singular, named victims threatens the narrative emphasis of the Museum's display: one of collective suffering engendering popular resolve and resistance, bringing prosperity for all in a new revolutionary (territorial) whole. This whole was, naturally, only that whole which was supported, arbitrated and authorised by the state.

To name a prisoner portrait was also problematic in light of the fact that the majority of S-21 victims were themselves Khmer Rouge cadres, suspected of traitorous activities or tendencies. That is, to identify an individual in the Museum's display also identified that individual as having possibly been Khmer Rouge. A noteworthy ellipsis within the larger political imperative to demonise the Khmer Rouge made such an identification of victims possible. This was the official, positive recognition of a small number of high-profile individuals purged at S-21 for their opposition, or perceived diversion from, policies or ideologies adhered to by Democratic Kampuchea's Party Central. At Tuol Sleng, this group emerged as martyrs of the true revolutionary state – the (future) PRK. This subtle canonisation centred on Hu Nim, former Minister of Information and Propaganda of Democratic Kampuchea. Hu Nim, a dedicated leader whose revolutionary life was well known to his comrades, was arrested in April 1977 and executed three months later.[36] For many years the Museum has singled out one of the bricked-in cells of Building C as having been the cell where Hu Nim was imprisoned. Hu Nim's confessions and cell are pictured in each of five versions of the Museum's visitor brochure used between 1980 and 1999.[37] Photographs of Hu Nim remain on display in Building D, as do images of two of his associates also purged at S-21: Koy Thoun and Hou Youn. The names of these three men, their office in Democratic Kampuchea, and confirmation of their execution, appear on a list of the 'upper brothers' which includes the names of those who remained powerful at their expense: Pol Pot, Ieng Sary and Khieu Samphan. Within this context, relatives of victims pictured at Tuol Sleng were able to approach the Museum authorities as if their loved ones had also been sacrificed for their fidelity to the future state.

Named or unnamed, the prisoner portrait photographs persist as macabre souvenirs of the efficiency of S-21. The standard composition of the images blurs different faces, ages and expressions, in turn forcing a consideration of the magnitude of the killing carried out by S-21. The isolation of each individual in the stark environs of the photograph invokes a sense of the collapse of community or society under the force of pure, reactionary governmentality. Roland Barthes explicates a general situation where photographs whose meanings are too 'impressive' – too affective or disturbing – are quickly deflected, resulting in a situation of aesthetic rather than political consumption.[38] In my own experience, non-Cambodian visitors to the Museum regularly comment on the aesthetic attributes of the photographs – their clarity or size, their obvious physical deterioration as exhibited objects. Such comments often come as prefacing or concluding remarks to those expressing their own reaction to the emotion, *or lack of emotion*, 'there in the faces'.[39] An understanding of photography as 'an art of non-intervention' whereby 'the person who intervenes cannot record [and] the person who is recording cannot intervene' is fiercely intimated in this area of the Museum.[40] The political import of the situation is clarified in thoughts of one's own inability to intervene on behalf of the victims, and of the photographer's non-intervention in the horror despite the emotion shown in the faces before him.

The portraits concentrate the intensity of what (now) has passed and of what (then) was about to become. Barthes relates a cognate response to a photograph taken in 1865 of a young man waiting in a cell to be hanged for an assassination attempt. Barthes is shocked by what he terms:

> the lacerating emphasis of the *noeme* ('*that-has-been*'): The photograph is handsome, as is the boy: that is the *studium*. But the *punctum* is: *he is going to die*. I read at the same time: *This will be* and *this has been*; I observe with horror an anterior future of which death is the stake. ... I shudder ... *over a catastrophe which has already occurred.*[41]

The S-21 photographs similarly gesture to an anterior space in which surveillance, interrogation and torture are the stake. A recognition of the *modernity* of S-21 as a horrific amalgam of repressive ideologies and techniques of physical and psychological violence toward victims is inescapable.[42] Paradoxically, S-21 appears more modern as a prison than Tuol Sleng does as a museum; the latter is beholden to the former for its 'best' exhibited images, for example. The portrait photographs may at first glance be confused with objects produced after 1979 as part of the curatorial project of the Museum (the Museum contains many photographic images taken after 1979, and photographs generally appear without a date or source). In this confusion, the Museum and the prison seem to coexist – with unsettling effects. Historian James E. Young has observed a similar operation in the work of contemporary German artist Jochan Gerz. Examining the Dachau Museum as it appears refracted through an installation by Gerz, Young sees:

> the uncanny resemblance between the language of 'administering memory' at the Dachau museum and the language that once adminis-tered the concentration camp itself. It was as if the Nazi's efforts to control the lives of the former inmates had become both the latent content and the method of the museum's exhibition of the past.[43]

Young interprets Gerz as suggesting 'that what we finally "learn" from such museums may be less about history than how to comport ourselves in its vicinity'. In order to break the unhappy confusion of the *experience of the museum* with the *history we've come to remember*, we should take care never to 'mistake one for the other, even as we cannot know one outside of the other'.[44] In the inter-stices of the Museum populated by such uncanny objects, histories and effects, questions arise for the visitor and theorist alike. What are the limits of the museum as a space of empathy? How is it that the museum and the death camp may casually share artefacts? What of the contradiction of a museum's bureau-cracy and archive being put to work to further visitors' understanding of a place when these same phenomena are central to the violence and terror of the past now represented?

### The King (and the) remains

In 1994, Cambodia's King Sihanouk requested that the government cremate the remains contained in the Museum's 'map of skulls' exhibit. The King's main rationale was that such a ceremony would honour the dead and allow their spirits to be re-born – following the beliefs of Khmer Buddhism. The King offered ten thousand dollars (US) for the cremation ceremony, and another ten thousand dollars to build a memorial *stupa* for the cremated remains. Importantly, the cremated remains were not to be retained on-site at the Museum, but were instead destined for nearby Wat (Temple) Botum. Sihanouk suggested that, after the ceremony had been completed, 'the role of the skeletons would be to bring our country to peace'.[45] The King's request invites an analysis of the relationship between the Museum, the dominant political party, the monarchy and Buddhism in contemporary Cambodia.

In 1991, Sihanouk returned to Cambodia after some thirteen years in exile. For many Cambodians, the expectation that normal life would soon return was symbolised by Sihanouk's homecoming.[46] Buddhist monks played critical ritual roles in many of the festivities staged for the Prince's return, and he himself resumed his royal role as supreme patron of the *sangha*.[47] Sihanouk also resumed his position as head of state with the presidency of the Supreme National Council in 1991. In one of the final chapters of the UNTAC (United Nations Transitional Authority in Cambodia) period, Sihanouk promulgated the new Cambodian constitution on 24 September 1993.[48] Sihanouk was central to the political and symbolic life of the 'reconciled' nation.

Prior to his Tuol Sleng request, during treatment for cancer in Beijing, the King had pledged a large sum of money toward the continued construction of a significant new religious structure – Preah Cakyamoni Chedi – at Wat Phnom in central Phnom Penh. The construction of the Chedi was to provide for the re-housing of a much-revered relic of the Buddha.[49] Following his pledge to Preah Cakyamoni Chedi, another communiqué was released by the King. This statement contained specific instructions as to the treatment of his *own* body on the occasion of his death. His funeral pyre was to be small and simple, with fresh flowers and natural timbers, and 'if possible, some sandal-wood'.[50] The King took the opportunity to forbid the government to invite foreign leaders to be present at any ceremonies of mourning as, he reasoned, 'our country is very poor and not equipped to receive [them]'.[51] Interest in the success (or otherwise) of the King's treatment in Beijing fuelled constant polit-ical speculation as to a successor to the Cambodian throne, implying that Sihanouk was close to death. However the presumption of Sihanouk's immi-nent death far from diminished his symbolic authority. Instead it reinforced a status already present in the traditional and persistent notion of Sihanouk as a mythic figure, a god-king.[52]

Following his generous gesture towards a relic of Buddha, and the arrange-ment of his own funeral, one meritorious in its humility, Sihanouk's next turn was to the question of the proper treatment of another set of remains, whose traces also provoked questions of national identity and sovereignty. In a third communication in as many months, the King requested the cremation of the Tuol Sleng remains. In doing so, the King sought to settle a number of ghosts. As Ledgerwood has argued:

> The king was trying to lay to rest not just the souls of the dead, but the deep divisions between the coalition partners in the new royal govern-ment – those placed in power by Vietnamese 'liberators' and those who fought a 'war of Liberation' against Vietnamese 'occupation'.[53]

It is likely that Sihanouk was aware of the volatility of his strategy. While simultaneously declaring an intention to avoid political activity on his return to Cambodia from Beijing,[54] Sihanouk engaged the new coalition government in what has become a controversial, long-running and unavoidably politicised debate. At the time of the request, Tuol Sleng Museum remained, some fifteen years after its inception, the central symbolic site of the founding of the (modern) Cambodian nation, the ruling Cambodian People's Party (CPP) and, officially, of the population's gratitude to Vietnam and the CPP for their defeat of the Khmer Rouge. Sihanouk's plea was bolstered by his own personal authority and the Khmer Buddhist dictate that, following death, cremation was the correct, indeed the *correcting*, practice.

The Royal Government agreed to the King's request. Further, the government made public its intention to create film and photographic records of the 'map of skulls' in preparation for its destruction. Given the post-election climate of political cooperation instigated by UNTAC, and Sihanouk's role at the apex of Khmer Buddhism, direct opposition by the CPP was politically unwise.[55]

Then, in a complete reversal, the King announced he would drop his request. This change was purportedly 'in response to a plea from the Central Committee of the CPP [to] keep the bones as evidence of the genocidal regime'.[56] This refusal of Sihanouk's request was somewhat depoliticised by its apparent origin in the hearts and minds of Sihanouk's own 'little people'; the state press agency reported that most Cambodians did not agree with the planned cremation and sought the maintenance of 'the history of Pol Pot's genocide against the people'; opinion had been garnered by 'polls conducted in 16 provinces and cities throughout the country', the results of which demonstrated that '83.20 percent [were] against [the cremation]'.[57]

It remains of key importance that there was the supposition of a national disquiet in Sihanouk's original request – such that, in being cremated, 'the role of the skeletons would be to bring *our country* to peace'.[58] In such a phrase, Sihanouk broadcast his own de facto recognition of Tuol Sleng Museum as a *national* monument. However the King's recognition of the remains as fused to determinations of future sovereignty and social stability was undermined by his insistence that these remains should be treated *like any other* – that is, subject to the formal religious requirement of cremation. Exhumed remains had everywhere been placed, uncremated, in local *stupa* and museums. These relics were *unlike any other*: they were designated as 'evidence' which indicted perpetrators and proclaimed the legitimacy and necessity of the new state.

Voices and interests both internal and external to Cambodia have repeatedly called for the cremation of the Tuol Sleng 'map of skulls'. As Homi Bhabha reminds us, 'counter-narratives of the nation … continually evoke and erase its totalising boundaries – both actual and conceptual – [and] disturb those ideological manoeuvres through which "imagined communities" are given essentialist identities'.[59] Running counter to the dominant political sentiments of contemporary Cambodia, an expatriate Khmer publication contends:

> In concentration camps or goulags [*sic*] of the world, there is not such a display of contempt towards the bones of the martyrs … It is necessary that UN and the great powers say openly if these bones of our martyrs are 'exhibits' for a possible court to trial the Khmer Rouge leaders.[60]

In 2001 Prime Minister Hun Sen signalled one possible resolution by expressing his willingness to call a National Referendum on the issue. But Hun

187

Sen cautioned that any future trial of former Khmer Rouge leaders must be concluded before such a Referendum, in case remains were needed as evidence before the court.[61]

The debate around the cremation of the remains currently displayed in memorials throughout Cambodia – and as to who might, or should, intervene on the issue – was thus a prolonged and complex one. In an unexpected final turn, however, after this article had gone to press, the controversy was brought to a conclusion. On 10 March 2002, the map of skulls was dismantled. The taking apart of the map was accompanied by a ceremony in which Buddhist monks performed prayers and chanting. The Museum's Director, Chey Sophera, was reported as saying that the decay of the skulls had hastened their removal. Chey Sophera also stated that by removing the skulls the Museum would 'end the fear visitors have while visiting the Museum'. It seems curatorial devices once considered essential to an understanding of the true horror of Democratic Kampuchea are now committing improprieties in their very frightfulness, and are considered antithetical to the peace-time encouragement of tourism. It has not been reported where the cremation of the skulls will take place, nor where the cremated remains might be finally placed. The map of skulls is to be replaced by a large colour map of Cambodia, identifying the location of mass graves and prisons created by the Khmer Rouge. A large 'photographic reproduction' of the map of skulls will also be displayed. Past comments of the King supporting the skulls' cremation were reported in the press, but he appears not to have made any direct comments on this most recent event.[62]

## Conclusion

As the naming of victims' portraits and the cremation debate attest, popular misgivings about the Museum see it as failing or perhaps even preventing correct cultural and religious practice – and thus social renewal. The Tuol Sleng Museum attempts to portray exceptional circumstances and events, at the same time as it services local political and geopolitical demands. Reification and remembrance are accommodated within the space of the Museum – but not because of a lack in specific 'historical' information or curatorial impetus. It is instead because the tangible and intangible consequences of the violence of Democratic Kampuchea can only be inadequately expressed, and are therefore unavoidably political. It is certain that the masters of the future will continue to contest the traces of violence that traverse the Cambodian landscape.

## Notes

1 The term 'Khmer' refers to the dominant indigenous ethnic group of Cambodia. The Khmer Rouge (Red Khmers) grew out of a group of young Cambodian leftist intellectuals trained abroad or by French Marxists in Cambodia in the 1950s and 1960s. See D.P. Chandler, *Facing the Cambodian Past: Selected Essays 1971–1994* (Australia: Allen & Unwin, 1996), p. 210. For most of the period of Democratic

Kampuchea (1975–1979), Cambodia remained under the control of an unidentified political party of the Khmer Rouge. The existence of this party, the Communist Party of Kampuchea, was not revealed until September 1977 – nearly two and a half years after Democratic Kampuchea was established. See Chandler, *Facing the Cambodian Past*, p. 229.

2  The 'S' stood for *sala*, or hall, while '21' was the number assigned to *santebal*, Democratic Kampuchea's security police, or special branch. See D.P. Chandler, *Voices from S-21: Terror and History in Pol Pot's Secret Prison* (Chang Mai: Silkworm Books, 1999), p. 3.

3  Chandler, *Voices from S-21*, p. 15.

4  Visitor brochure (Tuol Sleng Genocide Museum, 1999), p. 3.

5  Visitor brochure, p. 6.

6  G. Evans and K. Rowley, *Red Brotherhood at War: Vietnam, Cambodia and Laos since 1975* (London and New York: Verso, 1990), p. 154.

7  Evans and Rowley, *Red Brotherhood*, p. 161.

8  See Ministry of Culture, Information and Press, *Department of Ancient Temples, Conservation, Museums and Tourism Report* (Phnom Penh: People's Republic of Kampuchea, 1980); see also Chandler, *Voices from S-21*, p. 8.

9  See C.F. Keyes, 'Communist Revolution and the Buddhist Past in Cambodia' in C.F. Keyes, Laurel Kendal and Helen Hardacre (eds), *Asian Visions of Authority: Religion and the Modern States of East and Southeast Asia* (Honolulu: Hawai'i, 1994), pp. 43–74 and I. Harris, 'Buddhism in Extremis: The Case of Cambodia' in I. Harris (ed.), *Buddhism and politics in twentieth-century Asia* (London: Cassell, 1999), pp. 54–78.

10  See 'mapping' of these sites by the Documentation Center of Cambodia and the Cambodian Genocide Program (Yale University) at http://www.yale.edu/cgp.

11  Keo Lundi, Senior Guide, Tuol Sleng Museum, pers. comm., 2000.

12  The irony of the participation of S-21 survivors in public memory as staged through various artistic mediums and activities is that it recalls the type of work that afforded their survival, literally, *in the first place*. This small group of S-21 prisoners was required to sculpt busts and paint portraits of Pol Pot. Towards the end of 1978, they were entrusted with a task of monumental proportions. They were to construct 'an eight-meter-tall concrete statue of Pol Pot standing with farmers carrying flags and such' – intended to show the history of class struggle. The monument was never completed. At the request of the new government in November 1979 Vann Nath agreed to contribute a number of oil paintings to the Museum. See Vann Nath, *A Cambodia Prison Portrait: One Year in the Khmer Rouge's S-21* (Bangkok: White Lotus, 1998) p. 82. These painted works are displayed in Buildings B and D.

13  While I have noted that S-21 was not technically a prison, I do use the term 'prisoner' – in line with Chandler and others – to refer to individuals detained, tortured or killed at S-21.

14  W. Shawcross, *The Quality of Mercy: Cambodia, Holocaust and Modern Conscience* (New York: Simon and Schuster, 1985), p. 45.

15  Also a priority for the new government was the National Museum of Khmer Arts and Culture, which re-opened three months after liberation on 13 April 1979. See H. Peters, 'Cambodian History Through Cambodian Museums' in *Expedition*, vol. 37, no. 3, p. 52.

16  *Pol Pot's Legacies* (Hanoi: Foreign Languages Publishing House, 1979).

17  A. Huyssen, *Twilight Memories* (London: Routledge, 1995), p. 15.

18  M. Kundera, *The Book of Laughter and Forgetting* (London: Penguin Books, 1983), p. 22.

19  Association of South East Asian Nations.

20  Pol Pot, interview with Nate Thayer (1997), quoted in Chandler, *Voices from S-21*, p. 8.

21  Shawcross, *The Quality of Mercy*, p. 64.

22 This is Chandler's translation. He states: 'the collective leadership of Democratic Kampuchea [was] known as the Upper Organisation (*angkar loeu*), the Organisation (*angkar*), or the "upper brothers" (*bong khang loeu*) to outsiders and as the Party Center (*mochhim pak*) or leading apparatus (*kbal masin*) to members of the Communist Party of Kampuchea [the party of Democratic Kampuchea]'. See *Voices from S-21*, p. 15.

23 J. Pilger, *The Daily Mirror* (12 and 13 September 1979). Cited in Shawcross, *The Quality of Mercy*, pp. 139–41.

24 Evans and Rowley, *Red Brotherhood*, p. 155.

25 Ibid. (my emphasis).

26 J. Ledgerwood, 'The Cambodian Tuol Sleng Museum of Genocidal Crimes: National Narrative' in *Museum Anthropology*, no. 21, vol. 1 (1997), p. 89.

27 S. Thion, *Watching Cambodia* (Bangkok: White Lotus, 1993), pp. 181–182.

28 Personal communication with Chey Sophera, 2000.

29 Chandler, *Voices from S-21*, p. 27.

30 Ibid., p. 3.

31 Ibid., p. 27; see also Department of Ancient Temples Conservation, Museums and Tourism Report, 1980. The East German film group – of Herronofsky and Scheumann Studios, East Germany's only private documentary film company – first visited the S-21 site in 1979. The three films on Cambodia made by Herronofsky and Scheumann Studios were: *The Angkar*, *Jungle War* and *Kampuchea: Death and Rebirth*. See P. Maguire, *Facing Death* (New York: Columbia University Press, 2003). The 1980 Report also states that other negatives were to be taken to be printed in Vietnam.

32 Niven and Riley, in exhibiting a number of the S-21 prisoner portrait photographs in multiple international locations (including the Museum of Modern Art, New York, in 1997) and in producing the book *The Killing Fields*, have served greatly to increase the global exposure of the images. Many of these images, and others displayed only at Tuol Sleng Museum, were also included in a CD-ROM collection of the Cambodian Genocide Project of Yale University. The collection is now accessible via the internet website of the CGP (see n.10).

33 See R. Hughes, 'The Abject Artefacts of Memory: Photographs from Cambodia's Genocide', in *Media Culture and Society*, vol. 25 no. 1 (2003).

34 Ledgerwood, 'The Cambodian Tuol Sleng Museum', p. 90.

35 Chey Sophera, Director, Tuol Sleng Genocide Museum, personal communication, 2000.

36 See Chandler, *Voices from S-21*, p. 64.

37 In the most recent version of the Museum brochure (1999) the reference to Hu Nim has been omitted.

38 See R. Barthes, *Camera Lucida* (London: Vintage, 1993), p. 36. Veteran documentary film-maker Gerhard Scheumann, who led the East German film crew into Cambodia in 1979, was reportedly 'most impressed [by] the high technical quality of the [original] photographic work [of the S-21 portraits]' (Maguire, *Facing Death*).

39 Most often visitors reported that they had been moved by one or many of the various emotions 'evident' on the faces of the prisoners, nominated as: fear, courage, defiance, confusion, anger, distraction. Others insisted their own sadness and confusion arose as a result of what they perceived to be the passivity and 'unknowingness' of those pictured. Overall, the non-Cambodian visitor population overwhelmingly named the prisoner portrait photographs in Building B as the space in which they spent most time during their visit.

40 S. Sontag, *On Photography* (New York: Farrar, Straus and Giroux, 1973), pp. 11–12.

41 Barthes, *Camera Lucida*, pp. 95–96. In his text Barthes defines the 'field of cultural interest' of the photograph as its *studium*. The 'unexpected flash' which breaks or punctuates the photograph's *studium* is the *punctum* of the photograph. However, in the

1865 photograph, Barthes identifies a *punctum* 'which is no longer of form but of intensity, [it] is Time', p. 96.

42 On the question of the genealogy of S-21, Chandler writes: 'Comparisons have frequently been made between S-21 and the Nazi extermination camps. ... Writers who have examined the Nazi camps illuminate the culture of obedience that suffuses total institutions and the numbing dehumanisation that occurs, among perpetrators and victims alike, within their walls. [T]he Nazis, like the Cambodians, coupled [indifference] ... with the pleasure they derived from causing pain. The same callousness toward "guilty people" and similar bursts of sadism characterised, among others, the judges in the Moscow show trials in the 1930s, the perpetrators of the massacres in Indonesia in 1965 and 1966, the military torturers in Argentina, and those who organised the mass killings in Bosnia and Rwanda in the 1990s', *Voices from S-21*, pp. 143–144.

43 J.E. Young, *At Memory's Edge: After Images of the Holocaust in Contemporary Art and Architecture* (New Haven and London: Yale University Press, 2000), p. 124.

44 Young, *At Memory's Edge*, p. 124.

45 Sihanouk, cited in Peters, 'Cambodian History', p. 61.

46 S. Heder and J. Ledgerwood, 'Politics of Violence: An Introduction' in S. Heder and J. Ledgerwood (eds), *Propaganda, Politics, and Violence in Cambodia: Democratic Transition under United Nations Peace-keeping* (New York and London: East Gate, 1996), p. 12.

47 Keyes, 'Communist Revolution', p. 64. The *sangha*, or Buddhist order of monks, is seen as the exemplar, teacher, and embodiment of the *dhamma*, the message of the Buddha. See 'Communist Revolution', p. 44.

48 Heder and Ledgerwood, 'Chronology' in *Propaganda, Politics and Violence in Cambodia*, pp. 266–267.

49 This relic – a 'bone of the Buddha' – was brought to Cambodia by a delegation of Sri Lankan Buddhist monks as an expression of Buddhist kinship on the occasion of the 2,500th anniversary of the Buddha's death in 1957. See Mang Channo, 'Construction Begins on New Site for Sacred Buddha Relic', *The Phnom Penh Post*, 27 August 1992, p. 8.

50 Cited in 'King Calls for Prompt Cremation to Avoid "Rapid Decomposition" ', *Agence Khmer de Presse*, 11 October 1994, p. 3

51 'King Calls for Prompt Cremation', p. 3. The King requested only the Queen and several 'very close' and 'very loyal' people be present at his cremation, and that four Buddhist monks be ready to travel from Cambodia to Beijing or Pyongyang in the event of his death in either of these residencies. The statement also divulged that the King wished his final resting place to be the Silver Pagoda in the grounds of the Royal Palace.

52 The traditional Khmer King embodied a supreme religious being. His direct involvement in the agricultural, cultural and spiritual life of the nation via his symbolic interventions (organised around particular lunar moments or festival periods), and through his exemplary personal behaviour, provided for prosperity and peace throughout the Kingdom. See Keyes, 'Communist Revolution', p. 46.

53 Ledgerwood, 'The Cambodian Tuol Sleng Museum', p. 95.

54 Prior to the Tuol Sleng request, Sihanouk had stated that, on returning to his 'beloved country', he would 'serve the little people of Cambodia [in] social, humanitarian, water policy, public health, national education [fields]', and would not 'engage in political activity with anyone', *Agence Khmer de Presse*, 3 December 1994, p. 8.

55 It is also important to note here that King's request, and the government's initial acceptance, speaks plainly of the almost universally recognised importance in contemporary Cambodian society of the role of the benevolent dead. Demands of ancestral responsibility, essentially to feed the hungry spirits, are keenly felt by Khmer. This is especially the case during the fifteen day period of the Buddhist festival of

*pchhum ben* (the festival of the ancestors) which occurs in the period of *photrobot* (September/ October).

56 'King Sihanouk Drops Request to Cremate Bones', *Agence Khmer de Presse*, 19 January 1995, p. 2.

57 Ibid., p. 2.

58 Cited in Peters, 'Cambodian History', p. 61. My emphasis.

59 H. K. Bhabha, 'DissemiNation: Time, Narrative, and the Margins of the Modern Nation' in H. K. Bhabha, *Nation and Narration* (New York and London: Routledge, 1996) p. 300.

60 'Cambodia, Right of Death to Burials and the Puppet Regime: are the bones of our martyrs exhibits?' *Khemara Jati*, 17 April 2001.

61 This caution is evinced in Section 4 of the Report of the United Nations Group of Experts for Cambodia, 1999. (This Report investigates the scope and ramifications of a possible trial of former Khmer Rouge leaders with international assistance.) The Report states: 'The physical evidence most relevant for any proceedings can be divided into three categories: human remains, structures and mechanical objects, and documents.'

62 See *Associated Press* report 'Cambodia Skull Map Dismantled', 10 March 2002. Assistance in the creation of the new colour map will come from the Documentation Center of Cambodia.

# 10

# THE DEATH OF SOCIALISM AND THE AFTERLIFE OF ITS MONUMENTS

## Making and marketing the past in Budapest's Statue Park Museum

*Maya Nadkarni*

A pile of photographs taken by visitors to Budapest's Statue Park Museum (*Szoborpark Múzeum*) fails to capture any image of a statue or monument that does not include houses, billboards, or power lines in the background, or weeds growing in the gravel that lines the paths.[1] Moreover, the photographs do not isolate each object from its neighbours, and this serialization frustrates the claim any monument might make to uniqueness: its capacity to overwhelm time and space, and hence to transform an event in history into the eternity of myth. Only a close-up could achieve this separation, at the cost of not only fragmenting or distorting the image of the statue or monument, but also breaching the auratic distance such objects traditionally demand. Yet the prospects are no less discouraging if a wide shot is attempted, perhaps standing on the highway that borders one side of the park. This reveals many of the monuments as incongruously small, standing unsupported by the enormous bases upon which they once stood.

In other words, these images demonstrate the difficulty of attaining a visual perspective that does not transgress traditional expectations of how to encounter a monument. Rather than dominating the public spaces of the city's centre, these objects are isolated in a small park a twenty-minute bus ride from the centre of Budapest. Deprived of the tall pedestals that traditionally prevent close examination, many are mounted low on the ground, inviting physical as well as visual engagement. Missing as well are plaques that might narrate the monuments' individual histories. Instead, each is numbered and arranged with its neighbours according to common themes, to be deciphered with the purchase of a guidebook. There are no benches, greenery, or space to have a picnic. Instead, the park's main architectural features are symbolic rather than functional: the red brick façade that dominates the entrance, and the path that winds past the monuments in the shape of figure-eights (the mathematical sign for infinity). The façade's architectural grandeur deflates once it is identified as a false front with nothing behind it, and the 'infinite' path guides the visitor into a brick wall – architectural metaphors for both the aspirations and end result of the ideology that erected the monuments.

The visitor's inability to attain a 'monumental perspective', however, is more than an effect of the statues' spatial dislocation and the park's architecture. Rather, these monuments are unable to produce the effect of the monumental because the incontestable future they projected has failed to materialize. They are artefacts of a now-discredited regime: forty-one socialist-era statues, monuments, and memorial plaques transferred from the public spaces of Budapest after free elections removed the communists from power in spring 1990. Attributes considered inherent to the monument have thus fallen away because of their sudden descent into what Mikhail Yampolsky terms 'temporalization' – the abrupt insertion into historicity of what was previously experienced as an 'islet of eternity'.[2] Architect Ákos Eleőd's winning proposal for the park's design sought to materialize this historical and perceptual shift through the creation of a 'neutral' space that would inspire neither propaganda nor mockery. Arguing that a more 'tendentious' anti-propaganda park would occupy the same totalizing mindset that erected the monuments, he stated, 'I would like this park to be right in the middle: neither a park to honour Communism, nor a sarcastic park that provokes tempers, but a place where everyone can feel whatever they want. … People can feel nostalgic, or have a good laugh, or mourn a personal tragedy connected with the period.'[3] Such a park, he argued, open to its visitors' diverse memories of and relationships to the monuments, embodies the essence of democracy.[4] That is, while collecting the monuments serves the museum's function of documenting the aesthetic and historical politics of the previous era, the fact that the park itself could be created not only demonstrates the collapse of the communist regime, but also proves the democratic and civilized way in which it happened.

As this logic suggests, the decision to create the Statue Park Museum constructed – as much as it was constructed by – a narrative of Hungary's system-change,[5] and the transformations of history, temporality, and public space it was assumed to accomplish. Thus while Eleőd considers the park Hungary's only memorial to the end of communism,[6] the park also commemorates the historical and memorial politics of the 'founding' of postsocialism itself. In this chapter, I shall explore this process of 'making history' through the debates that resulted in the park, as well as examine the life of the park since its opening. The strategies used to promote the park, I will argue, challenge the rhetorical and architectural strategy of democratic openness and temporalization made visible in the photographs described above. Instead, the uncanny afterlife of the park's monuments, and the fantasies and memories they efface or unleash, suggest what has been lost in the civilized act of historical preservation, and what emerges to haunt postsocialist memorialization from an era years past its demise.

## The problem of communist monuments

Traditionally, monuments 'face two ways in time': while they instantiate official history by commemorating a past figure or event, their very durability projects a specific future as the culmination of this historical vision.[7] Signifying the inevitability of both past and future, the monument renders the present static and immutable. This is the source of Robert Musil's famous formulation that 'there is nothing in this world as invisible as a monument':[8] the monument effaces its own existence in the present because its hypostasis and temporal completion negate any potential for future transformation. Musil views this invisibility as a 'carefully calculated insult' to the figure or event commemorated; as James Young argues, the monument's ossification seems to discharge the community from an obligation to remember, and thus the very impulse to memorialize may 'spring from an opposite and equal desire to forget'.[9] Yet although this archival function may indeed transform the monument into a proxy rather than a spur to memory, its invisibility in the present is a function of its apparent eternity, and hence demonstrates its effectiveness in signifying the permanence of the regime that erected it. As such, the monument's memorial value usually only inspires attention as a marker within cyclical time: a site to commemorate holidays within the official calendar.

In democratic societies, the monument's invisibility also indicates the inconsequence of its bid for eternity in an environment where different political claims are always competing for public visibility. For authoritarian regimes, however, monuments are key elements of their 'hegemony of representation', in which signs and symbols do not represent their literal meaning, but through their ubiquity rather signify the immutability of the system itself.[10] In opposition to right-wing discourses that sought to disavow their modernity through nationalist narratives of historical continuity, communism was conceptualized as a break with tradition: an intervention in the course of history in order to construct it anew. Thus, while on a superficial level historical rhetoric and symbols served to give national justification to communist rule, these new histories also demonstrated the regime's mastery of the past and the ability to mould it to their will. And if the past was the servant of the politics of the present, the present was to be sacrificed to an imminent and yet always just-out-of-reach glorious future.

The quotidian present-day thus posed a challenge to this logic, which under Stalinism attempted to eliminate the very category of 'everyday life'. After Hungary's failed 1956 revolution against Soviet rule, however, one of the unstated compromises that would make Hungary 'the happiest barracks' in the former Soviet bloc was the regime-sanctioned retreat of individuals from public and political spheres into private arenas. While more peaceful than previous decades, this private life was characterized by a sense of inertia and eventlessness, of being left out of international trends and outside the 'global course of history'. In the words of historians András Gerő and Iván Pető, 'time seemed to have stopped: socialism was being built, but the construction process appeared to be uncompletable, never ending'.[11] By the end of the era, even the promise of a beautiful future had fallen silent, to be replaced by the everyday concerns of 'existing socialism'. Public monuments, rituals, and political symbols continued to buttress the faltering regime's ideological self-justification, however, until almost the last days of its rule.[12] While invisible in their iconicity, the monuments' function as indexes of the unchangingness of everyday life allowed them to take on prosaic (and often ironic) meanings in the urban environment they helped to organize.

The political changes in the former Soviet bloc transformed the stasis and calculability of everyday life into the unnerving acceleration of postsocialism, both exhilarating and frighteningly unstable. Such temporalization of the very structure of the present would seem to demand similar changes to the monuments that had attempted to organize its historical and temporal perception. Yet while images of toppled monuments and headless statues of Lenin dominated the imaginations of both the former Soviet-bloc states and their Western observers, as materializing the historical break represented by the political transformations, this issue of temporalization was more fraught in the Hungarian case. No shots were fired and few monuments vandalized during Hungary's system-change, which was negotiated from above between the communist government and its democratic opposition. As historian István Rév puts it, after forty years, Hungary's era of state socialism simply appeared to 'melt like butter in the late summer sunshine' of 1989,[13] and the reform communists (who had replaced the more than thirty-year rule of János Kádár after his forced retirement in 1988) quietly retreated after free elections brought a new government to power in spring 1990. 'By the time people began to realize it', observe Gerő and Pető, the era 'was already over'.[14]

The demise of socialism thus did not represent revolution, but the apparent end of the age of revolutions. Hungarians welcomed this break from the tradition of their painful and turbulent twentieth-century history, electing in 1990 a conservative coalition government led by the Magyar Demokrata Fórum (MDF) on the basis of its promise of 'peaceful power' (*nyugodt erő*) rather than radicalism. Thus, while elsewhere the destruction of communist monuments often functioned as a tool of popular rebellion, Hungary entered a new era with the majority of its monuments unscathed by the forces of revolutionary transformation.[15] Instead, the question of communist monuments became part of *post*socialist politics, and the debates concerning their fate became battles to determine the nature of the system-change and what was to follow.

For many Hungarians, the withdrawal and self-dismantling of the communist regime – even if as the result of public pressure – denied them the moment of catharsis. By 'killing itself instead of letting the people do it', Rév argues, communism even in death denied the Hungarian people the 'experience of their sovereignty'.[16] Indeed, local governments endeavoured to anticipate public demand by changing street names and planning the removal of monuments even before the communists left power. The communist city authorities themselves removed the main Lenin statue from Budapest in spring 1989, ostensibly for maintenance.

The absence of revolution, however, did not diminish its power in the national imagination, particularly in the terms of the events of 1956: a set of uprisings and bloody reprisals whose enforced absence from public discourse for more than 30 years only heightened its popular status as a touchstone of moral authority. Assaults on the visual symbols of Stalinism had played a fundamental role in 1956, providing one of the revolution's most important symbolic moments when, on the eve of the uprising, thousands destroyed a statue of Stalin in one of Budapest's main squares. The statue was sawed from its boots, dragged through the city streets, and eventually hacked into souvenirs. Following the system-change, several attempted to repeat this ritual in order to make political claims to similar revolutionary transformation and popular legitimacy. Unlike in 1956, however, these relatively isolated instances of vandalism or destruction were not spontaneous actions performed in the heat of revolutionary fervour. Instead, 1956 veterans or representatives of some of Hungary's countless new political parties orchestrated these demonstrations as media events, attempting to garner public attention and symbolic capital in the context of the election campaign.

While these demonstrators hoped to turn the system-change into a revolution that would purge the remnants of communism (or at least, to give the appearance of promising to do so), their actions failed to capture wide public enthusiasm. 1989 was no 1956, and, in an attempt to maintain the peaceful nature of the transition (*békés átmenet*), the main forces of the opposition wanted to evoke the spirit of 1956 without actually conjuring it up as a model for action. For them, the lack of violent upheaval or widespread iconoclasm indicated what was truly 'revolutionary' about the negotiated political transformation. Meanwhile, most Hungarians, taking similar pride in this peacefulness and legality, were unwilling to ally themselves with the radicalism represented by the destruction of monuments – which reminded them not of 1956, but of the iconoclasm and annihilating historical politics of the communists themselves when they took power. Defining the political transformation as Hungary's entrance into democratic Europe and a return to 'normality', they wanted to prove that they belonged to 'Western civilization', rather than the 'Eastern barbarism' of Russian communism.[17] Art historians and other professionals, on the other hand, objected not only to the defacements but also to the ongoing quiet removal of the monuments by local authorities. Given that memorials to Marx or to Soviet liberation can be found in some Western European cities, they argued, Hungary's communist monuments should similarly be allowed to remain, either as icons of shared Western values, or as artistic and historical documents of the previous era. At the very least, they demanded, the fate of these objects should be determined by democratic public debate, rather than default.[18]

As local governments across Hungary continued the methodical removal of communist monuments initiated under the previous regime, defacements (or threats to do so) in Budapest made the 'problem' of Hungary's communist monuments more pressing for its city government. What was at stake was not merely the fate of specific monuments, but how the political transformation was to be understood and re-enacted on the public space of the city: through democratic negotiation or through an act of compensatory destruction that would give revolutionary momentum to a political process otherwise lacking in definitive public events. This tension was visible in MDF's winning election campaign, which on the one hand promised 'peaceful power', but on the other hand promoted itself with campaign posters of a dustbin containing busts of Lenin and other communist relics with the slogan of a 'big clean-up' (*nagytakarítás*).

The idea for a statue park was first raised in an article published before the political transformation, and was later enthusiastically promoted by several political organizations as a moneymaking tourist attraction. Authorities soon recognized, however, that the idea represented an ingenious political compromise between those who wanted to demolish the monuments and those who preferred them to remain. Rather than erase the fact of the socialist era or allow the former regime's self-representations to go unchallenged, placing the monuments in a park would invest the monuments with new symbolic content, as not only documents of the aesthetics, ideology, and historical politics of the previous era, but also, by the very fact of their preservation, emblems of democracy and Hungarian cultural health. Creating the park would thus enable city officials to make the political transformation visible in public space, while preserving the very sense of legality that actually distinguished this transformation from others in Hungarian history.

In December 1991, Budapest's General Assembly met to vote on the statues one by one, according to opinions collected from local districts and the recommendations of the Assembly's Cultural Committee. Invoking the discourse of European democracy and legality, officials emphasized the necessity of discovering precisely which monuments 'irritated' the public, whose interests were set in opposition to those of the art professionals otherwise entrusted with the care of the monuments, and the vocal minority who sought to destroy them. Ultimately, they decided that public opinion was best reflected through removing the majority of Budapest's communist monuments on the basis of their ideological content. The following year, the Assembly solicited architectural proposals for a park into which to place the statues, and national and foreign media eagerly chronicled each dismantling and the protests – whether to accelerate the process or halt it entirely – that ensued.

## Architects of democracy

While the idea of a park was greatly praised abroad, it failed to appeal to everyone within Hungary: protestors wanted the monuments destroyed rather than 'honoured' in a park, while their opponents considered the park a quarantine or zoo that represented an anti-democratic expulsion of historical heterogeneity from the public spaces of the city. Even the reaction of the 'public', whose desires had purportedly determined the fate of the monuments, was similarly lukewarm. After all, the Cultural Committee admitted that few local governments had actually responded to queries concerning the fate of monuments in their districts. The representative of the Budapest Gallery charged with directing the monuments' removal later maintained in an interview that the decisions were simply based upon whether there was any objection to a particular monument – whether that objection was voiced by five people, or one thousand.[19] Even a poll conducted in autumn 1992 revealed that many city residents resented the expenditure of public funds on such a symbolic gesture, and the majority would have preferred nearly all the statues to remain.[20] Nonetheless, art professionals and city officials publicly stated their consent to the monuments' removal and reinstallation in the park. The ideal of democratic consensus through public participation and rational debate would prevail – but as a rhetorical device, rather than reality.

The real problem, however, was not how well the city's decision reflected the public's actual demands, but rather how this 'public' was constructed. As mentioned previously, the social contract of late socialism was based on relinquishing political participation in order to pursue one's private life relatively undisturbed. In this atmosphere of depoliticization and inattention to the literal meanings of state rhetoric,[21] public space became another site for producing personal meanings. While some read the monuments as painful evidence of foreign occupation, many others managed to live with the monuments as they did with the regime: a more-or-less peaceful co-existence, which most did not experience as intolerably oppressive. Thus, one reason the destruction or defacement of monuments failed to capture the popular imagination during Hungary's political transformation is because communist monuments had inspired not only anger, but also indifference, irony, or affection. Moreover, there were simply no more Stalins to tear down. Instead, the public space of late socialism was an increasingly heterogeneous mix of socialist realist kitsch and artistically ambitious monuments, bland state enterprises and colourful private shops, political posters and occasional commercial advertisements.

The difficulty of isolating the monuments' ideological elements from other less official meanings became clear in the two tropes used to characterize the 'problem' of communist monuments in media and government debates. On the one hand, there was 'Lenin' – not a specific monument, but the sheer quantity of Lenin busts, statues, and portraits that saturated visual space in the socialist era. For most Hungarians, the ubiquity and seriality of these Lenins represented the imposition of a foreign power and the banality of socialist-realist aesthetics. On the other hand, however, there was Osztapenkó, a monument to a Soviet captain, which stood on one of Budapest's main highways. A landmark in personal and social narratives of the city, Osztapenkó was naturalized into the landscape and viewed by many with great affection. As cultural critic Péter György writes,

> The Osztapenkó statue meant the beginning of a trip to the Balaton [a popular holiday spot]: and thus for at least two generations, it meant the beginning of vacation, prosperity, the Hungarian 'weekend.' For the younger generation, it served as Route 66. This is where they hitch-hiked: 'let's meet at Osztapenkó!' ... Captain Osztapenkó meant the *genius loci*, the *phantom of freedom*, independently of who this officer of the Red Army actually was.[22]

During the meeting of Budapest's General Assembly, some raised this and similar arguments to support the maintenance of the Osztapenkó statue and others whose cultural significance exceeded their political content. Others denounced such statues as symbols of oppression. Insisting that the Assembly's function was to reflect popular will rather than impose personal or professional viewpoints, everyone cited a different 'public' opinion of the statues to support their claims, ranging from those of colleagues, to local districts, to – in one instance – a barber.

What was at stake in this debate was not merely reconciling the different aesthetic, historical, political, and cultural aspects of Hungary's communist monuments, but the competing memories of the socialist era that gave rise to these different considerations. The comforts of 'goulash communism' made possible by the withdrawal from political participation had produced an uneasy sense of complicity with the regime that now rendered definitive moral judgments, of oneself or others, difficult to achieve. As several officials noted, analysis of the era and determination of the 'true' history of the events and figures commemorated by the monuments would have to wait for historians to resolve. Instead, claiming not to take sides or pass judgment on the era, the Assembly ultimately voted to remove almost all of the communist monuments under debate – including Osztapenkó. Despite their claim of historical neutrality, however, the Assembly's decision to efface the difference between a 'Lenin' and an 'Osztapenkó' nonetheless made official a specific historical interpretation of the monuments and their role in the recent socialist past that would be visible in their very absence from the cityscape.

In thus rewriting the collective experience of socialist-era monuments, city officials were probably the first to take seriously the monuments' ideological intentions since the regime that erected them. By accepting this communist reasoning in order to get rid of it, however, they unwittingly revealed the persistence of the logic of communist bureaucracy into the postsocialist era. The pretext of anticipating popular will corresponded to communist rhetoric that similarly claimed to act in the name of the people, and the exclusion of private strategies of everyday life from the public sphere of action and opinion resembled the division of public and private under socialism. That is, just as the elimination of political participation was the condition for privacy under late socialism, the postsocialist 'public' was similarly constructed as the arena of exclusively political concerns: decisions were to be based on ideological criteria and expel other considerations. And once consensus was reached, there was no room for other alternatives. Those who missed the statues could simply go to the park and mourn 'privately'.

## Making history

With the selection of Ákos Eleőd's plans for an anti-propaganda park, the Statue Park became, perhaps inevitably, a site of structural tension. On the one hand, the open, non-evaluative architectural strategy of the park, which Eleőd envisioned as an artistic, historical, and tourist centre, sought to actualize the discourse of democracy. The transformation of public space was intended to effect a transformation of the public that purportedly demanded the statues' removal, converting Hungary's citizens from atomized subjects to active participants in public life. The democratic character of this new public was to be visible in both the fact of the park itself and its architecture, which by collecting multiple and competing memories of the past would demonstrate a heterogeneity of opinion denied by the previous regime.

On the other hand, the story of the creation of the park itself is one in which public opinion and the history of the monuments were re-written to the exclusion of the monuments' personal and cultural significance. Such elimination deprived both the monuments and the Hungarian public of their specificity. Just as the General Assembly constructed 'public opinion' as politically determined and univocal, they sentenced monuments representing different historical periods, aesthetics, and political intentions to a common fate: a logic of commensuration that rendered the monuments generically representative of the socialist era. Thus, if the ultimate effectiveness of the monuments under communism was to function invisibly as generalized signs of the eternity of the present, here – in the park's role as a 'monument to transition' – the monuments function as similarly homogenized signs of historical break.

This re-monumentalization in the service of a new memorial project to disjunction rather than continuity suggests that what was most threatening about communist monuments during the political transformation was not the scandalous visibility of their ideological message, but rather the potential *invisibility* of this content to the newly democratized public. After all, the very assumption that the monuments were visible – that is, the existence of a 'problem' that needed to be solved 'correctly' – was the one element common to all the different public opinions concerning the monuments' fate. Acknowledging the potential invisibility of the monuments' ideological content and the domestication of other readings into social life would imply that temporalization had not occurred: the past was not actually over, or there was no consensus concerning the nature of the political transformation and when – if ever – real change took place. In other words, while countless Lenins proved the infuriating fact of Soviet occupation, it was perhaps even more pressing to remove Osztapenkó, who called attention to the ways forty years of socialism had become cosy and familiar.

This logic is therefore not merely the 'distancing' of the recent past, but the act of break that transforms the quotidian into history and denies the possibility of legacy. Once historicized, objects can then be recuperated according to a logic of preservation that fends off the prospect of unclean destruction through a clean removal in which 'something' is taken away but 'nothing' is lost. Indeed, in the case of the Statue Park Museum, the monuments gained additional, democratic content, and the urban life of the monuments is supposed to be retained in the memories of those who visit. But the very condition for this memory – and its archivization in the park – is pastness itself: the loss of the monuments' living presence in the everyday life of the city.

As Éva Kovács argues, in re-writing collective experience as history, the park allows its visitors to avoid remembering that they too were part of the regime. It thus facilitates forgetting as much as remembrance, for while not everyone wanted to remove the monuments, everyone wanted to remove the memory of Kádárism: their own pasts, memories, and attachments to socialism, in which most people were at the very least bystanders.[23] Thus, the heated debates about the monuments' future, which from one aspect appear to be an engagement with the past, from another point of view can also be considered a remembering in order to forget.[24] The Statue Park Museum did not necessarily solve the 'problem' of communist monuments, but it provided a ritual of closure that buried goulash communism in order to ensure its demise.

## Consuming memory

The Statue Park Museum opened in summer 1993, as part of Budapest's celebration of the second anniversary of the departure of Soviet troops from Hungary. Staged as a parody of a 1950s communist party rally, the opening received a great deal of media attention both in Hungary and abroad. Its subsequent maintenance, in exchange for its profits, was entrusted to a young entrepreneur, Ákos Réthly, who on the basis of the park's initial surge of visitors created a business plan that anticipated – as the Western press gleefully reported – making a capitalist profit out of communist icons.

Once the flurry of interest surrounding the opening died down, however, the park was initially unsuccessful in luring either foreign tour groups or Hungarians. And with ticket prices kept artificially low for a public accustomed to decades of state subsidy for cultural consumption, the park was dependent on state funds for the future maintenance and completion of its infrastructure. Given the park's political function as an end rather than a beginning, however, it was difficult to raise support for such initiatives. In fact, it was only in 2001 that the government agreed to complete Eleőd's original plans for the park complex, which in addition to finishing the park's construction will include restaurants, shops, and conference rooms organized around a memorial square.

In the meantime, Réthly focuses his marketing on what he terms foreign 'culture tourists', making his profit through a gift shop that sells historical books or tongue-in-cheek memorabilia, including postcards, tee-shirts, busts of Lenin, Red Army medals, collections of workers' movement songs, and a tin containing 'The Last Breath of Communism'. Framing the park with the consumption of such socialist realist kitsch has made it more marketable for Western European and North American visitors, who view the park as proof of both the oppressed socialist past that feared and hated these statues, and the democratic present that is free to laugh at them. Indeed, Western reports of the park opening often played into these fantasies of monumental ignominy: describing the park's architecture as a humorous 'theme park' or 'Leninland',[25] or romantically locating the park on a 'bleak' or 'windy' hilltop.[26]

As the images described in the introduction made clear, however, many of the monuments are neither silly nor scary. Stalin and János Kádár (who discouraged personality cults) are nowhere to be found, and a number of the forty-one monuments, memorial plaques, and statues simply commemorate local Hungarians. Despite the theme of the park's opening, which humorously evoked the atmosphere of 1950s *szocreál*,[27] the monuments themselves were erected between 1947 and 1988, and not all partake of the excesses of socialist realism. While factually inaccurate, however, the slippage between the park's sober intentions and the mythifying reactions it provokes indexes the West's own imaginative investment in socialist iconography. Just as the city authorities' desire to deal with communist monuments in a 'civilized' manner revealed Hungary's fantasies about entering a more peaceful, prosperous, and 'European' future, Western visitors brought to the park their own mass-mediated memories and preconceptions concerning the aesthetic and political barbarism of the communist past and the 'triumph' of Western capitalism.

While Réthly's marketing strategy is successful in confirming rather than challenging the ideological and visual expectations of his foreign visitors, the gift shop has a different appeal for locals. Consuming the past in humorous quotation marks became a fashionable cultural practice even before the park opened: for example, a communist-themed pizzeria called Marxim opened in 1991, and on 7 November 1990, the city of Szeged held a *szocreál* ball.[28] The magazine *Magyar Narancs* also hosted a 'memory-canteen' public action, where Budapest locals could again taste the kinds of the food once served in socialist factory canteens.[29] While such activities might seem to evidence the desire to return to the socialist era, the very speed with which these phenomena appeared after the system-change tells a different story. Making the socialism of yesterday equivalent to that of the repressive 1950s – a period that for decades had already been experienced as past – enabled Hungarians to overlook all that still remained from socialism in the postsocialist era (in institutions, behaviours, and structures of feeling, as well as in the landscape and material culture). Moreover, marketing relics of political kitsch as objects of amusement or affection cleansed them not only of their ideological signification, but also of any painful or uncomfortable memories that might be evoked in their consumers. Such souvenirs offer a vision of the past drained of its unpleasant content, and the appeal of this, in a country otherwise famously concerned with its history, seems undeniable. In other words, if the creation of the park – by transforming the monuments into 'history' – permitted certain kinds of forgetting, the recuperation of socialist-era kitsch through nostalgic consumption covers up such amnesia through the appearance of remembrance.

Yet while tourist guidebooks to the city now list the Statue Park Museum as a popular attraction, most Hungarians evince little interest in a visit.[30] Although they accept the park as a unique and 'civilized' solution to the problem of communist monuments, it is too far away from the city centre to be worth a visit, they tell me, and anyway, they already know what the statues look like. Those who do go call the park dusty and boring, a place outside of everyday life where time stands still. In the visitors' books, a common complaint is that the park doesn't contain every one of the socialist statues of Budapest. And where are the former street signs? The red star from Parliament? Rather than accept the park's mandate to present a representative collection of communist statues, these visitors are disappointed in the park's failure to provide a 'total environment' of memory implicit in its rhetoric of preservation. This sense that 'something' is missing thus challenges the park's logic of forgetting-through-memory, which denies the recognition of loss itself.

This tension between memorialization and commercialization in the park also reveals a shift in conceiving the nature of the Hungarian public from citizens to consumers: from democratic participants in political decision-making to individuals concerned with satisfying commodifiable desires.[31] What is lost, however, in this transition is the possibility of debate or the desire to build consensus. Those who find the park's playful marketing strategies painful or offensive to their own memories of socialism can simply choose not to visit or buy its products. Thus, while the park was built to collect competing memories, this logic of individual consumption evades the possibility of dialogue or confrontation.

## Conclusion: afterlives of state socialism

Promotional images of the Statue Park Museum, found on official posters, postcards, and pamphlets, as well as the park's website and informational CD, advertise the park with dynamic montages that present the statues photographed from extreme angles, excised from their physical setting, and tinted the traditional shade of communist red. Silhouetted against the sky, the monuments appear menacing, oppressive, and forbidden: a visual strategy that seemingly counters Eleőd's explicit aim to present the monuments neutrally, as documents of the aesthetic politics of the previous regime and evidence of democratic tolerance.

But like the Western reports of the park's opening, while these images fail to document the physical reality of the park, they tell another truth about the imaginative investment in the relics of state socialism. This is the temporality of the *ghost*, a trope apparent in international media coverage of the park, which viewed the park as a 'cemetery' or 'graveyard' of dead statues, only to re-animize these figures as 'poor giants', 'forlorn', and 'adrift in a suburban wasteland'.[32] If the park is a memorial to the transition, then it too is susceptible to monumental invisibility; ghosts, on the other hand, intrude upon and demand attention, warning of improper burial and unfinished business. As paradigmatic instances of the uncanny, ghosts thus do not reflect confusion between fantasy and reality, but rather the dreadful certainty occasioned when that which has been expelled and forgotten reappears.[33]

On the one hand, this trope is part of the marketing strategy outlined above, which humorously plays with the notion of ghostly danger precisely because there is no actual fear that the monuments, or the ideology they are perceived to embody, will return. On the other hand, the very commercialization of the notion of 'ghost' points to what it tries to cover up: that the past does haunt the present because it has not been resolved. After all, lack of interest in the park reflects the success of the debates that resulted in its creation: the feeling that communism is dead and gone, and there is no use in performing an autopsy by re-examining the era in terms of its history, politics, or personal and collective memory. This is perhaps why there has been less critical analysis of Soviet aesthetics than that of National Socialism, and why there have been few examples of counter-monuments in the former Soviet bloc that would try to engage critically with the memory and monumentality of the past era. (Even the very notion of temporalization, evident in the photographs that began this chapter, merely reverses rather than dissects the traditional logic of monumental signification.) Instead, the Hungarian monumental landscape now consists of an 'ideological patchwork'[34] of new monuments to heroes of the distant past alongside those reinstalled after spending the socialist era in warehouses.[35] And the sites where communist monuments once stood are no longer visible as absence, but have been over-written with new meanings within the social and personal geographies of Budapest.

If communism is dead, the rhetoric of preservation that created the park has not allowed mourning to occur, in the sense of acknowledging and coming to terms with what is gone. But this does not mean that Hungarians do not want to remember the past, but rather that the park, as a physical and discursive site, appears to be inadequate for remembering. Instead, the forgetting made possible by the construction of the park (among other such memory rituals of the early 1990s) has been the condition for the return of goulash communism as nostalgia: the uncritical attempt to resurrect past presence and imagined origins that forgets everything that was painful and difficult about that era. Unlike the consumption of kitsch described above, which distances the past through ridiculing its political symbols, this nostalgia is a gentler, more affectionate attempt (through cafés, films, albums, books, museum exhibitions, products, and advertising campaigns) to recapture the atmosphere, gestures, and emotions of an era now indeed experienced as irretrievable. As one Hungarian told me, the era was 'stupid, but nice: a part of my life'. And the stakes of such unwillingness to confront the compromises as well as the prosaic pleasures and material security of the past era became apparent in summer 2001. A poll conducted upon the suggestion of the president of the Hungarian Workers' Party (the marginalized successor to the communist party) revealed that more than 80% of Hungarians wanted to add one more monument to Budapest's cityscape, in the form of a memorial to János Kádár.

## Notes

1 This chapter is drawn from ethnographic fieldwork and archival research supported by a grant from the Fulbright IIE, a National Science Foundation Graduate Fellowship, and a fellowship from the International Dissertation Field Research Fellowship Program of the Social Science Research Council with funds provided by the Andrew W. Mellon Foundation. An earlier version was presented at the panel 'Articulating Memory and History in Eastern and Central Europe after 1989' at the American Anthropological Association meetings in Washington, D.C., 19 November 1997. My thanks to the participants and discussant Andrew Lass, as well as to Ákos Eleőd, Ákos Réthly, András Szilágyi, István Rév, and József Litkei.

2 Mikhail Yampolsky, 'In the Shadow of Monuments: Notes on Iconoclasm and Time', in *Soviet Hieroglyphics: Visual Culture in Late Twentieth-Century Russia*, ed. N. Condee (Bloomington: Indiana University Press, 1995), 97.

3 *New York Times*, 31 October 1993: 3.

4 Júlia Váradi, 'Szoborpark-történet: Váradi Júlia beszélgetése Eleőd Ákos építésszel', *Magyar Építőművészet* 2 (1994), 19–24.

5 I use the phrases 'political transformation' or 'system-change' (*rendszerváltás*) in order to avoid the rhetoric of transitology, which often presumes a unilinear process of 'transition' from the socialist era into a future predetermined by Western ideal-types of the free market and liberal democracy.

6 Ákos Eleőd, conversation with author, Budapest, Hungary, 11 May 2001.

7 Benedict R.O'G. Anderson, 'Cartoons and Monuments: The Evolution of Political Communication under the New Order', in *Language and Power: Exploring Political Cultures in Indonesia* (Ithaca: Cornell University Press, 1990), 174.

8 Robert Musil, 'Monuments', in *Posthumous Papers of a Living Author* (Hygiene, Colorado: Eridanos Press, 1987), 64.

9 James E. Young, *The Texture of Memory: Holocaust Memorials and Meaning* (New Haven: Yale University Press, 1993), 5.

10 Alexei Yurchak, 'The Cynical Reason of Late Socialism: Power, Pretense, and the *Anekdot*', *Public Culture* 9 (Winter 1997): 161–188.

11 András Gerő and Iván Pető, *Unfinished Socialism: Pictures from the Kádár Era* (Budapest: Central European University Press, 1999), 7.

12 Ibid, 10–11.

13 István Rév, 'Parallel Autopsies', *Representations* 49 (Winter 1995): 23.

14 Gerő and Pető, *Unfinished Socialism*, 12.

15 The following discussion of Hungary's communist monuments and the decision to create the Statue Park Museum is abbreviated from a longer version of this chapter, which analyzes government debates and Hungarian press coverage of this topic between 1989 and 1993.

16 Rév, 'Parallel Autopsies', 24.

17 For the productivities of this opposition between East and West in Hungarian discourse, see Susan Gal, 'Bartók's Funeral: Representations of Europe in Hungarian Political Rhetoric', *American Ethnologist* 18, no. 3 (1991): 440–458.

18 While some local governments carried out these changes in consultation with historians and the opinions of the community, for most the logic was simpler: when the communists took power, no one asked the people if they wanted these monuments; now that the communists are gone and the people have regained their sovereignty, the monuments must go.

19 András Szilágyi, conversation with author, Budapest, Hungary, 20 April 1998.

20 *Népszabadság*, 16 October 1992.

21 Yurchak, 'The Cynical Reason of Late Socialism', 163.

22 Péter György, *Néma Hagyomány: Kollektív felejtés és a kései múltértelmezés, 1956 1989-ben (A régmúlttól az örökségig)* (Budapest: Magvető, 2000), 306. My translation.

23 Éva Kovács, 'A terek és a szobrok emlékezete (1988–1990) – Etűd a magyar rendszerváltó mítoszokról', *Regio* 12, no. 1 (2001), 80.

24 Richard S. Esbenshade, 'Remembering to Forget: Memory, History, National Identity in Postwar East-Central Europe', *Representations* 49 (Winter 1995): 72–95.

25 *Boston Globe*, 11 October 1993: 2; *Daily Telegraph*, 6 July 1993: 13.

26 *Irish Times*, 7 August 1993: 8; *Reuter Library Report*, 27 June 1993; *Wall Street Journal*, 28 June 1993: 1.

27 *Szocreál* (an abbreviation of the Hungarian term for socialist realism) includes not only monuments but anything – speech, behavior, visual and material culture – that conjures up the atmosphere of the early years of socialism.

28 György Szücs, 'Not to Praise, But to Bury: The Budapest Sculpture Park', *Hungarian Quarterly* 35 (Autumn 1994): 102.

29 Péter György, *Néma Hagyomány*, 304.

30 Réthly claims that at least half of the park's visitors are Hungarian, but my own impression, based on periodic fieldwork at the park since 1996 and discussing this topic with locals, is that the figure is much lower.

31 Krista Harper, 'Citizens or Consumers? Environmentalism and the Public Sphere in Postsocialist Hungary', *Radical History Review* 74 (1999): 109.

32 *New York Times Magazine*, 2 May 1993: 46.

33 Mladen Dolar, ' "I Shall Be with You on Your Wedding Night": Lacan and the Uncanny', *October* 48 (Fall 1991): 5–23.

34 Szücs, 'Not to Praise, but to Bury', 101.

35 The fragmentation produced by this 'democratization' of memory is perhaps most visible in the number of competing memorials to 1956 located just metres from each other in the square around Hungary's Parliament.

# 11

# FROM CONTESTED TO CONSENSUAL MEMORY

## The Rock and Roll Hall of Fame and Museum

*Robert Burgoyne*

The Rock and Roll Hall of Fame and Museum, situated on the Cleveland water-front of Lake Erie, stands next to a naval reserve facility and a coast guard mooring station. As if to defend or lay claim to certain national meanings that might be seen as under attack from the Rock Hall next door, the naval reserve and coast guard have mounted an impressive outdoor museum of their own, consisting of fighter planes, missiles, antiaircraft guns and ships. A visitor to the Rock Hall might easily notice the unlikely juxtaposition of these two projects dedicated to the shaping of public memory, and be struck by the contradictions that immediately present themselves. Although both museums feature an ensemble of artefacts and monuments centred on appeals to memory, they present an initially startling contrast in their iconography and in their appeals to different imagined communities. The Naval Museum, with its outdoor displays of F1 and Blue Angel fighter planes, missiles, a submarine, a patrol boat, landing craft, and various antiaircraft guns and cannons, summons concepts of history and nation that seem to be diametrically opposed to the messages communicated by the Rock and Roll Hall of Fame and Museum, with its array of talismanic objects, including the guitars used by Jimi Hendrix and Buddy Holly, the sunglasses worn by Roy Orbison, and the sixth-grade report card of Jim Morrison. Despite their seeming opposition and incommensurability, however, these two sites are deeply linked in the US national imaginary, a connection that is made explicit in one of the first objects that greets the visitor to the Rock Hall: the enormous American flag that served as the backdrop for Bruce Springsteen's 'Born in the USA' concert tour. In the juxtaposition of weapons and the imagery of rebellion and protest, the two museums offer a strikingly dialogical iteration of the significance of public memory – and its contested character – in defining concepts of nation, history, and more abstract concepts such as 'freedom', a word which has very different meanings in the two settings I describe.

Public memory can be understood as a form of organized remembering, or civic remembrance. Although public memory is often associated with monuments to national trauma – the Vietnam Veterans Memorial or the Berlin Holocaust Museum are perhaps the most visible recent examples – the activity of organized remembering extends to numerous civic activities such as re-enactments, commemorative parades, heritage celebrations, and museum exhibitions. The process of constructing a past that is worthy of commemoration typically brings into relief an extraordinary range of perspectives about the past and how it should be remembered; in general, however, the struggle over the shaping of the past for the purposes of public commemoration can be distilled, in most cases, into three main currents of opinion, which can be characterized as the official, the vernacular, and the commercial cultural viewpoints. For the purposes of this chapter, I will define public memory as the construction of a past that emerges from the interplay of official, vernacular, and commercial cultural viewpoints and expressions. It can be understood as a body of beliefs and ideas about the past produced from the political give and take of competing groups, each of which has a distinct claim on the past and an interest in its representation. As John Bodnar writes, 'public memory is produced from a political discussion that involves ... fundamental issues about the entire existence of a society: its organization, structures of power, and the very meaning of its past and present'.[1] Public memory, understood as a shared vision of the past that is useful to the present and the future, serves to mediate the 'competing restatements of reality' that emerge from the clash of vernacular, official, and commercial interpretations of past experiences. Rooted in the contradictions of the social system – including conflicts between generations, between racial and ethnic groups, between different classes and different regions of the country, and between women and men – its function is to 'mediate the competing restatements of reality these antinomies express'.[2]

The Rock and Roll Hall of Fame and Museum provides a striking demonstration of the way public memory mediates competing interpretations of history, for it is explicitly engaged in shaping, out of one of the most turbulent and contested periods in US history, a past that can be celebrated by a wide spectrum of society, a past that is worthy of commemoration. To its credit, the museum refuses the easy solution of trying to bracket the music from the explosive social milieu in which it was formed. Rather, the political and social turmoil of the second half of the twentieth century is set forth as the necessary and shaping context for the emergence of rock and roll. Rendering the social tensions of the period in high relief, the museum's numerous video montages, audio installations, written texts, and multiple pictorial references dramatize the interlocking and reciprocal relationship of the youth movement, the civil rights movement, the Vietnam War, and the culture of dissent to the emergence of rock and roll.

In foregrounding the social context perhaps even more emphatically than the music itself, the Rock Hall conveys an overarching concern with defining the place of rock and roll in the larger narrative of nation. The museum's powerful appeals to memory are consistently directed toward national symbols and meanings, toward a national pedagogy, as it were, formed from the 'rags and patches' of remembered daily life.[3] But what stands out most clearly is the way the still vexed and highly charged debate about the meaning of the decades of the sixties and seventies for the US national narrative is rehearsed throughout the Rock Hall's exhibits: the ongoing cultural and political debate about how the recent past should be remembered permeates the Rock Hall's organization of space and its address to its audience. It thus provides a powerful example of the way public memory can be simultaneously multivocal and hegemonic in dealing with the fundamental issues concerning the 'entire existence of a society'.[4]

Two major themes concerning the place of rock and roll in the national narrative can be distinguished in the museum's presentation. On the one hand, the Rock Hall sketches the story of rock as a form of unifying spectacle, a story that echoes the traditional national narrative itself, a story of rebellion and redemption and an ever-widening acceptance of challenging material, an acceptance that now embraces minority musical styles, ecstatic performance modes, and myriad cultural differences – a story in which history is redeployed in the service of a memory-system whose goal is the settling of all disputes. But on the other hand, the Rock Hall also narrates, in a minor key, as it were, another kind of story about the music and the period, situating it persuasively and movingly in the context of history as 'what hurts', of history consisting of conflict, loss, and promise unfulfilled, a narrative that resists the imagery of reconciliation and consensus.[5] In attempting to integrate these discordant meanings into a unitary conceptual framework, the Rock Hall illuminates how commercial and official memory-narratives try to incorporate and reshape vernacular memories that often are formed around hard kernels of historical truth.

Three types or subsets of collective memory – vernacular, official, and commercial – can be distinguished in the memory-system of the Rock Hall. Vernacular memory can be characterized as the memories carried forward from first-hand experience in small-scale communities; it conveys the sense of what 'social reality feels like rather than what it should be like'.[6] It expresses a sense of loyalty to local and familiar places. The Rock Hall, for example, places special emphasis on the local communities that became the defining scenes of rock and roll. Collections of posters, advertisements, contracts, photographs, costumes, newspaper articles, etc., provide a vivid portrait of the texture of everyday life in specific locations such as Detroit, San Francisco, and Seattle, that at certain historical moments flowered into centres of musical and cultural style.

Official memory, on the other hand, is a commemorative discourse about the past that offers an overarching, patriotic interpretation of past events and persons. It is most often produced by governments or other civic institutions. As Bodnar says, it restates the reality of the past in 'ideal rather than in complex, ambiguous forms ... it presents the past on an abstract basis of timelessness and sacredness'.[7] Moreover, it seeks to neutralize competing interpretations of the past that might threaten social unity, the survival of existing institutions, and fidelity to the established order. In the specific cultural setting of the Rock Hall, however, official memory is not associated with the government or with traditional patriotism; rather, it is consonant with a kind of idealized generational memory that has emerged in recent years: official memory here revolves around the dominant narrative of the sixties and seventies as a period of countercultural political activism, a memory-narrative which provides the Rock Hall with one of its central organizing stories. Official memory in the Rock Hall is expressed in the form of a commemorative discourse that stresses the liberatory politics and anti-authoritarian stance of a period that has increasingly taken on the aura of the sacred, the timeless, and the ideal.

A third strand in the Rock Hall's memory-system can be identified with the commercial recycling of the past, a form of commemoration that increasingly takes the form of an appeal to heritage. Perhaps even more influential than official memory in the present day, commercial culture engages the discourses of memory by invoking commercial products and representations as an aspect of national heritage, through 'strategies designed to heighten a product's visibility, legibility to its audiences, and resonance as a specifically American good'.[8] Along with other institutions of American mass culture such as film and television, the music industry is zealously commemorative, often casting itself in the role of preserving the nation's past. The continuous recycling of stars, songs, and period styles, the use of older rock and roll hits in advertising and in political rallies and celebrations, the correlation on radio stations of songs from the past with audio clips featuring the voices of national leaders from earlier decades, the various attempts to revivify the Woodstock experience, and even Bob Dylan performing via satellite feed at the Academy Awards, attest to the reach and effectiveness of the discourse of heritage. National heritage culture works by 'selecting aspects of the past for commemoration, supplying historical context to explain their significance to audiences ... ensuring that it will continue to represent the nation's achievements across generations'.[9] In the Rock Hall, the narrative of heritage is most explicitly expressed in the Hall of Fame section of the museum space, where defiantly anti-establishment figures such as Jim Morrison and Jimi Hendrix are now commemorated as national icons, exemplars of American values. More generally, however, the theme of rock and roll as a 'specifically American good', as a form of national heritage, is in many ways intrinsic to the museum's mode of address.

The enormous American flag that Bruce Springsteen used in his 'Born in the USA' concert tour illustrates the way these different strands of memory are woven together in a single artefact. The symbol of the flag, in the context of the rock song and the rock tour in which it appeared, simultaneously evokes the iconography of protest, patriotism, outlaw culture, the working class, and the nation-state, fusing vernacular and national emblems within a commercial, popular medium – American rock music – that has extended itself around the globe. The flag that Springsteen used in the concert tour, now displayed at the entrance to the Rock and Roll Hall of Fame, is a memory symbol that speaks simultaneously to the registers of vernacular, official, and commercial cultures. Moreover, both the triumphal narrative of rock and roll and the narrative of resistance are fused here: the symbol of the flag in the context of the song, 'Born in the USA', poignantly registers working-class protest and pain at the loss of jobs and community in the global economy; but the song and the symbol also register its opposite – the triumph of American capitalism crystallized in the successful single, in the platinum album, and in the global reach of the rock video. As Bodnar says, it is a symbol that 'restates social contradictions in a modified form'.[10]

In the Rock and Roll Hall of Fame and Museum, the antinomies and social contradictions that have defined the second half of the twentieth century are woven into the texture of the museum; these contradictions are central to the Rock Hall's mode of address, which emphasizes conflict, cultural dissonance, and the political power and provocative aspects of rock and roll. Yet the Rock Hall's overarching message is one of reconciliation and social consensus. In the visitor's progress through the museum, a certain narrative trajectory can be discerned, a sequence of moves that posits rock first as a form of social contestation and ultimately as a form of cultural consensus: the unfolding narrative of the Rock Hall can be seen as a kind of social drama that attempts to resolve the tensions between official, commercial, and vernacular culture in the symbolic forms afforded by music, film, architecture, and collections of artefacts.

Soon after entering the main exhibit space of the Rock and Roll Museum, the visitor confronts a display entitled 'Don't Knock the Rock'; here, various 'official' denunciations of rock and roll are sampled and exhibited, including a large quotation displayed on a wall stating, 'The First Amendment should be suspended in the case of rock and roll.' Numerous other quotes in the same vein are also displayed, including fearful jeremiads by J. Edgar Hoover and Tipper Gore. In addition, television footage of fundamentalist preachers, talk show hosts, and conservative disc jockeys (one of whom makes a play on words by saying 'It's record breaking time at station XYZ' as he smashes 45 rpm records on camera) are broadcast, testifying to the evils of rock and roll and illustrating the official campaigns to suppress it.

Immediately following this display, the visitor encounters a series of panels showing the vernacular sources of rock and roll. Here, in a display entitled 'Come See About Me', local music scenes that burgeoned into internationally famous capitals of music and style are represented through collections of material artefacts and short tape loops that testify to the daily lives of the musicians and their fans. These displays are centred on scenes such as Memphis in the fifties, Detroit in the early sixties, San Francisco, Liverpool, and London in the late sixties and early seventies, New York in the eighties and Seattle in the early nineties. A placard on the wall underlines the importance of the urban and of the local to the development of rock and roll, describing rock as an urban music whose rhythms and chord patterns reflect the urban context, and insisting that 'no one can predict where the next influential music scene will come from. It might be your home town'.

The artefacts displayed here emphasize the local development of these music scenes – the clubs that spawned the musicians, the posters and advertising that circulated throughout the cities, the ticket stubs, the records and record jackets, the pages of notepaper on which songs and song lists were written, the clothing worn by the musicians, the instruments, and numerous publicity and personal photographs. This vigorous assertion of the importance of vernacular culture to the development of rock and roll is augmented by display cases on the opposite wall that cover the early blues and gospel influences on rock – the ancestors of rock and roll – whose music emerged in large part from rural settings.

These displays serve as an effective counterpoint to the censorship wall that inaugurates the visit to the museum. The vitality and sense of community celebrated in the exhibit's panels exposes the official denunciations of rock as almost phantasmal and hysterical. But the spatial proximity of the censorship wall and the local music scene panels also reveals a larger rhetorical message: the urban music scene display comes to signify not only the importance of the local and the vernacular to the emergence and development of the genre, but also signals an 'official' kind of memory-narrative regarding rock and roll. Superimposed over the sites dedicated to vernacular memory is another message – that rock was, and is, the authentic voice of the nation, that it expresses, in its multiplicity, urbanity, and energy the actual character of national experience. Covering the breadth of the continental United States, with Liverpool and London annexed as satellite states of this imagined nation, the music scene panels express not simply the importance of the local and the regional to the development of rock and roll, but rather the story of rock as an abbreviated version of the story of nation.

The music scene exhibition presents the musicians and clubs, the dancehalls and downtowns as part of specific organic communities, suffused with local color and influences. But they are also portrayed in terms of the emergence of a certain generational style, an alternative mode of cultural identity. San Francisco, Detroit, New York, and L.A. are characterized as a series of imagined communities formed by their unique, vernacular style of opposition to traditional authority, a form of opposition that confers prestige from below, an oppositional attitude that is no less present in the rockabilly precincts of Memphis in the fifties than it is in the San Francisco of the sixties and the Seattle of the nineties. Here, Jerry Lee Lewis, Jerry Garcia, and Kurt Cobain speak for an alternative sensibility that acquires meaning and coherence principally from its embedded or overt opposition to official national culture. From the early fifties onward, the panels suggest, the rock scene functioned as an alternative national text, replete with an alternative national history, featuring social trauma and collective striving, a legendary past, sacred places and fallen heroes, and a teleological orientation whose destination is a future in which 'your home town' may be the next breaking scene. Here, vernacular memory and what I am calling official memory are effectively linked, as local urban music scenes are concatenated to express an alternative history, based on style and prestige from below, of the latter half of the twentieth century.

The Rock Hall's powerful solicitation of vernacular memory, however, also brings to light symbols and meanings that cannot be readily shaped to the requirements of public memory. In its evocation of what George Lipsitz calls 'the emotions close to home', the museum also narrates another story of rock and roll, a story that retains a certain hard kernel of authenticity and fidelity to what social reality 'feels like'.[11] Counterposed to the rock-as-the-story-of-nation theme is another theme, one that is mainly relegated to the background of the narrative constructed here, a theme revolving around loss and oblivion. An essay by Roland Barthes entitled 'The Grain of the Voice' provides a way of approaching this idea. Barthes notes that a subtle sense of loss pervades musical expression. Imagining music as deriving from 'a body without a civil identity', he emphasizes the power of music to afford access to 'jouissance, to loss', the capacity of music to engage the suppressed emotions of madness and desire. Barthes spoke of the friction between music and language, of the materiality of music, of music not being expressive but rather coming directly from the body, of musical pleasure consisting in the loss of the subject.[12]

But the idea of rock and roll as jouissance – the story of rock as a story of ecstatic experience and nirvanic excess, of exaltation and oblivion, a story which is such a significant part of its meaning and appeal – poses a particular challenge to the museum's project of restating the rock and roll past as something that is worthy of commemoration. In fact, the museum dodges this theme almost entirely, making almost no reference to the hedonistic lifestyle, the quest for a higher plane of reality, the drugs, the outlaw sensibility, and the headlong pursuit of physical sensation that were so much a part of the rock and roll experience. The theme of Dionysian excess is merely hinted at, subtly suggested in the hundreds of motel keys collected by Timmy Schmidt of Poco, or in the video montage of frenzied performances that runs continuously in the main museum space.

However, the attendant theme of loss and regret is mobilized as part of the museum's message about the past and how it should be remembered. In the several memorial sites dedicated to fallen rock stars that ring the museum's main exhibition space, the lives and careers of musicians such as John Lennon, Jimi Hendrix, and Jim Morrison are commemorated in a way that reminds us that history is also about loss and disillusionment. These sites are suffused with the most palpable sense of poignancy: to see Jim Morrison's touching letter, written in grade school, to his mother; to see the Christmas Card he drew in fourth grade wishing his parents a 'cool Yule', with the parenthetical inscription 'You better get me something!' inscribed in the margin; to view his second and sixth grade report cards, attesting to his strengths in writing and literature; to see that he was class president in high school and that he won a letter in swimming, is to be struck by the fragility and unpredictability of life in the mid-century. John Lennon's commemorative shrine is also evocative: in addition to school report cards and early instruments played by his skiffle group, we also see the cover page of the literary magazine he founded in middle school, copies of his art work, and an early satiric poem written about Guy Fawkes Day. The Jimi Hendrix shrine is of a somewhat different order. There are no childhood or

214

family mementoes here, only official, music industry press releases, copies of recording contracts and posters, a guitar, clothing, photographs of Jimi in concert, and the official coroner's report on his death.

These commemorative discourses, with their poignant evocations of a small world, of 'emotions close to home', restate a view of reality that expresses the ordinariness and fragility of the musicians. No transcendent symbols are used and no appeals to greatness or generational leadership are made. Rather, the exhibits express the idea that the period, for all its convulsive creativity and emotion, was mixed with sorrow, regret, and sadness. Like the Vietnam Veterans Memorial, the shrines constructed here are mainly about love, loss, and unful-filled potential. Like the mementoes left at the Vietnam Veterans Memorial by parents, siblings, and friends, the shrines in the Rock Hall are composed of deeply personal items that give a sense of what reality 'felt like' in the sixties and seventies. The pitched conflicts that characterized these decades, conflicts between creativity and conformity, between rebellion and familial affection, between public stances against government power and private self-absorption and self-destruction, are expressed here in a form that originates in first-hand experience.

Here, the place of rock and roll in the larger national narrative takes on a different meaning, becoming the story of an interrupted narrative progress, of an unfinished evolution, of unfulfilled promise. In these commemorative displays the assertion of vernacular memory serves as an implicit challenge to the triumphal narrative celebrated by the museum. The museum's attempt to build a consensus in public memory is here challenged, forced to accommodate a different understanding of the place of rock and roll in the narrative of nation. In their own minor-key and muted way, these memorials refer us to the violence and to the trauma of the sixties and seventies, to the loss of community, to the rupturing of families, to the assassinations and the body counts and the division of the national civic body. They refer us to a traumatic national past that remains resistant to the project of shaping a past that is worthy of commemoration.

The contradictory narratives that emerge from the museum's range of discourses about rock and roll and how it should be remembered are character-istic of the way public memory is constructed, a process that involves an exchange of views and debate about the fundamental issues facing a society. Public memory's function is to mediate the 'competing restatements of reality' that emerge from the clash of official, vernacular, and commercial memory-narratives and from the social antinomies that they embody. In order to help people grasp and integrate these discordant meanings from reality, institutions of public memory such as the Rock Hall construct symbols or metaphors that condense multiple meanings and connections to social reality in a unitary conceptual framework, a conceptual framework that allows a consensus view of the past to emerge. In this chapter, however, I have tried to show how public memory as it is embodied in the Rock and Roll Hall of Fame and Museum reflects both the dominant social perspective and alternative ways of remembering, arguing that the Rock Hall incorporates official as well as vernacular forms of remembering. In the space that remains, I will consider a third strand in the Rock Hall's memory-narrative, one that visualizes the rock and roll past as a form of heritage – a heritage consisting in part of technological mastery and mass media influence – represented in a widely varied matrix of cultural forms.

This framework can be found in the Hall of Fame section of the museum space, which is actually a separate institution housed under the same roof. Sponsored by AT&T, the Hall of Fame has a distinct look and feel to it in comparison with the rest of the museum. To a much greater degree than elsewhere in the museum, the Hall of Fame redefines rock and roll as a form of electronic heritage culture in which video, film, and recorded music are used to highlight certain performers, sites, and events deemed to be especially worthy of commemoration. The spectacular representations in the Hall of Fame sector of the museum, in which film and video clips of the legends, pioneers and greatest stars of rock and roll are projected onto three 20-foot high video screens, devises an image-repertory in which rock is associated not only with the creative performers and their cultural and historical impact but also, and importantly, with the technological superiority of American culture. Here, the electronic media itself is celebrated as a form of national heritage.

The electronic heritage culture promoted by the Rock and Roll Hall of Fame thus differs in almost every way from the description of heritage given by the English MP as 'that which moulders', a description dating from an earlier period in which heritage was mainly concerned with country estates and scenic pathways.[13] Nor is it quite what the French Minister of Culture meant when he wrote: 'The notion of heritage is enlarging; Heritage is no longer the coldness of stone, the glass separating us from objects in museums; it is also the village laundry-house, the rural church, local speech and song, family photos, know-how and skills.'[14] Rather, the Rock and Roll Hall of Fame has more in common with the construction of national heritage described by Michael Bommes and Patrick Wright. Here, heritage is understood as 'a whole battery of discourses and images' that resonate throughout the culture's representations, including advertising and television programs. Heritage, as Bommes and Wright point out, is not historical, but rather a 'public structuring of consciousness'; it is a 'public articulation or staging of the past … of immense extent, variety, and ubiquity … a spectacular display in which "the past" enters everyday life'.[15] The past, in the perspective promoted by heritage culture, is no longer behind us, temporally inaccessible, but rather all around us, concrete and accessible, a place or a scene that one can visit.

But it is as an embodiment of advanced technology that the Hall of Fame exhibit most powerfully defines the heritage of nation. The extraordinary revivification of the pioneers of rock and roll, with their scratchy, monaural recordings now transformed by digital enhancement into brilliant and lush sonic experiences, leads to a sense that technology can defeat time, that it can overcome the ravages of age and decay, that it can present the past in a way that is true to its essence, but improved. The media industry itself, with all its technological and capital resources, becomes part of the heritage, part of the history to be celebrated. The Hall of Fame exhibit combines the allure of the Hollywood cinema with the immediacy of the rock concert in the service of a narrative whose content centres on creativity and freedom but whose form expresses the power of technology and capital. The combination of technology and capital that is so powerfully displayed in this exhibit testifies to the reach and impact of the media industries, and ultimately to the power of the nation. Presenting the past glories of rock and roll in a way that resonates with other popular stagings of history in the US, the Hall of Fame exhibit, like the cinema and the theme park, monumentalizes the past, giving the rock stars an emblematic status as icons who symbolize the nation's greatness; the American story is rendered as a grand narrative in which creativity, style, and the power of the mass media can overcome the social dissonance and loss, a narrative in which progress is concomitant with technocultural wizardry.[16]

The Rock and Roll Hall of Fame provides a striking illustration of national heritage culture promulgated not through antiquated buildings or aged artefacts but rather through the resources of electronic mass media. Here, the rock and roll elect, living and dead, are resurrected and transfigured through an extravagant electronic display presented on the three enormous video screens. The memory-narrative generated by the Hall of Fame begins when the visitor seats him or herself on the floor, an arrangement that serves as a canny reminder of the seating at an outdoor rock concert. As the video montage begins, a strikingly discordant visual metaphor or symbol is immediately and powerfully set forth: the initial scenes presented to the viewer give the impression that the Rock Hall is under military attack (perhaps from the Naval Reserve facility next door). Viewed from what seems to be a helicopter approaching from the Lake Erie side of the museum, the Rock Hall is visualized on the video screen as a glowing, fabulous pyramid under electronic targeting or surveillance, with visual coordinates superimposed on the screen. The sound of chopper blades, radio communications, and other electronic sounds give the definite impression of an impending missile strike or some other kind of aerial attack. As the camera circles around to the front of the museum, an explosion is heard, along with the sound of breaking glass, and an old fashioned television appears to fly out of the Rock Hall. On the screen of this television, which lands on the animated image of the patio that fronts the museum, appears the date, '1986', the year the Hall of Fame began electing members.

The symbolism of the Rock Hall under military attack condenses several discordant meanings. On the one hand, it can be read as a strategic invocation of rock's contested standing in official culture, recalling the imagery associated with Vietnam, or with the Gulf War. At the same time, however, the animated sequence has the look of a computer or video game, placing it in the context of another generation of youth culture. By framing the presentation of the rock and roll pantheon with aggressively high-tech and militaristic imagery, the Hall of Fame symbolizes rock and roll as somehow threatening, dangerous to the established order, a carrier of rebellious and subversive energies. But more to the point, I think, is the condensation of technological prowess associated with the military and the electronic potency associated with rock music. Ostensibly dichotomous, the imagery of military targeting and the imagery of rock and roll come together in a national heritage defined as a celebration of technocultural achievement.

Following this 'targeting' sequence a spectacular montage of concert performances ensues. Concert footage of the charter members of the Hall of Fame, which include Chuck Berry, James Brown, Elvis Presley, Little Richard, Jerry Lee Lewis, and others, unfolds on three screens filled with images set in a constantly shifting mosaic: images travel from one screen to the other, then suddenly open up to a full three-screen exposure, before migrating to a small corner of one or the other panels. This pattern is followed throughout the Hall of Fame tape presentation. Animated scenes of the Rock Hall under military surveillance or attack inaugurate each of the sequences of musicians' performances, which are organized according to the chronology of their induction into the Hall of Fame. Beginning with 1986, the presentation chronicles, mainly through concert footage, the group of musicians admitted into the Hall of Fame each year. The video montage also includes still photographs of early, pre-rock artists selected as especially important early influences on rock and roll, a move which converts musicians like Bessie Smith and T-Bone Walker from vernacular artists to something resembling nation-building pioneers. The montage also includes occasional photographs of producers and disc jockeys, such as Sam Phillips, Alan Freed, and Dick Clark, who have also been admitted into the Hall.

The variety of visual and sonic ideas presented in these montage sequences, which include fragments of historical images, scenes of performers in concert, graphic elements keyed to the historical period represented on screen, and celebrated songs brought together in a dazzling postmodern pastiche, can be seen as an exemplary expression of electronic heritage culture. Its repertoire of images combines metaphors and symbols of the nation – what Bommes and Wright call the macro-heritage – with the performance styles, the costumes, the sounds and the graphics of local music cultures – the micro-heritage.[17] The antinomy between official and vernacular understandings of rock music and its place in the national narrative is effectively mediated in the Hall of Fame montage, which recasts rock music as a form of electronic heritage, encompassing both the vernacular and the official forms of memory in an overarching discourse that can be compared to what Jacques Rancière has described as the grand collects of patrimony. From photographs and concert footage of John Lee Hooker and Janis Joplin to the American flag of the 'Born in the USA' tour the configuration of images, lyrics and songs, rendered in a high-speed and dazzling electronic display, orients rock and roll toward the unity of a mass cultural form of national heritage.

The Rock and Roll Museum and Hall of Fame is an example of public memory in the electronic age, an institution that strives to hold together vernacular memory – the memory of what social reality 'felt like' (including the conviction that rock was meant to change reality, a conviction that has, as Simon Reynolds writes, 'somehow slipped out of "our" hands, with rock becoming a system that now excludes our experience'), with the official, idealized memory of rock as a form of bohemianism 'cleansed of the fast living and self-destruction of earlier forms of rebellion'.[18] It mobilizes a range of discourses and messages about the past and how it should be remembered, all of which are brought together in the celebration of rock and roll as a form of electronic heritage, a monument to technoculture, in the Hall of Fame exhibit.

The Rock and Roll Hall of Fame and Museum stages a kind of journey from contested memory to consensual memory, choreographing the visitor's movement through various exhibits that culminate in the dazzling consensual ceremony of the Hall of Fame video montage. But the most powerful evocation of this movement from contested to consensual memory may not, after all, be found in the Hall of Fame presentation but rather in the museum shop, a space as popular as any of the exhibits. Here not much music is sold, although a wide and deep collection of CDs is available. Rather, a striking array of t-shirts, caps, jackets, coffee cups and beer glasses emblazoned with the Rock Hall logo provide a more immediate touchstone to memory. Here desire and materialism coalesce, as the members of the Nation of Rock outfit themselves in a set of uniforms or insignia, as the serious matters of life and death so surprisingly manifest in so many sectors of the museum are given over to a commercial cultural milieu of leisure and entertainment, and where even the seemingly inviolate message of the Stones' *Satisfaction*, with its defiant statement against material culture, appears to be reversed. 'Desire is no longer antagonistic to materialism, as it was circa the Stones' "Satisfaction" ', writes Reynolds, a point which becomes emphatically evident as the visitor moves from the subterranean twilight of the shrines to fallen heroes, to the half light of the Hall of Fame, to emerge, finally in the dazzling sunlight of the museum shop.[19] As the visitor departs the museum, and casts an eye backward on its glowing, translucent pyramidal shape, one finds in I.M. Pei's architecture a perfect fusion of classical and contemporary memory-systems: a pyramid in which are preserved the relics of our hallowed past which doubles, in its glassy opulence, as a mall or galleria, in which the choreographed circulation of traffic terminates in the tie-dye precincts of the museum shop.

## Notes

1 John Bodnar, *Remaking America: Public Memory, Commemoration, and Patriotism in the Twentieth Century* (Princeton, NJ: Princeton University Press, 1992), 14.

2 Ibid., 14

3 Homi Bhabha writes persuasively of the way daily life is transmuted into the symbolism of nation in 'DissemiNation: time, narrative, and the margins of the modern nation', in *Nation and Narration*, ed. Homi K. Bhabha (London: Routledge, 1990).

4 Bodnar, 14.
5 This phrase comes from Fredric Jameson, *The Political Unconscious* (Ithaca: Cornell University Press, 1981).
6 Bodnar, 14.
7 Ibid., 14.
8 Barbara Klinger, *Fortresses of Solitude: Cinema, New Technologies, and the Home* (forthcoming).
9 Ibid.
10 Bodnar, 19.
11 George Lipsitz, *Time Passages: Collective Memory and American Popular Culture* (Minneapolis: University of Minnesota Press, 1990).
12 Roland Barthes, *Image Music Text*, trans. Stephen Heath (New York: Hill and Wang, 1977).
13 This description of heritage is found in Michael Bommes and Patrick Wright, ' "Charms of Residence": The Public and the Past', in *Making Histories: Studies in History Writing and Politics,* eds Richard Johnson, Gregor MacLennan, Bill Schwarz, David Sutton (Minneapolis: University of Minnesota Press, 1982), 292.
14 Ibid., 299.
15 Ibid., 264, 266.
16 For a superb discussion of the fusion of heritage and technological prowess in the context of classic films re-released on cable television, see Barbara Klinger, *Fortresses of Solitude* (forthcoming).
17 Bommes and Wright, 268.
18 Simon Reynolds, 'Against Health and Efficiency: Independent Music in the 1980s', in *Zoot Suits and Second-Hand Dresses* (Boston: Unwin Hyman, 1988), 253.
19 Ibid., 254.

# 12

# *DEAD MAN*

## Film, colonialism and memory

*Chris Healy*

> Benjamin, in noting the achievement of film to extend our scientific
> comprehension of reality, also notes in the same breath that film
> 'bursts our prison world asunder by the dynamite of a tenth of a
> second, so that now, in the midst of its far-flung ruins and debris, we
> calmly and adventurously go travelling'. And it is here, in this trans-
> gressed yet strangely calm new space of debris, that a new violence
> of perception is born of mimetically capacious machinery[1]

In the opening scene of *Dead Man*[2] William Blake (Johnny Depp) – an accountant who will soon become a killer of white men, an outlaw, and a poet – is
making a long journey by train across the USA in the 1870s. Blake has left
Cleveland, recently dead parents and a fiancée who changed her mind to take
up a job at the Dickinson Metalworks in Machine, the town at the end of the
line. Here he will, in quick succession, be disappointed, loved and shot. For the
rest of the film he is joined by Nobody (Gary Farmer), a Native American character, as the two of them travel to the place where Blake and Nobody will die.
*Dead Man* offers the spectator a filmic world unlike that of any other Western. It
is a world populated by degenerate white men and a pair of lost souls; a shock-
ingly damaged world governed by despair where death is everywhere. At the
same time Jim Jarmusch's film is hauntingly beautiful, deeply emotional and
funny. It is also a film which explores the cultural work of remembering.

In his recent discussion of the emergence of memory as a key concern of
contemporary Western society, Andreas Huyssen offers a useful orientation to 'the
time consciousness of the late twentieth century'.[3] He suggests that on the one
hand contemporary culture is relentlessly cast as forgetful, its historical consciousness lost or anaesthetized. Yet on the other hand there is a seemingly endless
proliferation of discourses of the historic, of commemorations, of memorialising,
of genealogical and local historical enthusiasm, and an unceasing escalation in the
desire to preserve, record and document 'the past'. It seems that Western society's
memory culture suffers from a hypertrophy of both remembering and forgetting.
The 'great paradox', writes Huyssen, is that '[T]he amnesia reproach is invariably
couched in a critique of the media, while it is precisely these media ... that make
ever more memory available to use day by day.'[4] Huyssen's productive approach to

this paradox is to regard anxieties about a culture of amnesia *and* the accusation of musealization *and* the compensatory nostalgia of some critical work on memory as both true and insufficient accounts of the ways in which 'the relationship between memory and forgetting [are] actually being transformed under cultural pressures'.[5]

This chapter makes a small contribution to thinking about some of the cultural pressures brought to bear on contemporary remembering by considering how *Dead Man* deploys and contemplates mnemonic practices. In the first place I am writing against the common cultural prejudice that regards media in general, and film in particular, as having assaulted and diminished human capacities to remember.[6] By reducing film to merely commodified spectacle, such characterisations fail to take seriously the fact that 'whether we like it or not, the predominant vehicles of public memory *are* the media of technical re/production and mass consumption'.[7] Here I begin by considering an editing technique and some dialogue from the opening scene in order to suggest how, rather than destroying memory, *Dead Man* actually works with the mnemonic skills that film requires of its spectators and establishes a complex set of relationships between time, story and memory. Second, I turn to more explicitly political questions of memory by arguing that, as a generically historical film, *Dead Man* makes a significant intervention in the broad cultural project of remembering colonialism. By re-visiting both the film genre of the Western and by structuring the plot around a journey undertaken by an indigenous and a non-indigenous character as the main protagonists, *Dead Man* productively elaborates the repertoire available for critical postcolonial remembrance. Third, I argue that Neil Young's soundtrack to *Dead Man* enables us to consider how the film works not only with meaning and politics, but also with the affective aspects of remembering. Finally, I speculate on some of the other significant resources which *Dead Man* provides for attempts to imagine remembering as part of place-making.

## When do we remember? Time and memory

> The eagle never lost so much time as when he submitted to learn from the crow.
>
> (Nobody)

The cinema is, of course, one of the pre-eminent modern cultural spaces that relies on, works with, invokes, constitutes and transforms contemporary practices of remembering. From Georges Méliès to George Lucas, film-makers have indulged in the memory-work of 'taking' spectators to other times. The cinematic apparatus itself relies on formal spectatorial practices which are, in important respects, dream-like. In submitting to cinema narratives the spectator habitually experiences (at least) the temporalities of screen duration, story duration and plot duration(s) not only as plural but also as differential. The editing techniques on which narrative cinema depends are, at a fundamental level, concerned with the experience of time and the image. So, an array of conventions exist to elide, compress, distend, stretch, reverse and displace time. Memory and history are deeply implicated in these manoeuvres. As Turim writes of the flashback: 'If flashbacks give us images of memory, the personal archives of the past, they also give us images of history, the shared and recorded past.'[8] It is not surprising then that cultural critics from Kracauer to Jameson have granted the cinema a privileged role in the processes whereby 'time, history and memory become qualitatively different concepts in a media-saturated world'.[9] In part this is because, as Barbie Zelizer, writing about *Schindler's List*, puts it, 'Every once in a while, a movie arrives that appears to triangulate the link between culture, history and collective memory in peculiar ways.'[10] But it is also, as Foucault argued nearly a quarter of a century ago, because film seems to actually shape and define the terrain of popular memory.[11] Here I will argue that *Dead Man* is a historical film which avoids the historicism of much historical film by virtue, and through the creativity, of its engagement with *processes* of remembrance. Not content to replace one version of history with another, *Dead Man* begins by productively disorganising the commonsense separation of past and present. In effect it poses the question: when do we remember?

Before the opening credits roll, as Bill Blake's train travels in the diegetic present, taking him away from his melancholy past, *Dead Man* is immediately recognisable as a historical film. While he's on the train, Blake dozes and wakes, dozes and wakes, perhaps blacking out, perhaps dreaming, perhaps regressing but certainly travelling. Each time he comes to, he finds himself in a different place. Initially his travelling companions are respectably dressed business travellers – men and women from the city, although none quite as ostentatious as Blake in his plaid suit – then farmers, then men dressed in animal skins, and finally a few drinkin', gun-totin' wild men who only come to life in order to shoot buffalo from the moving train. The intercuts of the landscape echo the changing appearance of Blake's carriage companions. Apart from the tight close-ups of the train's wheels, the first exterior shots offered to the spectator are of richly forested country, then a scene littered with decaying covered wagons, then mountain country, empty desert country and finally ruined remnants of Native American dwellings. Yet while Blake is obviously a character in (another) time and space, simultaneously, both his sedentary body and his distracted perception appear to bounce around or shift rapidly through time. Blake drifts in and out of consciousness, his attention switching between the carriage, the landscape and his amusements (solitaire and the *Bee Journal*) on a dreamy journey. It is plausible, as more than one critic has suggested, that this opening scene is meant to convey a sense of Blake travelling back through time.[12] The train heading to Machine certainly takes him away from the East and the urban towards the West and the country, away from civilization to a world of violence and depravity. But rather than simply reversing temporality so as to articulate the time of the spectator and the time of the diegesis, *Dead Man*'s opening scene also creates a sense of Blake existing in or experiencing multiple temporalities.

*Dead Man* immediately brings these temporalities to the fore through both formal means and character dialogue. Formally, the snippets which constitute the opening sequence are cut together through a series of fades-to-black each time we leave Blake's journey and fades-up from black when we return. While there are strong elements of sonic continuity between these shots, the editing immediately produces a series of uncomfortable temporal discontinuities. Unlike a dissolve which can be used to 'slide' the spectator from one point in time or space to another, fade-to-black is a standard device to shorten plot duration by omitting intervals of story duration through an ellipsis which nevertheless produces an experience of temporal coherence. For example, the spectator might see two moments separated on screen by seconds which are hours or years apart in terms of the story. However the spectator holds these moments 'together' as part of a temporal continuum of the story. The use of fade-to-black in the opening scene of *Dead Man* is different. For a start the fades stay with a black screen for much longer than necessary in any conventional sense. So, even though the spectator is 'returned' to the train carriage, the duration of blankness makes the *mise en scène* seem both different and the same. This apprehension is accentuated by the repetitive use of fade-to-black. At this point in the film the spectator is not really being offered a narrative but being bumped around in time. The many 'blank' scenes are vertiginous. They produce a feeling of falling out of time, of time being fractured or perhaps disappearing. As Kent Jones puts it, the use of blackouts 'create[s] an effect of pockets of time cupped from a rushing river of life'.[13]

This formal strategy is echoed at the level of character and performance. Blake himself loses track of time in ways not unfamiliar to anyone who has undertaken a long train, bus or airline journey. When he wakes he is disoriented. He takes a moment to check his surroundings and his watch as he readjusts to the present in which he finds himself. Thus after the fades-up from black, the spectator re-joins a character who seems surprised by his surroundings, as though he is somewhere else. Perhaps, then, we are watching a number of different journeys made at different times, or a journey taking place over decades. Perhaps this journey has already taken place. Perhaps this is a memory rising from the dead.[14]

This last possibility emerges strongly in the only character dialogue of the opening sequence. After a majestic shot of the train emerging from a tunnel, Blake is approached by the train's Fireman (Crispen Glover) who, with soot-blackened face, appears like a deranged prophet emerging from the fires of hell or a gate-keeper to the underworld inspecting the latest arrivals. The Fireman sits opposite Blake and says to him in a speech part aside and part to camera:

> Look out the window. And doesn't this remind you of when you were in the boat. And then later that night you were lying looking up at the ceiling and the water in your head was not dissimilar from the landscape and you think to yourself, Why is it that the landscape is moving but ... the boat is still ... And also, Where is it that you're from?

This 'stoned rap', as Rosenbaum calls it, refers us to the final scene of the film in which Nobody places Blake in the carefully prepared sea-canoe and launches it into the ocean so that Blake can travel, as Nobody says, 'back to the place where all the spirits come from, and where all the spirits return'. Of course it is not uncommon for prospective aspects of a narrative to be disclosed at the beginning of a film. What is unusual here is that this disclosure is couched as if it were a memory. The dialogue presumes that both Blake and the Fireman already know the story's end, and know it not just as a possibility but as an intimate and personal memory. When the Fireman, who has never met Blake, asks whether the land-scape reminds him of being in the boat and recalls Blake's own thoughts, the spectator knows that the Fireman is situated outside of both story time and diegetic time. He cannot know what he appears to know not only because, in terms of the story, he isn't there when Blake is in the boat but because those events have yet to take place. Thus in more ways than one, this opening scene sets up remembering as communing with the dead.

To think of the film in these terms is to refuse what Miriam Hansen has called the 'compulsive *pas-de-deux*'[15] of lived memory versus media memory, real memory versus cultural industry representations of memory. Both the dialogue and the use of fade-to-black in the opening scene of *Dead Man* engage directly with temporal mobility as a characteristic shared by both memory practices and the cinema. Because remembering is a temporal manoeuvre, when we remember we simultaneously occupy both everyday time and the temporality of remem-bering. Because film expects its spectators to be adept in recognising and occupying different temporalities, it too requires temporal manoeuverability. *Dead Man* calls forth these capacities in a film which is both a meditation on memory and consists of snatches of memory. By deliberately confusing past and present, before and after, it operates in a Benjaminian sense to 'bring to consciousness those repressed elements of the past (its realised barbarism and its unrealised dreams) so as to place the present in a critical position'.[16] And that of course is precisely Blake's predicament–a man with a bullet lodged too close to his heart.

## Routed through Europe: mimesis, memory and history

Things which are alike, in nature grow to look alike.'
(Nobody)

If the horizon of *Dead Man*'s formal structure is, in part, concerned with time and memory, then the film's horizon of political contestation is overwhelmingly focused on the role of cinema, with all 'its omissions and distortions, displacements and possibilities', as having produced the public, mass-mediated memory of the American West.[17] Eventually the train takes Blake to Machine, where he goes to the Dickinson Metalworks only to find that his job has already been taken. That night, outside a bar where he spends his last coins on a bottle of whiskey, he meets Thel Russell (Mili Avital), a former prostitute who now makes and sells paper roses for a living. Later, when they are in bed in Thel's room, a surprise visit from her

225

former lover, Charlie Dickinson (Gabriel Byrne), results in him shooting Thel dead while trying to shoot Blake, who then shoots and kills Charlie. The injured Blake escapes from the town and wakes up in the morning pinned to the ground as Nobody tries and fails to extract the 'white man's metal' in his chest. Nobody and Blake then undertake a journey to their deaths, a journey which consumes the rest of the film, as the pair are pursued by marshals and three bounty hunters hired by Charlie's father (Robert Mitchum). From this point onward *Dead Man* is almost entirely concerned with the Western as a film genre and how that genre has shaped the remembrance of colonial relationships in the historical world of the American West. In the following section I will consider each of these themes in turn. I will argue that *Dead Man* remembers the Western as an exhausted cliché and re-places questions of memory at the heart of its attempt to represent historical relationships between indigenous and non-indigenous Americans.

There is no doubt that *Dead Man* is centrally related to the Western. Jarmusch has identified this in describing the Western as a 'kind of an allegorical open form ... a fantasy world that America has used to process its own history through – often stamping its own ideology all over it'.[18] Critics and cinephiles have delighted in identifying the forms of dialogue between *Dead Man* and the Western in terms of genre, *mise en scène*, character, narrative, shots, jokes, themes, motifs, fragmentary references, quotations and twisting. It is clear that the film functions first to identify its diegetic space as (related to) that of the Western. As Jonathan Rosenbaum has written:

> Part of the satisfaction to be found in the Western genre is the recurrence of a recognisable and elaborately furnished universe. *Dead Man* alludes to that universe at every turn without ever completely conforming to it: a revisionist impulse ... which comprises a kind of ongoing historical critique ... as if Jarmusch wanted to give us a version of the classic Western reconfigured as some sort of nightmare.[19]

For the most part, I think Rosenbaum's characterisation is accurate.[20] But the questions that remain unanswered by Rosenbaum are: what kinds of revisionism are involved here, what kinds of subversion, what kinds of historical critique? I think some of the answers lie less in the realms of semantics and more in the *qualities* which Rosenbaum, and others, identify in the film's relationship to the Western. It is remarkable how often the film has been described as featuring scenes which are 'off-kilter', how critics have found casting, characters or *mise en scène* 'slightly unsettling', or marvelled at how 'the sense of detail dislodges generic norms'.[21] Overall we can say that *Dead Man* is a film which uses aspects of the Western in order to make that genre and its conventions appear strange. In this sense *Dead Man* is not concerned with the American West as an actual historical space. Rather, the film's historical point of reference is the Western as a mythic space which has been crucial to how America's past has been remembered. Thus, it confronts the relationship between history and memory at one remove. Therefore memory plays a key role in *Dead Man* because the memories which are unsettled or made strange are our memories of the Western. The film relies on the spectator's cultural competency to recall plots, characters, dialogues, shots and *mise en scène* from the archive of the Western. The Western as a form of monumental history is then systematically appropriated, re-figured and disassembled throughout the film. What the spectator experiences is not an exercise in demythologisation but a return visit to broken-down fragments of the Western. That genre is remembered, repeated and worked through until the clichés are exhausted. The Western is replaced by 'a landscape that America the conqueror has emptied of its natives and turned into a capitalist charnel house'.[22] Paradoxically all that remains of the Western after *Dead Man* is the rubble of the Western in ruins.

While *Dead Man* is certainly a subversion of the Western (as both genre and 'history') it is equally a film about remembering colonialism and the West. These aspects of the film, perhaps its most emotionally central form of 'historical revisionism', are developed in and through the relationship between Blake and Nobody. They are remarkable characters. Blake, perhaps more than any other major white figure in a Western, is almost entirely passive. From the opening shot we know that there is no way he is going to 'ride in, clean up the town, and ride into the sunset'.[23] Johnny Depp's character dialogue, his performance and the ways in which he is shot produce a character whose face functions almost as a blank screen, on which we see reflected his mostly naïve and uncomprehending reactions to what occurs around him.[24] Gary Farmer is a powerful screen presence. His character's fabulous dialogue is beautifully woven into a performance which contrasts moments of distraction and attention. Nobody is the man in charge here. He controls the plot trajectory. He tries to save Blake's life and keeps him alive. Then, after they have become reacquainted, he leads the journey the two of them make to the place where Blake can 'pass through the mirror where the sky meets the water to the other side', and where Nobody too will die. It is Nobody who provides the occasions for Blake's adventures and moulds his responses. It is Nobody who tests Blake first in the wonderful scene with the trappers, then when he sends Blake on a vision quest after the peyote ceremony, and finally at the trading post. Nobody trains Blake to become a murderous avenger and a graveyard creator.

Importantly, the relationship between Nobody and Blake is structured by practices of remembering performed in a variety of different modes. The foundations of these possibilities are established in *Dead Man*'s productive confusion of William Blake (1757–1827) and Johnny Depp's William Blake. As we learn later in the film, Nobody has already met William Blake (1757–1827) through his books. So when he first hears Depp's Blake speaking his own name he exclaims, 'Is this a trick or white man's magic?' and asks, 'Is your name really William Blake?' When Blake replies in the affirmative, Nobody recites some of Blake's poetry. Blake says, 'I really don't understand.' To which Nobody replies with the wonderful line, 'Nobody understands. You were a poet and a painter and now you are a killer of white men.' The 'confusion' between the two William Blakes is not established as a case of a dumb Indian mis-recognising an identity so that the spectator can share a knowing joke at his expense. In fact Depp's character does not know of Nobody's William Blake, and although he subsequently affirms Nobody's vision of Blake later in the film, if anyone is ignorant of the existence of two Blakes it is Depp's William Blake. Instead once it is clear that the name actually inheres in Depp's character, it is Nobody who solves what might appear to be the problem of mis-recognition through two elegant moves.

In the first place, Blake is an amnesiac. As Nobody says later, 'It's so strange that you don't remember any of your poetry.' In this respect Blake stands in for Europe. His inability to remember directs us to the ways in which, at the most general level, relationships between memory, indigeneity and postcolonialism have overwhelmingly been thought of as pertaining to the domains of representation and the juridical. Thus colonialism has regularly been figured as pathologically amnesiac – forgetful of the damage of civilising, forgetful of the colonised, forgetful of the wounds and scars of colonising which persist in the present. Indigenous people, on the other hand, have often been figured as dogged rememberers – defenders of the memory of colonisation, maintainers of the histories of their survival and (often belatedly) witnesses to the (historical) fiction of the post in post-colonialism. As these fixed speaking positions become more dialogic, as they must in the face of even the most elementary attempts to reconcile the colonial and the putatively post-colonial, then, for the colonisers, remembering becomes a civic duty. Silence and surdity give way to truth-telling and listening. The colonisers must re-visit the 'Other side of the Frontier', recall the obligations of old treaties, recollect promises made and debts unpaid, acknowledge the violence of conquest and expropriation, and avow the veracity of indigenous memory.[25] However, to generalise this juridical model of memory across the entire social domain is to forget history's forgetting, to endlessly replay the positivist oscillation between remembering and forgetting, and reduce remembering to the role of truth-telling witness.[26]

It is precisely this fate which is avoided in *Dead Man*. Because Blake is transformed, energies which were once artistic are put to a different use: 'You *were* a poet and a painter, and *now* you are a killer of white men.' The dimensions and logic of this transformation become clear a little further along their journey. When Blake asks, 'Shouldn't you be with your tribe or something?' Nobody explains that as a young man he was captured by English soldiers, taken east across the USA and then to England. He tells Blake:

> I was paraded before them like a captured animal, an exhibit.
> And so I mimicked them, imitating their ways, hoping that they might lose interest in this young savage. But their interest only grew and so they placed me in the white man's schools.
> And it was there that I discovered, in a book, the words that you, William Blake, had written. They were powerful words and they spoke to me.

This monologue is shot as Nobody and Blake ride through a stark forest of white-trunked trees. Between compelling shots of the two riding towards camera, a series of fades-to-white bring up soft focus tableaux of the young Nobody being captured, caged, discovering Blake's poetry and then witnessing the destruction of Native American people on his journey back to his lands. Whereas, as I've suggested, fade-to-black in the opening sequence takes the spectator out of time, here fade-to-white takes the spectator out of the narrative and into the past as it actually happened. In other words here the film fuses memory and history – what is clearly a narrative of personal remembrance is seen by the spectator as a series of *verité* flashbacks. These intercuts are highly didactic in their use of Nobody's dialogue as an authenticating narration. While the tele-movie look of these scenes is stylistically off balance in terms of the rest of the film, they nevertheless guarantee this remembering as historically accurate. In narrative terms, Nobody's story provides a clear and compelling historical argument that takes us a long way from the world of the Western. It is clear that colonialism, in the form of English soldiers, breaks the connection between Nobody and his people. His capture and transportation to England brings Nobody into direct personal contact with Europe both literally and philosophically in that Nobody is connected to the world of European practices of exhibition (he's put on display) and knowledge (he is sent to 'white man's school'). In other words, both Nobody and Europe are changed by that encounter.[27] Yet when Nobody escapes and finally returns to his people they do not believe what he has seen. Europe thus disappears and, as we've seen, America forgets that it has forgotten its history of colonisation.

So, how does the relationship between Blake and Nobody remember colonialism? It is not unusual in the Western for a Native American character (or more broadly an indigenous person in other cinematic traditions) to be figured as in-between; perhaps as a guide, scout or 'soldier of fortune', perhaps as a character who mediates, translates or negotiates bargains between indigenous and non-indigenous peoples; perhaps as a hybrid character, out of place or shifting, dramatically mobile, treacherous or ambivalent. The flip-side of this ensemble is the non-indigenous character who is becoming not-white.[28] Both characterisations remind us that colonisation both required and produced actual inter-cultural performance by translators, emissaries, interpreters, brokers and so on. In some respects, particularly at the level of the story, Nobody possesses some of these potentialities. However he is, if not unique, then certainly distinctive in that Nobody is an historical emissary because of his relationship to Europe. Whereas Blake does not even remember that he has forgotten (his poetry), Nobody remembers both the violence of colonisation which 'America' has forgotten and the utopian beauty of 'Europe's' poetry. But in the journey which Nobody makes with Blake he is not simply mimicking some redemptive (European) journey.

In essence I think that their journey is one in which Nobody attempts to work with the magic of mimesis. *Dead Man* is full of mimesis and remembering as sympathetic magic: stones mimic the sun; men mimic women; actors (especially Robert Mitchum) mimic their previous cinematic incarnations who mimic bears;

pioneering journeys mimic modern journeys; 'Indians' mimic white people who mimic hippies who mimic indigenous people; an accountant mimics Nobody who mimics a poet; William Blake's weapon mimics his speech; even the 'Indian' and the 'white man's' villages seem to mimic each other. But Nobody's use of mimicry is far more involved and complex than any of these examples. Even when he episodically recites William Blake's poetry to the uncomprehending Blake who thinks it's just 'Indian malarky'; Nobody's mode of speech is more ritual than everyday. Nobody knows that the Blake he read in England has been forgotten in the world of the American frontier. When he re-discovers a man with the name (of) William Blake, Nobody attempts to harness through ritual the energies of William Blake by giving him a proper funeral so that his energies can be returned 'to the place of emanation [to] rejoin the identity of that place'.[29] Thus the return of William Blake to the sacred spirit-world might make possible a magical journey of William Blake from England to America. In the midst of a ruined landscape in which nobody seems to remember, an Indian attempts a critical postcolonial project. In their journey though many valleys of death Nobody and Blake re-enact the 'horror and violent legitimacy of sacrifice and gift'[30] that is colonisation not in order to transcend that history but, as I'll argue in the final section of the chapter, to find a way of living in the midst of death. Thus the mimesis with which *Dead Man* plays is not about copies, reflections or mirror-images. Instead the film stages a repetition of one colonial encounter (between Nobody and Europe) in relation to another (Nobody and Blake in America). The memory of the first is joined to the ritual of the second in the hope that the future might be transformed, magically.

## Affect and sonic memory

> It's so strange that you don't remember any of your poetry.
>
> (Nobody)

Neil Young's soundtrack to *Dead Man* has been subjected to high praise and considerable abuse. When the film was released many critics chose the sound-track as a focus for their hostile reaction to the film, describing it as annoying, distracting or even painful.[31] Disliking the film after a single viewing is, at least, understandable. It is a film which requires repeated viewing. The soundtrack, on the other hand, while not exactly brimming with Top Forty singles, is immediate, accessible and powerful, as well as capable of bearing repeated and attentive listening. As Jarmusch writes on the liner notes to the CD: 'What he brought to the film lifts it to another level, intertwining the soul of the story with Neil's musically emotional reaction to it – the guy reached down to some deep place inside him to create such strong music for our film.'[32] Of course, other film critics loved the music. Greil Marcus wrote perceptively in 'Ten reasons why Neil Young's *Dead Man* is the best music for the dog days of the 20th century' that,

'For a film set more than a century ago, an electric guitar, playing a modal melody, surrounded by nothing, sounds older than anything you see on the screen.'[33] More broadly, people know that Young recorded most of the sound-track over two days performing to a rough-cut of the film in a San Francisco warehouse. In a sonic world in which soundtracks often function as just another product spin-off, Young's status coupled to the power and distinctiveness of the improvisation have raised this soundtrack to quasi-legendary status.

Today, after sensorama and large format cinema, we take it for granted that the cinema is a space in which a sensual as opposed to a purely scopic body is mobilised. It is much less usual to think of remembering as affective in the sense in which the term has been deployed within cultural studies, to refer to a certain intensity of sensual, emotional and embodied experience.[34] But of course, remembering is affective. We know from the work of Francis Yates and others that in Western cultures, mnemonics has long been governed by interlocking regimes of training in the ordering of memory, image and language. A man might be remembered by associating his moustache with a memory image. Groups or sequences would be visualised in place, so the objects in a familiar room could hold and order memory images, as in the case of Matteo Ricci's memory palace.[35] Finally, linguistic associations, primarily those around spelling or rhyme rather than any quality of sound, have been recurrent in memory training. A woman named Smith could be remembered by associating her with an anvil. These mnemonic systems suggest two propositions: first, that Western culture's valorisation of the gaze is reproduced in mnemonic systems by privileging the visual, and second, that linguistic and spatial apprehension have been central to mnemonic systems. By implication then, a tradition of memory in the logic of seeing and writing will tend to exclude memory's reliance on other senses.[36] The soundtrack of *Dead Man* challenges this logic.

In formal terms the guitar component of Neil Young's soundtrack to *Dead Man* is, for the most part, an elaboration of a single tonal sequence in 3/4 time. It's melodic and chordal. It uses mid-range, harmonic and feedback sounds. It would be insufficient to note that there are moments when the sound-design performs relatively conventional roles in alerting the listener to moments of on-screen intensity or bridging scenes. The soundtrack is an empathetic and didactic counterpoint to the diegesis in that it anticipates and replies to various scenes. Yet even these feature more often as intense flashes of sound which, like star-bursts, explode into cascading showers of incandescent residual sparks. This improvised soundtrack is part 'Jim Hendrix's apocalyptic *Star-Spangled Banner* ... [and] in both shape and feeling, *Sometimes I feel like a Motherless Child*, pointing to the absolute aloneness of both Blake and Nobody'.[37] But the soundtrack also anchors the images, providing a kind of sonic datum for the entire film. For example in the opening sequences, as the sounds of the train wheels gradually give way to the fragmentary but insistent beginnings of Neil Young's guitar, it is as if these sounds are opening up the journey, inviting the listening spectator to travel. But this initial suggestion soon gives way not to another song and another moment, but to Young's repetitive re-working of the single theme which is looped and twisted.

In a wonderful essay on time in the gangsta film, Jodi Brooks has written that,

> Through the compression, loading, stretching and evacuation of time at the level of the shot itself, through editing, and through its practices of quotation, the contemporary gangsta film re-maps the temporal structuring of the everyday by searing a fissure in its surface. ... The key struggle in these films becomes a struggle over time itself.[38]

In *Dead Man* the sound and the editing operate together to produce an analogous struggle over time and an opening-up of memory spaces through repetition. Young plays with the theme meandering around yet holding it, stretching and meditating on the note. Crucially, Young's harmonics are never resolved, they are never finished but keep building, through repetition and echo until we reach the two moments of sonic crescendo in the film. The first comes when Blake and Nobody finally arrive at the Indian village where Nobody will acquire a sea canoe. By this time Blake has been shot again, and he is feeble and semiconscious as he walks towards the longhouse along the main street of the village, a street which echoes the main street of Machine. Here there is no diegetic sound other than the music, which is both smacked-out and trippy, a driving, angry and delirious approach to death. Second, as the final scene begins with the quietness of gently breaking waves, we hear Young's guitar returning to lovingly punctuate the words of Nobody and Blake as they speak of his final voyage. Then the guitar becomes a fog-horn issuing mournful, moaning, pained cries across the water; then, slowly, it returns to the theme that's still going, unresolved and echoic as the canoe moves off into deeper water, the sky filling the screen, the screen becoming dark. The music takes us to yet another place because like a persistent memory it operates to produce what Bakhtin described as chronotope, a quasi-autonomous time-space which in *Dead Man* gains the turbulent intensity of affect from the film score.[39]

To think in this way is to side with Bergson in insisting on the duration and present pasts of remembering, and against those for whom memory is primarily interpretive and associative.[40] But unlike Bergson, who drew a sharp delineation between cerebral and corporeal remembering, sensual memories confound such distinctions of mind and body. Because the body incorporates sensations across the boundaries which we imagine our skin provides, sound can both become and invoke body memory; it can be a bodily trace that might be summoned, but equally one which might come out, without bidding, in a sweat. Bachelard appeals to similar qualities in a passage from *The Poetics of Space*, where he writes of the memories of space, in this instance the rooms and places of childhood:

> I alone, in my memories of another century, can open the deep cupboard that still retains for me alone that unique odour, the odour of

raisins drying on a wicker tray. The odour of raisins! It is an odour that is beyond description, one that takes a lot of imagination to smell. But I've already said too much. If I said more, the reader, back in his own room, would not open that unique wardrobe, with its unique smell, which is the signature of intimacy.[41]

I read Bachelard's memories of the smells of space as an argument against history as disciplined knowledge. His emphasis is relentlessly specific. His terms, 'I alone', 'unique' (three times in a short passage) and 'beyond description', are all militantly anti-representation. It is an argument in favour of the sensual imagination that can be called on in order to re-member. The reader cannot smell Bachelard's raisins but must 'open that unique wardrobe', that is remember her own 'smell of raisins'. Memories of smell and sounds can have the dream-like qualities that Bachelard evokes, in part because language cannot inscribe their particularity. These kinds of memories recall that which history can neither grasp nor consign to the past. Their moment of apprehension, in the case of both smells and sounds, is situational yet as memories they are enduring in their presence, outside of chronology and certainly neither evidence nor markers of progress. Memories of smells, like Young's soundtrack, remind us of the anti-historical qualities of memory that we need in order to inhabit space and time through our bodies.

## Death and memory's present future

> Did you kill the white man who killed you?
>
> (Nobody)

*Dead Man* is a meditation on the centrality of death to our present pasts. In the first place, the film is super-saturated with death. At the level of the story, even if Blake is not already dead, he is both possessed by death and a killing machine. In the end the two main characters certainly die, as do most of the white characters. The *mise en scène* offers us endless images of coffins, skulls, dead animals and dead people, so that 'the West' becomes a kind of theatre of death. Underpinning the entire film is the haunting presence of the destruction of Native American peoples. Thus we both see and hear reverberations of the conquest of lands, the physical obliteration of peoples, the theft of children, the spread of disease, the threat Christianity posed to Native American visions, and the persistence of indigenous culture and communities. The world of the film is a deeply traumatised world. It is a world in which perhaps time itself is traumatised, so damaged that it is not yet possible to 'recover' historical experience. There is no justice, no peace and no redemption. *Dead Man's* deadly closure seems to propose that a different relationship to history might be sought in sacrifice.

233

In this sense *Dead Man* can be regarded as a cultural text that works creatively with and beyond what Huyssen described as the disabling binaries of *either* remembering or forgetting, *either* amnesia or memory overload. I've argued that the film's use of particular cinematic techniques produces a fractured and fragmentary experience of time which forces us to contemplate the proleptic functions of remembering. I've suggested that *Dead Man* revisits the Western and colonialism in ways that propose remembering as a culturally fluid process. The film asks the spectator to regard remembering as partial and unfinished; rhythmic, haptic and bodily; anticipatory and sliding; above all, affective as well as institutionally performative. Thus remembering becomes a mode of contingent place-making rather than the inscription of property rights behind patrolled frontiers. *Dead Man* offers a model of memory-work as part of the process of belonging, in this instance, learning to belong in worlds in which remembering the presence of colonialism *in the post-colonial* is an ethical necessity. It offers some suggestions about how remembering can be thought, sung, imaged and spoken in ways quite other than those of anachronism or evidence, confession or cure, guilt or innocence. It proposes some terms through which to think the difference of the poetry of anamnesis – not remembering or forgetting but remembering and forgetting as repetition and reiteration; remembering as necessarily sensory and affective, as mimetic and proleptic, as performative as well as traumatic, as trafficking and transacting in contradiction. *Dead Man* seems to me to offer a modest and affirming project of being in time – remembering as holding together present pasts and present futures in the contingent yet grounded moment of the present.

## Acknowledgements

Thanks to Paul Healy, Jodi Brooks and Brian Morris for comments and assistance with this chapter.

## Notes

1   M. Taussig, *Mimesis and Alterity: a particular history of the senses*, Routledge, New York, 1993, p. 32.
2   J. Jarmusch, *Dead Man*, USA/Germany/Japan, 1995.
3   A. Huyssen, 'Present Pasts: Media, Politics, Amnesia', *Public Culture*, 2000, vol. 12, no. 1, p. 27.
4   Ibid.
5   Ibid.
6   See, for example, D. Marc, *Bonfire of the Humanities: television, subliteracy, and long-term memory loss*, Syracuse University Press, Syracuse, 1995.
7   M. B. Hansen, '*Schindler's List* is not *Shoah*: The Second Commandment, Popular Modernism and Public Memory', *Critical Inquiry*, 1996, vol. 22, p. 310.
8   M. Turim, *Flashbacks in Film: memory and history*, Routledge, New York, 1989, p. 2.
9   Y. Loshitzky, 'Introduction', in Y. Loshitzky, ed., *Spielberg's Holocaust: critical perspectives on Schindler's List*, Indiana University Press, Bloomington, 1996, p. 3.

10 B. Zelizer, 'Every Once in a While. Schindler's List and the Shaping of History' in Loshitzky, *Spielberg's Holocaust*, p. 18.

11 M. Foucault, 'Film and Popular Memory', in M. Foucault, *Foucault Live: interviews 1966–84*, trans., J. Johnston, ed. S. Lotringer, Semiotext(e) Foreign Agent Series, Semiotext(e), New York, 1989. Originally published in *Cahiers du Cinema*, nos 251–52, July–August, 1974.

12 M. K. Hall, 'Now You Are a Killer of White Men: Jim Jarmusch's *Dead Man* and traditions of revisionism in the Western', *Journal of Film and Video*, 2001, vol. 52, no. 4, pp. 3–14.

13 K. Jones, '*Dead Man*', *Cineaste*, 1996, vol. 22, no. 2, p. 46.

14 These possibilities have been raised in G. Rickman, 'The Western Under Erasure: *Dead Man*', in J. Kitses and G. Rickman, eds, *The Western Reader*, Limelight Editions, New York, 1998, p. 400.

15 Hansen, '*Schindler's List* is not *Shoah*', p. 312.

16 Quoted in S. Buck-Morss, *Dialectics of Seeing: Walter Benjamin and the Arcades Project*, MIT Press, Cambridge, Mass., 1989, p. 338.

17 This formulation draws directly from Hansen, '*Schindler's List* is not *Shoah*', p. 312.

18 Jarmusch quoted in Rickman, 'The Western Under Erasure', p. 388.

19 J. Rosenbaum, *Dead Man*, British Film Institute, London, 2000, pp. 60–1.

20 The key exception consists of the ways in which *Dead Man* represents women. There are only two female characters with speaking parts, Thel and 'Nobody's girlfriend' (Michelle Thrush), both of whom exist principally for men to have sex with and only one of whom is likely to live through the story.

21 See for example Susan Kollin, 'Dead Man, Dead West', *Arizona Quarterly*, Autumn 2000, vol. 56, no. 3, pp. 125–54. These sentiments also fit nicely with Rosenbaum's persuasive argument about *Dead Man* as an 'acid Western', see Rosenbaum, *Dead Man*, pp. 47–62.

22 Jones, '*Dead Man*', p. 46.

23 J. Jarmusch quoted in T. Colbath and S. Blush, 'Jim Jarmusch Interview', *Seconds Magazine*, 1996, no. 37, http://members.tripod.com/~jimjarmusch/sec96.html.

24 Jarmusch's description of Blake in Rosenbaum, *Dead Man*, pp. 69–70 is interesting in this context:

ROSENBAUM: It's interesting how Blake picks up bits and pieces of his identity from other people in the film, including Nobody.
JARMUSCH: Yeah. He's also like a blank piece of paper that everyone wants to write all over, which is why I like Johnny [Depp] so much as an actor for that character, because he has that quality. He's branded an outlaw totally against his character, and he's told he's this great poet, and he doesn't even know what this crazy Indian is talking about. Even the scene in the trading post where the missionary [Alfred Molina] says, 'Can I have your autograph?' and then pulls a gun on him – and Blake stabs him in the hand and says, 'There, that's my autograph.' It's like all these things are projected onto him.

25 In political terms it's clear that these kinds of dialogues have resulted in significant but limited advances for indigenous people in autonomy, human rights and self-determination. Nothing in what I want to say aims to belittle such achievements or undermine the necessity of their further elaboration in the multi-faceted cause of justice for indigenous people. Indeed it remains important for indigenous people to be able to deploy realist, rational and historicist representations within juridical institutions and have them authorised.

26 See in particular G. Agamben, *Remnants of Auschwitz: the witness and the archive*, trans. D. Heller-Roazen, Zone Books, New York, 1999.

27  I'm thinking here of the way in which Europe is deployed in D. Chakrabarty, *Provincializing Europe: postcolonial thought and historical difference*, Princeton University Press, Princeton, 2000.

28  On becoming, see Gilles Deleuze and Félix Guattari, *A Thousand Plateaus: capitalism and schizophrenia*, trans. Brian Massumi, University of Minnesota Press, Minneapolis, 1987, pp. 232–309.

29  S. Muecke, 'Travelling the Subterranean River of Blood: philosophy and magic in cultural studies', *Cultural Studies*, 1999, vol. 13, no. 1, p. 15.

30  Muecke, 'Travelling the Subterranean River of Blood', p. 15.

31  See for example, P. Bell's review at, *http://www.24framespersecond.com/reactions/films/deadman.html*.

32  N. Young, *Dead Man: music from and inspired by the motion picture*, Vapour Records, New York, 1996.

33  G. Marcus, '[Dead Again]: Here are ten reasons why *Dead Man* is the best movie of the end of the 20th century', *Salon*, *www.salon.com/ent/feature/1999/12/02/deadman*, 2 December 1999.

34  B. Massumi, 'The Autonomy of Affect', *Cultural Critique*, 1995, vol. 31, pp. 83–109.

35  J. D. Spence, *The Memory Palace of Matteo Ricci*, Faber, London, 1985.

36  See F. Yates, *The Art of Memory*, Routledge and Kegan Paul, London, 1966.

37  Rosenbaum, *Dead Man*, p. 43.

38  J. Brooks, ' "Worrying the Note": mapping time in the gangsta film', forthcoming in *Screen*.

39  Mikhail Bakhtin, *The Dialogical Imagination*, ed. and trans. Caryl Emerson and Michael Holquist, University of Austin Press, Austin, 1981, p. 84.

40  H. Bergson, *Memory and Matter*, Zone Books, New York, 1988. See also G. Deleuze, *Bergsonism*, Zone Books, New York, 1991.

41  G. Bachelard, *The Poetics of Space*, Beacon Press, Boston, 1969, pp. 13–14.

# Part IV

# AND THEN SILENCE ...

## Introduction

*Katharine Hodgkin and Susannah Radstone*

Throughout this volume and its companion, memory appears in different and often contradictory shapes. Conservative and destructive, conciliatory and unforgiving, memory may serve as an implacable reminder of what some might prefer to see forgotten; or it may strive to forget it. It is at once the salve and the salt in the wound.

In this volume, with its emphasis on the past as a source of conflict and dissent, we have seen alongside contestation a simultaneous drive to consensus, and a need to transform the past in order to move on from it. But the move towards reparation and reconciliation rather than continuing conflict may leave gaps that cannot be filled, holes in the fabric of memory that simply have to be stepped over or around. If memory can appear as ghost at the funeral, reminder of the unmended past, it may also be an agent for the reshaping and reinvention of that past into more acceptable shapes. And reconciliation in its turn may be part of the necessary process of moving memory into history, however unsatisfying; or it may signal the existence of a hole whose presence is unmendable and will prevent any such move.

These dilemmas of silence and recognition are explored by Luisa Passerini in the chapter that concludes the volume. Passerini highlights the ethical problems underlying these debates: is self-deception in the cause of reconciliation preferable to a relentless clarity of recollection? What difference does it make if oblivion is willed by a community, or imposed from 'outside' that community? How is silence different in the public or the private sphere? Drawing on examples across Europe and beyond, Passerini reminds us of the ambivalent force of memory and forgetting.

# 13

# MEMORIES BETWEEN SILENCE
# AND OBLIVION

*Luisa Passerini*

## Introduction

The title of this essay draws attention to some of the characteristics of memory in our time. Firstly, the plural 'memories' alludes to the multiplicity of cultures and languages which flows from the diaspora of peoples throughout the world today, a multiplicity which we hope will come to incorporate a full sense of mutual respect, so that multiculturalism, multilingualism and multiracialism are not just empty words. The title also alludes to the multiplicity of layers in any process of representation, which cannot be exhausted by the old metaphor of a dual relationship between reality and its image – and memory is above all a form of representation. Secondly, although the term 'silence' is an ambivalent one, we can start by taking it literally to indicate what is pre- and post-sound, particularly the area around the word, the space where speech is located. Thirdly, 'oblivion' is a word chosen on the basis of the assonance with my language, Italian, where '*oblio*' is a word in common use, as 'forgetting' is in English. The Latin root '*oblivisci*', which has given rise also to the French '*oubli*' and the Spanish '*olvido*', means 'to take away', while the English 'for-get' and the German '*ver-gessen*' literally mean 'to receive away'.[1] This significant expression implies a mixture of passivity and activity, close to the original meaning of '*oblivisci*'. Although from certain points of view 'oblivion' and 'forgetting' can be considered as equivalent terms, the former indicates a state of mind, while the latter is used to mean a process which can take place at various levels, and which includes daily life more easily than does the former.

Finally, silence and oblivion are often confused if memory is analysed as narration, be it oral or written. Something may be unsaid because its memory has been actually repressed – by trauma, contrast with the present, conflicts of individual and collective nature – or because the conditions for its expression no longer (or do not yet) exist. Sometimes the change in these conditions may break the silence and allow memories to be expressed, while at other times silence can last for so long and under such conditions that it may contribute to the effacing of memory, and induce oblivion. At the same time, however, silence can nourish a story and establish a communication to be patiently saved in periods of darkness, until it is able to come to light in a new and enriched form.

The method adopted in my discussion is that of an itinerary, a journey through many different cases which have at one time or another been studied for their problematic relevance to memory. The argument is thus drawn out of an accumulation of examples which I have encountered over years of reflection on memory.

## Memory of memory, forgetting of forgetting

St Augustine, in his fourth-century *Confessions*, observed the peculiar and bewildering nature both of memory itself, and of the relationship between memory and oblivion: memory is based on a self-reflection – 'I remember that I remember.' It is the memory of oneself, of one's soul, of one's story through time: 'I remember with joy a sadness that has passed.' Augustine remarks on the universality of memory – which belongs even to animals and birds, otherwise they could not go back to their nests and occupations – but he also points out the paradox of memory: we cannot look for something we have lost unless we remember it at least in part. However, the intertwining of memory and oblivion is such that Augustine confesses himself bewildered, and has to turn to God for illumination: God is beyond memory, however immense memory is.[2] The paradox of memory relates not only to the history of the individual, but to the history of whole civilisations. Yosef Yerushalmi, in a talk given in 1987, commented that he had for some time resisted the invitation to give it, because of the required topic, '*Usages de l'oubli*' ('The uses of forgetting').[3] His resistance was based on the memory of the risk of forgetting the Torah in ancient Israel, but was also inspired by the loss that the very development of a specifically Jewish religion and culture had involved for other cultures. In fact, when monotheism took root in ancient Israel, all the vast and rich world of the Near East religions and mythologies was forgotten, and only the caricature described by the Jewish prophets survived, as idolatry reduced to the adoration of wood and stone. And then even the forgetting was forgotten, with an irretrievable loss.

These self-reflecting expressions are clues to understanding the chain of representations in which the process of remembering/forgetting consists. It is indeed a process of representations of representations, where any step refers to or mirrors another one, and where the subject moves between as well as creating multiple layers of representations: the subject cannot receive representations without creating new ones, in other words it cannot communicate without contributing to this multiplicity. As Augustine and Yerushalmi in different ways write, both memory and forgetting are multiple processes in time and perception.

As scholars we meet with similar problems in our researches, although formulated in more modest ways. How can we find traces of forgetting and silence, since they are not themselves observable? We know that certain silences are observable only when they are broken or interrupted, but we want nonetheless to find them; we do not want to perpetuate the suppression of what has been until now deemed unimportant, nor to reinforce what is already hegemonic. Similar problems haunt us in daily life. Martha Gellhorn beautifully described an instant of uncontrollable memory, which suddenly took her from a happy moment near the Red Sea back sixty years:

> I was sitting in the big inner courtyard of the New Tiran Hotel, Naama Bay, south Sinai … Without warning or reason I was in a room in Gaylords Hotel in Madrid. It was winter, late 1937 at a guess … From Madrid, my memory took me without pause to Prague. It was right after Munich …

She concludes her reverie with the question: 'What is the use of having lived so long, travelled so widely, if at the end you don't know what you know?'[4] It seems essential, in order to keep a sense of oneself, to make an act of self-reflection, not to leave memory or oblivion to automatism: therefore we must remember to remember and to forget, just as we must try to know what we know.

The French ethnographer Marc Augé, in his book *Les formes de l'oubli*, quotes the psychoanalyst J. B. Pontalis on forgetting and remembering.[5] What is repressed, Pontalis says, is not a piece of memory – *un souvenir* – supposed to be able to re-emerge intact through chains of associations, like the *madeleine* in Proust (or rather, as some interpret the story of the *madeleine* in Proust). All our memories are screens, but not in the traditional sense, as traces of something they reveal and hide at the same time. What is registered on the screen is not directly the sign of a piece of memory, but a sign of absence, and what is repressed is neither the event nor the memory nor even single traces, but the very connection between memories and traces. From this perspective, our task as researchers can be defined in the following way: '*dissocier les liaisons instituées*', to break institutionalised links in order to establish risky ones, '*des liaisons dangereuses*'. Put another way, when trying to understand connections between silence and speech, oblivion and memory, we must look for relationships between traces, or between traces and their absences; and we must attempt interpretations which make possible the creation of new associations.

## This century, this continent

When one ventures into the universe of memory, one must be aware of the starting point of the itinerary – which may be very different from the destination – and the position of the travelling subject. The perspective from which I speak is rooted in the European literary and scholarly tradition, and takes place in the temporal context of what Eric Hobsbawm has defined as the 'short twentieth century' (needless to say, my approach follows a very different historical route to Hobsbawm's), from the First World War to the end of the century.[6] In using the term 'European' I am aware that European culture is today very incomplete, and that in my case the points of reference are limited to just a few of the many

European countries. However, at least the intention is to make reference to a common European cultural space, hopefully now in the process of being created.

As for the temporal dimension, this century has a very specific relation to the processes of remembering and forgetting. Anna Rossi-Doria, in a brief but rich study of history and memory in the case of deportation, remarks that the twentieth century has been for the most part a time of cancellation of memory, and that it has prolonged the tendency to remove the past – a process Walter Benjamin analysed as deriving from the crisis of memory and experience typical of modernity.[7] This cancellation is associated with totalitarian regimes, but they are not the only ones to practise it; it can easily happen in democratic or transitional political regimes, as we will see.

However, any operation aiming to cancel memory cannot help being also an effort to produce another set of memories, to replace the previous one by force. The field of memory is a battlefield in many ways, and it would perhaps be more apt to say that this century has given rise to a contradictory mixture of memory and oblivion. *Theatres of Memory* by Raphael Samuel offers a fine illustration of the growth but also the ambivalence of forms of memory, where memory can turn into a form of oblivion, between nostalgia and consumerism.[8]

An example of the double character of memory, and how it can be exalted and erased at the same time, can be found in Hiroshima's transformation into a site of pleasure and urban entertainment. Lisa Yoneyama, in a study conducted in 1986–90, analysed the ruling aesthetic in Hiroshima's renewal as one of brightness, comfort and cleanliness. The town was becoming a future-oriented megalopolis and an international site of commerce and consumption, where the 'dark and gloomy' was turned into the 'bright and jovial'. In the official cartography of memory, concluded Yoneyama, there is seldom space for death, anger, sorrow or pain.[9] It is not by chance that the first example chosen for the present itinerary does not come from the European territories; this choice is a reminder that the memory of Europe, within which I work, must be placed in the context of the world, and if my focus here is European, I will at least give a few signals that this broader horizon is present in my mind and research.[10]

Returning to Europe, the mixed character of our century's relation to memory is particularly sharply revealed in the contrasting repercussions of Nazi persecutions and mass killings on different cultures and peoples.[11] The Roma were killed by the Nazis in huge numbers. Estimates vary between almost one hundred thousand and one million, but these questions cannot be reduced to quantity; whatever the exact figures, countless Roma were swallowed up by what in their language is called *Porraimos*, the devouring, and many more were subjected to torture and to medical experiments by the Nazis. However, these mass crimes were not addressed at the Nuremberg trials, where no Gypsy witnesses were called; as late as 1995 only one Nazi had received a sentence for crimes against Gypsies. According to Isabel Fonseca, while the Jews have

241

responded to genocide with 'a monumental enterprise of remembrance', the Roma have reacted with an 'art of forgetting', a peculiar mixture of fatalism and the urge to seize the day.[12] Among the Roma, 'forgetting' does not imply complacency; rather, it suggests sometimes buoyant defiance. Fonseca attributes their silence to the fact that they seem to have no sense and no need of a great historical past. Very often their memories do not extend beyond three or four generations – perhaps a legacy from the days of travel, when the dead were literally left behind, an attitude which continues to serve people who even when settled are hard-pressed to survive. Therefore the Second World War and the *Porraimos* are within memory, but for the moment they have given rise to no significant tradition of commemoration or even of discussion, as if there were among the Gypsies a lack of interest for their eventful and tragic past. This may be in the course of changing, but the original attitudes towards remembering and forgetting seem to have been very different in the two cases of Jews and Roma.

This contrast between defiant silence and monumental remembrance seems to me expressive of our time, and a version of the double character of the century in this respect. But let us not forget that before monuments of memory were built to the Shoah, a long period of silence about it had to be gone through: debate over its historical significance and its place in the heritage of the West developed very slowly. Genocides were considered monstrous exceptions in the Western tradition, both by the antifascist literature and even by the critical analyses of the Second World War.[13] The obscure side of that tradition was relatively hidden during the decades of the cold war. The importance of Hannah Arendt's *The Burden of Our Time*, written in 1951, which made it clear that understanding genocide is the burden that our century has imposed upon us, was recognized only in the 1970s.[14] In fact this burden was accepted by very few for a rather long time.

Again, while it must be kept in mind that the very concept of genocide is problematic if extended too much, the task of understanding genocide cannot be carried out only within the boundaries of Europe. We should not forget that other genocides have been perpetrated by all sorts of peoples through history, and in particular by Europeans against the peoples of other continents – one major instance being the colonisation of South America, for which the term has been explicitly used.[15] However, we do not need to go very far from Europe in order to find signs of both the violence of colonialism and the silence imposed upon it: an example follows.

## Silence as repression of memory and imposed 'amnesia'

In mid-August 1999, *Le Monde* published a long article and an editorial concerning a very significant case of public silence in the Europe of the second half of the twentieth century:

Hidden for years by the authorities, the truth about the repression of a demonstration organised by the Algerian Liberation Front in Paris in October 1961 begins to emerge more clearly in a report prepared by the Solicitor General of the French Highest Court of Appeal. On the basis of judiciary archives, having obtained a special right of exception to the one hundred years rule [he disclosed] that at least 48 people died at the hands of the police in the night between the 17th and 18th [of October]; for a long time the official count was three.

The article went on to explain that at the time the government had been informed of the facts – i.e. that hundreds of people had been thrown by the police into the water of the Seine – through a note sent by the Prefet de Police to the Cabinet of the Prime Minister, but it had preferred to maintain silence on the events. Therefore *Le Monde* holds the authorities responsible for this 'amnesia' and recognises the importance of coming to terms with it, more than forty years later, in order to contribute to the 're-establishment of Franco-Algerian relationships'.[16]

In fact, in this case the effort on the part of the authorities to hide their own responsibilities and to conceal the implications of the massacre for the relationships between the French and the colonised, between Europeans and non-Europeans, led to an oblivion in public memory which was part of the general disappearance of the Algerian War from French collective memory.[17] Books and films tried repeatedly to reveal the dynamics of the affair. But the film *Octobre à Paris* (Jacques Panijel, 1962), in which those who had survived the massacre were interviewed, was immediately put under censorship, and banned for the following ten years; while among the documents of France Presse which were made available to researchers, the dossier on October 1961 was missing.[18] We will never know the exact number of dead, but witnesses talk of more than 300 Algerians who disappeared on that occasion. Some were probably deported to Algeria; an estimate of around 200 dead seems plausible.[19] The story of the memory of that event is the story of a struggle against a silence intended to impose oblivion, an imposition which succeeded only partially. Moreover, 'silence was the refuge of many Algerian workers', observes Jean-Luc Einaudi, who reports the moving encounter he had with one of them in Algeria. The man still bore the consequences of that night, his right eye having been blinded by a policeman who had fired at his head; the night after the interview, the man could not sleep, and the following day he refused to go on, telling Einaudi: 'I do not want to remember.'[20] Forced silence and oblivion had reached even those directly involved in the events.

If such public (and extending to the private) 'amnesia' is imposed by the authorities, very often it requires some sort of complicity on the part of those who, not being in a position of power, accept and prolong an imposed silence. Such a complicity is revealed by Marilyn Young's research on the Korean war in the United States, which gave rise to a silence of a similar nature.[21] The Korean war took place between 1950 and 1953; it was as brutal as the Vietnam war, and its casualties were almost as high (and occurring over a shorter time); but it did not lead to a similar re-examination of national identity and purpose. Young's project, to understand this absence in history and public opinion, includes an analysis of the role of some intellectuals of the period, as exemplified by a symposium in the *Partisan Review* in 1952. These intellectuals did not want to take into account the unpopularity of the war; they preferred not to 'mar the immaculate essence of the American triumph in the Second World War', and not to challenge the power of the nationalist narrative to cushion and mute. Memories of the Korean war reappeared only after Vietnam – as if memory were a living substance where one wound has repercussions on the whole, and where associations with latent aspects are often possible at a later time – and the first oral history of the Korean war dates from 1988. This war has rightly been called 'the forgotten war'. Even events such as the massacres of hundreds of civilians perpetrated by American troops – for instance that of 23–26 July 1950 at No Gun Ri, which involved a majority of women and children – have been revealed only very recently by the Associated Press, following research and interviews carried out by one Korean and two American journalists.[22]

Europe too hosts a wide range of examples – almost too many to choose from – of imposed silences, large and small, involving individuals as well as communities. One could refer to the silence imposed in 1988 by British television upon 'Mother Ireland', a film exploring how Ireland was portrayed as a woman in Irish culture and how this image developed as a nationalist motif.[23] Or one could refer to the silence which the Catholic hierarchy tried to impose on the courageous priest of a Piedmontese village in the province of Cuneo (Borgo San Dalmazzo), don Raimondo Viale, who during the war tried to save many Jews and assisted partisans – but also Fascist spies – who had been condemned to death. Don Viale was repeatedly reproached and threatened by the Catholic authorities for refusing to allow the memory of those times (and his own part in them) to fade, and in 1970 he was suspended *a divinis* (banned from celebrating mass and preaching from the pulpit), ten years before being declared in 1980 one of the 'Righteous' of Israel. In 1998, his biographer Nuto Revelli reminded readers that the archival documentation on don Viale at the Curia of Cuneo and at the Vatican was censored, and not yet available to researchers; and that don Viale, even in the long interview which he gave, seemed to have internalised the imposed silence.[24] The breaking of other silences is documented by papers given at the 'Frontiers of Memory' conference where this chapter was initially presented, such as the major work done by Alessandro Portelli on the combination of silence and memory concerning the massacre at the Fosse Ardeatine in Rome.[25]

I want here to discuss two examples of silences which were broken in opposite ways. They have been chosen on the premise that the most interesting cases are those where silence is not an imposition by an authoritarian regime, but a self-decided attitude taken by a whole community or society. In this situation, however, some individuals in the interstices of society may resist, and their voices try to break the collective silence. This has been the case with poetry in Germany over the last few decades. Following 1968, the literary movement in West Germany known as *Neue Subjektivität* established a link between individual and collective memory, between the Nazi past and the present, asking that the silence over the responsibilities of the past should be broken. At the same time, in this individual rediscovery of the collective tragic past, women's voices became more numerous in poetry. Meanwhile in the eastern part of the country literature (and especially poetry) was able to break silence in a different way, because – being seen as a subjective mode – it could evade censorship more readily than other genres. Here what made the difference was the type of imposed 'oblivion': in East Germany it was not a literal silence, but rather an institutionalisation of the memory of the victims of Nazism, collected together under the general term of 'antifascists', against which counter-memories not allowed in 'objective' public space could be introduced in poetry.[26]

A more recent German example of the continuing role of poetry in the game between memory and oblivion is Heiner Müller's 'Seife in Bayreuth' ('Soap in Bayreuth'), a poem composed in 1992, after the annual neofascist demonstration in honour of Rudolf Hess, Minister of the Third Reich and supreme commander of the SS.[27] Müller's poem starts with a memory of his childhood: having heard adults say that in concentration camps the Jews were turned into soap, he started hating the smell of soap. Now, the poet says, he lives in a clean and tidy flat, with a shower 'MADE IN GERMANY' which could wake the dead, and when he opens the window he can smell soap. '*Jetzt weiss ich, sage ich gegen die Stille*': 'now I know' – continues the poem – 'now I say against the silence/what it means to live in hell and/not to be a dead man or a killer. Here/AUSCHWITZ was born in the smell of soap.' The fact that the poem was composed after the fall of the Berlin wall implies that reunification has made even more acute the problem of the memory of the German past. What seems particularly important in this example is the crucial connection established between individual and collective memory, between the public and private spheres; the role of the individual in reestablishing a collective sense of the past is very significant for the complex relationships between silence, memory and oblivion.

The name of the German literary movement reminds us that there are not only objects of forgetting and remembering, there are always subjects of these processes, subjects whose attitudes are crucial in determining how silence is to be broken: certain forms of oblivion point to a lack of identity or to an effort to cover up some of its components. This is relevant also for my second example, concerning emergence from the silence imposed by totalitarian regimes, such as that of the former Soviet Union. Maria Ferretti describes very convincingly the drama of memory in breaking that silence – which was never complete, thanks to the dissidents – in her account of Russian society confronted with its past.[28] To reflect on the memory of the Soviet Union and its terrible experience of repression, camps, extermination – an experience which lasted much longer than Fascism and Nazism – reminds us of the comparative 'silence' with which Western Europe regards this memory: while all sorts of cultural and historical remembrance evoke the crimes of Nazism and Fascism, comparable markers of the crimes of Stalinism are much fewer. This is probably due not only to the greater complexity of Stalinist oppression in historical terms, but also to the Western European left's insufficient acknowledgement and investigation of its own past.

This relative 'silence' can be juxtaposed with new forms of silence in Eastern Europe. For example, after 1990 Dina Khapaeva interviewed a group of young Russian 'Westophiles' – businessmen, journalists, professionals – all under 35, and all in favour of a Western-oriented development for Russia.[29] Their interviews and self-presentations both idealise and identify with the West; not only is the memory of Stalinism not problematised, but that past is not presented as part of their identity; it is treated as a stranger's past, the past of another people. Meanwhile the present is imprecise, transitional and unforeseeable, and the future seems to be largely foreseeable only as a projection of the subject's hopes. The present ends up being excluded from the horizon of temporality, an exclusion which is essential in order to save the perfection of the ideal image of the West ('everything in the West goes well for ordinary people', states one of the interviewees), fixed in its perfection, incorruptible by the passing of time. The cost of this operation is the loss of the role of the intelligentsia through the loss of its own consciousness. As the Spanish political theorist Perez-Diaz has noticed, there is a close link between the formation of a 'democratic public sphere' and the memories of the individuals who give life to it: if the memory of the past is trivialised, this leads to 'individus manqués', incomplete and forgetful individuals who can easily become prey of totalitarian movements.[30]

## Silence as full of memory, nourishing and projecting it to the future

Another Spanish scholar, however, Paloma Aguilar, takes an opposite view of silence.[31] She draws an interesting contrast between what she calls the 'patologìa amnésica de los españoles' about the Civil War in the political public sphere, on the one hand, and the many representations of the same topic in the fields of film and literature, on the other. In the period of transition after Francoism (after 1975, and especially 1978), it became essential in political life to forget the rancours of the past in order to consolidate democracy in Spain. A collective traumatic memory, which had been transmitted from generation to generation (generational transmission was crucial, since more than 70 per cent of the population had not lived through the war), had to be put aside in a period of great risk and uncertainty. Although there was a tendency to activate that memory on the basis of alleged similarities between the 1930s and the 1970s, the use of silence prevailed in politics – sometimes linked with an almost superstitious fear of repeating the same mistakes. According to Aguilar, this silence had its frustrations, but it helped to establish a democratic dialectic, and especially made it possible to avoid the use of the past as a weapon in political struggle. Let us remember, in order to understand the full sense of this silence, that the time of the dictatorship in Spain has been called 'a time of silence', when 'an imposed quarantine or silencing signified the continuation of [the civil] war as a work of cultural destruction'.[32] In the light of this imposed oblivion, the use of silence after Franco's death seems acceptable in politics only if it is considered alongside other levels of public life, such as the cultural and the academic, where the war was a privileged theme after 1978.

Aguilar's discussion calls to mind Nicole Loraux's analysis of civic memory in ancient Athens – during the fifth century BC – in response to the need for the community to reestablish its unity by prohibiting the use of a conflictual past.[33] A negative command, '*mé mnesikakeìn*' ('do not remember suffering'), prohibited the memory of bad things, and was intended to give priority to the political – a civil version of forgetting evil and moving on from mourning. Loraux also recalls the end of the Odyssey, when Ithaca is plunged into a civil war by the news of the death of the pretenders, but Athene stops Ulysses from fighting and the gods make an appeal to forget not only the misdeeds of others but especially one's own rage and desire for revenge. Refusing to forget is ultimately all-powerful because it has no limits, and in particular it does not accept the limits of the interiority of a subject. But in the Athens of the fifth century it was politics which in the end decided the uses and limits of memory.[34]

These examples remind us of communities where there is still a perception of a common good to be saved or restored, where corruption has not reached the roots of the social and political contract, and where solidarity can be (re)established between the individual and the collective. In such a situation silence has the function of making it possible to distance oneself from the past – not necessarily to forget – in certain areas of public life, while in others the remembering goes on. It is difficult for us to accept such presuppositions, and I personally incline to share Yerushalmi's suspicion of public silences. However, we must not rule out the possibility that an enjoined silence in the public sphere can have a positive meaning.

It is easier to think of the positive meanings of silence in the personal and private sphere, which is illuminated by literature and poetry. If literature can have social and political reverberations when breaking silence, as we have seen before, the same may be true in keeping silence. 'The difficult terrain between individual memories and collective remembrance' has been explored in the light of cognitive psychology, social psychology and social patterns of action and behaviour, the terrain shared by *Homo psychologicus*, *Homo sociologicus* and *Homo agens*.[35] I would like to add to the territory indicated by these figures the area inhabited by *Homo poeticus*, understanding of course this term in its original meaning comprising both *vir* and *femina*.

The Italian writer and poet Cristina Campo, remembering her childhood in the interwar period, beautifully evokes its silences: '*Sulla tavola bianca e rotonda, nelle veglie estive all'aperto in giardino, il silenzio rivestiva il suo reale valore, che è quello di accumulare potenze*'.[36] ('On the white round table, in summer wakings outside in the garden, silence took on again its real value, which is that of accumulating potency'). This sentence, uttered in a tone of memory, directs us towards the positive aspects of silence in its relation to memory: it takes strength, sometimes, to keep silence, the silence which allows for meditation and reflection, for absorption of meaning from the environment and projection towards the future.

In a similar vein, I have been thinking of memories transmitted without verbalisation, such as those incorporated in gestures, images and objects: the transmission of how to cook (by imitation, not on the basis of recipes), the memories of the body – of both traumas and pleasures – the memory of laughter, the memory conveyed through family names given to the newborn. One can think of photographs, portraits, letters. Or of the custom of keeping a minute of silence in order to commemorate somebody who has died. Or of silences in a psychoanalytic session. All these are examples of silences which are connected with remembering, not with forgetting. Finally, silence is essential in order to remind us that memory is not only word, it is the 'embodied memory' enlivened by intersubjectivity.[37]

Assia Djebar, the Algerian writer, returned repeatedly in her poetry to her decision to write in French while at the same time defending Algerian culture, during the period from the late 1950s to the late 1990s.[38] A poem published in a book with the subtitle 'A reflection at the margins of my francophony', gives various replies to the question: 'Why do you write in French?'. Djebar starts by reminding us that she had more than two languages: she had Berber, Arab, French, and the language of the body, '*un corps de femme qui se meut au-dehors*', a woman's body which moves outside, and which is not a single woman's body but is included in a chain of women's bodies. The author goes through the memories of her mother, her grandmother, her great-grandmother, through a memory populated by women, a '*traversée en mémoire féminine*' ('a journey in feminine memory'). The poem, called '*Entre corps et voix*' ('Between body and voice'), describes '*ce tangage des langages/dans le mouvement d'une mémoire à creuser/à ensoleiller*', 'this seesawing of languages/ in the movement of a memory to be excavated/ and illuminated', a memory at the border between body and voice. Memory is a woman's voice for this poet, but it is also '*mémoire de l'eau, plutot mémoire des sables, silence*', 'memory of water, or rather memory of sand, silence'.[39] This is another way of saying that there can be memory within silence and memory through silence. But it is also a reminder that memory is gendered, and women's memories and silences offer different continuities and repetitions, through the specificities of their experiences in different times and spaces.[40]

To continue with the reminder that 'memory is more than words', music has much to teach us about silence. The composer Luigi Nono has called attention to a 'listening to silence' which can have a social and political meaning, that of listening to the other: '*Le silence. Il est très difficile à écouter. Très difficile d'écouter, dans le silence, les autres. Au lieu d'écouter le silence, au lieu d'écouter les autres, on espère écouter encore une fois soi-même*'.[41] ('Silence. It is very difficult to listen to. It is very difficult to listen, in the silence, to others. Rather than listening to silence, rather than listening to others, we hope to listen once more to ourselves.') Silence may contain an appeal to go beyond ourselves, in relation to the present as well as the past. It may signal a suspension of the daily noise, of the customary sounds, and express attention, in the sense of approval or disapproval. George Steiner has written about silence as 'the only *decent* response to the violations of human speech' perpetrated by Fascism and Stalinism.[42] Among various types of silence (the final logic of poetic speech, the mystics' 'ineffable', the exaltation of action), he includes that of defiance of 'a time like the present', tracing it back to the First World War.[43]

We can understand these words on the basis of our experience of silence as oral historians and interviewers, when we listen to our interviewees. In a larger sense we can take them as inviting us to listen to those cultures and peoples which have not yet been listened to enough. Women's studies, for instance, was born out of such an inspiration, as was subaltern studies, to give two important examples. In both cases, the endeavour implied silencing the traditional hierarchies of historical knowledge and its objects in order to open up new ways of listening.

We can also understand Nono's and Steiner's reminders of the importance of silence as warnings never to use or analyse memory without situating it in a context of silence. This has different meanings in various fields. For the work of cultural historians it means recognising the fragmented nature of memory, its complexities, and the necessary complexity of the required approach: one should work as if memory were more than words and yet at the same time concentrate on the textual analysis of what traces of memory we have: 'Not all silences are equal and they cannot be addressed in the same manner; any historical narrative [is] a bundle of silences, the result of a unique process, and the operation required to deconstruct these silences will vary accordingly.'[44] Historians can decide, as Trouillot points out, according to their sources and objects of research, whether to reveal a silence, or make a silence speak for itself, or unravel silence as a mask of conflicts. Taking silence into account means watching out for the links between forms of power and forms of silence. It means, finally, looking more deeply in those aspects of memory which have to do with oblivion.

My own experience of using silences for history is that many of the silences we observe are relative and we must understand them as such: for instance there may be a silence of existing historiography confronted with workers' culture, or a silence of women's studies in comparison to women's oral tradition, or a silence of the mass media where poetry is able to speak. It is constitutive of the definition of a silence to find out its limits, its context, and its reference: in respect to whom and to what is it a silence? Who can define it as such? At the same time, we also experience in our researches, as well as in public memory, the frustration resulting from the loss of memory, large and small, which all our efforts do not seem capable of reducing. Very often, especially when researching those who lost and were repressed, we have the experience of finding people, ideas, books which seem to have completely disappeared, which have vanished leaving only scattered and tantalising traces, in spite of all our efforts.

I think we could all agree on this: that silences, oblivions and memories are aspects of the same process, and the art of memory cannot but be also an art of forgetting, through the mediation of silence and the alternation of silence and sound. But what are the implications of this finding for our work on the continuous set of transformations which is memory? I believe that we should turn our attention and our discussions in two main directions: one is the effort to build a new history (or a new anthropology, or whatever discipline we are concerned with) that takes into account the dialectics of memory, silence and oblivion; the other is the search for the limits of our disciplines in these fields, bearing in mind Schachter's reminder of 'memory's fragile power', where power as well as fragility, compelling force as well as failures, are present at the same time.[45]

Examples of the first can be found not only in those works that explicitly intend to be 'histories of forgetting',[46] but in those histories which set memories in the context of confrontations with power, and of various forms of oblivion. For instance, Shahid Amin has analysed the history and memory of a violent confrontation between police and peasants that took place on 4 February 1922 at Chauri Chaura, a small market town in north India, in which Gandhian peasants resorted to violence.[47] Amin has 'arranged and rearranged' local remembrances against the authorised texts of court records and other official sources, challenging both the version of colonialist history and the stereotyped incorporation of the event within the narrative of the Great Freedom Struggle in post-colonial history. His exemplary work shows the multiplicity of memory and the possibility of its use for a new type of history, where 'incongruence with known facts [is] not construed as a lapse of memory, but rather as a necessary element in the stitching together of the story'.[48]

For an example of the second direction, approaching the limits of the discipline, I look outside the realm of history, to that of psychoanalysis. In Wilfred Bion's *A Memoir of the Future* (1975–80), the future enters the theatre of the mind, and is connected with memory.[49] On this stage there are continuous dialogues between the various characters, one of which is called Memory. In one scene, Memory is woken up by a conversation between two girls, Alice and Rosemary, and reminds them that some of the things of the past that they were mentioning (black stockings and 'practical' shoes) come from the unconscious. It is the mention of those things past which has woken Memory up, but when she (I take Memory to be feminine) starts speaking, the two girls fall asleep. Memory then declares that she has been born in sin, and proceeds to talk about the past with Roland, who is just waking up (chapter 15). These alternations of sleep and waking give the sense of various levels of representation in this scene. But we have already been told (chapter 14) that the land of sleep, of the unconscious, of the forgotten can be identified with either the past or the future. Memory is therefore situated between the two.

A clue to this suggestive image can be found earlier in Bion's writing, in the 1967 'Notes on memory and desire'.[50] Here Bion distinguishes sharply between, on the one hand, memory and desire – which have to do respectively with the past, 'what is supposed to have happened', and the future, 'what has not happened' – and, on the other hand, something he calls evolution, which has to do with psychoanalysis and takes place eminently in the present ('every session attended by the psychoanalyst must have no history and no future'). Memory is the past tense of desire, anticipation its future tense, and both are obstacles to the present-oriented attitude which is the only one which allows the *unknown* to emerge in any session. 'Evolution' has a superficial resemblance to memory, which must be watchfully avoided by the psychoanalyst. The former is 'the experience where some idea or pictorial impression floats into the mind unbidden and as a whole'; the latter is the 'response to a deliberate and conscious attempt at recall' and it has to do with 'those aspects of the mind that derive from sensuous experience'. As historians or anthropologists or cultural critics, we deal with this memory and with the experience which is its basis, although we are excluded from coming across the 'unknown'. Keeping in mind these limits is essential for those who want to deal with memory, oblivion and silence.

## Concluding remarks

This itinerary has led us from ancient Greece and ancient Israel to Hiroshima, then on the paths that the gypsies followed through Europe and to the camps where the effort to exterminate them and the Jews took place in the interwar period; to Paris in the early 1960s, and to Korea and the USA in the 1950s. It has touched on Ireland, Italy, Russia, Germany and Spain in the last three decades – with reference to memories of the previous half a century – and finally on India in the 1920s; it has alluded to Algeria and Latin America. The route, therefore, has gone back and forth between various European countries, and to a lesser extent between Europe and other parts of the world; but the focus has remained on the twentieth century and the European continent.

However, I am not arguing here for a specificity of European memory, a question which requires much more discussion and thought.[51] To pursue this direction, one would have to take into consideration at least two directions of research: the impact of accelerated processes of mediatisation, and generally of change in the field of communication, on the contemporary phenomenon of proliferation/cancellation of memory; and the relationships between memory and guilt – for colonialism, for persecutions and massacres. But for the moment, I am just indicating some links, some connections. The unsystematic nature of the itinerary is accounted for by the unsystematic nature of memory; in other words, I have followed my own associations, which are however grounded in a common patrimony of studies and knowledge. While this itinerary is linked to my own personal idiosyncrasies, and also to chance, the choice of places and times is based on considerations that I believe are shared with others, such as a concern with Europe and its memory and their place in a world context. Many similar itineraries could be drawn which might be more or less complete than mine, but they would probably go through similar points, because the dialectics between memory and silence in this continent cannot avoid colonialism, totalitarianisms and wars, and their sites within and outside Europe. Yet this dialectics includes also many personal aspects, involving the bodies and minds of individuals in times of peace.

To conclude on a personal note, I think that it is no accident that one of my very first projects in oral history was concerned with certain forms of silence among Turin workers on the subject of Fascism. I am convinced that it was my decision to pay attention to such silences on the part of the narrators that led me to understand the importance of other aspects of their testimonies – on which existing historiography was silent in its turn.[52] It is as if it is only by listening to silence that we as oral historians can learn the special language which allows us to be on the same wavelength as our interviewees.

## Acknowledgement

I would like to thank Ron Grele, Rosalind Delmar and Richard Waswo for their bibliographical suggestions. Liliana Ellena read the draft and provided useful comments.

## Notes

1 Harald Weinrich, *Lethe. Kunst und Kritik des Vergessens*, Beck, Munich 1997. (I quote from the Italian edition, *Lete. Arte e critica dell'oblio*, il Mulino, Bologna 1999, Introduzione.)
2 St Augustine, *Confessions*, X, 13, 14, 16.
3 Yosef H. Yerushalmi, 'Réflexions sur l'oubli', in *Usages de l'oubli. Contributions au Colloque de Royaumont*, Seuil, Paris 1988, pp. 7–21.
4 Martha Gellhorn, 'Memory', *London Review of Books*, 12 December 1996.
5 Marc Augé, *Les formes de l'oubli*, Payot, Paris 1998, pp. 32–34.
6 Eric Hobsbawm, *The Age of Extremes: the short twentieth century, 1914–1991*, Abacus, London 1995.
7 Anna Rossi-Doria, *Memoria e storia: il caso della deportazione*, Rubbettino, Soveria Mannelli 1998.
8 Raphael Samuel, *Theatres of Memory*, Verso, London 1994.
9 Lisa Yoneyama, 'Taming the Memoryscape: Hiroshima's Urban Renewal', in Jonathan Boyarin (ed.), *Remapping Memory. The Politics of TimeSpace*, Minneapolis-London, University of Minnesota Press 1994.
10 However, I also wish to say that I have chosen as a focus of cultural intervention that of criticising eurocentrism from within; see Luisa Passerini, *Europe in Love, Love in Europe: Imagination and Politics in Britain Between the Wars*, Tauris, London 1999.
11 Inga Clendinnen, *Reading the Holocaust*, Cambridge University Press, Cambridge 1999.

12 Isabel Fonseca, *Bury Me Standing: The Gypsies and Their Journey*, Vintage, New York 1996.

13 Eleni Varikas, 'Le fardeau de notre temps: Pariah et critique de la modernité politique chez Arendt', in Marie-Claire Caloz-Tschopp (ed.), *Hannah Arendt, les sans-Etat et le 'droit d'avoir des droits'*, vol. 1, Harmattan, Paris 1998.

14 Hannah Arendt, *The Burden of Our Time*, Secker & Warburg, London 1951.

15 Annette M. Jaimes, 'Introduction: Sand Creek: The Morning After', in M.A. Jaimes (ed.), *The State of Native America: Genocide, Colonization, and Resistance*, South End Press, Boston 1992.

16 *Le Monde*, 13 August 1999: 'Octobre 1961: mensonge officiel', pp. 1 and 5, and editorial 'Les fautes du passé', p. 14, author's translation.

17 Antoine Prost, 'The Algerian War in French Collective Memory', in Jay Winter and Emmanuel Sivan (eds), *War and Remembrance in the Twentieth Century*, Cambridge University Press, Cambridge 1999.

18 Anne Tristan, *Le silence du fleuve. Ce crime que nous n'avons toujours pas nommé*, Au nom de la mémoire, Bezons 1991.

19 Jean-Luc Einaudi, *La bataille de Paris. 17 octobre 1961*, Seuil, Paris 1991.

20 Ibid., p. 292.

21 Marilyn Young, 'Memories of Vietnam and Korea'. Talk given at the European University Institute, Florence, 6 June 1997; thanks to Marilyn Young for permission to quote from this unpublished paper.

22 Sylvie Kauffmann, 'Des soldats américains auraient massacré des centaines de civils sud-coréens en 1950', *Le Monde*, 3–4 octobre 1999.

23 Anna Davin, 'Introduction' to Irish History Feature, *History Workshop Journal* 31, Spring 1991; Anne Crilly, 'Banning History', *History Workshop Journal* 31, Spring 1991.

24 Nuto Revelli, *Il prete giusto*, Einaudi, Torino 1998, p. 106. See also Luisa Passerini, 'La memoria orale: l'opera di Nuto Revelli e la sua ricezione', *Rivista dell'Istituto Storico della Resistenza in Cuneo e Provincia*, no. 55, pp. 21–48, 1999.

25 'Frontiers of Memory' conference, London, September 1999. Alessandro Portelli, *L'ordine è già stato eseguito. Roma, le Fosse Ardeatine, la memoria*, Donzelli, Rome 1999.

26 Anna Chiarloni, 'Introduzione', *Nuovi poeti tedeschi*, Einaudi, Torino 1994.

27 Heiner Müller, *Die Gedichte*, Suhrkamp, Frankfurten Main 1998.

28 Maria Ferretti, *La memoria mutilata. La Russia ricorda*, Corbaccio, Milano 1993.

29 Dina Khapaeva, 'L'Occident sera demain', *Annales: Histoire, Sciences Sociales*, 6, Nov.–Dec. 1995, pp. 1,259–70.

30 Victor Perez-Diaz, *The Role of Civil and Uncivil Nationalisms in the Making of Europe*, ASP Paper 27 (b), Madrid 1999.

31 Paloma Fernandez Aguilar, *Memoria y olvido de la Guerra civil española*, Alianza Editorial, Madrid 1996.

32 Michael Richards, *A Time of Silence. Civil War and the Culture of Repression in Franco's Spain*, 1936–1945, Cambridge University Press, Cambridge 1998, p. 2.

33 Nicole Loraux, 'De l'amnistie et de son contraire', in *Usages de l'oubli. Contributions au Colloque de Royaumont*, Seuil, Paris 1988, pp. 23–47.

34 Ibid., pp. 39, 44.

35 Jay Winter and Emmanuel Sivan, 'Setting the Framework', in idem (eds), *War and Remembrance in the Twentieth Century*, Cambridge University Press, Cambridge 1999.

36 Cristina Campo, *Sotto falso nome*, Adelphi, Milano 1998, p. 191.

37 Jonathan Boyarin, 'Space, Time, and the Politics of Memory', in Jonathan Boyarin (ed.), *Remapping Memory. The Politics of TimeSpace*, University of Minnesota Press, Minneapolis 1994.

38 Assia Djebar, *Ces voix qui m'assiègent ... en marge de ma francophonie*, Albin Michel, Paris 1999.

39 Ibid., pp. 152, 158.

40 Sherna Berger Gluck and Daphne Patai (eds), *Women's Words. The Feminist Practice of Oral History*, Routledge, New York and London 1991; Ritu Menon and Kamila Bhasin, *Borders and Boundaries. Women in India's Partition*, Rutgers University Press, New Brunswick, N.J. 1998.

41 Luigi Nono, *L'erreur comme nécessité*, in *Ecrits*, Bourgeois, Paris 1993, p. 256.

42 George Steiner, *Language and Silence. Essays 1958–1966*, Introduction 1984, Faber and Faber, London 1985, p. 15.

43 Ibid., p. 69.

44 Michel-Rolph Trouillot, *Silencing the Past. Power and the Production of History*, Beacon Press, Boston 1995, pp. 27–28.

45 Daniel L. Schachter, *Searching for Memory: the Brain, the Mind and the Past*, Basic Books, New York 1996.

46 As in Klein's title: Norman M. Klein, *The History of Forgetting: Los Angeles and the Erasure of Memory*, Verso, London & New York 1997.

47 Shahid Amin, *Event, Metaphor, Memory. Chauri Chaura 1922–1992*, Oxford University Press, Oxford 1995.

48 Ibid. p. 198.

49 Wilfred R. Bion, *Memoria del futuro. Il sogno* (Italian translation of *A Memoir of the Future: The Dream*, 1975, and *A Key to A Memoir of the Future*, 1980, revised edition 1991), Cortina, Milano 1993.

50 Wilfred R. Bion, 'Notes on memory and desire', *The Psychoanalytic Forum*, 2, pp. 272–3, 279–80, reprinted in Elizabeth Bott Spillius (ed.), *Melanie Klein Today*, vol. 2: *Mainly Practice*, Routledge, London 1988, pp. 17–21.

51 On this see e.g. Gérard Namer, *Memorie d'Europa. Identità europea e memoria collettiva*, Rubbettino, Soveria Mannelli 1993.

52 Luisa Passerini, 'Work Ideology and Consensus under Italian Fascism', *History Workshop*, 8, 1979; *Fascism in Cultural Memory*, Cambridge University Press, Cambridge 1987.

# INDEX

Aboriginal children 6; separation from parents 15, 101–2, 142–7
Aguilar, Paloma 247, 248
Algerian Liberation Front: demonstration in Paris and massacre (1961) 244
ambivalent nostalgia 82–5, 93
Amin, Shahid 251
amnesia: and denial of shameful pasts 16; silence as repression of imposed 243–7; *see also* silence
ANC (African National Congress) 157
Antze, Paul 97–8, 153
Anzac 140
apartheid 158
Appelfeld, Aharon 79
Arendt, Hannah: *The Burden of Our Time* 243
Aretxaga, Begoña 132
Armistice Day 10
Arregi, Agurtzane 123
Asuländer, Rose 81
Athens, ancient: civil memory in 248
atrocity tales: and Finnish Civil War 42, 45, 49–52, 53
Attwood, Bain 146–7
Augé, Marc 241
Augustine, St: *Confessions* 240
Australia 136–49, 142–7; adopting of 'strategic victimhood' by indigenous peoples 147–8; authority of the witness 140–1; commemoration of massacre of Armenians by Turks in 136; criticism of dominance of memory in public debates 147–9; different understanding of relationship between past and present by government and sufferers 143–4; domination of memorial culture in national consciousness 102, 140, 143; and historical consciousness 139, 149; living memory through the generations 139–40; offering of reward by Lee for return of videos and films 137; and question of 'authenticity' in remembering 148; and rhetoric of 'forgetting' 144; separation of aboriginal children from parents 15, 101–2, 142–7; 'stolen generations narrative' 145–6; use of psychoanalytic terms 148
autobiographical documentaries 14, 110–16
autobiography 9, 13; connected to collective history 111

Bachelard, G.: *The Poetics of Space* 232–3
*Bad Day at Black Rock* 113
Barthes, Roland: 'The Grain of the Voice' 214; on photographs 184
Basque nationalist women 8, 15, 100–1, 120–32, 169; collective memory of and collective 'Spanish' memory 120–1; connection between painful and pleasurable memories by second interviewee 126; difficulty in putting memory into words by second interviewee 125–6; dreamlike-quality of memories of violence 124; gendered meaning of memories 101, 126–7; interplay between private and public memories 15, 101, 121–2, 128; and myth of strong mother 127; personal memories of political violence

255

flashbacks 223
folk stories 23, 25
Fonseca, Isabel 242–3
forgetting 173, 221, 239, 251; of
    forgetting 240–1; rhetoric of 144;
    and the Roma 243
Fosse Ardeatine *see* Rome massacre
Foucault, M. 223
France: and massacre of Algerians in
    Paris (1961) 244
Franco, General 130, 131, 132
Franklin, George 107
Franklin-Lipsker, Eileen 107, 109
Franzos, Karl-Emil 80
Freed, Alan 218
Freud, Sigmund: on night dreams 124;
    on Rome 11; on trauma 106, 114
Friedlander, Saul 110, 116, 141
Frisch, Michael 116
'Frontiers of Memory' conference xiii-
    xiv, 245

Gallipoli 140, 141
Gellhorn, Martha 241
gender: and memory 101, 126–7, 249
genealogy: importance of to memory of
    war 68
generational motifs: as core element of
    official commemorative ceremonies
    in Canada 61–4; use and purpose of
    in *The Valour and the Horror* 59–61
generational transmission: of
    memory 10–11, 14, 26–7, 58, 59,
    74, 247 generations 9–11; living
    memory through in Australia
    139–40
genocide 243
Germany: poetry in 246
Gerő, András 195
Gerz, Jochan 185
Glenney, Donald 58
*Globe and Mail, The* 70
Gooder, Haydie and Jacobs, Jane M.
    144, 148
Green, Anne and Troup, Kathleen: *The
    Houses of History* 3
György, Péter 199–200
Gypsies 242–3
Gzowski, Peter 73

Haebich, Anna 143, 147
Hamilton, Carrie 8, 15, 100–1, 120–32
Hamilton, Paula 7, 15, 101–2, 136–49

Hansen, Miriam 225
Hartman, Geoffrey 57
Havill, Lorna 139
Healy, Chris 13–14, 16, 173, 222–34
Heimo, Anne and Peltonen, Ulla-Maija
    13, 14, 25–6, 42–53
Helen 161
Hendrix, Jimi 211, 214–15
heritage 211, 216
Herman, Judith: *Trauma and Recovery*
    106
Herron, John 146
Hershman, Lynn 104–6, 109, 114–15
Hiroshima 242
Hirsch, Carl 80, 81, 83, 86, 86–91, 92,
    93
Hirsch, Lotte 79, 80, 81, 83, 86–91,
    92, 93
Hirsch, Marianne 68–9
Hirsch, Marianne and Spitzer, Leo 12,
    15, 23, 27, 79–94
historians: and memory 141–2
historical consciousness 137, 139, 141,
    142
historical writing 14
history: family 4; oral *see* oral history;
    public 3; relation between memory
    and 1-3, 4–6, 7–8, 9, 130, 138–40,
    141–2; relation between nationalism
    and 169; resistances to trauma-
    centred 159–62; resistances to
    writing of as therapy 162–5;
    transforming traumatic memory into
    therapeutic 157–9
*History and Memory* (film) 110–14
'history of trauma' 114
Hitler, Adolf 115
Hobsbawm, Eric 137, 241
Hoffman, Eva 85
Holocaust 6, 7, 98, 101, 108, 116, 142,
    143, 148; application of to
    Cambodia's genocide sites 180–1;
    and oral testimony 108–9; and
    'politics of denial' 107
Hou Youn 183
Howard, John 143, 144
Hoy, Claire 73
Hu Nim 183
Hughes, Rachel 15, 170–1, 175–88
Human Rights and Equal Opportunity
    Commission's National Inquiry
    (HREOC)
    42, 144, 146, 148